The Siege
of Strasbourg

The Siege
of Strasbourg

Rachel Chrastil

Harvard University Press

Cambridge, Massachusetts ▪ London, England

2014

Cataloging-in-Publication Data available from the Library of Congress

ISBN: 978-0-674-72886-8 (alk. paper)

For my parents

Contents

Note to the Reader

"German" and "Germany" refer to the German states collectively before 1871 and to the German Empire after 1871. "Strasbourgeois" and "Strassburgers" refer interchangeably to the people of Strasbourg. Prior to 1878, the French word *siège* was spelled *siége*.

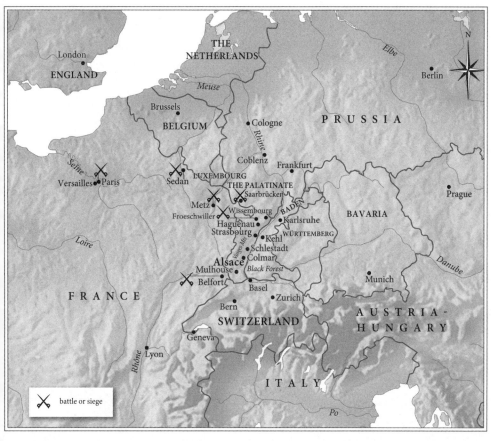

Alsace and the Franco-Prussian War

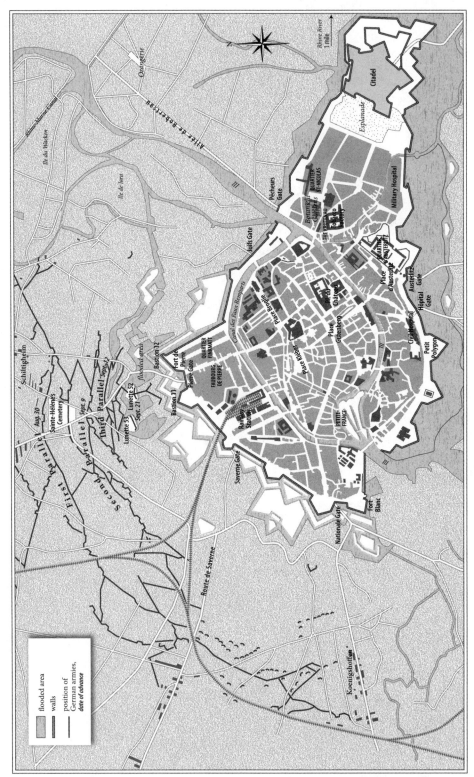

Besieged Strasbourg

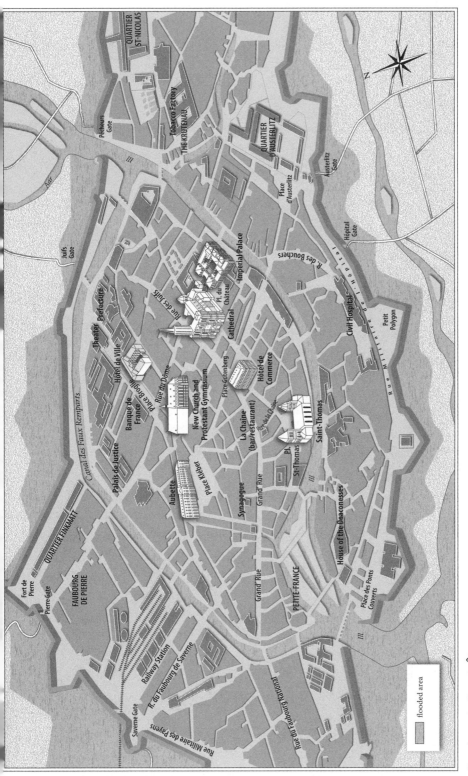

Strasbourg's Grande Île

The Siege
of Strasbourg

Introduction

I N JULY 1870, UNDER the shadow of war, the citizens of the French border city of Strasbourg carried on the business of everyday life: moving cargo, studying medicine, hauling water, brewing beer, and giving birth. By early August, Strasbourg, "the city at the crossroads," came under siege. It had been caught in the war between France and the German states—often called the Franco-Prussian War—that unified Germany under Wilhelm I and his chancellor Otto von Bismarck, sealed the reputation of Prussian military leader Helmuth von Moltke, and undid French Emperor Napoleon III. Civilians in Strasbourg suffered six weeks of bombardment that left hundreds dead and thousands homeless. Sometimes despairing, sometimes resilient, the women and men of Strasbourg served in hospitals and patrolled the streets, hid in their cellars and confronted the authorities. They witnessed and shaped the modern development of both warfare and humanitarianism. Then, on the morning of September 28, the people of Strasbourg woke up under German rule.

This is the story of that fateful siege and the civilians who survived it. It is an ensemble piece in which a dozen individuals play a prominent part, including nurses, generals, clergy, and politicians.[1] We will meet a mother torn between patience and action, a redeemed political exile dodging bullets to sneak into the city, and a French general divided between his duty to hold firm and his desire to protect "innocent" women and children. These individuals responded to the siege in a variety of ways, from the cynical to the melodramatic, from the spiritual to the mundane. During this critical time they debated the right course of action: What, if anything, justifies the bombing of civilians? Are cultural sites legitimate wartime targets? Should civilians be allowed to evacuate, and if given the chance, should they go? When may a city honorably surrender? How should newly occupied civilians interact with their conquerors? Many in Strasbourg believed that, at its heart, the siege presented a choice between barbarity and civilization, between war and humanity. They stood at the crossroads of the future of Europe.

"May God Protect This Tower"

In that summer of war, the summer of his seventieth year, Frédéric Piton regularly gazed across the city rooftops from Strasbourg's rose-colored cathedral, the world's tallest building. He ascended 332 winding steps to reach the platform, a large open space located at the base of the cathedral's lone tower. For half a century, during his many years as a bookbinder and a librarian, he had made this spot his second home. From there, Piton could gaze over the maze of medieval alleys punctuated by large open squares, the red-tiled roofs of shops and apartments, the stone façades of monumental civic and religious buildings. It wasn't a particularly green city, and the narrow streets disallowed vast perspectives. Even the Grand'Rue curved so precipitously that its length and cardinal direction remained elusive. Amid this somewhat geometric tangle, Piton could just perceive the Ill River and its canals wrapping around the Grande Île on which the cathedral stood. To the west, the edges of the city melted into the fertile plain of Alsace below the Vosges Mountains, while to the east the Rhine River glimmered and, further, the Black Forest beckoned.

Over the course of several summers in the early 1850s, Piton had drawn a 360-degree panorama of Strasbourg, a work that he eventually published as part of his celebrated 1855 *Illustrated Strasbourg*. Piton realized, however, that this panorama offered only the illusion of understanding. It fooled viewers into thinking that looking was the same as knowing, when in fact the perspective masked more than it revealed.

Looking down into the "labyrinth of houses grouped at my feet," Piton tried to imagine the people who had constructed them, but found that "the past extended like a veiled tableau before my imagination." Piton longed to break out of the prison of the present time.[2]

Piton was not the first (or last) whom this panoramic view tantalized. When Johann Wolfgang von Goethe arrived in 1770 to study in Strasbourg, he made a visit to this spot his first priority. Looking over the city produced wonder and fear, arising not just from the giddy sensation of height but also from anticipation of the unknowable future: "Such a fresh glance into a new land in which we are to abide for a time has still the peculiarity, both pleasant and foreboding, that the whole lies before us like an unwritten tablet. As yet no sorrows or joys which relate to ourselves are recorded upon it; this cheerful, varied, animated plain is still mute for us; the eye is only fixed on the objects so far as they are intrinsically important, and neither affection nor passion has especially to render prominent this or that spot. But a presentiment of the future already disquiets the young heart; and an unsatisfied craving secretly demands that which is to come."[3]

To mark his presence on the precipice of the inevitable but invisible future, Goethe scratched his name into the rose sandstone surface of the surrounding guard walls. His name stands alongside those of other visitors, including philosopher Johann Gottfried von Herder and poet and scientist Joseph-Louis Gay-Lussac. Voltaire, too, was not so enlightened as to forgo this act of self-assertion, though his name now bears lightning scars.[4]

Frédéric Piton was intrigued less by the unknowable emotions of the future than by the city's rich past. With the confidence of a nineteenth-century autodidact (his formal education had ended at age thirteen), Piton believed that he could master the city's history through the guidance of books. Armed with volumes from the New Church library where he worked, when Piton beheld the rooftops again, he saw the invisible layers of history awaken, the succeeding generations jostling with one another inside and out of the city's shops, churches, and great houses. Piton told the history of his city in four dimensions: two in the maze of streets, a third from the heights of the cathedral, and the fourth through cascading layers of time.

In the city's architecture Piton saw living elements of the natural and social world. He was awestruck by the cathedral, with its delicate, intricate pink stonework reaching skyward, and by the city that produced such a wonder. "This temple," he wrote in *Illustrated Strasbourg*, "conceived with wisdom, executed with force, dazzlingly beautiful, is the symbol of a well-constituted society that rests on the immutable bases of prudence, foresightedness, justice, equity, charity and common devotion. This tower is the robust mirror of the destinies of generations who have lived in its shadow; like them, many times beaten by storms, by the impetuousness of wind, many times caressed by the first and last beneficent rays of the sun. . . . May God protect this tower, may it protect those who live in its shadow."[5]

Strasbourg inspired devotion in its inhabitants and admiration in its visitors. In the eyes of many, Strasbourg modeled the successful European city and all that it implies for the quality and richness of life. From its position just west of the Rhine River, Strasbourg connected European centers of production through a series of canals and railroads. Trade provided the financial undergirding for workshops, cheery taverns, and flourishing civic institutions. Within the France of Napoleon III, Strasbourg's cultural life ranked second only to Paris and surpassed the capital in its ability to bridge French and German intellectual circles. "It was a place," writes Anthony Steinhoff, "where one could see a Parisian company perform at the opera one night, and participate in a conference about the latest German medical discoveries the next."[6] The public statues of printer Johannes Gutenberg and revolutionary general Jean-Baptiste Kléber, both dedicated in 1840, symbolized this complex cultural heritage. Gutenberg embodied Strasbourg's deep intellectual roots, entrepreneurship, and centuries as an independent, Germanic city within the Holy Roman Empire. Kléber, who fought alongside Napoleon in Egypt, stood for Strasbourg's commitment to French revolutionary ideals and military heroism. After all, it was in Strasbourg that Claude-Joseph Rouget de Lisle wrote the "Marseillaise."

With a population of about 77,000 civilians and 8,000 soldiers, Strasbourg was large enough to retain anonymity and surprise, but small enough to make visible its network of political, military, religious, and economic leaders. It teemed with common soldiers yet charmed visiting aristocrats. The city divided between rival Protestants and Catholics, who both enjoyed long-standing institutions and large congregations. A small but significant Jewish population made the city one of the most religiously diverse in Western Europe. The leading urban center of the region of Alsace and the capital of the department of the Bas-Rhin, Strasbourg attracted intellectuals, officers, theologians, and publishers. It was a city worth fighting for. When Strasbourg came under siege, its active and influential inhabitants refused just to watch their city burn.

French or German?

Strasbourg helps us to understand civilians at war within a European context: not just France, not just Germany. It is a major hub in the Greater Rhineland, the region that flows with the Rhine River from the Alps to the North Sea. Today the Greater Rhineland includes Belgium, Luxembourg, and parts of Germany, France, the Netherlands, and Switzerland. Its rivers, ports, and canals have facilitated the passage of goods and people for millennia, from Julius Caesar to Charlemagne to Napoleon. In the nineteenth century, Rhineland coal and steel sustained the formidable German army and forged the Eiffel Tower. Strasbourg lay at the crossroads. From its position just west of the Rhine, it both connected the Mediterranean with Northern Europe and protected a passage to the headwaters of the Danube and thence to the Black Sea. Parisians traveling to Munich or Vienna and Italians heading to Belgium or Britain all passed through Strasbourg.[7]

In the midst of this dynamic economy, Strasbourg developed a complex heritage and an elusive identity. Despite the reality of cultural intermingling along the Rhine, the river has often been mythologized as a boundary between peoples. Under the Roman Empire, Strasbourg—then called Argentorate—formed part of a zone of contact along the Rhine that attracted both Romans and a diverse mix of non-Romans. Yet Julius Caesar invented the idea that the Rhine formed a border between Gallia and Germania. Ever since, peaceful transaction has at times given way to conflict. During the late Middle Ages, the burghers of Strasbourg asserted their independence from princes and bishops, even as the city remained part of the Holy Roman Empire. In the sixteenth century, the city created a new identity for itself as a leader in the Protestant Reformation, but religious conflict weakened the city's claim to independence.[8] In 1681, Louis XIV incorporated the city into France, but he could not stamp out Protestantism and did not prevent Strassburgers from continuing to speak German and Alsatian (a Germanic language). While France claimed Alsace for itself, many on the eastern side of the Rhine believed that Strasbourg remained a German city "in its essence *[Wesen]*."[9] With the rise of nationalism in the eighteenth and nineteenth centuries, the Rhineland once again became the site of competition, a frontier between supposedly different cultures and ways of life, and a "natural" boundary between the French and German nation-states.

By 1870, Strasbourg and the surrounding region of Alsace had belonged to France for nearly two centuries but remained culturally ambiguous. Many inhabitants of Strasbourg identified more closely with Alsace than with either France or any German state. They also shared affinities with nearby Swiss cities like Zurich and Basel due to their common heritage as formerly independent cities within the Holy Roman Empire. They furthermore maintained economic, cultural, and familial ties with the Grand Duchy of Baden, a small, independent Germanic country that bordered Alsace along the Rhine. As nationalists on both sides of the Rhine tried to claim Strasbourg, they used language as a measuring stick. French administrators from "the interior"—from west of the Vosges Mountains—disparaged Alsatian as a patois, a lower form of language. The linguistic frontier between French speakers and Germanic speakers ran somewhat west of Strasbourg. In 1832, only 10 to 14 percent of Strasbourg's children spoke French, but some Strassburgers could speak Alsatian, German, or French, depending on the circumstances. In the 1860s, driven by a nationalistic desire to equate Frenchness with French literacy, the central government in Paris tried to introduce French in Alsatian schools, with modest success.[10]

We do not have reliable statistics about Strassburgers' spoken language in 1870, but even if we did, it would be difficult to draw correlations between language and class, religion, or national sentiment. Traditional nationalist frameworks—France for French-speaking

Catholics and Germany for German-speaking Protestants—do not apply. Many Protestants spoke French, and many Catholics spoke Alsatian. French tended to be the language of the educated upper class, army officers, and state employees, but many wealthy and professional Protestants spoke Alsatian.[11]

To complicate matters, many Alsatian speakers associated themselves firmly with the French revolutionary tradition but saw Germany as their spiritual and cultural homeland. Max Reichard, a Protestant vicar who wrote in German, acknowledged his allegiances both to France, the political ruler for almost two centuries, and to the German states, the "cradle of our church."[12] Frédéric Piton also embraced his city's complex heritage, "where the two languages are both cultivated, and where, among the enlightened and instructed population, the practical spirit of the French is wedded to the profound spirit of the Germans."[13] Whatever the governing elite in Paris might say, language did not determine identity.

The more we study Strasbourg, the clearer it becomes that the question of whether it identified more closely with France or Germany is beside the point. Like Gaza or Kashmir, Alsace was a contested region that encourages us to rethink the framework of nation-states. It reveals that national identity is constructed over time, through the deliberate actions of governments and cultural leaders as well as through the sentiments and experiences of the inhabitants. Local, regional, and international identities also mattered.

Soldiers, Civilians, and Violence

Over its long history, Strasbourg has experienced countless battles, from the long period of Roman conflicts, to sixteenth-century religious war, to the endgame of the Napoleonic adventure. A well-known folk song evokes Strasbourg's military legacy:

O Strassburg, o Strassburg
du wunderschöne Stadt
darinnen liegt begraben
so mancher Soldat![14]

O Strassburg, o Strassburg
You beautiful city
Inside lies buried
Many a soldier!

Despite this long history of war, the crisis that the inhabitants of
Strasbourg faced in the summer of 1870 came as a shock. By the second
half of the nineteenth century, Europeans' tolerance for violence in everyday life was declining. Pain and suffering increasingly took place behind
closed doors, while respect for corpses grew. In 1832, France outlawed
the branding of convicts and moved executions from public squares to
courtyards or out of cities altogether. Urban streets, illuminated by gaslight and patrolled by policemen, increasingly evoked pleasure and
safety.[15] Violence became a sign of dysfunction as "the incomprehensible and blind forces of massacre came to be seen as unacceptable and
even obscene."[16] Legislators and social theorists increasingly viewed
fights and beatings as social ills amenable to treatment and reform.
Women and children were believed to be particularly vulnerable and
therefore in need of protection from everyday acts of violence.[17]

Extraordinary episodes of civilian violence and distress also seemed
on the wane. Civilian life rested on stability, order, and predictability.[18]
With the growth of European states interested in keeping their populations alive and fed, "life was less of a risk and more worth living."[19] In
France, bread riots were now a memory. A full generation separated the
civilians of 1870 from the armed citizen-combatants of the revolution of
1848.[20] Following the repression of the protests to Louis-Napoleon's
coup d'état in 1851, French civilians experienced the 1850s and 1860s
in relative peace.

With this decreased tolerance for civilian violence came the belief
that civilians should no longer be the victims of wartime violence.
Although civilians in Strasbourg encountered soldiers frequently in
their everyday lives, they believed that their own fate should no longer
be entwined with that of the military. By the nineteenth century, many
Europeans had come to view war as an exceptional experience in which
civilians took little part. War, many believed, ought to be circumscribed.
Military personnel alone had the duty to put themselves in harm's way,

for they alone had been trained to defend themselves and to kill. Civilians, it was thought, should be allowed to go about their business while the war unfolded somewhere else, on the battlefield. They were not supposed to kill or be killed.[21] (Increasingly, Europeans believed that even soldiers deserved to be treated as neutrals once they were wounded or ill.)

But the decline in violence was illusory. The aristocracy had not given up the duel, and the bourgeoisie increasingly took up the practice. Intimate violence continued to be condoned—and acquitted by juries— as "a popular system of retributive justice."[22] In addition, states emerged from the long revolutionary period of 1789 to 1848 stronger than ever, with a greater capacity for violence and a willingness to use it. The European state claimed, but did not achieve, a monopoly on violence as police forces professionalized and standing armies grew in status and numbers. New technologies—such as long-range, highly accurate rifles and cannon—allowed for unprecedented devastation in warfare. Anyone paying attention to the Crimean War, the U.S. Civil War, or the Austro-Prussian War would have observed the increasingly destructive capacity of wartime violence.

Civilians did not escape, either. Armies in 1870 were prepared to use their new weapons against enemy civilians or even their own people. The French state soon made a strong claim to dispense violence in the name of order: in one bloody week in May 1871, the army crushed the revolutionary Paris Commune and killed thousands of civilians; meanwhile, in Algeria, the French army killed 20,000 Arabs and Kabyles as it put an end to an anticolonial uprising.[23] It was nearly impossible to maintain the distinction between soldiers and civilians in war, and especially difficult when an army tried to capture an entire city. To complicate matters, some civilians believed that they had the right to take up arms to defend themselves from invasion; military leaders could not agree upon the proper response to such actions. All in all, the sharp line that many civilians believed to exist between themselves and soldiers proved less durable than they had hoped. Bertrand Taithe tells us that in the nineteenth century, "the boundary between the military and the civilian sphere—in effect, between the social orders of war and of peace—became more blurred and porous than ever before."[24] A vast gap

widened between civilian intolerance of wartime violence and the potential for harm against them. When civilians became the targets of wartime violence, it shocked Europeans to the core.

The War

Just what kind of war did the inhabitants of Strasbourg face? How did
the conflict between France and the German states compare with the
world wars of the twentieth century? The rapid mobilization and
extreme combat violence stunned contemporaries. After France declared
war on Prussia and its South German allies (Baden, Württemberg, and
Bavaria) on July 15, 1870, railroads and streamlined bureaucracy rushed
troops into battle. A British minister witnessing mobilization in
Darmstadt observed, "The present war is one without parallel in the
history of civilized nations. . . . An entire people has been suddenly
called from its daily avocations to take a personal part in a struggle,
which promises to be the bloodiest and most deadly on record."[25] In six
months, 139,000 French and 52,627 German soldiers died—more than
double the number killed in a comparable period of the U.S. Civil War.[26]
The death rate for soldiers was high: in the German armies, 30 per
1,000 soldiers died, nearly the same as during World War I (34 per
1,000). Yet the Franco-Prussian War lasted only six months, so a far
smaller percentage of the population mobilized for battle.[27] Nor did the
war entail the conversion of private industry to the production of bombs,
tanks, uniforms, and all the matériel of war.

In the opening weeks, the German armies steadily gained ground,
pausing only to lay siege to dozens of French cities, including Strasbourg.
In the bombardments of these cities, the Prussians destroyed priceless
libraries and damaged sites of worship. Many French and Germans
viewed the conflict in nationalistic terms, a war between peoples rather
than between rulers; in German rhetoric, the war helped to found a new
German Empire and served as revenge on France for the national humiliation of the Napoleonic era.[28] At the outbreak of war, the French government forced some 80,000 German migrants living in France to leave
the country, much as enemy nationals were expelled in later wars.[29] Yet
the conflict contained meanings beyond nationalism; many observers

applied regional and religious interpretations of war and suffering. Hatred did not cross into the dangerous desire for the complete destruction of the enemy.

As the war continued, it anticipated but did not reach the horrors of twentieth-century wars. After the pivotal battle of Sedan on September 1, the Prussians captured French Emperor Napoleon III and 80,000 of his soldiers. Yet these soldiers did not expect to be exterminated upon surrender or imprisonment, as Soviets did during World War II. After Sedan, the French underwent a political revolution, overthrowing Napoleon III in favor of a republic. But the revolutionaries did not attempt to completely remake society in the manner of the Bolsheviks; the war had not ripped French society apart. The nascent French republic rebuilt its army and sent guerrilla fighters into the field, calling for "war to the last extremity," but nevertheless agreed to an armistice long before reaching the vanishing point of total destruction. In northern and eastern France, civilians felt the terror of occupation and died as hostages. The Prussians burned the entire village of Fontenoy in retaliation for partisan resistance. Paris came under siege for four months of cold and scarcity. But in many areas of France, and in all of Germany, civilians went about their business and did not suffer from rationing, hunger, or systemized murder. The French finally surrendered on January 28, 1871.

The Franco-Prussian War clearly did not share all the characteristics of the wars of the twentieth century, but it shaped the experiences and attitudes that made those catastrophes possible. It was one of the first conflicts in which both sides had signed the Geneva Convention and in which both sides failed to live up to it. When the Prussians targeted civilian noncombatants in the bombardment of Strasbourg, they made possible Dresden, Leningrad, Sarajevo, and Gaza. When civilians accused Prussia of breaking the "laws of war," they anticipated war crimes trials at Nuremberg and The Hague. When bombs destroyed libraries and set the cathedral on fire, they prefigured the destruction of cultural heritage in Leuven, Rheims, and Baghdad. And when Swiss humanitarians intervened on behalf of besieged civilians, but unwittingly helped Prussia conquer Strasbourg, they paved the way for the ambiguous successes of the Red Cross and Doctors Without Borders.[30]

Strasbourg lay at the heart of the conflict. When German forces entered French territory in August, Strasbourg was the first major city they targeted. For six weeks, from August 15 to September 27, the armies of Prussia and Baden bombarded Strasbourg. German bombs killed three hundred citizens, wounded three thousand more, and caused enormous damage to public and private buildings, including the cathedral roof and the irreplaceable libraries housed in the New Church.[31] The siege exhibited the important issues raised during the Franco-Prussian War in microcosm: the targeting of civilians, the destruction of cultural sites, the revolution in the midst of war, and the sacrifice of one's own civilians for the cause. The siege alone did not determine the outcome of the Franco-Prussian War, of course, but the symbolism of Strasbourg elevated its importance in the minds of French and German alike. The loss of Strasbourg, along with the rest of the region of Alsace and most of neighboring Lorraine, was one of the most important consequences of the war. The transfer of Strasbourg from French to German hands heralded the rise of a powerful new German Empire.

Humanitarianism

To ordinary civilians, the violence of the siege of Strasbourg seemed like an illegitimate use of force, breaking the unspoken "laws of war." Furthermore, protective traditions that might have shielded civilians fell short. No international agreements restrained armies when they confronted civilians. At that time, the Geneva Convention, the prime example of international humanitarian law, only addressed sick and wounded soldiers and their caregivers. Just War Theory did not hold sway over military or political leaders and had not been affirmed in contemporary treaties. Charities failed as they were cut off from sources of funding and disrupted from their normal activities. Europeans had not yet articulated civilians' right to wartime protection as a fundamental human right. Military custom and regulations relied on the suffering of civilians and offered little protection. Prussian General August von Werder counted on women's terror during bombardment and fears of rape should the city be taken by assault, and assumed that the plight of women would influence male decision makers. But according to French military regulations, the commander, General Jean-Jacques-Alexis Uhrich, could not capitulate to save civilians. The people of Strasbourg were caught without recourse to national or international law.

In the midst of these difficulties, a group of Swiss dignitaries proposed a new response: humanitarianism. Humanitarianism was a particular expression of human sympathy characterized by an emphasis on aiding victims, the physical movement of humanitarians to the site of suffering, and the belief that concrete action could alter the status quo and confer transcendence.[32] Many factors contributed to the development of humanitarianism, including Enlightenment projects of social betterment, ethical imperatives to help strangers, and the valorization of sympathy, along with mass media, rapid transportation, and advanced fundraising techniques.[33] In the 1850s and 1860s, during the Crimean War and the U.S. Civil War, a few Europeans and Americans began to apply humanitarian aid to soldiers. Prior to 1870, however, wartime humanitarian aid had not been extended to civilians.

In order to understand the development of civilian-oriented humanitarianism, we need to look to the context of nineteenth-century gender and combatant status, particularly as they relate to the concept of "victims." In a siege, everyone can be a hero, and everyone can be a victim. But not everyone agrees on who fills which role. The people of Strasbourg suffered during the bombardment, but this did not mean that they identified themselves as victims. Rather, they saw themselves as actors trying to make the best of a difficult situation. They tended to shift "victimhood" onto others: civilian men transferred it onto women and children; women placed victimhood on children and wounded or imprisoned soldiers. Women acted as caregivers not only to replicate traditional roles or to embody the nation, but also to escape the characterization of victim.[34] The fact that individuals defined others as victims and acted accordingly is precisely the reason that the siege played an important role in the development of humanitarianism. The fact that they saw themselves as actors, just as we like to see ourselves, and preserved their experiences in writing, is why we need to know more about their activities. This siege gives us the rare opportunity to hear the voices of the recipients, not just the givers, of humanitarian aid.

Strasbourg's civilian men often claimed that women and children were the primary victims of the Prussian bombardment. But they were wrong. Prussian bombs killed far more civilian men than women. This error fit with the dominant gender paradigm. Just as nineteenth-century women faced exclusion from politics and increasingly from economic life, they also were no longer supposed to be touched by war. Men were supposed to protect and provide for their wives and children. Civilization itself, it seemed, depended upon shielding women and children from wartime violence.

The (supposed) divide between martial and civil spheres in times of combat deepened and complicated this gender regime. The civilian-military split did not line up precisely with the division between women and men: many men in Strasbourg had never served in the army.[35] Civilian males found themselves caught in the middle, expected to protect women but unable to truly do so. They felt "anguish" and "embarrassment" at their inactivity, much as they did during World War I.[36] When the Swiss delegation offered to help women and children to depart, the men of Strasbourg particularly welcomed it: women would depart, and civilian men could resume their focus on the siege without worrying about their families. Humanitarian aid emerged in part as besieged males tried to shift the label of victimhood onto their wives and daughters, many of whom in turn resisted that categorization. The perceived status of women, who were believed to both protect civilization and need saving themselves, resonated with the paradox of liberation and paternalism characteristic of humanitarianism.

▪ ▪ ▪

The chapters ahead introduce a series of concepts to help us think critically about civilian wartime experiences: the reconfiguration of urban space, the physical and social definition of outsiders and insiders, the distinction between suffering and victimhood, the definition of well-being, the expressions and limitations of various protective traditions, and the debate among timeless ethical traditions over the right course of action. Throughout, we will examine the different perspectives of men and women, and of soldiers and civilians. In essence, I will ask in various ways, what do people living together in a city owe to each other during times of crisis?

In 1870, civilians made hard choices, sometimes sacrificing their energies for others, sometimes acting creatively and resourcefully, other times succumbing to despair and anger. Neither superhuman nor dehumanized, the civilians of Strasbourg offer insight into life in a city before, during, and after the disturbance of war. This book could be seen as a tale of defeat about a city brought low and incorporated into enemy territory. But when standing at the crossroads, we can see many possibilities in the story of Strasbourg, including one of resilience.

CHAPTER ONE

The Grey Areas

O N JULY 12, 1870, seventy-year-old Frédéric Piton wrote a personal letter to Emperor Napoleon III. Alarmed at rumors that France was preparing to declare war on Prussia, Piton sought to register his disapproval. He opened with a formal introduction in which he presented his many loyalties and experiences: "As an elderly man, loving humanity and the *patrie* above all; a citizen involved with the political agitation of this century; a state employee, having taken an oath to the government; [and] an Alsatian . . . I believe it is my duty to present to Your Majesty the present supplication."[1] Bookbinder, artist, and librarian, Piton straddled Strasbourg's many divides: a civilian living in a fortress city, a craftsman who moved in intellectual circles, a Freemason steeped in Strasbourg's religious heritage, a born Protestant—working in and living next to the Protestant New Church—who frequented the Catholic cathedral, an Alsatian speaker who could write in French, and a loyal Frenchman who also respected his neighbors across the Rhine in Baden. Piton was adept at negotiating the grey areas.[2]

The war crisis had begun earlier that summer, when King Wilhelm of Prussia and his Minister-President Otto von Bismarck tried to place one of the members of the royal Hohenzollern family on the Spanish throne. Napoleon III objected to this encirclement. Frédéric Piton saw this as a flimsy excuse for conflict and entreated the emperor "not to unleash the horrors of war on peaceful Europe and . . . to take advantage of a more favorable moment, of a more plausible reason, for attacking Prussia."[3]

Piton could remember the last time Prussia and France had gone to war. In 1814, just as Piton was taking up his father's trade of bookbinding, Strasbourg was besieged by the Allies seeking to dislodge Napoleon. A year later, the city welcomed Napoleon from exile during the Hundred Days and came under siege again. Piton had survived the privation and boredom of both sieges, and recognized that even victory could sow the seeds of future conflict.[4] He did not disloyally suggest that France could lose a war against Prussia, but everyone knew that it was possible. Four years earlier, Prussia had decisively defeated Austria in just a few weeks, settling the question of which was the dominant Germanic country.

Piton particularly worried about breaking relations with Baden, the German state located just across the Rhine from Strasbourg. Badenese and Strasbourgeois lived together, worked together, and intermarried; cousins living on either side of the Rhine maintained strong ties rooted in common language and religion. Just a decade earlier, Napoleon III and leaders in Baden had worked together to construct the Rhine Railway Bridge, bringing the promise of more trade and prosperity.[5] Piton feared that nationalist rhetoric could turn Baden, along with neighbors Württemberg and Bavaria, against France and into the arms of Prussia, "And then! What blood, what ruins!"[6] He apparently did not realize that all three states had already been obliged to sign treaties with Prussia.

Piton admitted that he had no hope of changing Napoleon III's mind: "Although my feeble voice is the expression of truth and conviction, I know that it will exercise no influence, but it is for the acquittal of my conscience that I have the honor of having Your Majesty hear it."[7] Indeed, Piton's petition had no effect. Although Prussia withdrew its bid to control Spain, Napoleon III encouraged his foreign minister to press King Wilhelm never to make such an attempt again. This bit of diplomacy, or lack thereof, only made matters worse. Wilhelm snubbed the French ambassador to Prussia, and Bismarck doctored a telegram to make the encounter seem unforgivably rude. The French press called for redress. Bismarck now embraced war as an opportunity to forge a unified German Empire with Prussia and King Wilhelm at its head.

France voted for war credits on July 15 and formally declared war on July 19. As required by treaty, Baden, Württemberg, and Bavaria joined Prussia against France.

In the three weeks that followed, Strasbourg burst with activity. Soldiers and matériel made their way to the city, the headquarters of the First Army Corps, as civilians tried to contribute to the war effort. Meanwhile, the grey areas that Piton had negotiated so well for seventy years operated under new rules. The neighboring state of Baden turned from partner to enemy. The military tried to separate soldiers from non-combatants, even as civilian men sought to join the National Guard. Confessional rivalries intensified, although people of all faiths joined the Red Cross. In the excitement and confusion, many hoped that Strasbourg would launch France's victory against the Germans.

Life at the Crossroads

In the summer of 1870, a determined pedestrian could walk the whole of Strasbourg from end to end in about an hour. It was difficult, however, to pass through the city without yielding to the temptation to slow down. Ice cream and military music on Place Broglie and the outdoor booksellers on Place Gutenberg diverted many a pedestrian. Strassburgers congregated at annual events such as the horse market or the Grand Fair of Saint-Jean. The city's 85,000 inhabitants were divided by religion, politics, social position, gender, and military status—yet they lived and worked in constant interaction.

In the words of François Igersheim, the walled city recalled "not Athens, but Sparta."[8] One in every ten inhabitants was a soldier, about 8,000 men.[9] Military personnel and civilians shared physical space and wove their fortunes together. Yet after fifty-five years without war, civilians did not expect to share the same fate as the soldiers that they encountered every day. The French army consisted primarily of professional soldiers who had joined through the draft and re-enlisted with the help of hefty bonuses. Most civilian men had never served. Young, educated bourgeois viewed a seven-year term in the army as an obstacle to their professional goals, and those who were drafted often bought out their service. On the eve of the war, civilian men and women in

Strasbourg thought more about earning a living, enjoying their leisure, and practicing their faith than about violent international conflict.

Few industries operated within the city—Mulhouse to the south was Alsace's industrial capital—other than breweries, tanneries in Petite France, small clothing firms, producers of foie gras, a few candle makers, and the large tobacco-processing plant. The city government self-consciously limited heavy industry and the attendant problems of worker unrest and overpopulated slums. Instead, Strasbourg's wealth came from trade. All manner of goods from books to straw hats passed through the hands of merchants, porters, drivers, deliverymen, postal employees, and shipping clerks.

The wealth generated by trade supported a variety of professions. Notaries and municipal administrators, university professors and military officers, publishers and insurance brokers all enjoyed prominence, while businessmen, lawyers, and doctors held the highest status. Many in these social strata enjoyed connections in Paris and Mulhouse, Le Havre and Frankfurt. Those from Frédéric Piton's milieu joined the ranks of highly trained glaziers, tailors, and tinsmiths or increasingly worked as white-collar employees serving hotels or insurance companies. Those less skilled became porters and peddlers or served beers and sauerkraut at Strasbourg's many brasseries and cafés. Suburban market gardeners provided vegetables to the urban center. Domestic servants—many bourgeois households employed two—lugged water and wood up the stairs to serve the kitchen and warm the parlor.[10]

Civilians of all kinds worked near or with military personnel. Within the citadel, a squat brick pentagon with a starburst of protruding bastions, civilians ran cafés, a bakery, a grocery, a tobacco store, a school, and a church. When market farmers and tradesmen brought their goods through any city gate, they passed barracks and a guard. Commanding General Auguste-Alexandre Ducrot and his staff held offices in the Aubette on Place Kléber, the open square on which regiments showed their colors and where civilian shopkeepers sold their wares. Doctors and medical students worked at the military medical school near the cathedral.[11]

Strasbourg's rich and poor lived side by side in most neighborhoods throughout the city. Artisans, bankers, politicians, and porters

inhabited the same streets, even the same buildings. The only impover-
ished areas lay in the sickle of land south of the Ill, near the Civil
Hospital, and in the Krutenau, east of the Grande Île. Social mixing did
not necessarily lead to social harmony, but it did mitigate the possibility
of neighborhood divisions; it is difficult to imagine a neighborhood-
based uprising like the Paris Commune in Strasbourg.[12]

Whatever their occupation, Strassburgers stopped by their favorite
drinking establishment after hours, during lunch, or even before hours.
Strasbourg contained some 61 cafés, 68 brasseries, and 1,393 cabarets—
all spots for libation and conversation. Regulars discussed the upcoming
elections, debated the Opera Director's contract, and engaged in illicit
gambling. Schutzenberger's place drew students and workers, while the
tailors preferred café Schneider. Some brasseries attracted socialists,
republicans, and the inevitable police surveillance. Almost daily, young
historian Rodolphe Reuss and his companions dropped by La Chaîne,
located near the large commercial houses on the Grand'Rue. Some brasseries became institutions: the City of Paris, the Three Kings, the
Dauphin, and the Golden Eagle.[13]

As evening fell, bourgeois leisure moments were dedicated to the
simple pleasures of comfortable togetherness. Arthur Faes, the son of a
fabric merchant, recalled that his family dined around six o'clock.
Afterward, men frequently gathered at their Circle to smoke, chat, and
play billiards with family and friends. Rodolphe Reuss belonged to a
men's club known as the Commercial and Literary Casino. Located in
the Hôtel de Commerce on Place Gutenberg, this exclusive club provided a lending library and rooms for reading, conversation, and playing
whist. Faes's father often brought books from his Circle's library back
for his mother. She likely had spent the evening sewing in the company
of other bourgeois wives with a cold glass of syrup-flavored water as
refreshment. Often, their homes echoed with pianos, wind instruments,
and melodic voices. Alternatively, the children, sugary from sweets and
chestnuts, went for a walk with their father. In Faes's memory, everyone
returned safely to their homes and beds as the bell chimed ten o'clock.[14]

The social elite enjoyed rather more exclusive entertainment: din-
ners, dances, and social calls to mark the new year. The three most
prominent imperial representatives—Prefect Baron Marie-Joseph-
Auguste Pron, Mayor Théodore Humann, and Commanding General

Auguste-Alexandre Ducrot—hosted winter balls that drew local aristo-crats like the Pourtalès or Renouard de Bussierre families.[15]

Not surprisingly, tension arose between the empire's men and the educated, bourgeois French-speaking Protestants who considered them-selves the city's natural leaders. Nobody embodied the empire more than the prefect of the Bas-Rhin, Baron Pron. Born the son of a general in Metz in 1820, Pron secured his first prefectural appointment at age thirty-two, just as Napoleon III consolidated his empire. His annual income of 40,000 francs put him among the top 5 percent of prefects, and as the central government's representative, his first loyalty lay with Napoleon III. The ideal prefect was supposed to bring local notables into the imperial fold, but Pron had a history of alienating them: back in 1852, his arrogance had quickly earned his transfer out of the Sarthe. Posted in the Bas-Rhin since 1855, Pron had not succeeded in win-ning over Strasbourg's bourgeoisie. They despised his dismissive atti-tude, his "habitual insolently jovial air."[16] Imperious, fatuous, and nefarious, Pron always seemed to slither out of responsibility for unpop-ular policies.[17]

Rather than supporting the empire, local civic leaders formed a republican opposition. Many of the men who were to play important roles in the siege or record the most vivid memoirs came from this milieu: doctor and future mayor Emile Küss, historian and diarist Rodolphe Reuss, journalist and politician Auguste Schneegans, among many others. They came from long-established families and possessed enough cultural and intellectual clout to head many of the city's institu-tions and to irritate Pron. Their world was that of the opera, the univer-sity, and the Commercial and Literary Casino. Educated at the Protestant Gymnasium, many developed their bonds of friendship and appetite for service as Freemasons. Frédéric Piton hovered in and around this envi-ronment; as a retired librarian, he did not have the influence of a busi-nessman or newspaper editor, but he knew them well through the New Church and the Masons.

Political debate between and among Bonapartists and republicans was facilitated by Strasbourg's two dual-language papers of record. *L'impartial du Rhin—Der Unparteiische am Rhein,* edited by Paul Raymond-Signouret and published by Berger-Levrault, provided the imperial regime's perspective. The moderate republican *Le courrier du*

Bas-Rhin—Niederrheinischer Kurier, under editor-in-chief Charles Boersch, was the largest and most important newspaper in the Bas-Rhin (though it printed only 3,000 copies per issue). Thirty-five year old journalist Auguste Schneegans kept his pen sharp and his beard trimmed as he attacked clericalism and looked for opportunities to influence.[18]

Yet the political divisions were far from absolute, particularly within the municipal government. Mayor Théodore Humann, an Orléanist—his father had served King Louis-Philippe as minister of finances—managed to win the mayoral nomination from Bonapartists and earn the respect of moderate republicans.[19] Born in 1803, Humann fit a contemporary description of the ideal mayor of Strasbourg: "a man with status in the community because of his wealth and connections, sufficiently influential to attach the city to [the Empire], sufficiently devoted never to constitute a force against us . . . [and] Catholic without being intolerant."[20]

Religious tolerance was prized because in Strasbourg one was never more than a few steps away from a house of worship: six Catholic and seven Lutheran parish churches, one Reformed Protestant church, and a Jewish synagogue on rue Sainte-Hélène. It is true that, in the previous decade or so, priests, pastors, and rabbis had worried that their congregations failed to attend services regularly. Most citizens of Strasbourg, however, remained immersed in a complex web of religious symbolism, education, and rites of passage. Strasbourg was a Catholic diocesan center, the seat of the Lutheran Directory and General Consistory for all of France, and the home of a Reformed and a Jewish consistory. As of 1866, Strasbourg's 28,800 Protestants lived alongside 43,800 Catholics and 3,100 Jews. They encountered each other in every neighborhood and profession in the city; the mayor was usually Catholic, with the first adjunct mayor usually a Protestant, and a Jew as one of the other three adjuncts. Still, members of the different confessions did not mix socially: marriages between Protestants and Catholics were rare, and between Christians and Jews almost nonexistent.[21]

Strasbourg's central religious landmark was its rose-colored cathedral. Today, visitors to the cathedral speak in hushed tones, but for centuries, it reverberated with joyous noise, contentious shouts, and the sounds of everyday life. For decades after the start of construction in

1254, the clink and hum of hammers, chisels, winches, and pulleys mingled with Latin mass, lively markets, and town meetings. During the Reformation, the cathedral shifted hands several times. At times, Lutheran hymns echoed to the far ends of the transepts. In a period of Catholic control, local Protestants raucously interrupted mass until armed men and the heavy tread of their boots restored order by command of Emperor Charles V himself. Once, the cathedral echoed the laughs and yells of children taking their snowball fight into the nave and the *pfff* of cold, wet projectiles hitting the frocks of priests at the altar.[22]

Over the centuries, the cathedral's white sandstone facade grew pink, and its spire survived the changing times. When the French attacked Strasbourg in 1678, one of the three cannonballs launched into the city hit the cathedral, an event deemed so momentous that the city fathers installed a plaque in commemoration. In 1681, Louis XIV demanded the return of Strasbourg's most prominent building to the Catholics. Then came the Revolution and a new era of demolition and construction in which revolutionaries called for an end to religious superstition. The cathedral took on a new purpose: a Temple of Reason. The heads of stone kings crashed to the ground, while a rocky monument to nature weighed upon the altar. The revolutionary leadership nearly voted to remove the spire altogether, but it was saved when an anonymous citizen argued that a red Phrygian bonnet of liberty be placed on top to inspire revolution across the Rhine in Baden. After a decade of turmoil, the cathedral returned to the Catholic Church in 1800 as part of Napoleon's religious settlement. Lightning damaged the roofs, pillars, and spire many times over the years, setting the roof on fire in 1759 and destroying a statue of the Virgin Mary. Despite repeated calls for the installation of a lightning rod—Benjamin Franklin himself approved the project in 1780—it took a massively destructive hit in 1833 to jolt the city into action. Few people ever reached the top of the spire, attainable only by a ladder of iron bars extending out above the city. Cathedral workers undertook the perilous task to mark important occasions with a flamboyant gesture, like the balloon that one worker attached to the spire on the day in 1852 that the railroad line from Paris first opened.[23]

A center of spiritual and public life, the Protestant New Church, seen here from Place Broglie c. 1860, housed two major libraries. (Archives de la Ville et de la Communauté urbaine de Strasbourg)

The New Church, Strasbourg's second largest religious space, contained two libraries and was physically attached to the Protestant Gymnasium that educated so many of Alsace's prominent citizens. The New Church had originally served as the church of the Dominicans and had later become an arsenal and a storage facility before definitively coming under Protestant control in 1681. With four pastors, including pietist Franz Haerter, the church welcomed Lutherans of varying theological persuasions. On Sunday mornings, the bells of Protestant churches peeled for fifteen minutes, calling congregations to worship. When Haerter delivered the sermon, he attracted three thousand faithful.[24]

Strasbourg's rich and poor, republicans and Bonapartists, Catholics, Protestants, and Jews coexisted within the city walls. When the bombs fell at the end of the summer, they hit people across social groups indiscriminately.

A Berlin!

The declaration of war changed everyone's summer plans. High-rolling society vacationing in Baden-Baden reluctantly left the casinos and water cures and returned, via Switzerland, to serious business in Strasbourg. Fifty trains passed through the station every day, bringing men and matériel to form the First Army Corps. Soldiers of all kinds converged on Strasbourg: regulars, artillery, cavalry, Zouaves, and the North African corps known as *Turcos* that "aroused general admiration."[25] Reserve soldiers in the Mobile Guard left their vegetable gardens, bakeries, and brasseries to rejoin their regiments. Some 350 customs agents, too, were called up to scout for enemy sentinels.[26] Piton saw his first machine gun on August 3, "this terrible engine that has been hidden until now with such jealous care and whose destructive action—which nothing, it seems, can resist—is said to assure us victory."[27] Journalists also hastened to Strasbourg, hoping to be the first into Prussia following France's victories. Major Parisian newspapers sent reporters, including Camille Pelletan for *Le rappel* and Jules Claretie for *L'opinion nationale*.[28]

Commanding General Ducrot was called up to lead the First Division of the First Army Corps. Command over Strasbourg fell to the square and stocky General Jean-Jacques Alexis Uhrich. Like the citadel, Uhrich was solidly built, with the interests of France at heart, but outmoded and inflexible. A native of nearby Phalsbourg born in 1802, Uhrich had served in Spain, Algeria, Crimea, and Italy, but he had never been called to defend his own people. Uhrich had retired from active duty in 1867, but at age sixty-eight, he volunteered to serve again and arrived in Strasbourg on July 21. One observer described the general as the kind of man that "you would pass ten times without noticing, but once you noticed him, you would never forget."[29] Even Uhrich's detractors believed he embodied the best characteristics of the French soldier: noble, loyal, proud, and forthright, with a firm handshake and a straightforward gaze. He was a good choice to command a city that was supposed to serve as a frontier depot, a stop on the way to the real action.[30]

In the evenings, soldiers loitered on Place Broglie in gas-lit cafés alongside civilian men and women, drinking, toasting, eating, smoking, singing the "Marseillaise" within earshot of the site where it had been

General Jean-Jacques Alexis Uhrich. Photographer probably Eugène Appert. Armand Dayot, *L'invasion: Le siège 1870, la commune 1871* (1901). (Charles Deering McCormick Library of Special Collections, Northwestern University Library)

written in 1792—and everyone shouting, *A Berlin!* Prefect Pron strutted about in uniform and kepi, followed by Jean-Baptiste-Emile-Henri-Camille, Count de Malartic, his general secretary and primary toady.[31] The rattle of sabers and the clink of glasses punctuated lively conversation. Dr. Henri-Etienne Beaunis recalled, "What enthusiasm and what festivities! . . . The handshakes of men, the smiles of women, the encouragement from all parts."[32] In hindsight, the doctor claimed, "Alsace was perhaps the only province where enthusiasm was spontaneous and not artificial."[33]

Not everyone was so excited. Twenty-eight-year-old Rodolphe Reuss, a teacher of history at the Protestant Gymnasium, sneered cynically at the empire and the motivations of his compatriots. He hoped to watch this war between two despots detachedly, recording his impressions in a scrapbook of newspaper clippings. When students of the Gymnasium offered their school prize moneys to go toward the care of wounded soldiers, Reuss commented that this "spontaneous" patriotic gesture only demonstrated the prodding of their elders.[34] A patriotic street demonstration on July 16, proudly reported in *L'impartial du Rhin,* left Reuss cold: "It was just street hooligans and girls howling in the streets."[35] Much as Parisian artists made the "flirty, vacuous, self-serving" young woman—*la parisienne*—a staple of their siege illustrations, Reuss indulged in misogynistic dismissals of his female compatriots.[36] He rejected the notion put forth in *L'impartial* that the young women in the demonstration had chastely gone home by eleven o'clock. No, they were off the streets because "they had made their choice" among the young men.[37]

Reuss was also disgusted at the arrival of drunken Alsatian reservists, who often lacked housing, food, and knowledge of their commanders. This embarrassing state of affairs, captured so clearly later in Emile Zola's novel *The Debacle,* was not entirely the fault of the reservists, who had been ordered to converge on points of concentration located far from their supply depots. Reuss heard that one man came home to find eight soldiers foraging in his garden, and others complained of servicemen begging in the streets. Market women responded pragmatically, setting up a large kettle of food for the hungry soldiers.[38]

Now that Strasbourg was at war, civilians prepared to protect themselves, their families, and their soldiers from harm. Strasbourg, along with eastern France, resolved to defend the country, if not Napoleon III's empire. But how? The French model of service encouraged the notion that military and civilian spheres were separate. Yet warfare necessarily drew civilians into combat, whether in fields, forests, or besieged cities. Furthermore, the French had a history of enlisting the service of all citizens in times of national crisis. In 1793, during the wars of the French Revolution, the revolutionary government had called on young men to serve in battle, women to make tents and clothing and tend to the wounded, children to gather linen, and the elderly to preach courage and revolution. If war could be seen as conflict between two nations of people, and not just between two rulers, the door was opened for civilian involvement of all kinds. But French civilians had not faced war on their own territory since 1815. What course of action should they take?[39]

The National Guard and the *Francs-Tireurs*

Civilian males seeking an active role in the war could volunteer for the National Guard or the *francs-tireurs*. Units of the National Guard, a volunteer force dating from the Revolution, usually served in their place of residence, patrolling the streets and maintaining order. Only men without previous military experience were eligible to enlist, as those with a record of service were to be reintegrated into the regular army. In recent decades, the National Guard had become the domain of the bourgeoisie, many of whom enjoyed the uniform and the reputation without the inconvenience of far-off military service. The war crisis heightened the urgency to join and led the National Guard to open its ranks to the working class. Three thousand men rushed to sign up. No matter that most of them had never shouldered a rifle, no matter that military technology and strategy had made untrained recruits obsolete: with memories of Valmy and 1848 as ammunition and sustenance, they planned to guard the city gates, man the ramparts, and defend their homes. They would elect their own officers and maintain an egalitarian spirit.[40]

The reality of the National Guard failed to live up to this republican fantasy. The empire of Napoleon III had no interest in arming its political opponents. Although Prefect Pron called for the formation of a National Guard unit on July 29, he dragged his feet when it came to organizing and arming the volunteers. Staunch republicans deplored the waste of so many valuable, idle men. Auguste Schneegans signed up on the second day of recruitment, but neither he nor any of his fellow republicans received a rifle, nor were they called upon to actually patrol the streets. When the four battalions of the National Guard finally met on August 8, Rodolphe Reuss and his fellows stood around disorganized in the rain for two hours before being sent home. Furthermore, republicans disagreed among themselves over just who should be allowed to join. Radicals steeped in revolutionary memories believed that any able-bodied man ought to be able to take up arms to defend his city; could the army not use thirty thousand men? For Schneegans, however, only the propertied men had an interest to protect. He based his calculation of wasted manpower on the number of electors—12,315—

dismissing out of hand eighteen thousand other men. Nobody in Strasbourg suggested the inclusion of women in the National Guard.[41]

Republicans furthermore were disappointed to find that the National Guard dripped with empty self-importance. When Reuss signed up on August 1, the recruiter asked which rank he desired. "Everyone wanted to be at least a sergeant or a corporal," he discovered, and "applicants for the rank of lieutenant or captain were numerous."[42] Reuss had already authored two books—on Protestantism in Bohemia during the Thirty Years' War and on witchcraft in early modern Alsace—but he had no experience to qualify him as an officer. The National Guard looked to him like another example of the empire's willingness to distribute honors without doing the job.

Eventually, Uhrich assigned the volunteers primarily to the task of keeping order within the city, especially around the mayor's office on Place Broglie and by the prison near the canals of Petite France. Uhrich did not entrust the National Guard with crucial duties. With the exception of a battalion of volunteer artillery, guardsmen stepped nowhere near the ramparts.[43] They received inferior rifles, little ammunition, and scant instruction, left (in the words of a disgruntled republican) in a state of "premeditated disorganization."[44]

Strasbourg's *francs-tireurs,* comprised of experienced riflemen, formed later, in mid-August, to serve as sharpshooters in the advanced defensive works.[45] Like the guardsmen, these guerrilla fighters occupied an ambiguous space between soldiers and civilians. The imperial government sanctioned the formation of their units and approved war credits to help pay for them, but their uniforms, organization, and operations functioned outside of the regular armed forces. Nationwide, some 57,600 men volunteered for 300 *franc-tireur* units.[46] On August 18, Frédéric Piton picked up his rifle and went to enlist but was disappointed to see that the others were all "young men unknown to me who were mostly interested in the question of Tyrolean hats and armbands with hunting horns."[47] He returned home without signing up. Although discussion of the makeshift uniform annoyed Piton, proper clothing was of deadly importance. The Prussians did not consider an armband to be sufficient indication of combatant status and threatened to execute any captured *franc-tireur.* After September 11, the Strasbourg units wore the uniform of the National Guard.[48]

The debates over the National Guard and the *francs-tireurs* revealed confusion regarding the line between civilians and soldiers. Civilians believed it their duty to protect themselves, regardless of experience. Uhrich distrusted an armed and angry population, whatever their politics, but finally acknowledged a need for enhanced forces of order. The safe and strict line between soldier and civilian had to be renegotiated.

For his part, Piton hoped that he could help protect France by keeping watch from the cathedral platform. But in late July, General Ducrot prohibited civilian access, redefining the space as belonging solely to the armed forces. Rejected, Piton tried to climb atop Saint-Thomas or the New Church, but found that they, too, were off limits. Nor could civilians enter the citadel. In the end, Piton had to settle for the vantage of his attic to observe movements below—and later, to watch projectiles falling from above.[49]

Red Cross Volunteers

In anticipation that Strasbourg would soon treat soldiers wounded on Alsatian battlefields, institutions all over the city converted their buildings into hospitals: the synagogue, the New Church, the two Catholic seminaries, the Protestant seminary attached to Saint-Thomas, the Franciscans, the Freemasons, the Gymnasium, the Catholic Lycée, the Petites Soeurs des Pauvres, the Deaconesses, and the Imperial Palace (today, the Palais Rohan) all prepared to shelter wounded men from the early days of August.[50]

At first, sectarian rivalry marred these efforts. The French-language Calvinist Reformed Church of rue du Bouclier refused to offer its space. With room for only thirty beds, Pastor Christian Karl Paira questioned whether the small amount of support justified the damage it could inflict on the Reformed Church. He feared that his parishioners would turn to one of the many Lutheran churches if their single Reformed church became a hospital. Max Reichard, a vicar at the New Church, worried that Catholics would distrust anything associated with Protestantism.

Lutheran Rodolphe Reuss characterized a rival Catholic committee as exclusive and forced.[51]

Despite this mistrust, all the makeshift hospitals soon came under the umbrella of the Strasbourg branch of the Red Cross. The Red Cross had been founded in 1863 in Geneva, and the first French committee had followed three years later. The Red Cross went hand-in-hand with the 1864 Geneva Convention, signed by twelve nations including France and Prussia, which protected sick and wounded soldiers as well as the doctors, nurses, religious personnel, and volunteers who cared for them. In 1870, Strasbourg's branch of the Red Cross existed primarily on paper. Like most other local committees, it sprang to life only when war threatened and found that it had to improvise its response. It soon became organized under the leadership of Jacques Kablé, a balding man with a little moustache and glasses. A lawyer by training and the head of an insurance company, Kablé embodied the moderate republican opposition and the competent leadership of Strasbourg's businessmen. Despite grumbling from Pron over the liberal politics of the Red Cross leadership, the organization managed to establish its headquarters on the ground floor at the Imperial Palace, just south of the cathedral.[52]

One of the largest Red Cross hospitals, the 150-bed hospital at the Protestant Seminary, came under the purview of the Deaconesses. The women of this society, which was founded by Pastor Haerter of the New Church in 1842, dedicated their lives to caring for the sick, educating young women and girls, and sharing their prayers and bread. They lived in community in the neighborhood near Saint-Thomas, just west of the Civil Hospital and not far from the establishments of the Catholic Sisters of Charity and the Sisters of Saint-Vincent de Paul. Unlike nuns, *diaconesses* did not take a perpetual vow. Still, the choice to enter the organization was not taken lightly; they could leave only after a year's waiting period. Celibacy was understood—they lived outside of the conjugal couple—although as good Protestants, they did not view celibacy as an elevated Christian state. They took neither a vow of poverty nor a salary, and their community took care of their needs. They did not take a vow of obedience but rather freely consented to the leadership of their elected sister superior. By 1867, 114 women served as deaconesses in and around Strasbourg.[53]

At the declaration of war, the Deaconesses prepared to "[dress] the wounds of the body and [pour] the balm of Christian consolation on bruised souls."[54] Like the other Red Cross hospitals, they depended upon private donations and faced personnel difficulties. Although the Deaconesses themselves were experienced in caregiving, the other well-meaning volunteers were often ill equipped. Moreover, despite the able leadership of Mlle Henriette Keck, the Deaconesses had to submit to the authority of a director of the Red Cross's choice.[55]

In addition to fixed hospitals inside the city, the Red Cross also prepared twelve mobile hospitals to tend to the wounded on battlefields outside. Antoine Zopff, a handsome man with longish dark hair and a drooping moustache, oversaw the organization of doctors, medical assistants, medications, linen, and food. Zopff raised the suspicions of many due to his association with the Freemasons and his promotion of secular education through the Strasbourg Circle of the French Teaching League. Still, his energy and ability to work with others won praise across the political spectrum. Every day from August 5 to 15, a convoy left Strasbourg for northern Alsace, including a total of thirty-four doctors. Not all of them returned; as it became clear that Strasbourg itself would become a target, the Germans did not allow doctors to reenter the city.[56]

Inter-Confessional Tension

Clergy in Strasbourg also became involved in the war effort. Protestants and Catholics prayed, at the emperor's behest, for France, Napoleon III, and his son, the imperial heir. Pastors and priests served as military chaplains.[57] Max Reichard decided to make his wartime contribution the distribution of New Testaments and spiritual tracts to French soldiers. He organized a group of fellow Protestants, who happened to be of Swiss origin, to circulate the literature. On August 2, the police arrested four of these men as German spies. They were dragged through the city streets, subject to threats and hollers. Reichard argued for their release, but the police were adamant: some of the literature had been printed in Berlin, and the missionaries' notebooks appeared to contain coded information about regiments and equipment. "Tracts" in spy-speak stood for "Zouaves," while "New Testaments" signaled "cannon."[58] Only their Swiss origin saved the men from a death sentence. After two weeks in jail, they were expelled from the city without papers and made their way to Basel.[59]

As this episode suggests, Strasbourg remained a city divided along confessional lines. Although elsewhere in France the most important religious tensions arose between Catholic monarchists and secular republicans or between formal religion and unorthodox expressions of spirituality such as scientific séances, in Strasbourg, the far more important fault line fell as it had for centuries between Catholics and Protestants. In the 1840s and 1850s, Catholic political leaders attempted to take control of the Saint-Thomas Foundation, the organization that financially supported the Gymnasium, the Protestant Seminary, and the city library held in the New Church. In the 1860s, the city tried to give the church of Saint-Pierre-le-Jeune to Catholics. None of these attacks succeeded, thanks to the vigorous response of Protestants, but they were not forgotten.[60]

The doctrine of papal infallibility, which Catholic leaders adopted at the first Vatican Council in early 1870, provided another opportunity for inter-confessional rivalry. Bishop André Raess, who staunchly supported papal infallibility, returned from the Council in triumph on June 2, 1870. Mayor Humann, Malartic, and the Catholic vicars met Raess at the train station and were soon joined by a crowd of lay Catholics. Raess processed to the cathedral with bells ringing from the parish churches.[61] Protestants watching the spectacle mocked the "insensible" doctrine as out of touch with the modern world and amenable to authoritarian rule.[62]

In this climate, some saw the conflict between France and the German states as a holy war between Catholics and Protestants. Catholic children taunted Protestants that they were going to take their houses.[63] Reuss heard rumors of a telegram from Baron Pron to Empress Eugénie that complained "the Protestants are helping out the Prussians."[64] Others protested that Bishop Raess prayed for victory from the Holy Virgin, "as if Protestants, Jews, and even Arabs [Muslims] did not fight for the same cause."[65] Later, some claimed to have seen spies signaling to the enemy from the bell towers of the Protestant churches of

Saint-Thomas and Saint-Pierre-le-Jeune.[66] Max Reichard's attempt to extend spiritual comfort to soldiers, and perhaps win over a few Protestant converts, elicited more ire than praise in this sensitive city.

"Misfortunes in Life That No Mortal Can Anticipate"

Not all civilians volunteered for the war effort. Many focused instead on protecting their family and property. One woman, vacationing in Colmar with her two children at the declaration of war, faced a terrible dilemma: should she remain outside in an unprotected city, or return to her home in Strasbourg and face the possibility of a siege? The woman recounted her inner debate in a handwritten memoir created probably in October 1870. A good mother, she wrote, must protect her children from danger, "but there are nevertheless some misfortunes in life that no mortal can anticipate."[67] Although this woman did not sign her name, her unedited manuscript—dedicated to her two young children—provides riveting detail about survival during the siege. Call her Catherine Weiss.

Before examining Weiss's story further, it is worth noting the rarity of her memoir. Even in a city with a high literacy rate, such as nineteenth-century Strasbourg, it is difficult to find sources written by women, artisans, or laborers. An individual who takes pen to paper requires not only literacy and leisure time, but also a certain sense of self. The existence of a memoir indicates the author's capacity for self-reflection and desire to employ a written narrative as a tool for understanding. A memoirist enjoys a healthy belief in her or his own worth, creativity, and freedom.[68] But writing a memoir is not enough; it must also be conserved. Publication was more common for male diarists such as Piton and Reuss, whose memoirs can be found today in a variety of libraries. Weiss's memoir was never published. Fortunately, it was conserved in Strasbourg's municipal archives.

Furthermore, the social networks of the poor and of females—even of middle-class women like Weiss—are not as visible in the historical record as they are for the male elite. The male civilians that we have encountered so far were all linked through well-documented institutions. Reuss attended school and taught at the Gymnasium attached to the New Church where Piton worked and Reichard served as vicar.

These men appear in official documents and in each other's memoirs. We can establish club memberships, and therefore social networks, even for organizations known for secrecy like the Freemasons. It is much more difficult to find out who spoke to whom on the city streets or who frequented a market stall or shared information over a beer at the local bar.[69] We may wish to know more about Weiss, but there are many thousands of Strasbourgeois whose experiences are even harder to uncover.

Suffering from chronic ill health, Weiss took the waters every summer in Soultzbach, a small village fifty-five miles to the south of Strasbourg, while her husband stayed in the city for work. By July, however, Weiss and her children had already left their usual summer refuge due to an outbreak of typhoid fever. They were renting a house near her parents in Colmar, an open city, when the war began. Weiss's father urged her to stay. She disagreed, hoping that a stronghold would better protect her children.[70]

Weiss rejoined her husband at their apartment in Strasbourg's city center on July 25, well before the siege set in, but she did not fully unpack her bags for another week. Torn between her father's warnings against spending the war in a stronghold and her husband's assurances that the city was unassailable, Weiss watched and waited. Every day, she walked past the growing camps of French soldiers. She later admitted that she could hardly have imagined that "all these handsome men [would be] killed or wounded" or that France truly could have been invaded. "When you do not know what war is," she continued, "these ideas cannot come to mind."[71] Weiss alternated between calm and fear through those early weeks of the war.

Like the civilians in Zola's *The Debacle*, Weiss compared the evidence before her eyes against the rhetoric of French invincibility.[72] As the first week of August passed, Weiss sought comfort in observing the military's preparations. Palisades went up around the approaches to each of the city gates.[73] In the Orangerie to the northeast of the city, dockworkers from Brest and Toulon created an embarkation point into the canal leading to the Rhine and toward German territory. Smoking their pipes and singing plaintively, they set stones, tied rope, and readied anchors. But Weiss wondered, Where were the boats? Was it possible that, three weeks after the declaration of war, this essential piece of equipment was still not in place? Her husband shook his head and reassured her that her fears were ungrounded. True, France had fallen victim to an "odious reign," but "we were still the first nation of the entire world."[74] She would not explicitly contradict her husband's opinion, but his words only reassured her "by half."[75]

Weiss had good reason to worry. The boats, which were "platonically intended to operate against Mainz," never arrived.[76] Defensive preparations were even worse. As the French army assumed it would win the war on German territory, most of the soldiers converging on Strasbourg saw the city as a point of departure. They were preparing to attack the German armies out in the field, not digging in for defense.[77]

"Contradictory Rumors, Great Anxiety"

At the outset of war in mid-July, everyone expected France to initiate the first offensive. The French standing army of 400,000 regulars could, in theory, prepare for combat weeks before the Prussian reserve-based army reached its full strength. The Prussian army depended on the universal conscription of twenty-year-old men for three years, followed by four years of service in the reserves and an additional five years in the National Guard *(Landwehr)*. With this extensive reserve system, the Prussian army could eventually call up more than one million men, but mobilization would take several weeks. The French hoped that their army of experienced men would counteract the Prussians' youth, education, and discipline.[78]

Napoleon III, eager for military glory and jealously mistrustful of his most capable marshals, insisted on taking personal command of the French army, despite the gallstones that nearly incapacitated him. He placed the bulk of his army in Lorraine, near Metz, in preparation to strike the Prussian armies north of the border. Meanwhile, he ordered the First Army Corps to Strasbourg, from which it could invade Baden to the east. In those early days of the war, France hoped that Austria-Hungary would join in an attack on the south German states.[79]

Napoleon III put Marshal Patrice MacMahon, the Governor-General of Algeria, in charge of the First Army Corps. When MacMahon arrived in Strasbourg from Algiers at the end of July, he found his divisions still

disorganized. Soldiers foraging for food in local gardens were a far cry
from a disciplined force prepared to attack. By this time, Strasbourg had
only 40,000 men, not the 100,000 required. Notions of an invasion of
Baden dissipated as an alliance with Austria-Hungary failed to materi-
alize. Meanwhile in Metz, hopes for a rapid drive north faded when
Napoleon III found himself with only 100,000 rather than the expected
150,000 soldiers.[80]

As July turned to August, Napoleon III and his advisors struggled
to formulate a new plan. When divisions from the emperor's army finally
did attack the German village of Saarbrücken on August 2, they achieved
a minor, temporary victory that distracted them from solidifying a
defense against the rapidly strengthening Prussian armies.[81] It proved to
be the only French incursion on German soil. The following day,
MacMahon's First Army Corps left Strasbourg and headed north
through Alsace, leaving Uhrich with only one regiment, the Eighty-
Seventh, along with pontonniers, artillery, and a handful of sailors.[82] As
the French still had no war plans, the First Army Corps prepared—
poorly—for all contingencies. It stretched along the eastern side of the
Vosges Mountains in order to stay in contact with Napoleon's corps to
the northwest and protect Strasbourg to the south. MacMahon's four
divisions each stood ten to twenty miles apart, too far to come to each
other's aid in the event of an attack.[83]

Meanwhile, Chief of the Prussian General Staff Helmuth von Moltke
mobilized the three Prussian armies along a hundred-mile arc between
Karlsruhe and Coblenz. Moltke had spent a decade preparing his army
for this invasion, sending Prussian general staff officers to France to
study their forts and map their territory. Moltke hoped to deliver a quick,
decisive blow in the late days of July, but he, too, had to wait impatiently
for his forces to gather strength. By August 3, Moltke had amassed
320,000 soldiers on the border, with one million reservists at the ready,
an army three times larger than the one he had deployed against Austria
just four years earlier.[84]

The Prussian Third Army was the southernmost of Moltke's armies,
about fifty miles distant from the other two, positioned in Baden and the
Palatinate to swing into France at the northeastern tip of Alsace. In command was Crown Prince Friedrich Wilhelm, King Wilhelm's son and a

hero of the 1866 Prussian victory over Austria at Königgrätz. His 125,000 men included the Fifth and Eleventh Corps of Prussia, two Bavarian corps, and a division each from Baden and Württemberg. The incorporation of these soldiers into Moltke's army confirmed Prussian dominance over the south German states. Four years earlier, Baden, Württemberg, and Bavaria had all fought alongside Austria against Prussia. After Austria's defeat, Prussia had managed to annex or domi-nate the north German states and levied a hefty war indemnity on the south German states. Upon France's insistence and due to the vested interests of the local elite, Baden, Württemberg, and Bavaria formed a nominally independent South German Confederation. Nevertheless, these countries acknowledged Prussia's undeniable military superiority. Baden adopted the Prussian needle gun and trained its officers within the Prussian corps. The Badenese even appointed Prussians to high government posts, including the minister of war and the chief of the gen-eral staff. By 1868, Bismarck had forced mutual defense treaties on the south German states, and in 1870, these treaties called the soldiers of Baden to invade neighboring Alsace. German loyalties were in the pro-cess of realignment.[85]

In the first week of August, the Prussian Third Army launched the war's first major offensive. It first sought to dislodge MacMahon's First Army Corps. This encounter unfolded in two stages: first, a small clash at Wissembourg on August 4, followed by a larger battle at Froeschwiller on August 6. The Third Army caught the French division at Wissembourg under General Abel Douay completely off guard. Although the French Chassepot rifles decimated Prussian frontal attacks, the Prussians vastly outnumbered the French 50,000 to 6,000, attacked their flanks, and closed off their line of retreat. The inhabitants of the town initiated the surrender. In order to save themselves and their town, civilians lowered the drawbridge and let in the Bavarians.[86]

Back in Strasbourg, forty miles south of Wissembourg, Rodolphe Reuss pulled out his pen. "The most contradictory rumors are circu-lating about a battle at Wissembourg," he recorded on August 4. "Great anxiety."[87]

When MacMahon learned of this loss, he ordered the four divisions of the First Army Corps to regroup at Froeschwiller, where he and the second division were already headquartered. Advance units of the Prussian Third Army ran into them on August 6. On both sides, rifles and heavy artillery inflicted appalling losses: the Germans suffered 10,500 casualties, and the French 11,000. In the end, the Third Army's numerical superiority carried the day. Crown Prince Friedrich Wilhelm now had an open path through the Vosges Mountains to Lorraine and a chance to catch Napoleon III's army. But before he turned west, he sent Prussian and Badenese divisions south to take Strasbourg.[88]

Around seven o'clock on the evening of Saturday, August 6, Rodolphe Reuss heard the alarm. Loud, cacophonous bells called everyone outside, maximizing the rumor and panic. Someone cried out that the enemy had crossed the Rhine. Others claimed that the Prussians were already at the city gates. An hour later, the first convoys of French wounded arrived. On foot or in carts, bloodied and poorly bandaged, these soldiers had traveled thirty miles from Froeschwiller on their own, without officers or medical personnel: armored horsemen without armor or horses, "ragamuffin *Turcos*," artillerymen who had abandoned their cannon—all of them dirty and cursing their commanders.[89] The festive atmosphere came to an end.

Catherine Weiss cried tears of pity for this sad parade of damaged men. In her eyes, the spectacle aroused a sense of unity among the citizenry, "old and young, rich and poor."[90] In contrast, Reuss the cynic saw only chaos and anger. The next day, upon reading in a newspaper that "the alarm sounded to stop the panic," Reuss commented, "That's completely false: the panic took place because they sounded the alarm."[91] In the midst of these emotions, doctors tended to the wounded, most of them suffering light wounds that did not require amputation. The most serious casualties could not make the journey to Strasbourg: they remained on the battlefield pleading for help for two more days.[92]

More chaos was to come. In the wake of the soldiers, peasants from surrounding villages poured into the city, their linens and furniture in tow. Red Cross ambulances staffed with the city's surgeons rushed out of Strasbourg toward the scene of battle. Uhrich hastily integrated the influx of dispirited, disorganized soldiers from Froeschwiller into a new regiment. Meanwhile, the German armies drew closer. On the next day, August 7, General Uhrich declared a state of siege.[93]

■ ■ ■

Prior to the war, Frédéric Piton had been able to make peace with ambiguity; now, he had to reconfigure his categories. In the space of just a few weeks, the war called into question three ways that Piton had formerly made sense of his city. First, Piton had seen the people of Baden as his brothers. Alsace and Baden had been two richly interconnected regions along the Rhine, neighbors able to coexist despite Alsace's long incorporation into France. They now had transformed into mere subparties on opposite sides of a conflict between two great powers. Soldiers from Baden came to attack Strasbourg.

The distinction between soldier and civilian had also changed. During peacetime, the lives of soldiers and civilians in Strasbourg were integrated. The lines between the two had long been blurry but comprehensible. Now, the war sharpened the spatial lines—Piton no longer had access to the cathedral platform or the citadel, and the only soldiers now visible in public were wounded—but the grey zone of their proper activities became more contested. As the besieging armies drew closer, everyone became a target—and more civilians wanted to act. Both men and women volunteered for the Red Cross. Men with no prior military experience had the opportunity to join the National Guard, a possibility that does not even seem to have occurred to a woman like Catherine Weiss, though their contributions were minimal and circumscribed. Piton's inability to volunteer as a watchman was symptomatic of a larger issue: civilian men wanted to contribute to the war effort but found few opportunities to do so.

Finally, before the war, Piton had moved easily, physically and intellectually, between the panoramic view from the cathedral and the labyrinth of the city streets. He had found liberation in his studies of Strasbourg's past. Now he faced limitations in all four dimensions. Confined within the city walls, unable to rise above the streets, and metaphorically cut off from the past and future, he was trapped in the realities of the present. Piton did not know when he would next see anything beyond the city limits. Betrayal, vulnerability, and confinement: before the first bomb landed in Strasbourg, the war shook Strasbourg's civilians.

CHAPTER TWO

Insiders and Outsiders

O N AUGUST 7 AT three o'clock in the afternoon, as German armies began to invade the suburbs and encircle Strasbourg, *Le courrier du Bas-Rhin* published General Uhrich's declaration of a state of siege. The decree unlocked an afternoon of panic. Grocers and bakers sold out, despite the fact that they should have been closed on a Sunday. Citizens took it upon themselves to arrest and "horribly mistreat" a supposed Prussian spy.[1] By Monday, the gates were shut and a curfew enforced, bringing to an end all the music and movement. "How grim are the streets in the evening," lamented Max Reichard. "No one on Place Broglie. . . . Only here and there a few people whisper to each other and speed quickly home."[2] The town fell eerily silent after so many weeks of whistles and steam. No one sang the "Marseillaise" anymore. The railroads now only served the military. No more letters, no more newspapers—at least not through official channels.[3] Even a naval officer found himself cut off: "We found ourselves . . . completely deprived of news as if we were in the middle of the sea."[4] When the municipal council asked about news from the outside, Prefect Pron reportedly replied, "News, news, I don't have any, and anyway I have to go piss!"[5]

Nobody in Strasbourg had expected a siege. It had been over fifty years since the Napoleonic Wars. *L'impartial du Rhin* had declared on July 21, "Nowadays . . . one no longer wastes one's time laying siege to strongholds."[6] After Froeschwiller, plans to use Strasbourg as a platform

41

for victory out in the field upended. Uhrich's top advisors became a defense council. The battle came to Strasbourg.

Just as the outbreak of war had reshuffled the use of urban space and social relations between soldiers and civilians, the state of siege created new insiders and outsiders. Whereas the city at peace prized circulation and movement, the city under siege turned every entrance and exit into a tense negotiation. The city walls became a literal barrier between those outside, who were among the first to experience the German occupation, and those inside, who anticipated bombardment and fire. The siege created figurative insiders and outsiders as well: military exigencies excluded male civilians from power, and civilians took on a gendered division between those deemed "useless" and those capable of protecting their neighborhoods. Fear of spies, those outsiders who have penetrated the inside, grew stronger. In the week before the first bombs fell, the spatial and gendered definitions of belonging became more important than ever.

How to Besiege a City

In 1870, siege warfare combined centuries-old customs and procedures with modern artillery. Military commanders on both sides followed highly ritualized customs and conventions that had been largely codified by the eighteenth century. Following these customs, commanders generally avoided open fighting and communicated with each other through polite, formal letters delivered by their protected intermediaries (parlementaires). The besieging army slowly approached the stronghold by creating a series of trenches and earthworks, called parallels. A carefully engineered parallel protected the besieging army's flanks from the city's defenders, even as the attackers entered into firing range. Eventually, the besieging artillery drew close enough to blast into the fortifications and create a breach that could be penetrated in a final assault. Once the besiegers had opened such a "practicable breach"— the formal phrase appeared in any discussion on siege warfare—they expected the defenders either to surrender or to submit to days of pillage. Alternatively, if their artillery failed to open the fortress, besiegers waited until the defenders starved.[7]

Meanwhile, the defenders hunkered down, rationed their food, volleyed their own projectiles, and hoped for relief from the outside. They depended upon the thick walls that had encircled their cities for generations. In the late fifteenth century, after the arrival of gunpowder, European cities began to build fortifications that could withstand artillery bombardment. Sébastien Le Prestre de Vauban, Louis XIV's chief military engineer and designer of Strasbourg's fortress, brought these innovations to the height of rationality. His fortifications took on massive proportions, capable of storing enormous quantities of food and supplies. Across France, Vauban's deep defensive line of fortresses eventually included some three hundred fortified and garrisoned strongholds. Strasbourg's fortress dated from the 1680s. Low, thick, angled walls along with gunports, outcroppings, and a polygonal shape maximized defensive capabilities. Lunettes—half-moon shaped fortifications that jutted out into the surrounding plain and connected to the main defensive walls by narrow land bridges—provided cover for defensive artillery. Such vast fortresses could require a besieging army to build siegeworks extending twenty-five miles or more in diameter. Early modern sieges could take months, if not years, to conclude: in Flanders, the Spanish blockaded the port of Ostend from July 1601 to September 1604.[8]

Besieging armies historically relied on the suffering of civilians in order to take a city. Men and women faced different perils and expectations in siege warfare, and these differences affected military strategy. For centuries, the primary threat to civilians came in the form of starvation and thirst. Since food traditionally went to male defenders first, women and children were often the victims of hunger. In the early modern period, the inhabitants of besieged cities could expect little mercy upon capitulation. Rape and pillage were the expected norm, especially if the city was deemed to have resisted longer than required by honor, that is, after a practicable breach had been created. Women were the primary victims of rape. Customarily, victors considered this sort of "plunder" their right. In an era predating reliable state funding for armies, the plunder of food and money played an essential role in the wartime economy. The suffering of civilians and especially of women was therefore fundamental to siege warfare.[9]

In early modern sieges, the armies of both the besiegers and the besieged were responsible for thousands of noncombatants: the civilians of the fortress city in question and the legions of camp followers attached to the besieging army. As John Lynn has documented, European armies prior to the late 1600s routinely carried noncombatant men, women, and children in tow—often numbering as many as the soldiers—who provided basic services and companionship to the soldiers; the women often participated in and managed the plunder, and were subject to the physical risks of life near a battlefield.[10] The presence of noncombatants on each side meant that both armies risked harming those who did not engage in battle. Just War theorist Francisco de Vitoria, noting that non-combatants might sometimes be legitimate targets in war, included both the "innocent people" inside a fortress city and the camp followers out-side: "If a town be wrongfully besieged and rightfully defended, it is lawful to fire cannon-shot and other missiles on the besiegers and into the hostile camp, even though we assume that there are some children and innocent people there."[11]

In many ways, the siege that unfolded in Strasbourg looked like sieges from earlier eras. The besieging army approached slowly and methodically, and the attackers depended on the pain of civilians in order to achieve their goal. As we shall see, however, the siege differed qualitatively from older sieges. Structural changes in European armies beginning in the seventeenth century had centralized military power; consequently, armies were paid more regularly and did not rely as heavily on plunder. Furthermore, besieging armies no longer brought legions of women and children in their wake. The Prussian and Badenese armies were comprised almost exclusively of soldiers. This change meant that only the besieged army had to protect noncombatants. The balance of "innocents" had shifted in favor of the besieged people of Strasbourg.

Modern Artillery

In the early days of August, as Prussian forces approached, the inhabit-ants of Strasbourg may have recalled newspaper accounts of the French siege of Puebla, Mexico, in 1863 or perhaps remembered stories about the siege of Vicksburg in the same year during the U.S. Civil War. For most French people, however, the most salient example of a siege had taken place fifteen years earlier and a thousand miles away, when the French and British together had besieged the Russian port of Sevastopol during the Crimean War. It was a long, brutal episode. Although the French and British vastly outgunned the Russians—they lobbed 400,000 more shells into the city than the Russians could return—and although they killed some 100,000 Russians in the process, Sevastopol took a year to fall. Due to their modern fortifications and precision firearms, the Russians successfully turned back French and British assaults. When the city finally fell in September 1855, the French public in Strasbourg and elsewhere celebrated with bonfires and illuminations.[12]

The siege of Sevastopol illustrated the devastating power of modern artillery. The arms race of the nineteenth century centered on firepower. Smooth-bore muskets and field guns gave way to rifled weapons, whose grooved interiors allowed projectiles to move farther, faster, and more accurately. Breech-loading weapons could be refired more rapidly than traditional weapons that were loaded through the barrel. In 1870, the French army held the upper hand in rifles and had developed the machine gun, but the Prussians countered with the latest artillery: the steel Krupp cannon. The German model fired more quickly and further than the French bronze cannon, cast in 1859 but already outmoded. The standard Prussian field gun was a six-pounder, while the heavy artillery lofted shot weighing up to twenty-four pounds, compared with four and twelve pounds on the French side. Due to improved rifling and loading capabilities, "the Krupp guns had three times the accuracy, twice the rate of fire, a third greater range, and many times the destructiveness of the French guns."[13] This artillery helped to transform the nature of warfare. In 1814, artillery fire had accounted for one out of every five combat casualties, but by 1914, the ratio grew to three out of four.[14]

The Prussian artillery could choose among several kinds of projectiles. They could send solid shot, shells filled with gunpowder, or shells filled with gunpowder and bits of metal. Although British artillery officer Henry Shrapnel had invented the latter back in 1804, many civilians had not yet been exposed to it. In a post-siege letter to his distant

German cousin, who had presumably performed his military service, Strasbourgeois Emile Schmitt wrote, "You probably know what shells are. I did not know but have since learned."[15] Prussian shells were fitted with percussion fuses that exploded on impact, meaning that the Prussians could launch their projectiles from any range and expect to damage whatever they hit (the French used inferior time-fuses, preset to explode at 1,300 or 3,000 yards). The Prussians achieved unprecedented, though by no means perfect, accuracy due to careful training under General Gustav Eduard von Hindersin. Prussian artillery could inflict damage from two and a half miles away. Furthermore, in order to protect their artillery, the Prussians used the new tactic of indirect fire. Instead of sighting their targets visually, they calculated the angles of fire and shot at targets from a relatively safe, concealed position. How could Strasbourg defend itself?[16]

The Walled City

French officers focused their defensive efforts on the city walls and citadel. While Frédéric Piton used the cathedral's platform to provide his four-dimensional perspective on the city, military officers took a different approach. They imagined the city as a two-dimensional geometric form whose strong and weak points could be understood from the distance only achieved by maps. "If one glances at the map of Strasbourg," wrote ship's captain Bergasse du Petit-Thouars, "one sees that this place represents an isosceles triangle, oriented lengthwise from east to west, with the acute angle pointing to the Rhine and formed by the citadel."[17] The Ill River cut through the two long legs of the triangle, flowing in from the southwest under defensive works, splitting into two branches— the northwestern branch called the Canal des Faux Remparts—that surrounded the Grande Île, and then meeting up again and flowing out next to Pêcheurs Gate in the center of the northeastern side of the triangle.

Strasbourg's city walls, massive structures filled with earth, defined the three sides of the triangle. A system of lunettes, earthworks, and forts added reinforcement. The base of Strasbourg's triangle, facing northwest, bristled with such structures, including two forts on either extremity, Fort de Pierre to the north and Fort Blanc to the south. Three city gates opened through this line of defense: Pierre Gate and Nationale Gate (also called Blanche Gate) near the two forts, with Saverne Gate in the middle. The citadel lay opposite the base of the triangle, at the very eastern tip. When Vauban designed the citadel in the 1680s, just after Strasbourg came under French control, its thick walls defended the army against resentful citizens as well as against the Holy Roman Empire.[18] Bergasse du Petit-Thouars had to admit that "it would have been more natural" to place the citadel of Strasbourg north instead, near the suburb of Schiltigheim.[19] As Vauban himself had acknowledged centuries before, Pierre Gate in the northwest corner of the city remained a weak point.[20]

Although Strasbourg had once been a first-class fortress, it had not been updated since Vauban's time. In the 1860s, the commanding general at Strasbourg, Auguste-Alexandre Ducrot, had traveled incognito to Prussia to investigate their fortresses. The results confirmed his worst suspicions: Strasbourg could no longer compete. Ducrot composed memoranda calling for new fortifications, but no repair work or maintenance was performed. Officials suspended an 1869 plan to construct new, stronger barracks in the citadel due to lack of funds. By 1870, the defenses no longer provided sufficient shelter from long-range heavy artillery and could not protect the civilian center from bombardment.[21]

In addition, the French army in Strasbourg lacked precisely the maps that would have allowed them to use geographic information effectively. As Uhrich complained to Prefect Pron, the maps of Strasbourg published by Berger-Levrault had been flying off the shelves ("they are at the moment sold out") and into German hands ("please tell them to temporarily stop selling these maps").[22] It was said that Uhrich himself had to borrow a map from a local lawyer.[23]

Although they were outmoded, Strasbourg's earthworks provided the best hope for defense from Prussian heavy artillery. In order to break through, the cannon had to aim down into the base of the earthworks. To achieve such a low angle, artillerymen were obliged to draw close to the fortress, within the range of accurate French rifles and 250 front-loading cannon atop the ramparts.[24] The Prussians needed to build protective parallels in order to bring their cannon close enough, and that would take time. Despite its long range and firepower, the Prussian artillery could not immediately blast its way into Strasbourg.

Still, the French found it difficult to stop the Germans from preparing their artillery for attack. The French were outmanned and outgunned, with only 17,000 men—many of whom were not regulars, but mobile guardsmen, national guardsmen, firemen, customs officials, or sailors—against 40,000 on the German side.[25] From the beginning, the scattered war effort meant that Strasbourg could not hope for external reinforcements. Prefect Pron's plea to Empress Eugénie garnered this reply: "I thank you for your telegram, I communicated it to the council of ministers; but I fear that there is nothing to be done."[26]

Walled In

Strasbourg's defensive walls can also be viewed from the perspective of civilians. For centuries, the city walls had defined the limits of urban space and the related taxes, privileges, and loyalties. In the fifteenth century, the city walls lay just beyond Strasbourg's Grande Île, extending northwest to encompass the neighborhoods of Saverne and Pierres, south just beyond the Civil Hospital, and east around the neighborhood known as the Krutenau. After Strasbourg's annexation to France in 1681, Vauban extended the walls further east to enclose the military esplanade and the citadel. By 1870, these same walls contained a population that had doubled in size.[27]

In the mid-nineteenth century, the city walls formed the immovable backdrop as municipal leaders in Strasbourg became attuned to trends in urban planning. European municipal leaders increasingly believed that urban planning should take a holistic approach, encompassing railroad depots, roadways, parks, marketplaces, and sewers. All of these elements should work together to move people and goods in and out, making the city center healthier and more amenable to the generation of wealth. Most famously, Baron Georges Haussmann, the prefect of the Seine, reimagined Paris as a body in need of circulation and air. Napoleon III dreamed of "major arteries opening, populous areas becoming healthier, rents tending to get lower as a result of more and more building, the working class getting richer through work, poverty diminishing through better organization of relief, and Paris responding to its highest calling."[28] Backed by the imperial state and sustained through the wealth of France's banks, French municipal leaders in cities large and small saw infrastructure as the bedrock of prosperity and political stability.

Strasbourg, too, invested in infrastructure and developed into a modern transportation hub. Steam-powered navigation came to the Rhine in 1825, and in the decades following, new canals linked the Rhine to the Rhône, Ill, and Marne Rivers. As rail connections opened to Basel (1841) and Paris (1852), the city became the nexus of rail lines leading east to Germany and south to Switzerland. In 1854, a new street, rue de la Gare, plowed through old neighborhoods to connect the train station to the city center. These changes solidified Strasbourg's position as a major inland port, France's stake in the Rhineland economic power-house. Modern construction, including the train station and the Banque de France on Place Broglie, embodied the city's dependence on trans-portation and commerce. Under mayors Charles-Louis Coulaux (1852–1864) and Théodore Humann (1864–1870), Strasbourg's streets widened, their names and numbers were increasingly standardized, building codes became stricter, waste collection improved, and new sidewalks facili-tated travel within the city's neighborhoods.[29]

One final change illustrates the growing influence of modern trade. Traditionally, the city gates closed each evening at ten o'clock. Anyone stuck outside had to wait to enter until the wee hours of the morning: three o'clock in summer, an hour later in winter. The army liked to close the doors at night to discourage the entrance of beggars or thieves. Customs agents liked it, too, because they did not want to staff the gates all night. But businessmen and travelers lobbied to keep the gates open to facilitate late-night train travel. In 1863, the Ministry of War finally decreed the permanent opening of the gates of all French strongholds.[30]

Amid these changes, the city walls stood impassive. Nobody talked seriously about tearing them down. Military strategists may have been willing to leave the city gates open during peacetime, but they were not prepared to abandon them all together. The military imperative remained paramount, and the municipality also had good reasons to maintain the fortress. Walls permitted the collection of taxes on goods entering the city and prevented the construction of new working-class neighborhoods. As the Germans armies drew closer, the walls presented the best defense of Strasbourg.

Suburban Invasion and Occupation

Outside the fortifications, suburban villages, small industrial centers, and large aristocratic parks lay open to invasion. In recent years, Strasbourg's semi-industrial suburbs had mushroomed, responding to the garrison's demand for machinery, leather, and beer. By 1866, the suburbs surpassed 15,000 inhabitants. This population prepared for the oncoming Prussians as well as they could. Farmers rushed the harvest, and schoolchildren gathered linens and dressings. In Schiltigheim, less than a mile north of Strasbourg's Pierre Gate, the Strasbourg committee of the Red Cross set up a mobile hospital while Pastor H. Magnus sought consolation in the psalms. But the local governments had received no instructions from the imperial authorities on how to interact with the invaders. The decision to resist or cooperate rested with village mayors.[31]

Advance Badenese dragoons rode into Schiltigheim at seven o'clock on the morning of August 7. This action triggered Uhrich's declaration of a state of siege in Strasbourg. On August 9, a German intermediary approached the French outposts to formally request capitulation. Uhrich refused. Two days later, the French military watch atop the cathedral spied the approach of the full Badenese division. With their telegraph wires cut, the watchmen were helpless to warn the suburbs about these 25,000 soldiers, but villagers already knew that they were in danger. The Badenese soon occupied Oberhausbergen, Mittelhausbergen, and Niederhausbergen, along with Eckbolsheim and Koenigshoffen to the southwest. They spread eastward to take the canals of the Ill and the Marne and eventually encircled the entire city. Upon arrival in a suburban town, soldiers set to work digging earthworks, installing cannon, and stacking cannonballs in pyramids. Farmers from the south German states brought hundreds of poplar trees and other material for the earthworks.[32] The Badenese stood alone before Strasbourg from August 11

to 17, making painfully clear that Baden had allied with its former enemy
Prussia against its Alsatian neighbors. Everyone knew that Prussian
reinforcements were coming.[33]

The invasion brought normal life in Schiltigheim to a halt. "Nobody
worked any more," recalled brewer Emile Ehrhardt. "One lived in the
street searching for news; imaginations were overheated."[34] Breweries
stopped producing, but they continued to sell their wares both to local
clientele and army suppliers.[35] Stories abounded of Badenese spies who
knew the area all too well.[36] Many Badenese soldiers had recently
worked in local brasseries, and when they asked for beer, they refused
the drinks they were served: " 'Not that one,' they said, 'but the one from
the little vault,' and they indicated perfectly the storage room that
held the best quality [beer]. It was easy for them to know; they had
brewed it themselves."[37]

On the evening of August 14, the rumor spread that the Germans
planned to destroy Schiltigheim overnight. Immediately, people,
wagons, and carriages clogged the streets. "The fear, the loud cries of
pain that this news brought, cannot be described," recorded Pastor
Magnus.[38] With other town leaders and clergy, he sought answers from
the Germans but received no guarantees of safety. Ehrhardt and his
brother tried to send their parents and children away, but eventually, the
family and several neighbors decided to stay. They huddled together in
their brewery, hardly daring to sleep. At three o'clock, a terrible explosion woke them. Fearing the worst, they rushed down into their vaulted
cellar amid "an indescribable brouhaha in the courtyards and staircases."[39] The next morning, they learned that the Germans had blown
up the bridge des Quatre-Colonnes on the canal near the Orangerie, less
than a mile east.

As it turned out, the Germans did not destroy Schiltigheim, but the
rumor had seemed plausible to inhabitants who had been hearing fearful
stories during the previous week. On August 7, German forces had
entered Haguenau, about twenty miles north of Strasbourg. Someone
fired from a window, and this infuriated the Germans: "Their rage knew
no boundaries," reported one mobile guardsman.[40] They burst into
houses, sabers first, pillaging flour and animals, searching for the

culprits. Villagers now were forced to quarter soldiers, sometimes ten or twenty at a time. As the Prussian army advanced, it burned property, shot peasants, and took village leaders hostage.

To Alsatians, this scene seemed to belong to the sixteenth and seventeenth centuries, when soldiers survived through pillage and quartering. To the Prussians, however, the encounter in Haguenau was the unfortunate but necessary consequence of villagers' refusal to acknowledge that they had been occupied. As Prussian soldiers approached Alsatian villages, Crown Prince Friedrich Wilhelm tried to establish martial law. He expected civilians to refrain from any violent act of resistance against his soldiers and to withhold any aid to "the enemy"—the French army. The Germans reserved the right to execute French civilians on the spot for shooting at German soldiers, spying, destroying bridges or canals, or misleading the German army. In addition, any town associated with the guilty party could be taxed. Inhabitants furthermore had to supply bread, meat, fat, coffee, tobacco, and alcohol for each soldier, and oats, hay, and straw for each horse, as well as any other requisitions German officers deemed necessary. The Red Cross hospital was partially evacuated to Strasbourg, and several others (though not all) were abandoned or closed by order of the German authorities. German military doctors set up their own hospitals.[41]

For the Prussians, in other words, invasion led swiftly to occupation. The distinction is important because an invasion can be justifiably resisted, whereas an occupation demands pacification in the name of order. In instructions issued on July 25, the Prussians claimed to occupy territories as soon as their army was present, even before they had established an effective administration. They argued that noncombatants had no right to defend themselves or to resist. From the Prussian perspective, the curtailment of civilian resistance would prevent an uncontrollable spiral of violence. Civilians were civilians, and soldiers were soldiers—even if they had been farmers or clerks in the reserves just weeks before. This capacious definition of occupation had appeared in an 1870 (prewar) treatise by German military theorist Felix Dahn. The Governor General of Alsace, Lieutenant General Friedrich Alexander von Bismarck-Bohlen, reasserted these proscriptions on civilian resistance in a proclamation dated September 12. They were confirmed in the German Military Penal Code of 1872. The Prussians were particularly concerned about the volunteer *francs-tireurs,* guerrilla sharpshooters whom the Germans considered to be rebellious civilians. As the war continued into the fall and winter, *francs-tireurs* picked off soldiers, sowing suspicion and nervousness.[42]

Many French civilians believed they had the right to resist the encroaching army. In the words of one Alsatian, the Prussians displayed "the hypocrisy of Tartuffe and the cruelty of the barbarian."[43] Auguste Schneegans protested vigorously that the Prussian declarations were no more than cynical promises establishing rules that they expected to be broken, the better to punish French civilians.[44] In Strasbourg, the Prussian proclamations suggested that a prolonged civilian resistance to the siege could prove devastating should the city then fall into Prussian hands. At the same time, the warnings hardened opposition to the Prussians. By August 8, Rodolphe Reuss discovered within himself "the specific fiber of French patriotism in the face of danger. For me, I never before understood so well that, despite all the high esteem in which I hold the *esprit* of Germany, politically I would be very unhappy to belong to it."[45]

"Useless Mouths"

With the suburbs invaded, Uhrich tried to implement defensive flooding. In times of emergency, the region's many waterways and canals allowed for engineered flooding just north, south, and east of the city walls. Thanks to its swampy surroundings, Strasbourg had depended on this method of defense for centuries.[46]

This time, however, Uhrich was not able to maximize the defensive potential of floods. In theory, the military forbade construction on the glacis—the bank gently sloping away from the fortress—so that attackers would be exposed and emergency flooding would cause minimal damage. But during the 1850s and 1860s, nobody enforced this precaution. All along the canal leading north out of the city from Juifs Gate, country houses, garden hedges, and fences presented Uhrich with a dilemma: Article 248 of the French military regulations empowered him to undertake any necessary defensive measure without fear of indemnity, but Article 245 ordered him to make flooding the least damaging possible to the inhabitants and their property. Ever cautious, Uhrich sought authorization from the minister of war to open the floodgates. But, in a demonstration of the late Second Empire's crisis of leadership, Uhrich never received a clear answer. The Ministry of War changed hands on August 10 from Pierre Charles Dejean (who had served for twenty-two days) to Charles Cousin-Montauban, Comte de Palikao (who would serve for twenty-six days). The delay and the many buildings and hedges allowed enemy soldiers an easier approach for reconnaissance. The Germans gained enough information to start bombarding the city before they fully encircled Strasbourg.[47]

Uhrich was castigated for delaying this key defensive move, but once he put it into effect, civilians bemoaned the destruction of homes, vegetable gardens, and flour mills. Starting on August 16, battalions of French soldiers and organized civilians began to tear down buildings to prepare for the flood. Some of these houses and gardens belonged to the wealthy, while others were the only property of working people. Le Bon-Pasteur, a convent located near the citadel, came down as well. Inhabitants had forty-eight hours to leave.[48]

Uhrich also turned his attention to the internal civilian population. French military regulations provided little guidance. At the declaration of a state of siege, the military commander was supposed to expel "useless mouths, foreigners, [and] those deemed dangerous," and ensure food for the civilian population.[49] Civilians were aware of these priorities, as *Le courrier du Bas-Rhin* published the military regulations on the morning of August 7. First, following Article 245 of the military regulations, Uhrich authorized the expulsion of foreigners. Workers originating from Baden who had served in cafés quickly departed. Dr. Henri-Etienne Beaunis regretted most of all the departure of the Badenese "Gretchens," with their blond braids and red arms, who served cold and frothy beer. Some Germans who had lived for years in Strasbourg stayed on out of loyalty to their adopted city. A full week later, on August 14, Uhrich ordered such individuals to present themselves to the police in order to receive a permit if they wished to stay, but he was in no position to root out every foreigner.[50]

Second, Uhrich invited those without a "serious" interest in Strasbourg to depart, although he did not explicitly address the definition of the "useless mouths" that were expected to leave. To Uhrich's mind, the distinction between soldier and civilian remained clear, but he could hardly order 77,000 noncombatants to evacuate, and he did not have the means or the authorization to provide any support: no trains, wagons, provisions, or passes.

Individuals and families had to decide for themselves their course of action. They only enjoyed a small window of opportunity to escape. The last train left on the morning of August 9, less than two days after Uhrich's declaration of a state of siege.[51] Many proudly refused to depart, calling railcars out of the city the "train of cowards."[52] Feeling a rush of courage, Catherine Weiss refused to leave, despite her husband's insistence. Weiss later became consumed with guilt for this decision, which exposed her children to the siege. "It was a crime," she confessed.[53] "We constituted what was commonly called 'useless mouths.' "[54] Weiss bitterly regretted that she had not left in order to give food to soldiers and resented the country folk who "had the deplorable idea" of seeking refuge inside the city walls.[55] One hundred fifty-two refugees tried to find shelter in the citadel, bringing their furniture and precious objects for safekeeping.[56] To their minds, they had a "serious interest" in escaping the invading soldiers. Departures and entrances by foot and by cart became more difficult as the week wore on. By August 15, the Germans completely encircled Strasbourg, preventing anyone from passing through the gates without special permission.

Next, Uhrich established his authority over the civilian hierarchy. Following military regulations, he declared that all powers went to himself as commander, except those that he delegated to civilian authorities. The prefect, the mayor, and all other civilian positions would continue in their administrative functions, but they would have to execute the general's directives, and the prefect would report daily to Uhrich. The justice system was expected to function as usual, though certain crimes— such as insurrection and treason—would be handled through the military courts.[57]

Journalists felt shut out of this arrangement. Paul Raymond-Signouret, the editor of *L'impartial du Rhin,* complained that throughout the siege he received "no precise information on local affairs, no official document on the operations of the defense. It seemed that the vast majority of inhabitants had no right to know what was going on, even exclusively inside the walls."[58] He suspected in this silence a nefarious plot to demoralize the population. Understandably, Uhrich refused to supply Raymond-Signouret with officers' reports, despite the editor's promise to publish only non-compromising portions. The journalist was appalled that Uhrich preferred to share these reports with the minister of war first. Raymond-Signouret wanted Uhrich to defend Strasbourg with the utmost martial rigor, yet the editor also believed that civilian leaders such as himself should be privy to the decision-making process.

The food situation exemplified the gap between what the officials knew and what they told the public. Although Uhrich did not address provisions in his August 7 decree, his defense council assessed the question immediately. The food supply was adequate for 60 days, and bread rations could extend for an additional 120 days. Uhrich sent two squadrons and two infantry companies to the suburbs to secure one hundred head of cattle and other provisions. The news was not yet dire, but most people were not aware of the adequate food supply. They only knew that the cost of sugar, coffee, and rice was rapidly rising. The price of butter increased, too, without the supply from the dairies of the Black Forest across the border in Baden. Categorized as "useless mouths," men and women wondered if they could add anything of value to the encircled city.[59]

"Spies Everywhere"

As the siege began, Uhrich also had to concern himself with the loyalty of Strasbourg's inhabitants. Despite nearly two hundred years of French rule, he feared that some citizens would prefer the city to regain its status as an autonomous city-state. Imperial authorities particularly suspected local republicans of disloyalty. "The opposition . . . has caressed the idea of a separation of Alsace from France," argued Malartic.[60] Perhaps such ideas would make Strasbourg's native leaders less loyal to France and unwilling to sacrifice for the imperial cause.

Did some citizens of Strasbourg want to surrender immediately? Even if they did not seek independence from France, some might have found the idea of surrender to be the best course of action. After all, a siege brought destruction and a strong possibility of starvation, rape, and pillage. Perhaps capitulation would be the best option. No published diarist, journalist, or politician dared to voice such an opinion in August 1870, but thirty years later, the memoir of a longtime resident (published in German Strassburg) mentioned a petition, signed by four thousand residents as of August 8, calling for immediate surrender. The "rich and very respectable" Herr L., who had gathered many of the signatures, placed his wife, children, home, and business above all else, particularly since Napoleon III had dragged France into this misfortune.[61]

Such a petition, if it existed, could not hope for any hearing. The French commanding officer was required to resist to the utmost any internal pressure to capitulate. "He must not forget," the regulations stipulated, "that military law condemns with the death penalty and military degradation the commander . . . who capitulates without having forced the enemy to pass through the slow and successive stages of sieges, and without having repulsed at least one assault through practicable breaches."[62] The plight of civilians ought not to figure into the decision. Rather, the commander was to "employ the inhabitants . . . [and] make use of their edifices, houses and all materials."[63] On August 11, the military authorities requisitioned coal and wood and called upon workers to help maintain the fortifications.[64] Civilians were pawns of military strategy rather than a prize to be safeguarded.

A joint proclamation from Uhrich and Pron on August 10 reflected the military regulations, and indeed, went further: "Disturbing rumors and panic have been spreading in recent days, involuntary or by design, throughout our brave city. Some individuals have put forth the thought that the fortress should surrender without firing a shot. In the name of the courageous and French population we protest energetically against these cowardly and criminal weaknesses. The ramparts are armed with 400 cannon. The garrison is composed of 11,000 men, without including the National Guard. If Strasbourg is attacked, Strasbourg will defend itself—so long as there remains a soldier, a hunk of bread, a cartridge."[65]

This proclamation took a hard line: refusal to capitulate until death, in opposition to those who took a pragmatic view regarding the health and safety of the city. Defense "so long as there remains a soldier, a hunk of bread, a cartridge" went far beyond the military regulations' requirement of defense through one assault on a practicable breach. As we shall see, Uhrich eventually distanced himself from this position, to the point where he did not include the August 10 proclamation in his memoir of the siege.

Some civilians embraced this staunch position. Journalist Raymond-Signouret later claimed that the "immense majority of the population . . . was resolved to firmly second the military authority and to resist to the last extremity."[66] His only problem with the August 10 proclamation was that it revealed to the enemy that some citizens of Strasbourg hoped for capitulation.

Despite such pronouncements, most people did not know what to expect or how to wait. Days of unease led to violence directed against the remaining German inhabitants. In a city where many people spoke French, German, and Alsatian, loyalties were difficult to discern, and the population "saw spies everywhere."[67] Bergasse du Petit-Thouars was warned of a plot (real or imagined?) to blow up the Mairie.[68] On August 13, a crowd attacked the founder of the anticlerical Teaching League, a French citizen.[69] Others experienced the first week of the siege in a daze. "We continued to wander through our little occupations," remembered Weiss. "We walked through the streets up through August 15."[70]

At Brasserie Lipp

While General Uhrich focused on defenses, Mayor Humann and civilian neighborhood leaders turned their attention to the protection of property. Most terrifying was the threat of fire, which even in ordinary times consumed buildings almost every week.[71] Some neighborhoods were constructed entirely out of wood. In a fire, staircases acted like chimneys, pulling the flames through an entire structure in minutes. The municipality engaged six elderly watchmen as fire lookouts. They lived and worked atop the cathedral platform, in a small eighteenth-century house with six sleeping chambers and a common stove. Every fifteen minutes—all day, every day—after having rung the quarter hour, the aged guardians made the tour of the platform, scanning the horizon for signs of smoke. In the event that they spied a fire, they rang the tocsin—an alarm of multiple bells—and indicated the direction with a red flag during the day, a lantern at night. Trained professional firefighters rushed to the fire, usually to find that they could save only the neigh-boring buildings.[72]

To prepare civilians for the increased risk of fire, Humann (jointly with Uhrich) issued a decree on August 12 calling on renters and prop-erty owners to ready sand, towels, and basins of water to throw on flames. Each house furthermore had to organize night watches, ready to fight fires and alert the municipal firefighters stationed at eight locations around the city.[73]

Within days, citizens voluntarily extended this responsibility by forming neighborhood fire patrols. The faubourg de Pierre took the lead—perhaps owing to its location in the northwestern, most vulner-able quarter of the city, a square bounded by the ramparts on two sides, the railroad, and the canal. As the volunteers explained in a letter to Mayor Humann, "The faubourg de Pierre contains several industrial establishments . . . that contain easily flammable material, such as wool, wood, lime, straw, etc. Almost all of these establishments possess their own pump."[74] One hundred twenty men signed up on the night of August 14. Drawing on the organizational and political slogan of their fathers, *Aide-toi, le ciel t'aidera* (Heaven helps those who help them-selves), these men agreed to nightly watches of fifteen men.[75] From ten o'clock until five the next morning, they met at the brasserie of M. Lipp and sent out regular patrols of three or four men—unarmed but wearing an identifying red and white armband. Lipp was not allowed to sell his wares after closing hours; the fire patrol may have been an exercise in sociability, but it was not supposed to encourage all-night drunkenness. Proprietors brought their own pumps to Lipp's courtyard. At the first sign of fire, the patrol warned the municipal firemen and the neighbors and started to douse the flames themselves until the professionals could take charge. The statutes clarified that the organization remained "com-pletely private and [could] not on any pretext impede the work of public services, including the National Guard."[76] The volunteer firefighters could not become a back door to soldiering or revolution.

In the following week, nine more neighborhoods, covering the rest of the city, formed similar organizations. Those listing their member-ship claimed between 100 and 180 volunteers, so perhaps over 1,000 men in total took part. No occupations were listed, but they were all men of property, or at least men with a fixed address. Each patrol operated out of a brasserie that stored their collective water pumps. Rodolphe Reuss's hangout, La Chaîne, headquartered the fire patrol for the southern corner of the city, including the famous Protestant church of Saint-Thomas.

Humann announced on August 14 that the city's gas supply was shutting off. No more gaslight in the evening for fear that a bombardment would cause massive explosions. Once again, the war emergency led private individuals to act collectively: inhabitants were invited to use their own candles and lanterns to light the way. Traditionally, such collective illuminations marked a celebration. The resulting glow from windows high and low gave Strasbourg the eerie atmosphere of a festive city.[77]

"Like an Arrow into the Eye"

On August 14, the besieging army got a new commander: Prussian Lieutenant General August von Werder. Werder did not have the physical appearance of a warrior. He had always been small and slim, with a weak chin and a round, slightly extended nose. Now sixty-two years old, his hair had thinned and his jowls lengthened.[78] But no one missed the power of his eyes. One admirer noted, "Werder dressed unimpressively; his hat and his cloak had experienced many storms; the only shine on him was the Orden pour le mérite and his flashing eyes."[79] Even to his enemies, Werder's gaze sank "like an arrow into the eye of his interlocutor."[80]

Born in 1808, Werder entered the army at age eighteen. He trained as a cavalry officer in Potsdam and moved easily through the higher social circles during the relatively peaceful early decades of his career. In 1866, after forty years of service, Werder finally enjoyed his brilliant moment at the victory over Austria at Königgrätz. His supporters, including Crown Prince Friedrich Wilhelm, admired his energy and clearheaded focus.[81]

Werder arrived outside Strasbourg fresh from the victory at Froeschwiller, where he had led the divisions from Württemberg and Baden.[82] Helmuth von Moltke's orders to Werder were short and to the point: "The mission of Your Excellency is to render yourself master of this place as quickly as possible."[83] Moltke's directive did not provide much guidance regarding the techniques that Werder was authorized to employ. Nor does it appear that Bismarck tried to weigh in on the procedures at the siege of Strasbourg, as he later argued for the swift bombardment and storming of Paris.[84] Werder himself had not studied the latest developments in siege technology. "He well remembered from his war school days," wrote a sympathetic biographer, "that a siege requires parallels and batteries, but the monstrous progress that besieging artillery has made just in the last decades, and the resulting changes in engineering, were to him only generally known."[85]

With these limitations, Werder relied upon the advice of his closest officers: engineering commander in chief, Major General von Mertens; Lieutenant General von Decker, who oversaw siege artillery, with his whiskers flowing beneath his balding head; and the Badenese chief of staff, Lieutenant Colonel von Leszczynski, who served as the Chief of the General Staff of the besieging army.[86]

As the German armies drew around the city, rain and fog hampered the placement of siege artillery. Nevertheless, starting on August 13 or 14 (reports conflict), field artillery sent the first shells into the city. It is unclear just what these isolated attacks were intended to achieve in terms of siege strategy. Shells hit both military targets—lunettes 44, 52, and 53—and civilian neighborhoods near Nationale Gate and Saverne Gate, neither of which suffered sustained attacks. One projectile fell down a chimney and exploded inside a house on the rue du Marais-vert. At least two men and two women were wounded; one of the men, a worker named Ulrich, died of his injuries.[87]

Civilians reacted to the first bombardment with a mixture of dread and fascination. Despite the violence, recalled Schneegans, "One examined, with a sort of unalarmed curiosity, the debris of this projectile, whose construction seemed strange, even to the French artillery officers; one studied its form; one calculated its properties; one admired this ingenious invention and this perfect workmanship."[88] Already, the story of the bombardment began to take on certain characteristics: the Prussians seemed to be able to achieve precision bombardment directed at specific buildings.[89] One observer described the victims as "women and children," even though the first fatality was a man.[90] But after a week of mounting tension, the concrete appearance of these first bombs seemed to calm nerves. "'Here we are then,' everyone seemed to say on that day, 'the hour has sounded,'" wrote Schneegans.[91] And yet, the possibility of an all-out bombardment of the city center still seemed unreal. Catherine Weiss and her family lived within a ten-minute walk of the first explosions, yet she felt that she and her children remained safe. These shells seemed to be an aberration. The people of Strasbourg tried to comfort themselves with the thought that the Prussians would not want to damage a city they sought for their own.[92]

Saint-Napoleon's Day

Monday, August 15, was a national holiday: Saint-Napoleon's Day, the annual celebration of an invented saint to boost support for the imperial regime. Napoleon III needed help in Strasbourg. Although government-sponsored candidates routinely carried Strasbourg's electoral district, they regularly faced a healthy republican opposition led by those who still remembered the ideals of the revolution of 1848. In the spring of 1870, voters had an additional opportunity to express their discontent. Over the previous several years, Napoleon III had relaxed his authoritarian regime, notably allowing the right to strike (1864), a freer press (1867), and the right to assemble (1868). On May 8, 1870, the emperor cannily held a plebiscite to approve of these and other changes, realizing that only the hardcore republican opposition would be willing to vote against liberal reform. Electors nationwide supported the new quasi-parliamentary regime by 83 percent, but in Strasbourg, the results were mixed: 6,322 yes to 5,501 no, with 6,000 abstentions.[93]

Saint-Napoleon's Day presented an opportunity to paper over such divisions. The first and greatest Napoleon had persuaded the Catholic Church to canonize a Roman martyr named Neopolis, whose name day just "happened" to coincide with both Napoleon's birthday and the Feast of the Assumption, a traditional holy day in the Catholic Church. Cities across France used the celebration to boost civic pride and honor local heroes. In Strasbourg, the festivities typically began with the pealing of bells across the city, military salvos at dawn, and a Te Deum.

The city gave a place to its religious minorities but assured the dominance of the Catholic Church: services at the Lutheran New Church, the Reformed Church, and the Synagogue at nine o'clock anticipated the eleven o'clock mass at the cathedral. The day's events included a fair, a military review on Place Kléber, a river regatta and nautical show, and fireworks displays in the park at the Robertsau and over the cathedral. As the central element of Strasbourg's civic pride, the cathedral tower remained illuminated at night. The holiday also hardened the republicans' disgust at the imperial regime. All "serious" people laughed, said Schneegans, at the festival's stupidity.[94]

This year, as Saint-Napoleon's Day approached, Uhrich and Pron jointly called for a prayer for the soldiers, drafted as follows: "On August 15, after the Te Deum, the Religious Authorities are invited to have public prayers said for the relief of these brave wounded soldiers and for those who have died have gloriously succumbed to the enemy to rest in peace."[95] On August 14, Uhrich and Pron issued a new pronouncement: "Rumors that have taken on a certain consistency seem to indicate that certain individuals are preparing a hostile demonstration for August 15. There are only two possible positions in our current grave circumstances: Friend of France or her enemy."[96] This warning "profoundly shocked" the population. Republicans later claimed that no one had been planning a demonstration, given the gravity of the military situation.[97]

No demonstrations did take place. Events were limited to the religious services. Flags covered the cathedral, but there was no sign of jubilation. Charitable organizations that ordinarily participated in the festivities, like the Protestant Deaconesses, declined in light of the seriousness of the war. In the New Church, the presiding preacher could not bring himself to ring out a Gloria, and chose instead Psalm 130, the sorrowful lament De Profundis, to shame the listening imperial authorities. Many members of the municipal council refused to attend the Te Deum.[98]

In the afternoon, citizens calmly took their holiday promenades under the blazing August sun. Who would think, asked Max Reichard, that this population was ready to face the difficulties to come?[99] Weiss recalled that the "cursed day passed lugubriously and silently. The approach of misfortune covered the city with a black veil."[100] As more details regarding the battle of Wissembourg trickled into the city, many spent the day spewing invectives at Napoleon III and criticizing the military's performance. Why had officers eaten ice cream on Place Broglie instead of preparing for war?[101] When Prefect Pron visited the hospital at the Protestant Gymnasium, someone asked him about the shells and the wounded. According to Rodolphe Reuss, Pron responded, "What a laugh!"[102] Whether or not Pron in fact uttered such a callous response, the war clearly intensified hatred for the regime. There were no fireworks this year.

■ ■ ■

It is not clear why, late that night, the Badenese field artillery in Koenigshoffen lobbed the first shells squarely into the city center. The Badenese had completed their encirclement of the city that evening, but Werder's siege artillery was not yet in place, and the Prussian divisions had not fully arrived.[103] The siege logbook for August 15 simply states, "Von Troben's battery shelled the city during the night, without however the [battery's] firing being observed."[104] The entry implies that the first shells were fired without a coordinated strategy.

Nobody inside Strasbourg missed the bombardment. They startled out of bed at half past eleven o'clock.[105] Catherine Weiss and her husband considered moving their children into the cellars, but they remained above ground until the bombs ceased half an hour later. Weiss did not yet realize that a bomb could penetrate the roof without warning. The next morning she "learned just what a shell is, and its murderous effects."[106] Steps away from her door, projectiles had mangled and killed neighbors inside their homes. Weiss's sister-in-law's house had also been hit, though nobody inside was injured. This family moved in with Weiss, and the entire group moved to the ground floor for safety.

"It's a savage war!" declared Frédéric Piton.[107] The bombardment had reached into the very heart of the city, the neighborhood around the cathedral. Piton and other diarists began to tally the streets and monuments damaged, a preoccupation taken up throughout the siege: "the Banque de France, Café Bauzin; houses on the rue des Echasses, rue du Dôme, rue des Hallebandes, rue des Serruriers, rue des Chancelles, the Mint. . . ."[108] For the first time, too, shells damaged a symbolic building—they shattered the glass roof of the Banque de France on Place Broglie, the site where Rouget de Lisle had composed the "Marseillaise." And, to general indignation, the shelling had come without warning.[109]

After a week of anticipation, the siege had truly begun. With Badenese and Prussian soldiers encircling the city, the fortress walls now divided those outside and subject to occupation from those inside facing bombardment. Civilian men volunteered as night watchmen and *francs-tireurs* to distinguish themselves from "useless mouths," spies, and cowards. Republicans hardened their opposition to the imperial regime, while General Uhrich's proclamations never seemed to hit the right note. The placement of August von Werder at the head of the besieging army soon led to the shelling of civilians. August 15 marked a turning point in the siege. Many repeated the macabre joke: they had gotten their fireworks display after all.[110]

CHAPTER THREE

Every Twenty Seconds

W ITH THE DANGER of bombardment no longer in doubt, Catherine Weiss moved her household to the cellar. She and neighbors from the building used screens to divide their new sleeping quarters into three spaces: one for the ladies, one for the men, and one for refugees from burned-out neighborhoods. They laid the floor with boards and carpet to guard against the damp and lit lamps and candles to make the cellar like home. Still, Weiss worried that the air quality suffered from the cesspools below—not to mention the men's cigars.[1]

Weiss and her family sought this refuge soon after the Saint-Napoleon's Day bombardment. Shells now fell on the city every night. From the German perspective, the period from August 15 to 24 was merely the time of investment during which General August von Werder maneuvered his artillery into place and developed his strategy. Any shells were incidental. In their war coverage, German newspapers did not include more than a paragraph on Strasbourg during this time. The nocturnal shelling soon escalated, however: from August 24 to 27, Werder tried to compel civilians to demand capitulation through an intense, destructive nighttime bombardment of the city center. When that strategy failed, Werder turned to the traditional form of siege warfare in which he primarily aimed his cannon at the ramparts in order to effect a breach. Many shells still fell on civilians. This "regular siege" (so called for following the rules), during which shells and bombs fell day and night, lasted for a month. In total, over the course of forty-four days between August 15 and September 27, the Germans sent 193,722 projectiles into Strasbourg, an average of one every twenty seconds.[2]

The nuances of the Prussian strategy appeared less obvious to those inside the city. For many Strasbourgeois, the entire period stretched out unbearably with little relief. Weiss's building caught fire three times, but was saved each time thanks to firefighters paid five francs per night to keep watch.[3] Sometimes the bombardment threatened to bury her alive. The worst night came on August 24, when the intense bombardment destroyed the beloved New Church along with its libraries and the adjacent Protestant Gymnasium. This terrible episode in the history of Strasbourg awakened fears of unbridled destruction. To Weiss, it seemed that the Last Judgment had arrived.[4] As cultural and sacred objects turned to ashes, Auguste Schneegans warned that "one day, History will report that in the year 1870, civilization stopped suddenly in its march, and humanity fell back by two centuries."[5] It seemed that the horrors of the Thirty Years' War had returned.

The German use of long-range artillery came as a shock to civilians after two generations of relative peace. It anticipated the characteristics of warfare we often associate with the world wars of the twentieth century: the destructiveness of impersonal heavy artillery, the psychological trauma of constant shelling, and the impossible choices that civilians must make. In the first month of the war, civilians had experienced the conflict primarily through their own complex relationships within the city, including the fluctuating grey areas between soldier and civilian and the intensifying difference between insiders and outsiders. During the nighttime bombardment that peaked on August 24, new crucial questions came to the fore. To what protections were civilians entitled? And why did the Germans decide to bomb civilians anyway?

"A Terrible Wake-Up Call"

In 1824, workers in the New Church discovered and restored a series of frescoes, each one designed to remind their viewers of unavoidable death. The images dated from the late fifteenth century, not long after

Gutenberg's time, when the building had belonged to the Dominicans. In each vignette, Death whisked away with gleeful impunity the old and the young, the lowly and the powerful, the worldly and the pious. Death did not appear as the cartoon skeleton with scythe and hourglass but rather as a living creature of skin and sinew, draped in a shroud, whose baldness only served to make him more real, an ever-present figure in daily life. Death's simple costume contrasted with the sartorial choices of the two young men caught in his bony arms. Lavish doublets, coiffures of ringlets, and immodestly short coats marked them as the wayward youth of Columbus's day. The frescoes reminded the viewer that no one would be spared, not the nun "imploring forgiveness for some peccadillo," not the imperial couple engaging in quiet conversation.[6] The frescoes underscored the unpredictability of existence, save for this common human experience. Reflect and repent, pray and prepare: these were the messages from the Dominicans of centuries past.

The frescoes remind us that the people of Strasbourg had long experience with mass, unpredictable death. Even as recently as the Second Empire, the death rate had outstripped the birth rate in several years: 1852–56, 1861, and 1868. Although Strasbourg's population rose from 64,000 to 77,000 during the Second Empire, this growth came almost entirely from immigration. Respiratory diseases and fevers killed many. In 1854 alone, 550 inhabitants died of cholera.[7] Looking back, however, the people of Strasbourg believed that the bombardment had disrupted a peaceful and prosperous era. Catherine Weiss later wrote, "One would never believe, dear children, while living peacefully during the summer in the fields of the green mountains, in winter around a hot stove, that upheavals, cataclysms of this kind could happen, and that the hand of mankind created them." Weiss omitted from her recollections any indication of earlier epidemics or hardships: "For me, too, [the war] was a sad education. Not any more than you had I made such an apprenticeship. I drifted peacefully down the course of life, without a care, without fear of shipwreck."[8] In her memoir, and perhaps in her memory as well, Weiss depicted life before the war as serene and uneventful. Similarly, Dr. Henri-Etienne Beaunis, writing in 1887, remembered passing the summer of 1870 "amidst the greenery and the flowers" of his suburban village garden. The pleasures of working under the arbors, napping in the grass, and fishing at leisure all came to an end with the declaration of war.[9] The year 1914 does not hold a monopoly on European memories of bucolic prewar summers.

In 1870, Strasbourg's civilians had not experienced war firsthand for two generations. During the 1814 and 1815 sieges, civilians died of typhus and suffered malnutrition, but they were not bombarded.[10] Since that time, Strasbourg had been spared international conflict. Despite periods of internal revolution and knowledge of conflicts abroad, many French in these years deepened their conviction that the fates of civilians and soldiers should differ. Psychologist Ludger Lunier believed that by 1870 "the material well-being and the relative tranquility that [civilians] enjoyed had dis-habituated them, so to speak, from ideas of war and militant politics."[11] Before August 15, many Strasbourgeois, like Schneegans, still hoped that "all of this would end, as in 1814 and 1815, with a pure and simple blockade and by a few battles outside the city that citizens would observe from atop their attics through their telescopes."[12] In retrospect, argued military theorist Charles Thoumas, "war seemed like a distant evil that city-dwellers did not have to suffer directly, or like the concern of an army, whose glorious operations one followed with patriotic interest, but with which one did not have to be concerned other than to administer praise and blame. The bombardments were, for the inhabitants of the besieged cities, a terrible wake-up call."[13]

The restored frescoes of omnipotent Death still adorned the walls of the New Church in 1870 when the building was converted into a temporary hospital. As bombardment became a reality, the wounded and their caregivers needed no reminders of the randomness and unpredictability of death. Most neighborhoods in Strasbourg were socially mixed, so rich and poor both suffered. The worst destruction occurred in the western neighborhoods of Saverne, Pierre, and National. The bombing from Kehl brought destruction to the northeastern Saint-Nicolas neighborhood, including damage to the tobacco plant and the church of Saint-Guillaume. The two neighborhoods that the rich largely avoided, south and east of the Grande Île, happened to be the most protected neighborhoods. As the frescoes indicated, wealth, power, and piety offered no guarantee of safety.[14]

Yet death in the form of bombs and shells was both more concrete and less personal than its representation in the frescoes. Just as soldiers in the trenches struggled with random shellfire some forty years later, civilians in Strasbourg tried to cope with horrifying uncertainty. French civilians enjoyed very little control over their situation. Technology could not warn them of impending explosions. The tocsin did not sound. Many civilians responded by overestimating Prussia's capabilities. One rumor held that Prussian shells contained a poison that rendered wounds incurable. Another claimed that the Prussians could precisely target certain buildings, particularly with the aid of the Badenese who knew the city so well. Still another story maintained that the Germans aimed at areas that had caught fire in order to prevent firemen from putting out the flames. (It was probably true that projectiles sometimes hit the same place multiple times, but this was less a consequence of artillerymen's skill than of their immobility.)[15]

In an era before airplanes, satellites, or even incandescent light bulbs, the appearance of man-made objects streaking against the night sky inspired fascination and dread. The experience of bombardment was so novel that authors took pains to explain, sometimes in minute detail, the sights and sounds of projectiles. Each salvo started with a long whistle that "resembles an intermittent buzzing in ones' ears . . . and . . . varies according to its rotation."[16] Frédéric Piton, watching from his rooftop terrace, learned just how long it would take to hear the thunder of cannon from each suburb.[17] "A flash illuminates a point," wrote journalist Paul Raymond-Signouret, "then a long silence that lasts 3, 4, 5, 10 seconds . . . during which one sees the gleaming streaks traced in the night by the fuses . . . then, suddenly, the dull noise of the [cannon's] detonation, which arrives almost at the same time as the striding shudder of the air under the effort of this heavy mass; then again, but almost instantaneously, the detonation . . . of the projectile itself, which has just burst as it hit an obstacle, and whose mass or fragments have destroyed some section of wall, or massacred some human creature, perhaps a relative, perhaps a friend."[18] Schneegans sarcastically ascribed an artistic sensibility to the Prussian bombardment strategy, which proceeded "from the smallest to the largest, as professors of aesthetics recommend to those who want to produce effective works."[19] The "autopsy" of a thirty-kilogram projectile revealed its inner workings: a capsule filled with flammable material at the cone ignited on impact, causing an interior tube filled with gunpowder and sulfur to explode. Surrounding the tube, within the canister, 450 sulfur-sprinkled lead balls awaited the explosion that would recklessly disperse them in all directions.[20]

Soon, inhabitants discerned the difference between bombs and shells. Imperial secretary Malartic noted that bombs were too heavy to reach the city center. They fell only as far as the rue Brûlée and near Saint-Pierre-le-Jeune, several hundred yards north of the cathedral. "When a bomb falls, its effect is terrible," he explained. "Its great weight (150 kil.) is augmented by the height of its fall; it pierces a house from the attic to the cellar and can even break through ordinary vaulted ceilings; then, exploding, it blows up the entire interior, floors and roofs, without leaving anything but the four shaking walls. But this effect is limited. Half of the surface area of the city is in courtyards, gardens and streets: therefore half of the bombs do not fall on buildings."[21] Shells posed a greater danger, for they "follow an almost horizontal parabola; [a shell] is never wasted, because it continues its path until it hits a house, where it bursts. Its explosion occurs in every direction; the splinters penetrate even very thick walls."[22] It might take half an hour for all the debris from a given projectile to fall. Soon, the city was covered with rubble, smoke, and dust. In the morning after, the brave and the desperate tried to collect scrap iron, sometimes inadvertently coming too close to an unexploded shell. Disarming these devices required patience, care, and a lot of water. Publisher Oscar Berger-Levrault advised immersing the projectile in a tub to dampen the gunpowder. But if the liquid failed to turn black like ink, the shell should be carefully set aside until the end of the siege. It was too dangerous to carry projectiles to the sappers now.[23]

In the Cellars

Soon, nobody felt safe in the upper stories of their homes. Those whose buildings had been destroyed or whose cellars had flooded moved to public spaces, like the theater, only to be displaced again when those buildings were struck. One man paid thirty francs per day to shelter his family in a neighboring cellar. The lucky ones, like Catherine Weiss, could stay in the cellars of their own buildings. Some set up elaborate spaces, filled with papers, furniture, and precious objects.[24] One woman described her careful arrangements: "Curtains and screens were put in place to safeguard propriety; five beds were prepared in the central cellar; twenty-five beds, large and small, were set up in the two subbasements to the right and left. Our provisions and our personal belongings are piled in every cellar."[25] No amount of screens could provide the same level of privacy as their own apartments. Out of modesty or to allow a quick exit, many slept in their clothes. Damp, dark, and narrow, these cellars often did not get fresh air. Sacks of dirt and dung provided additional protection but made the cellars smaller and smellier.[26]

Some individuals chose to stay underground for the duration of the siege, but most only descended into the cellar at night. In Weiss's building, three families—thirteen people—washed and took their meals together on the common ground floor. At first, Weiss occasionally ventured up to her own apartment on the second floor to check on the servants. Her domestics presumably continued to cook and do the laundry, though it is not clear whether they slept downstairs with the others. On these daytime visits upstairs, Weiss told herself she was helping to keep up everyone's courage, and she took the opportunity to carry down armloads of clean clothes and linens.[27]

After one frightening episode, however, Weiss stopped these excursions out of fear of leaving her children even for a few minutes. Emile, Marie, and their cousins were playing in the building's inner courtyard when a projectile landed. Weiss had no time to pick up her children before the explosion. Fortunately, the children had happened to run into the building at just the right moment. From then on, Weiss refused to allow them out of her sight, even though she recognized that this attention caused them to "wilt like flowers kept away from air" and that she herself visibly weakened under the strain.[28]

Every evening around eight o'clock, Weiss faced a terrible dilemma. A night in the cellar protected her children from a random shell but entailed the risk of burying them alive. Weiss always made the choice to descend to relative safety underground, keeping shoes on Emile's and Marie's feet in case of a quick evacuation. She took comfort in the fact that her children slept happily, "conscious of nothing."[29] Across the partition, men dozed in chairs or stayed up smoking and talking. Some nights passed more calmly than others. In one particularly grim hour, the frequency of the bombs made their deaths seem inescapable. Weiss and other women, she reports, succumbed to overwhelming anxiety. In a moment of panic, Weiss tried to escape the cellar in the dark with Emile in her arms and Marie holding onto her skirt, but her neighbors held her back.[30] "Fear is not reasonable," she later reflected. "It catches you in spite of yourself. It is a contagious evil."[31]

Meanwhile on the ramparts, the French military was already starting to feel demoralized. In a small sortie on August 16, the French attempted to dislodge the Badenese from the Illkirch Bridge but found themselves easily overpowered. The hapless French, retreating back into Strasbourg, left three large guns behind, which the Badenese recovered to their great joy. Since the French failed to break out of the fortress, they had no choice but to use artillery to try to push back the approaching Prussians. In this, too, they struggled to be effective. The Prussians hid their artillery and moved them every night.[32] "It was a horrible spectacle," recalled French Captain Bergasse du Petit-Thouars. "One heard the sharp note of the cries of children that dominated all the rest. . . . We were there, unable to do anything, because we felt that shooting blindly at the gleams of the shots, at an uncertain distance, would only burn munitions uselessly."[33] The citadel caught fire on August 20. On the night of August 23, the Aubette on Place Kléber also burned, forcing Uhrich and the defense council to move to the Hôtel de Ville on Place Broglie. That same night, the arsenal burst into flames. Some thirty-five thousand percussion fuses were destroyed, costing the fortress several days' worth of ammunition.[34]

No wonder that Max Reichard of the New Church compared Strasbourg with besieged Jerusalem, whose destruction happened to be featured in the service of August 21. He recorded in his journal, "We are experiencing today what that is and what it means!"[35] Weiss lamented, "War, dear children, is the worst plague that God in his anger inflicts on us, it is made up of . . . all the evils united, of all kinds, known and even unknown. . . . It is a study of destruction . . . [and] they are perfecting this ferocity. For it is no longer an art. One does not fight anymore, one kills."[36]

Protective Traditions

As the bombs started to fall, the superior of the *petit séminaire,* Father
Mury, published a letter of lament in *L'impartial du Rhin.* Did this bombardment, he asked, follow the "laws of war"?[37] The short, technical
answer is *yes.* In 1870, no internationally acknowledged "laws of war"
applied to the treatment of ordinary civilians. Bombarding the civilian
center and destroying cultural edifices were legal. Yet for centuries theorists had tried to inject justice into the practice of warfare and shield
noncombatants from abuse and violence during war. In the ancient
world, long-standing customs spared conquered women and children
from death, even if only to enslave them. Ancient Hindu texts, early rab-
binical Jewish law, medieval Islamic jurists, and the Christian Peace of
God all agreed that noncombatants should be protected in war. In medieval Europe, secular custom conceived of war as a contest between
equals in which noncombatants should not be involved.[38] As far back as
697, Adomnán, the abbot of Iona, proclaimed that the Irish church, its
buildings, and clergy ought to be spared from war's violence.[39] In
Strasbourg, when journalists, doctors, and religious personnel like
Mury objected to the Prussian bombardment of civilians, they continued this tradition.

Two protective frameworks tried to adapt these long-standing customs to war among modern nation states: Just War theory and international humanitarian law. These traditions, each of which included
ethical, social, and legal components, hoped to limit and regulate warfare through a series of compromises and negotiations, though they did
so based on different assumptions and using distinctive mechanisms. In
1870, each proved unable to prevent the bombardment of civilians.

Just War theorists sought to mitigate the unnecessary suffering of
combatants and noncombatants alike. Sixteenth-century Christian
theologians Francisco de Vitoria and Francisco Suárez distinguished
two strands of lawful behavior in war: the appropriate reasons for going
to war *(jus ad bellum)* and the proper conduct during war *(jus in bello).*
Few would argue that the declaration of war in July 1870 followed the
precepts of *jus ad bellum;* neither France nor Prussia could be said to be
using force to counter injustice or protect an innocent third party.[40] But

what about *jus in bello,* right conduct once war had begun? *Jus in bello* included limitations on *who* could be the targets of violence (discrimination) and *what* forms of violence were acceptable (proportionality). Armies were limited in terms of both the kinds of weapons and ammunition to be employed and the appropriate times to use them. The Just War tradition followed a "distinctive, case-specific form of argument" based on natural law in which leaders evaluated each situation according to its particular characteristics in a form of argumentation called casuistry. The method tried to achieve a balance between guiding moral principles and the admission of "exceptions, compromises, and the clash between desire and reality."[41] In other words, limitations on warfare were not laid out for all cases in a set of hard-and-fast positivist *a priori* rules.

Early modern Just War theorists recognized that "military necessity" could at times legitimately justify violence, but they believed that the prudent restraint of warfare usually yielded the best results. Hugo Grotius's *De jure belli ac pacis,* first published in 1625, argued that it was possible, natural, and in a nation's best interests to follow lawful behavior in war. Grotius and other early modern jurists, including John Locke and Emmerich de Vattel, developed Just War theory and incorporated it into international law systems.[42]

By the late eighteenth century, philosophers had developed a theory of war that fell more or less in line with the relatively limited combat practice of that period. States would go to war, but they would also recognize that they should not use any more force than necessary. Geoffrey Best explains that this later-Enlightenment consensus aimed to mitigate but not eliminate civilian suffering: "Civilians and their property would suffer in wartime, partly because it was in the natures of war and the war-waging human beast that they would suffer, partly because there were good philosophical reasons why they should share the suffering; but military discipline, political good sense, moral self-respect, and humanitarian sentiment concurred to enjoin that this suffering and damage should be kept to the necessary minimum."[43] This delicate balance between discipline and permissiveness proved difficult to achieve, particularly in the case of siege warfare, in which civilians and soldiers shared the same space.

The Just War consensus, incomplete as it was, fell apart during the French Revolution and Napoleonic Wars. David Bell argues that new forces, particularly nationalism and the utopian desire to remake the world by cleansing it of its corruption and weakness, made unrestrained warfare against one's enemies philosophically and psychologically more attractive. If only we could defeat the evils in the world, the thinking went, we could then achieve a lasting peace. Warfare between 1792 and 1815 created a generation of Europeans for whom combat was a "test of a person's very essence, his moral qualities and intentions."[44] Just War distinctions between combatants and noncombatants eroded as nationalists argued that ordinary civilians ought to take up arms to spread liberty and defend the nation against invaders.

Meanwhile, states resisted Just War limitations through the claims that positive law was more valid than natural law, and that war should be used to the utmost in order to achieve political goals. These claims, associated with Prussian military theorist Carl von Clausewitz, argued that if a state needed to perform certain acts of war to fulfill a political goal, then it had the right to do so. In contrast with the nationalists, Clausewitzian positivism argued that noncombatants had no business in a combat zone, but if they interfered with a military campaign, they would suffer violent retaliation.

In the mid-nineteenth century, the quest to develop internationally binding agreements to limit war's violence revived, this time along positivist lines. Europeans now sought to codify right action in war, making concrete and permanent the protections that Just War had tried to derive from moral principles on a case-by-case basis. This was international humanitarian law. Such a code of conduct would limit both the nationalist fervor of people's armies and the Clausewitzian attitude that the ends justified the means. The 1864 Geneva Convention, a seminal and much cherished act of international law, established important limitations on the conduct of war. As signatories, both France and Prussia were to protect wounded and sick soldiers along with the people who cared for them, including civilians. The idea behind the Geneva Convention was not new; in the 1700s, commanders had commonly signed pre-battle agreements to set aside protected field hospitals for wounded soldiers and their caregivers.[45] However, the Geneva

Convention applied not just to one battle or war, but also theoretically to any future combat. It was the first effort to create pre-existing international treaties protecting civilians during war.

Hailed as a sign of civilization's progress, the Geneva Convention worked imperfectly in practice. It was like covering a mattress with a fitted sheet that is too small and full of holes; just when one corner seems covered, another pops up, and the holes rip wider the longer the ordeal drags on. Often commanders mistrusted, ignored, or were unaware of the convention. During the Franco-Prussian War, the Germans claimed that the French violated the treaty at least thirty-two times.[46] In a bid to follow the letter of the convention without changing his strategy, Werder asked Uhrich to evacuate the Military Hospital, as it was hidden from view and easily hit. He suggested that Uhrich establish a military hospital near the Civil Hospital south of the Ill River and fly a flag above it. Uhrich responded that he would leave the hospital in place but add the flags of France and of the Red Cross.[47]

Civilian observers in Strasbourg believed that Werder purposefully disrespected the Geneva Convention.[48] Public discourse about such violations had not yet developed the notion of unintentional but unfortunate collateral damage; nor had it distinguished between individual soldiers and their commanding officers. Instead, any discussion over the imperfect implementation of the Geneva Convention assumed that the commanders were to blame, and that they knew precisely what they were doing. Malartic went so far as to assert that the flag of the Red Cross attracted extra shelling![49]

Even with the best of intentions, just how were German artillerymen to avoid hitting Red Cross hospitals? Any home that took in wounded soldiers claimed the right to immunity through the unfurling of an improvised Red Cross flag. Miss Jacot, the English tutor to the four Herrenschmidt children, carefully sewed a Red Cross flag out of one of their few remaining tablecloths, but she recognized that it offered little real protection.[50] Small or obstructed Red Cross flags might not be seen, cannon precision was imperfect, and hospitals used for any military purpose opened themselves up as fair game. With fifteen Red Cross hospitals scattered among the major edifices of Strasbourg's city center, it was not easy to avoid them.

Even if the Geneva Convention had been followed to the letter, it still did not offer any protection to non-caregiving civilians. This position left many questions unanswered. Was Werder obligated to allow civilians to depart? Or would this give the French such an advantage as to undermine Werder's military goal? Was the bombardment of civilians an egregious crime or a permissible act of "military necessity"? Despite a lack of formal legal protection, many in Strasbourg believed that noncombatants, especially women and children, should be spared the worst ravages of war. They anticipated the views of political philosopher Michael Walzer, who argues that a siege is only "morally possible" when soldiers on both sides "help civilians leave the scene of battle."[51] They felt in their guts that the "laws of war" existed.

"The Bombardment is Fully Justified"

When we start to examine the Prussian motivation for bombing Strasbourg—particularly for the intense bombardment that started on August 24—it is difficult not to recall the atrocities of later German wars. We might be tempted to compare Strasbourg to the Nazi siege of Leningrad during World War II. But a look at the Directive of the Nazi Command issued on September 29, 1941, shows that the two sieges differed significantly. The Directive states that Hitler had "decided to wipe St. Petersburg [sic] off the map. . . . It is proposed to establish a tight blockade of the city and, by shelling it with artillery of all calibers and incessant bombing by the air force, level it to the ground. . . . In this war that is a matter of life and death, we are not interested in the survival of even a fraction of the population of so large a city."[52] The siege eventually killed 700,000 Soviets. Clearly, the German actions in Leningrad do not help us to understand Strasbourg, at least not in a simplistic way. Leningrad far outstripped Strasbourg in its duration, brutality, and intentionality. The inhabitants of Leningrad were believed to belong to a lesser race, worthy of extermination. In contrast, the Prussians saw the people of Strasbourg as long-lost brothers of the German nation; the Prussian military sought order and victory but did not want to destroy the city altogether. Yet some of the attitudes that underpinned the decision to bombard Strasbourg were consistent with those that allowed the

German army to commit atrocities all over Europe in the twentieth century. These attitudes included the importance placed on achieving victory on the field as quickly as possible, a reliance on new and devastating technology, and the belief that the enemy will break under psychological pressure.[53]

We do not have Werder's personal account of his decision to bombard the civilians of Strasbourg, so we have to look further to understand the attitudes, habits, and external dynamics that shaped his choices. A single, brief telegram from Helmuth von Moltke provides an entrée into this decision. Werder telegrammed Moltke on August 19 for guidance on how best to take Strasbourg. On the following day, he received this reply: "The bombardment of Strasbourg, even executed from Kehl, is fully justified, if one can by this means obtain capitulation. But this cannot be judged from here."[54] Four days later, Werder started the three-night, all-out bombardment of Strasbourg's civilians. What underlying assumptions did this telegram convey?

First, the Germans and the French differed in their definitions of "the bombardment." For the civilians of Strasbourg, the entire period from August 13 to the capitulation on September 27 might be included in "the bombardment." They experienced the period of August 24 through 27 as particularly horrific, but they did not differentiate it from the shelling either before or after. A shell fired from a field artillery gun killed just as surely as a bomb from heavy artillery. When German observers discussed "the bombardment," they meant only the period from August 24 to 27, when their guns aimed specifically and unrelentingly at the civilian center. Moltke's telegram refers only to this kind of bombardment; Werder would not have needed Moltke's advice on whether or not it was justified to target the city walls in a traditional siege.

Werder's decision to bombard the city center indicated a turn away from the traditional slow, methodical method in which armies would gradually approach the city, build trenches and earthworks, pick off defensive lines, create a "practicable breach" in the defenses, and thus trigger an honorable capitulation. This slow method was likely to succeed but might stretch out over months.[55] Werder's troops would not be able to fight in other battles that might help bring the war to a successful conclusion. They would slowly eat up their own supplies and become demoralized by prolonged inaction. The longer the soldiers waited and the more they suffered from the French defenders, the harder it would be to control them at the siege's completion. The victory would turn ugly if German soldiers succumbed to the temptations of rape and pillage.

Werder also feared that a prolonged siege would turn deadly for his own soldiers if civilians continued to fight after the walls were breached. This was the situation that the French had faced when they besieged Saragossa, Spain, during the Napoleonic Wars. In June 1808, the Spanish army and civilian defenders resisted two French assaults, followed by a two-month siege and bombardment. The French withdrew only to return in December with reinforcements. Meanwhile, the people of Saragossa built stronger fortifications and held firm despite the shells and a typhus epidemic. When the French finally broke into the city in January, civilians fought them from house to house. As David Bell relates, the assault unfolded in horrific and surreal scenes: "French troops advanced while shielding themselves with huge folio volumes recounting the lives of the martyrs, taken from a convent library. During a rainstorm, the French took shelter under painted and varnished canvases of the crucifixion. In monastery basements, men drowned in floods of oil and wine from huge, earthenware containers shattered by explosions. Ancient cadavers were literally blown from their tombs."[56] Only in mid-February, after 50,000 had died, did the city surrender.

Werder wanted to avoid creating a Saragossa. In a letter to his brother he explained, "Humanity to the citizens of Strasbourg means inhumanity towards my soldiers."[57] With some of the world's best artillery at his disposal, Werder possessed the means to undertake a different form of siege warfare. Instead of focusing on the fortress walls, he could bombard the city center, which he hoped would terrorize and demoralize the civilians, encourage internal division, and lead to a quick capitulation. This tactic was not entirely new; commanders had sometimes intentionally bombarded the civilian population in the wars of the eighteenth and nineteenth centuries. But the technique had not become the norm for siege warfare.[58] The latest in long-range artillery coupled with concerns about a slow and messy traditional siege allowed Werder to bombard civilians.

The phrase "if one can by this means obtain capitulation" suggests two assumptions. First, it posited that civilian bombardment could lead to capitulation; distressed by death and destruction, civilians would either convince or force Uhrich to surrender. The strategy relied on psychological factors, namely the idea that French civilians, particularly women, did not possess the fortitude necessary to withstand bombardment. As Isabel Hull has argued, the German army erroneously made this assumption time and time again, such as during the Great War when Supreme Command believed that unrestricted submarine warfare would lead to the collapse of British morale. Werder may well have been encouraged in this assumption by Uhrich's proclamation of August 10, which had revealed that some civilians were willing to capitulate.[59] This strategy furthermore ignored the French regulations, which followed centuries of tradition and would have been well known to Werder, that prohibited a commander from surrendering until after the walls had been breached.

The second assumption is that the likelihood of capitulation should be the most important factor in Werder's decision. This is not surprising; after all, armies exist in order to achieve military goals. Yet the need to take Strasbourg speaks to both the special prestige of the Prussian army during its decades of European dominance and the symbolic and strategic importance of this particular city. More than in other nations, the Prussian army became a heroic symbol of the political goal of national integration.[60] Following the ideas of Clausewitz, the army acted as an arm of politics, undertaking its operations professionally and ruthlessly to the best advantage of the state. Like all European armies of the nineteenth century, the Prussian army enjoyed more money, manpower, and technology than ever before.[61] It had achieved two striking (though not flawless) victories against Denmark and Austria. Since 1866, Chief of General Staff Helmuth von Moltke had answered directly to the king, with little interference from civilian leaders, not even Bismarck.[62]

The capture of Strasbourg would enhance the army's role in building the German nation-state and justify its organizational independence. Such a victory would give the Prussians an incalculable advantage in any negotiation and open the possibility of the outright annexation of Alsace, a goal that Moltke had cherished for over a decade.[63] Bismarck had begun to consider that idea seriously since the summer, and both public opinion and high-ranking officials leaned toward the same conclusion.[64] Historian Heinrich von Treitschke famously argued in 1870 that Alsace and Lorraine "are ours by the right of the sword. . . . At all times the subjection of a German race to France has been an unhealthy thing; today it is an offense against the reason of History—a vassalship of free men to half-educated barbarians."[65] The capture of Strasbourg would also support operations in the broader field that would lead to the successful conclusion of the war. Werder needed to prevent Strasbourg from launching an attack on Baden and keep supply lines from Baden clear to support German incursions further south.[66] The Germans were not particularly keen to tie up their soldiers on a siege and therefore hoped that Strasbourg would fall quickly.

Securing Strasbourg would bring more glory to the Prussian army and allow it to achieve the overall goal of defeating France. The pressure to fulfill these goals may have encouraged Werder to justify the human cost of civilian bombardment. In a letter to his sister Charlotte dated August 25, Werder acknowledged that bombardment was "a harsh measure . . . but I can't do otherwise, for Strasbourg should and must by the shortest path at all costs be taken. You can imagine how hard the matter becomes for me."[67]

Moltke and Werder also viewed the bombardment as "fully justified" because they saw the civilians of Strasbourg as enemies by virtue of their presence in the fortress. As such, they believed, civilians enjoyed few rights and could not take up arms themselves. As Uhrich repeatedly refused Werder's requests for surrender, the Prussian general believed that he was allowed to take the fortress by force. Collateral damage to civilians was not his concern.

The Lieber Code, a set of military regulations issued by the United States during the Civil War, offered a concurring perspective. Officially titled "Instruction for the Government of Armies of the United States in the Field," U.S. Army General Order No. 100 was issued on April 24, 1863, and popularly named for its author, German-American jurist Francis Lieber.[68] Best known for its provisions limiting the poor treatment of prisoners of war, the Lieber Code also provided guidelines on civilians, particularly during siege warfare. It argued that civilians were integral to the enemy's strength and therefore legitimate targets. "War is not carried on by arms alone," hence "it is lawful to starve the hostile belligerent, armed or unarmed, so that it leads to the speedier subjection of the enemy." A besieging army had the right to "drive . . . back" civilians who left a stronghold "so as to hasten on the surrender."[69] As for bombardment, the Lieber Code did not distinguish the city center from the fortress walls, and it allowed besiegers to bombard without warning: "surprise may be a necessity."[70] The code encouraged the besieged and bombarded population—but not the besiegers—to protect "classical works of art, libraries, scientific collections, or precious instruments, such as astronomical telescopes, as well as hospitals."[71] Although the Prussian army was in no way beholden to an American regulation, the Lieber Code sparked intense debate among Europeans, which Moltke and Werder could not have missed.[72] The Lieber Code sought to limit warfare, but it did not curtail civilian bombardment.

In claiming the legitimacy of civilian bombardment, Moltke ignored several additional possible objections. He did not discuss the possibility of foreign disapproval, which might affect Germany's diplomacy in the future (though later during the siege of Paris, Prussian Crown Prince Friedrich Wilhelm opposed the shelling of civilians for that reason).[73] He did not address the potential damage to irreplaceable cultural objects. Furthermore, he did not consider the psychological effects that the bombardment might have on the soldiers doing the killing, whether in their future lives as civilians or as officers who would later shape policy.

Moltke's concluding sentence, "But this cannot be judged from here," suggests that he allowed Werder some flexibility in the manner in which he carried out orders. It also disarms the French accusation that the Prussians undertook a single-minded plan to destroy the civilians of Strasbourg. Moltke demanded rapid results, but he did not want his generals undertaking wasteful operations before their men and equipment were fully positioned. They should not bow to political pressure from Bismarck and start a job they could not finish due to lack of ammunition; Werder needed to exercise judgment.

Other Prussian generals vehemently disagreed over the efficacy of civilian bombardment. During the debate a few months later over whether to bomb Paris, General Leonhard von Blumenthal went so far as to declare that such a strategy was not effective: "In 1849, I saw Fredericia bombarded for three days without any result. By superior order, in 1864, I had to bombard the redoubts of Düppel for four weeks with excellent artillery, without noticing the least advantage for the final goal. . . . In this campaign, Toul and Phalsbourg were vigorously bombarded and nevertheless we had to retreat without a definitive result."[74] General Edwin von Manteuffel expressly forbade the bombardment of civilians in Mézières, "which only cause[s] loss of life and destruction of property, without obtaining any military result."[75] The officer in command of engineering before Strasbourg, General Schulz, also disagreed with the bombardment policy.[76] The final decision rested with Werder.

Why did Moltke state that bombarding Strasbourg was justified "even from Kehl"? We do not have the precise wording of Werder's August 19 telegram to Moltke, but other events illuminate the question. On the morning of August 19, around seven o'clock, Badenese artillery batteries outside of Kehl sent shells across the Rhine and into Strasbourg. Werder apparently did not order this bombardment; the commander in Kehl had assumed that Werder wanted it as soon as the batteries were in place. By ten o'clock, French General de Barral, who oversaw artillery operations, ordered fire on the Badenese batteries as well as on Kehl itself, an open city.[77] Werder realized that the French would be willing to kill German civilians in Kehl if artillery fire came from that side of the Rhine. It seems plausible that Werder wanted to confirm with Moltke that it was acceptable to put the civilians of Kehl in harm's way in order to achieve the capitulation of Strasbourg. Moltke assured Werder that he could bombard Strasbourg "even from Kehl," suggesting that Badenese civilians were expendable "if one can by this means obtain capitulation."

Moltke's telegram emphasized that the goal of obtaining Strasbourg overrode concerns about civilians, whether French or German. Moltke and Werder were willing to try the strategy of intensive civilian bombardment; they could find justification in the Lieber Code and were not constrained by other international agreements or treaties. Yet, despite their emphasis on taking Strasbourg quickly and through force, Werder and Moltke both wanted to limit warfare. Werder did not want the siege to turn into all-out, hand-to-hand slaughter, and he did not want to be put in the position of using violence against armed civilians. And, unlike the besiegers of Leningrad seventy years later, Werder was not ordered to be as destructive as possible.

Among the civilians of Strasbourg, Werder quickly won a poor reputation: "A man of small stature, dry, skinny," wrote Schneegans, "his anger is formidable, and, in truth, it seems that he rarely comes out of it. . . . [But] he calms down, they say, just as quickly as he becomes irritated, and those who have seen him more closely assure [me] that his reputation for ferocity is singularly exaggerated. However it may be, Strasbourg only saw the bristling sides of this man of war."[78] Inhabitants of Strasbourg blamed Werder personally for the bombardment and especially distrusted his promises to spare the city.[79] In a letter afterwards, Werder complained to his sister that he was called "a hellish wretch" for his decisions at Strasbourg, but he told her, "I wasn't that at all."[80] He believed that he had followed the right course of action.

The Traditions and Customs of War

Werder had reason to think that he deserved a better reputation. After all, in the days preceding the bombardment of August 24, he followed military traditions carefully in all his dealings with Uhrich. Military custom, enshrined in national legal codes governing warfare, was supposed to provide an honorable way for sieges to unfold, from investment to capitulation. The respect for intermediaries (messengers between the sides), the formal construction of parallels, the personal request as the primary tool of negotiation, and the goal of a "practicable breach" were intended to lend an air of propriety to this deadly undertaking. Werder and Uhrich maintained constant, polite, barb-pointed correspondence throughout the siege. They composed messages in their own languages and relayed them via a mounted courier, whose approach into enemy territory remained protected so long as he rode at a slow pace accompanied by a white flag. They identified themselves with their weapons and defenses—speaking of "my artillery" or "my walls"—which heightened the illusion that their relationship followed the same rules as polite society. But they did not openly discuss war's violence and the horror of killing and being killed.[81]

Werder and Uhrich took these customs seriously, even though such communication gave away the element of surprise. Indeed, their correspondence was honorable precisely because it acknowledged reciprocity.[82] Military expediency was not Werder's only motivation, even with the influence of Clausewitzian positivism. Both men also understood that their messages were subject to high scrutiny. Not only did they take care not to reveal too much to the enemy, but they also wanted to cover themselves in case of a future investigation into their actions. Much of their correspondence consisted of negotiations over the protocol for messengers, demands of capitulation and refusals to give in, individual requests for safe passage (usually for officers' families), and admonishments over the practice of warfare. They also attempted to politely intimidate each other. It was typical for Werder declare, as he did on August 20, "I have the honor to announce to you that the French Imperial Army, after two preceding battles, was attacked and totally beaten on August 18 by H. M. the King of Prussia."[83]

However, military custom provided little guidance on the treatment of civilians in sieges; a cynical reader might view it as no more than a polite cover that allowed commanders to do whatever they deemed necessary. As we saw earlier, the French regulations simply required "useless mouths" to depart before the city was fully invested. After investment, did the customs of war constrain commanders from bombardment? Did military custom provide any opportunities for civilians to flee to safety?

Werder believed that so long as he had formally demanded capitulation and given prior warning of bombardment, he had fulfilled his duties according to the customs of war. Uhrich and Werder's exchanges regarding Kehl illustrate their delicate understanding of proper bombardment. When the French bombed Kehl on August 19, Werder protested to Uhrich that Kehl was "an open city and not fortified" and that Uhrich had acted "against any kind of the rights of men. . . . Such a manner of making war," he continued, "which is unheard of in a civilized nation, forces me to hold you personally responsible for the consequences of this act."[84] Werder did not mention that the French bombardment of Kehl occurred after the Germans had already shelled Strasbourg.

Uhrich countered that it was Werder who had "contravened the laws of war and the norms of civilized peoples" when he sent bombs into Strasbourg without warning, resulting in the deaths of "inoffensive city-dwellers, women and children. . . . Notably, eleven young orphan girls, who occupied the same room in a convent of sisters, were struck in a very cruel manner. Six are dead and the five others leave little hope of recovery."[85] Uhrich hoped that the orphan girls would distract attention from his own actions, or at least balance them out, even though the bombing of Kehl was apparently not intended as a direct retaliation for the orphanage bombing. He furthermore argued that Kehl was not really an open city at all, but "a military post surrounded by two forts and sub-mitted, consequently, to all the resulting dangers of war."[86]

Werder did not accept this explanation. He dismissed the notion that Kehl was anything but an open city. More importantly, since an intermediary had requested Strasbourg's capitulation and mentioned the possibility of bombardment on August 8, Werder believed that the Germans had done their duty: "I am therefore obliged to make the observation that, from our side, no omission of the customs of war and of the rights of man has been made."[87] Werder argued that his bombard-ment was acceptable because of the previous warning, whereas Uhrich's bombardment of Kehl violated the customs of war because it came without warning. This episode caused considerable embarrassment to French civilians who had hoped to maintain the high ground. In his memoirs, Schneegans erroneously (or deceptively) placed Kehl on August 29, after the period of intense bombardment of Strasbourg.[88]

On the question of whether or not to allow civilians to leave a besieged city, military custom offered little guidance. Once the Prussian forces had cinched the line around Strasbourg, civilians inside had few opportunities to depart. Some civilians attempted to escape in the wake of the intermediaries' white flag.[89] More commonly, women with mili-tary connections petitioned Uhrich to intercede directly with Werder on their behalf. Each individual request passed under Werder's scrutiny and judgment. The flood of demands soon became too much. By late

August, Uhrich found it impossible to "make the choice from among all the women who request departure."[90]

Meanwhile, on August 20, Werder had received Moltke's authorization to bombard Strasbourg. Without mentioning this telegram, Werder wrote to Uhrich: "I invite you, in the name of humanity, to avoid a useless effusion of blood and to save the beautiful city of Strasbourg, for which we still yet have amicable, neighborly sentiments, from the destruction that awaits."[91] Uhrich resolutely refused. "I would make great sacrifices to save Strasbourg from the effects of the bombardment and siege," he wrote on August 21, "but I cannot sacrifice my honor and my duty: your heart of a soldier will understand this and I am certain that at this moment, although I have not had the honor of meeting you, you have some esteem for me and for the brave officers at my side."[92] Uhrich and Werder had become deadly enemies, but they respected each other's adherence to protocol.

In this same communication, Uhrich decided to gamble a request: he asked Werder "to authorize women, children and the elderly to leave the city."[93] This request fell within the scope of military custom in that Uhrich appealed to Werder's personal generosity. "The sympathy that you profess for Strasbourg," he continued, "makes me hope that you will welcome this plea."[94] Werder responded, "Sir, I entirely approve and I well understand the thinking of your honored letter of the 21st of this month. I perfectly conceive the painful feelings mingling the duty of the soldier with anxiety for 80,000 exposed citizens. The fortifications of large cities have their weakness in the suffering of the population, which is exposed without shelter to the enemy's cannonballs. . . . The exodus that you wish of a part of the population would thus augment the strength of the fortification; that is why I am not of a mind, as painful as it may be for me, to grant your request the answer that, in the interest of humanity, I would like to give."[95]

Military strategy trumped Werder's proclaimed sympathies. He recognized the tension between Uhrich's duty to his military regulations and his desire to protect innocent civilians, and he sought to exploit it. For their part, Uhrich and his defense council, following military regulations, agreed "unanimously and energetically" to hold firm despite Werder's refusal to allow a civilian exodus.[96] On August 22, Werder formally declared his intention to bombard "the city and the fortress," requesting and receiving acknowledgement from Uhrich.[97] Thus, military commanders on both sides operated under the assumption that the suffering of civilians would shape and color the siege's denouement.

At dawn on August 23, citizens read the following posted proclamation, issued jointly by Uhrich, Pron, and Humann: "Inhabitants of Strasbourg. The solemn moment has arrived. The city will be besieged and submitted to the dangers of war. We appeal to your patriotism, to your virile energy, in order to defend the capital of Alsace, the advanced sentinel of France. . . . Friends! Courage! The *patrie* has its eyes on us!"[98]

The proclamation did little to explain the situation or prepare civilians for the bombardment to come. Years later, Reuss recalled "the flabbergasted expressions of the good people reading this proclamation, posted in two languages, at the corner of the street across from my window, walking away shaking their heads, because they did not understand what that could mean!"[99] He opined, "The military and civilian authorities would surely have done better to announce frankly, in a manly way, what awaited the people of Strasbourg; they preferred to address them with a few absolutely vague and high-sounding phrases."[100] Raymond-Signouret, too, longed for the facts of the siege "followed by some good and sincere words of encouragement."[101] Piton also reacted to Uhrich's August 23 poster with scorn. Hadn't Paris already abandoned Strasbourg to its fate?[102] Uhrich must have realized his misstep; he did not include the proclamation in his memoirs. Military custom on its own could do little to ameliorate the situation of Strasbourg's civilians.

Burning *The Garden of Delights*

Frédéric Piton left his diary aside for four days in late August. He tried to start again on August 27: "Ah! The hard days that we have just passed! How many ruins piled up in this short amount of time!"[103] For three nights, August 24 through 27, the Prussians undertook an intense, deliberate bombardment of Strasbourg's urban center, sending more than four thousand shells each night into the heart of the city. The first night, August 24, was the single most destructive and symbolically powerful moment of the entire siege. At seven o'clock in the evening, German artillerymen took their positions at batteries tucked behind protective earthworks.[104] Caked in mud, they served a twenty-four-hour unbroken shift in the dark and the rain with "scarcely enough time to take a bite of bread and a drink from a field flask."[105] A battery of six guns was expected to fire four hundred shots during one shift. Retaliation from the French defenses caused the Germans horrific injuries and amputations of leg and arm.[106] "It is a very burdensome and also dangerous task," reported journalist Julius von Wickede from the scene, "but the brave artillerymen perform it with delight and joyful sacrifice."[107]

German artillerymen could not see the results of their action, but in the New Church cellar, hundreds of people felt and heard it firsthand. Elise Reichard, the daughter of pastor Franz Haerter and wife of vicar Max Reichard, was in the basement kitchen when the church was hit. "A most terrible blast sounded over our heads," she recalled, "and two seconds later a bright flame lit up the whole courtyard, all the way down into our cellar!"[108] She and the others ran upstairs to find the whole complex on fire—church, Gymnasium, libraries, Red Cross hospital. As shells continued to fall, tiles from the church roof rained into the courtyard with "the most peculiar, terrible noise that I have ever heard!"[109] Fortunately, the hospital staff was able to move the wounded and the homeless to the deep cellars in the Imperial Palace.

Instead of seeking safety herself, Reichard joined a bucket chain alongside Deaconesses, maids, teachers, and hospital staff. Their efforts were in vain. Reichard watched the last roof tile fall off and the dome collapse, along with the small tower with its silver bell. "It will no longer call us to church on Sundays," she wrote, "nor will its bright voice mix with the ringing of its sister at the cathedral to honor the Lord!"[110] Soon, the organ gave one last "deep, wistful note," no longer to move its listeners under the skilled master's hands, no longer to provide the *continuo* to their days.[111] In just a few hours, the church in which Elise Reichard's father had preached for forty years was gone.

For many, the loss of the libraries weighed even more heavily than that of the New Church. Early Reformers had founded this center of learning, the second largest library in France, out of a desire to wrest

As the New Church and libraries burn, two men care for a wounded or exhausted man, and a woman flees with children. In the background, two soldiers read posters of the latest news. Auguste Münch, *Guerre de 1870: Siège et bombardement de Strasbourg* (1870). (Archives de la Ville et de la Communauté urbaine de Strasbourg)

education away from clerics. It began as a repository for the Gymnasium, the oldest educational institution in the city, which gave courses starting in 1538.[112] Eventually, a second collection, the City Library, served the purpose of forming intellectually and morally educated civic leaders.

Frédéric Piton knew the libraries of the New Church well. He lived on rue du Temple Neuf and worked for the library from 1821 to 1853, a span of years that included two revolutions and a coup d'état.[113] But in his eyes, these episodes in modern history paled in the glow of this rich collection. The New Church represented a particular culture of the book that was already disappearing in the era of cheap, mechanized publication, liberalizing press laws, and expanded primary education. Resisting the trend, rare book collectors of the period prized scholarly knowledge bound in well-preserved leather and "studded with small gold-covered nails."[114] For bibliophiles, the New Church libraries, aged yet alive and growing, provided a tangible connection between past and present.

The libraries of the New Church developed and thrived primarily through human transformation and death. Volume after volume of literature, philosophy, and law entered the library at the passing of its original owner, a profoundly human transfer of knowledge. Books entered unwillingly, too: during the 1790s, revolutionaries confiscated the collections of convents, monasteries, and fleeing nobles. Works of history and archeology, heraldry and diplomacy, travel and theology slowly filled the shelves and demanded greater space. Piton's *Illustrated Strasbourg* grew out of his study of many of these volumes. By 1870, the library had acquired a collection of over 400,000 volumes and thousands of manuscripts, including "treasures that could never be replaced."[115] Its most famous piece was also one of its oldest, the *Hortus deliciarum (The Garden of Delights)* of Herrad of Landsberg. The twelfth-century abbess had created an encyclopedia filled with broad knowledge and minute detail, illustrated with numerous miniatures. The illuminated manuscript was so valued that scholars in Berlin wrote the military authorities to implore their care toward the library.[116]

Beyond its scholarly importance, the library symbolized the city's history and shaped its identity. Thousands of incunabula, books printed in the fifteenth-century infancy of publishing, reminded Strasbourgeois

The lone tower of the cathedral looks over the ruined New Church. Gustave Fischbach, *Le siège de Strasbourg: Strasbourg avant, pendant, et après le siège* (1897). (Charles Deering McCormick Library of Special Collections, Northwestern University Library)

of their link to Gutenberg, who had lived in Strasbourg in the 1440s. Festivities in 1840 marked the "invention of printing in this city" (a claim that was probably an invention itself), and the banners carried by craftsmen during this celebration guarded the bookshelves in one of the main reading rooms. In addition, the library had accumulated historical artifacts from Gallo-Roman coffins to Kléber's sword, including Strasbourg's collection of constitutions and documents from Gutenberg's conflict with the inheritors of his former partner. A bronze kettle of friendship from Zurich and the large Phrygian bonnet that had graced the cathedral spire in the 1790s reminded visitors of the city's loyalties. Even the windows told a story: the fourteenth-century stained glass marked the city's prosperity during that period.[117]

The Prussian bombardment destroyed this monument and everything it contained. All was lost, every page. Cinders retained the shape of sheets of paper just long enough to tease before disintegrating into dust. Commentators noted melodramatically that only Kléber's sword had survived.

Civilization under Siege

The next morning, volunteers struggled to contain the New Church fire with awkward water pumps and bursting tubes. They resorted to the bucket chain, with Gymnasium teacher Rodolphe Reuss doing his bit for five hours in the morning and again after lunch. That afternoon, exhausted from failing to save the place that had been his church, his school, his employer, and his intellectual home, Reuss stopped at the Commercial and Literary Casino and found himself alone in its reading rooms. "Thinking of our beautiful Library," he later reported, "of so many work projects for the future destroyed by these Vandals the Prussians, I began to cry with rage: it was one of the saddest moments of my existence."[118]

Reuss did not doubt that the Prussians had deliberately targeted the library. He obsessed over their uncanny ability to aim their cannon "with a diabolical precision," "a marvelous precision," a "truly stupefying precision."[119] A later rumor held that German commanders had provided their gunners with erroneous charts in order to fool them into targeting cultural sites. The purveyors of this oral tradition apparently did not want to blame the artillerymen so much as their sly commanders.[120] After all, "soldiers only act by the orders of their leaders," believed French journalist A.-G. Heinhold.[121]

Was the bombardment intentional? Given the technology of 1870, the Prussians probably could not have aimed their cannon so precisely as to hit the library. With all the incendiary material raining upon the city, it is no surprise that a building full of books caught fire. No records indicate that the Prussians explicitly intended to destroy the library. (Ironically, the archives of the Prussian Army that might have shed more light on this question were destroyed on April 14, 1945, when the Allies bombed the Heeresarchiv in Potsdam.[122]) Nevertheless, the fact remained that the library was gone and the German bombardment was responsible.

Intellectuals like Reuss and Piton found the loss of the libraries' collections almost unbearable. The repository of Strasbourg's own history was gone. A Germanophile professor of the Protestant Seminary wrote to a German friend, "As we again look ahead to the future we are ready to shed tears of blood, those of us who count ourselves among the more

The ruins of the Library and New Church. For many of Strasbourg's elite, the destruction of the libraries symbolized Prussian barbarism and a return to the destructive wars of the past. Auguste Münch, *Guerre de 1870: Siège et bombardement de Strasbourg* (1870). (Archives de la Ville et de la Communauté urbaine de Strasbourg)

cultured and elevated part of the local citizenry. . . . Strasbourg is done for! Nothing can bring back to our town its old literary reputation, nothing can connect it anymore with its beautiful past."[123] Furthermore, the libraries' collections were not just a local or even a French treasure, but one that belonged to all of civilization. The maintenance of knowledge in privileged repositories remained central to the European sense of self and civilization.

The loss of the library also indicated yet another weakness in the protections to which civilians felt entitled. We have already seen that civilians in Strasbourg could depend on neither legally recognized rights nor military customs to shield them from war. For many, hope for protection lay in something far more fundamental: the nebulous construction known as civilization. In particular, they expected that the accumulated educational, religious, and social structures of the nineteenth century had formed leaders who possessed an internal moral compass and did not need external laws to tell them that killing children and destroying libraries were wrong.

Looking back from the twenty-first century, we might think that the expanded range and capacity of nineteenth-century artillery would have unleashed a backlash against civilization. We live in a post–World War II world and are accustomed to science fiction visions of technology's dangerous implications. But in 1870, most observers did not fear that civilization had gotten out of control. The notion that efficient weaponry ought to lead to shorter and more humane wars still prevailed.[124] Distrust and fear of technology was not a common thread in civilian anger at the bombardment; such a response would not dominate European culture until after the Great War.

Instead, observers believed that the Prussian military in general and Werder in particular had deviated from civilized behavior and reverted to standards left behind in the 1600s. Ignoring the devastating sieges of the French Revolution or the Crimean War, Schneegans argued that the Prussian tactics belonged to the Thirty Years' War and the destructive conflicts of Louis XIV. Schneegans repudiated the "barbarities" of the past, even of France's past, arguing that "humanity must have progressed" in the previous two centuries. If the Prussians were willing to burn cities, "won't they go further? Why wouldn't they return to the excellent practices of Tilly, who systematically had women raped and children killed? . . . And why wouldn't they massacre prisoners, as they used to do? All of these acts were formerly considered to be acts of good and honest war."[125]

For Schneegans, Prussia jeopardized the civilizing progress of the previous centuries. He wrote, "Let's turn our backs on the future of humanity . . . ! Let's turn back on the path that our fathers had cleared for our civilization, and let the brambles grow! Progress is a chimera, civilization is just a word, man is a crude beast."[126] How could it be that Germany, "in the middle of the nineteenth century, renewed the horrors that she condemned in the seventeenth and eighteenth centuries in her enemies, that are a mournful and desolating anachronism, and will be a dark spot on its annals?"[127] As some Europeans came to believe that pain and misery were man-made, rather than part of God's mysteries, it became logical to blame suffering on the deliberate actions of backward-looking individuals or cultures. The horrors of war represented not the emergence of "modern" warfare so much as the reemergence of the past. Civilization was moving backward.[128]

For Reuss, the civilization embodied in the libraries of the New Church contrasted with the barbarity of King Wilhelm, "an old, imbecilic monarch, who believes himself to be the representative of divine right on earth." Hypocritical and decrepit, Wilhelm appeared to Reuss as living evidence of the dangers of monarchical power. Reuss protested that "nobody, I must say, nobody would have thought it possible that in the middle of the nineteenth century a nation that claims to march at the head of civilization [and] a Christian sovereign could give the order to reduce temples and churches to ashes."[129] Reuss's republican sensibilities encouraged him to view monarchical political systems as inherently antithetical to all that was good about European civilization.

Like many of his contemporaries, Reuss thought of Germany as the home of authentic *Kultur* and the literary, musical, and philosophical achievements embodied in Goethe and Beethoven.[130] Reuss feared that "Germany's intelligent and serious men, its scholars, artists and writers," risked seduction by the charms of military victory.[131] "It was logical, as well as barbarous," wrote Reuss, "and the war showed us that our enemies held logic more dearly than humanity."[132] Schneegans did not even hold General Werder completely responsible for the bombardment, for "the man that the uniform suffocates is better than he wants to appear." Since Schneegans erroneously believed that Werder had been ordered to bombard Strasbourg, Werder himself became a victim of Prussian militarism who "only knows his orders" and "executes them whatever the cost."[133] Schneegans had hoped for better from Germany, a country "more civilized that the others, more instructed, wiser, and Protestant besides, and delivered from the domination of priests, full of idealistic aspirations and vehement indignation against the vices of the modern Babylon."[134] Over the following decades, Martha Hanna explains, many French scholars became convinced that Germany experienced "cultural schizophrenia" between the profound philosophies of Kant and the materialistic militarism of Moltke.[135]

Werder's choice to bombard therefore seemed to take on specifically Prussian characteristics. It hardened national lines and reconfigured and simplified civilians' loyalties. In the words of Bertrand Taithe, "The complex apportioning of responsibility boiled down to a banal story of good and evil."[136] August 24 was the moment, according to one professor, that French culture finally became dominant in Alsace![137] Journalist Raymond-Signouret believed this bombardment signaled a difference between French and Germans; if the French invaded German territories, they would not do the same, as "the French character is too chivalrous to allow itself to be led to such excesses."[138] Of course, such protests ignored the French way of spreading "civilization" through military conquest and violence, as practiced during the revolutionary period in Europe and in France's invasion of Algeria.[139]

The destruction of the library forced the emotional engagement of those who, like Rodolphe Reuss, had hoped to remain detached from a war between two monarchs. As he sat brooding in the Casino, Reuss felt a powerful new sentiment rise within himself, at odds with the cosmopolitanism of scholarship: "We felt our voice break off in sobs and, in our heart, we felt rise one of those furious national hatreds believed to have been now forgotten and that will not be snuffed out anytime soon."[140] He called for revenge against the loss: "Ah! If eternal justice is not a vain name, the hour and the day will come, when such attacks will be judged and punished as they merit! To the rear, we will say in turn, to the rear with soft complacencies and misplaced sentimentality! If they are barbarians, let us treat them as barbarians: they will only reap what they have sown!"[141]

Reuss took comfort in the belief that "Europe and the civilized world" of the future would "note under the deceptive varnish of this intellectual culture, of which they show themselves so proud, the native barbarism of a race where at all times, and most often without shame, Might makes Right."[142] However devastating the loss today, however vast the hole in civilization appeared, civilization remained a constant whose values of scholarship, books, and the continuity of knowledge would endure and pass judgment.

Reuss's notion of history allowed him to imagine a future that transcended the present. Whatever damage occurred in the service of barbarism, he believed that those who cared about the human experience as expressed in literature and philosophy would prevail. Love of ideas remained a constant, indeed, notwithstanding catastrophic setbacks such as the destroyed library, each year marked an increase in the tangible evidence of the human devotion to scholarly inquiry. Reuss had no doubt that the judgment of history would fall in his favor, rendering the Prussian successes in Strasbourg small and ironic. Reuss believed that he could win the war of words, for words themselves would transcend the logic of military strength. The history of the world may be, as Friedrich Schiller wrote, the world's court of judgment, but the standards would be cultural rather than martial. So long as people continued to read and write, the library at Strasbourg would symbolize an incalculable loss, but that loss presaged creation, as a cropped plant produces new shoots at the cut.

Reuss took the first step himself, in writing out his account of the library's destruction and its meaning for Strasbourg on September 19, while still under siege. He placed this essay as the preface to his wartime journal: "If these lines are the last to leave my plume, if, like so many others more brave and more useful to their *patrie*, I am not to survive the catastrophe of my unfortunate birthplace, I would be happy to have been able to protest again against so many horrors in the name of the *patrie*, of humanity, of science and of justice."[143] Written protest emerged as Reuss's sole outlet for revenge. "Whatever may be the fortunes of our unfortunate fatherland and our dear province, whatever may be the destiny that awaits us tomorrow," he wrote, "I applaud in my conscience for having been able to raise the cry of indignation again."[144] He ultimately came through that dark night with an even stronger faith in the power of reason and historical judgment.

■　■　■

After August 24, Strasbourg began to draw the significant attention of German newspapers for the first time. "The conditions of the poor inhabitants of the city must be dreadful," acknowledged a newspaper in Cologne.[145] The Berlin *Volks-Zeitung* published reports from German-leaning Strasbourgeois who were dismayed that a fellow German and Protestant country had destroyed the New Church.[146] Few people on either side noted that the New Church had burned on Saint-Bartholomew's Day, the anniversary of the infamous sixteenth-century massacre of French Protestants; after all, Strasbourg had not been part of France in 1572, and this time, the perpetrators included Protestants, too. The meanings and motivations for violence against civilians had changed since the wars of religion. The Prussians now justified bombardment as a quick way to achieve military objectives. Few constraints tempered their actions. Neither the older Just War tradition nor the newly emerging system of international humanitarian law had convinced nations to accept guidelines for the treatment of besieged civilians. Military custom, too, had traditionally limited civilian departures from besieged cities. Uhrich's ill-advised bombardment of Kehl did not facilitate negotiations, but in any case, there was little hope that Werder would acquiesce to a civilian exodus. Werder's insistence that the customs of war allowed him to trap civilians in the city was not just an excuse; it was the way that war worked.

The gap was wide indeed between the expectations of the civilians and the existing formal protections, not to mention actual military practice. Civilians had no doubt that the bombardment they experienced—especially on August 24—lay outside the norms and customs that defined humane treatment. "Outraged humanity expects additional expiation for the atrocities committed around Strasbourg and within its walls," wrote Rodolphe Reuss.[147] It seemed to many that civilization had receded back to the seventeenth century, "to the era of great crimes committed against humanity."[148] The accumulated European inheritance of knowledge and history—"civilization"—proved to be powerless, at least in the short term, against modern artillery. The French did not protest against the siege itself so much as against the "barbaric, savage" means of bombardment.[149] When Strasbourgeois evoked the "laws of war," they argued that war ought to follow both the "laws of nature" and the "laws of nations," which to them included the protection of all "innocents."

In the decades that followed, many Europeans came to view civilization itself as the source of Europe's wars and excesses. But in 1870, according to observers of the bombardment of Strasbourg, civilization remained the touchstone for the best possible world. But civilization had failed to form leaders who would make morally correct decisions, and war threatened to erode Europe's progress. In the aftermath of the intense bombardment of August 24, Strasbourgeois struggled to make sense of the experience while facing the reality that they remained under siege.

CHAPTER FOUR

Victims in the Eye
of the Beholder

FTER THE DESTRUCTION of the New Church, Rodolphe Reuss
continued to fight the fires, and Catherine Weiss cautiously
reemerged from her cellar. A few days of uncertainty followed:
Would Strasbourg continue to resist? Then, Werder change his strategy
from nighttime intense bombardment aimed at the city center to the
"regular" siege in which artillery focused day and night on the fortress walls.

Although Reuss, Weiss, and their families survived, many others
were not so lucky. The six-week bombardment killed 861 soldiers and
about 300 civilians, left some 10,000 homeless, and created a host of
new physical and psychological trauma. Military medicine had not kept
pace. Men, women, and children all lost limbs, lay feverishly in hospital
beds, and coped with long hours of bombardment. Everyone suffered,
but in the eyes of contemporary observers, not all suffering was equal.
Some people were considered victims—innocent bystanders caught in a
violent act—whereas others were passed over in silence. In other words,
suffering is a condition, whereas victimhood implies that certain suffering is unjust. In the siege of Strasbourg, gender, age, and combatant
status determined the difference. Most accounts of suffering came from
adult civilian males, particularly journalists and doctors reporting in literature intended for wide public consumption. Their descriptions did
not always tell the whole story. In their eyes, children, women, and

wounded soldiers—but never civilian males—suffered as victims of wartime violence. Similarly, observers praised the collective heroism of civilian women simply for going about their everyday tasks and for feminine
activities and characteristics, but rarely extended the same admiration
to civilian men. These interpretations of victims and heroes profoundly
shaped the solutions that civilians offered to help their city and its inhabitants survive.

"Worse Than Attila"

On the morning of August 25 at two o'clock, as the New Church still
burned, Werder sent the following message to Uhrich: "Monsieur. You
have seen over the course of two days the damage I have inflicted on the
city, the defenses and the citadel, with a weak part of my artillery. When
the day begins, I will hold fire to give you time to reflect on whether you
now want to grant me surrender of the place. If this is the case, I beg you
to send me a response by noon."[1] Confident of his success, Werder also
sent a directive to all the siege personnel under his command, reminding
them to respect the inhabitants of the city, which "in earlier times
belonged to our common fatherland."[2]

These instructions proved premature. Without delay, Uhrich
responded, "My walls remain standing and I cannot dream of rendering
a place that honor and the interests of France command me to defend to
the last extremity."[3] It did not matter that the library had burned or that
thousands were homeless. The physical state of the walls was the only
consideration, and Uhrich knew that his honor and perhaps his life
depended on his ability to maintain this standard.

From their new offices in the Hôtel de Ville, Uhrich and the defense
council assessed their limited options. The forces in Strasbourg were
too small to organize a sortie, and they had little hope of replacing the
35,000 percussion fuses that had been lost to fire. The general telegrammed Minister of War Charles Cousin-Montauban, Comte de
Palikao, for orders. The minister assured Uhrich that the Prussians
would not sustain the bombardment of the previous night, for "the
Prussians always start with a bombardment, hoping to demoralize the
city. It is only after this attack that the regular siege begins, from which

the place suffers less."[4] Bolstered by these words, Uhrich and the defense council knew they had to continue fighting. When Werder demanded surrender once again on August 26, the defense council united in saying, "Strasbourg will defend itself to the end!"[5]

Werder had counted on the civilian population to pressure Uhrich into capitulation. What did civilians think and feel during these intense days? Auguste Schneegans expressed the mixed emotions of living through a bombardment. Before the bombs fell, he recalled, "one could reason coolly, and one told oneself that Strasbourg was lost." But then, once the siege began, everything changed: "Lost or not, what does it matter? We must hold on to the last extremity."[6] He found himself imagining all kinds of improbable solutions, such as sending all men, women, and children out to fight or ransoming themselves to Prussia. Frédéric Piton recorded in his diary that although the inhabitants of the city suffered piteously, "in every group filling the streets, the firm resolution dominates that they will not let themselves be knocked down, they will resist to the end."[7]

Of course, the citizens of Strasbourg had never been a unified block. Despite his bravado, Piton betrays a hint of debate: the resolution to hold firm "dominates," implying that other opinions had been voiced. Indeed, the population's reactions can only be understood as multiple and contingent. In the afternoon of August 25, several hundred citizens met at Place Broglie and proceeded to the Hôtel de Ville, where they requested that Mayor Humann accompany them to confront Uhrich at headquarters. They demanded arms for a sortie and protective pillboxes to protect their wives and children so that they could fight "to the last extremity."[8] One man preferred to die *en masse* fighting the Prussians rather than be picked off one by one by the shells.[9] Uhrich refused to allow this massacre. At the same time, the citizens also requested that a delegation, including Humann, be sent to Werder to "appeal to his sentiments of humanity, to tell him that a general gathers little glory by burning a city and ruining a peaceful population, and that cannon are made to aim at ramparts and not at houses and churches."[10] They hoped for mercy without surrender. Uhrich realized that such a meeting would be tantamount to capitulation and therefore denied their request.[11] In their accounts of this episode, some observers emphasized surrender, others stressed the desire to fight, while still others put the two together. They sought any resolution to the distress of bombardment.

More important than the precise demands is the confrontational nature of this episode. A conflict arose between Uhrich and the population over the conduct of the siege. Uhrich prevailed due to his military position, but he now had to deal face-to-face with the people of the city he defended. A crisis of authority was brewing.

Just a few minutes after this confrontation, André Raess, the seventy-six-year-old bishop of Strasbourg, came to Uhrich to ask permission to intercede with Werder.[12] Raess was accustomed to careful negotiations. Born during the Terror, educated in the widely distrusted Jesuit tradition during the reactionary re-Christianization of France, and strongly ultramontane in his convictions, Raess nevertheless managed to avoid conflict with the state. During his long tenure as bishop (1842–1887), Raess survived the revolution of 1848, the siege of Strasbourg, the transition to German rule, and Bismarck's *Kulturkampf.* Raess's admirers saw him as a champion of the church, guarding its independence from political power. His detractors noted that he adapted a bit too readily to the changing regimes, using flattery and intrigue to promote his ambitions and win honors. Raess had reason to believe that he might be able to persuade Werder to change his course.[13]

Uhrich approved Raess's intervention. Although the general had just turned down a similar request to send Mayor Humann, he believed that intervention on behalf of the people, rather than the municipality, was acceptable.[14] During the night of August 25–26, Raess traveled to the furthest outposts of the city. But Werder refused to meet with the bishop, deeming him (in Moltke's words) "unqualified to negotiate."[15] The Prussians only wanted to deal with military authorities, and certainly not with a Catholic bishop. Instead, Raess spoke with Leszczynski, who refused to allow the departure of women, children, and the elderly and declined a ceasefire until Uhrich was prepared to negotiate a surrender. Raess returned to the city empty-handed and severely disappointed.[16]

Raess's failure became one of the episodes from Strasbourg that German journalists were most likely to report. The story first appeared in regional newspapers, including the *Karlsruher Zeitung,* the *Kölnische*

Zeitung, and the *Badische Landeszeitung,* and later made its way to the readers of the Berlin-based *National-Zeitung.*[17] Journalists usually made sure to mention that after the bishop was escorted back to Strasbourg, the French shot at the German escort and damaged the parliamentary flag.

On the French side, the bishop's thwarted intervention provided further fodder for anti-Prussian rhetoric and added to Werder's monstrous reputation. Raess had hoped to step in where the municipality and the military had failed. In reference to the famous fifth-century meeting in which Pope Leo I had successfully turned back the Huns, Raess reportedly quipped, "I am not Saint-Leo, but I found worse than Attila."[18]

That night, just one day after the destruction of the New Church, the cathedral over which Raess had presided for almost thirty years caught fire. The flames devoured the large straw mats in summer storage up near the platform from which Frédéric Piton had so often gazed. When the fire reached copper roofing, the flames took on blue and green tints, casting an eerie glow upon the city. Melted lead flowed out of the mouths of gargoyles.[19] By two o'clock, the entire length of the roof was engulfed in flames, far beyond the reach of firemen's pumps. Fiery fingers reached up toward the tower and the spire, the alternating light and shadow making their forms appear grotesque and overgrown. German artillerymen, watching from their trenches, could see the lacy cathedral stonework "like a skeleton in bright illumination."[20] Some saw a vision of the Virgin sway over the cathedral tower, her veils flowing through the smoke.[21] It all proved too much for Bishop Raess. He fell gravely ill and did not recover until the winter.[22]

Only one good piece of news emerged: the cathedral's interior was spared severe damage. Its famed astronomical clock survived unharmed. Time had not stopped; this moment would pass.[23]

Compromises

By the morning of August 27, municipal leaders were ready to bargain. Following a strategy session at the restaurant La Chaîne, Mayor Humann, Charles Boersch, Alphonse Saglio, and Jules Sengenwald

The cathedral on fire. The firefighters did not have the equipment to reach the flames on the roof. Auguste Münch, *Guerre de 1870: Siège et bombardement de Strasbourg* (1870). (Archives de la Ville et de la Communauté urbaine de Strasbourg)

presented their plan to Uhrich and Pron.[24] The bombardment and the rumors of impending relief from the outside had pushed them to a desperate and eminently bourgeois measure: the city would offer Werder 100,000 francs to provide four or five days of relief.

Uhrich and Pron refused immediately. Pron, whose head wound from a near miss with a shell had become a badge of honor, played the role of the worldly leader who understood the larger strategy far better than these provincial councilmen. He scoffed at the suggestion that 100,000 francs could buy off the Prussians. "We'd better talk of at least a million," he said. In any case, "the offer will be interpreted as a sign of extreme terror."[25] Uhrich agreed that such a request lacked dignity and would encourage the enemy to increase its firepower.[26] Furthermore, Uhrich dashed the hope of imminent relief from the outside.

Municipal councilmen now felt that it was every man for himself. Jules Sengenwald believed that it was clear that Strasbourg would eventually capitulate, perhaps after suffering an all-out military assault and "all the extremities and calamities" that would follow. He feared for the safety of his daughter and mother-in-law. With his house in the thick of the falling bombs and his nights spent in a dank and narrow cellar, Sengenwald felt that Uhrich now asked him to "be resigned to the sacrifice of our fortunes, our affections and our lives." It was too much for this family man. After all, "not a member of the defense council had his family near him, the prefect had placed his children in safety, the mayor had just been able to have his wife and daughter leave, and I, who had the means to save my daughter from the horrors of the siege, I should have to abandon myself to passive resignation?"[27]

Up to this point, Sengenwald's duties as a municipal councilman and as president of the chamber of commerce had tied him to Strasbourg, but by the last days of August, neither group was still meeting. He later admitted, "The solicitations of my heart were stronger than political suggestions." So Sengenwald, over sixty years old and unable to take up arms for his city, packed up his family and decamped for Basel: "I believe I thus acted as the situation, and duty, and family proscribed, and if I was not at the same time able to do an act of civic duty, it is because there are circumstances in life when one cannot reconcile contrary duties."[28] Just how he secured escape from Strasbourg is unclear.

Sengenwald and many others were ready to negotiate, but from the German perspective, the bombardment had not achieved its desired effect; the people of Strasbourg had not been able to pressure Uhrich to capitulate, and Werder did not have the ammunition to continue his all-out bombardment much longer. Werder scaled back and began the regular form of siege warfare, focusing on the defenses while still sending bombs into the center of the city to lower morale.[29]

The regular siege, which lasted from August 27 to September 27, entailed the methodical construction of parallels. In crews of four thousand, German soldiers stealthily dug zigzag trenches some four and a half feet deep in the loamy soil. The first parallel, about seven hundred feet northwest of the fortress walls, near the Pierre Gate, was completed in the night of August 29–30. By September 1, they began the second parallel about three hundred feet closer, cutting right through Sainte-Hélène's Cemetery.[30] A French sortie in the early morning hours of September 2 slowed their progress; two battalions of the French Eighty-Seventh Regiment exited at Saverne Gate, hoping to destroy the enemy's artillery strongholds and spike their cannon. But as the columns approached, they were greeted with German rifles. The French left behind 151 casualties and only managed to capture 5 Prussians.[31]

The Prussians took up their shovels again and completed the second parallel on September 9. Now they were in a position to bring their cannon close enough to slowly blast through the earthen fortress walls. German newspapers from Cologne to Berlin reported that the besiegers were making progress and expected the city to fall soon.[32]

On Rainbow Street

Meanwhile, hospitals in Strasbourg cared for the sick, wounded, and dying. The Military Hospital, located near the citadel on the eastern side of the city, handled wounded soldiers. By the end of the siege, this facility had cared for more than eight hundred sick and wounded, up to fifty new cases per day in the worst periods. The Civil Hospital, on the city's relatively protected southern edge, treated a total of 344 civilians. Both of these permanent hospitals lay within the city walls but outside of Strasbourg's Grande Île.[33]

In addition, fifteen smaller temporary Red Cross hospitals, which the authorities had initially mistrusted, became indispensible once the bombardment began. Altogether, 1,568 soldiers and civilians found treatment with the Red Cross (the records do not indicate the percentage of each). The Red Cross operated in centrally located churches, schools, and religious orders, as well as in the synagogue and the Masonic lodge. They were closer than the Civil Hospital to where wounded people were likely to be, but as a result, they were subject themselves to bombardment and fire; the destruction of the New Church and its Red Cross hospital made this danger clear. The Red Cross furthermore stationed doctors and nurses at each of Strasbourg's seven gates and at a prominent hotel, which served as a central office from which victims were directed to various hospitals. Altogether, hospitals treated more than 2,700 sick or wounded soldiers and civilians, almost 3 percent of the wartime population. Many more civilians may have been treated at home. Estimates of the total number of civilian wounded range from six hundred to two thousand.[34]

By the end of the siege, 861 soldiers from the French garrison died: 270 killed outright in battle or on the ramparts, 177 of wounds in the Red Cross temporary hospitals, 268 of wounds in the Military Hospital, and 146 of illness. These numbers come from registers at the site of later burial and may not include soldiers who were buried immediately or whose families happened to live in Strasbourg.[35]

About three hundred civilians died due to the bombardment, most of them either immediately or shortly after sustaining injury. The official Civil Register listed 279 names, but Reinhold Wagner, a German analyst, argued that 27 of these "civilians" had, in fact, served military functions as mobile guardsmen, national guardsmen, or customs agents. However, the Strasbourg Aid Committee claimed that the Civil Register missed at least sixty-two deaths that were only reported to the Aid Committee by families asking for assistance. Therefore, they believed that at least 341 had been killed.[36]

Strasbourg was fortunate in that it did not suffer from severe epidemics. Still, in the final five months of 1870, the number of deaths due to illness—1,912, including the mother of journalist Paul Raymond-Signouret—more than doubled the comparable average from the previous five years (947). Lack of milk for young children, the strain and close quarters of living in cellars, the stagnate waters of the Ill River and canals, and later, the disappointment of the capitulation may have contributed to higher rates of disease.[37]

How did Strasbourg's civilians make sense of this overflow of suffering? Journalists employed their most graphic and emotional descriptions for the following incident in the early phase of the nighttime bombardment. In the early morning of August 17, a shell struck the Asylum of Saint-Antoine, a girls' orphanage on rue de l'Arc-en-ciel, Rainbow Street. Raymond-Signouret reported, "Two young girls were killed instantly; the shell literally decapitated one of them; nine others were horribly wounded and mutilated . . . the legs of four of them were almost entirely detached and held on only by shreds of quivering flesh. Two were amputated from the left leg below the knee, another from the left thigh; the first two recovered, the other succumbed. Three of these poor children were so shredded by the debris of the projectile that they expired after a few hours of atrocious suffering, supported by the most touching resignation."[38] Another woman, struck in her bed on the night of August 17–18, lost both her legs. Five nights later, a shell hit the Stahl household, wounding Mme Stahl's two sisters. One of them lost both of her arms.[39]

These incidents confirmed prejudices about the nature of civilian war victims. Observers across political and national lines repeatedly argued that the shells hit primarily women and children. Schneegans recalled, "While the city thus perished, the walls of the fortress were intact; and while children agonized on all sides, hardly any soldiers were wounded on the ramparts."[40] War, he believed, "should be an open struggle, soldiers against soldiers, citizens against citizens, but not men against children, women, the elderly, the powerless." The Prussian bombardment could not help but harm "the innocent, who cannot defend themselves, who cannot flee, and whose martyrdom is not a feat of some kind of valor, but of a particular cowardice of the enemy."[41] Imperial functionary Malartic lamented, "Women and children were hit in their houses, in the streets."[42] When German journalists mentioned civilian victims explicitly—a rare occurrence—they too stated that the victims were women and children.[43]

However, despite the unusual statistics created by the girls' orphanage disaster, civilians killed by the bombardment were overwhelmingly and consistently adult males. Altogether, 170 of the 289 civilian deaths for which we have demographic information were male adults.[44] The same held true for the wounded. Between August 13 and September 27, the Civil Hospital treated far more men than they did women and children combined: 212 men, 110 women, and 22 children. The Civil Hospital also handled the remains of civilians killed instantly by shells or shrapnel. Here, too, the victims tended to be male: fifty-five men, nineteen women, and thirteen children.[45] Why more men than women? A diarist provided a likely explanation: "Many heads of households, in order to not expose his domestics, went himself to gather the daily provisions."[46] Whereas Catherine Weiss described life in the cellars, male diarists frequently referred to their exploratory walks through the rubble and their encounters with other men in public spaces. Men were more likely than women and children to be out in the open streets, and particularly during the regular siege, men were far more likely to be killed.

How do we explain the gap between reality and rhetoric? Of course, distress over harm done to women and children in war was nothing new. This narrative was strengthened by the ambiguous status of civilian males in nineteenth-century war. Men were expected to respond to attacks with courage and shield women and children from harm, but as noncombatants, men had few options for defending their towns or protecting against modern weaponry. Part defense mechanism against their own unacknowledged suffering, part tacit recognition of their failure to protect their wives, sisters, and offspring, part refusal to see women as partners in this situation, the rhetoric of civilian men shifted the role of victim onto women and children. Coded for innocence and domesticity, women provided a stark contrast to the steel and shrapnel of long-range artillery.

When authors described female victims, they emphasized either women's gentle resignation to the loss of their earthly bodies or women's inability to cope with bombardment. French surgeon Henri-Etienne Beaunis argued, "Women and children . . . more imprudent and losing their heads more easily, lost the presence of mind necessary for saving themselves in time."[47] Authors were not concerned with other issues we might expect, such as treatment, psychological challenges, or rates of recovery. Most did not dwell upon realistic and graphic descriptions of women's physical wounds, and no one attempted to capture the inner life or experiences of a wounded woman. Instead, women and children became a foil for Prussian aggression.

Meanwhile, the hundreds of male civilian casualties received almost no mention. This silence reveals contemporary limitations of representation: civilian men could not be inserted into the prevalent simplistic binary with female civilian victims on one side and aggressive Prussian soldiers on the other, so they were not discussed much at all.

In Praise of Women and Men

How did the victim narrative affect the praise of women and men? Some women resisted the victim narrative, but even so, the dominant story about the besieged women of Strasbourg rested firmly on gendered terrain. Observers celebrated women's actions in the collective, particularly when they were safely feminine in nature. Women could be considered heroic for simply going about their business during the bombardment. Civilian men's actions were almost never mentioned, except for those like firefighting that were nearly on par with the danger of soldiering. These definitions of heroism, like the definitions of victimhood, rested on the notion that men and women differed fundamentally.[48]

Cécile de Dartein, a bourgeois single woman of twenty-two years, did not see herself as a victim. She claimed in the privacy of her diary to rank among the city's courageous. In her entry at the outset of the siege, Dartein reported that Strasbourg contained three groups of civilians: "the brave, the fearful [and] the Prussians"—German sympathizers. The latter two groups were more numerous than she would have wished, but she reported that the "battalion of the brave, who are the smallest in number, [are] well resolved to hold on with the garrison."[49] Given an opportunity to leave the city, Dartein and her sisters and mother decided to stay in Strasbourg, because they would not abandon their home or Cécile's brother Henri, a *franc-tireur*.[50] Dartein never suggested that she would engage in combat, but she made it clear in her words and her actions that she aligned herself with the brave. Indeed, even women who suffered while crowded in the cellars could transcend the state of victimhood. The interactions among them may have been fortifying, consoling, or edifying. Like survivors of the siege of Leningrad, they may have experienced the ordeal as "a time when people knew how to be together, to take care of one another, to share to the bitter end."[51] For her part, Catherine Weiss focused on protecting her children. In her eyes, it was they, not she, who were the true victims of the siege.

In a slightly different tone, naval captain Bergasse du Petit-Thouars praised women's capacity to perform public tasks under fire: praying and nursing. Even under a "rain of iron and fire," Bergasse du Petit-Thouars constantly saw women out in public: "You saw them intrepid and trembling pressing into the churches, where they prayed to God all-powerful to save them by a miracle, [and] in the hospitals, where they multiplied near the sick and wounded."[52] It is easy to agree that the selfless nursing of women like the Deaconesses deserves praise. We might be tempted to dismiss the contention that prayer is heroic; it may seem condescending to place female heroes in a position of supplication instead of action. Yet prayer—especially public prayer in the parish church that necessitated a dangerous journey through the streets—required emotional fortitude and symbolized the victory of resolution over despair. For some observers, prayer was both a feminine and a heroic act.

Not only did Bergasse du Petit-Thouars praise women for performing female-coded tasks, he also described them as stereotypically feminine, "quivering from limb to limb with each detonation."[53] And yet, according to Bergasse du Petit-Thouars, women refused to surrender, subverting Werder's strategy to exploit women's fear. Frightened and strained, women approached the captain to ask, "Isn't it true, monsieur, that we won't surrender?"[54] Heroic women have often been characterized as unsexed or masculine, their feminine characteristics stripped away; such was the case for female warriors from adolescent Joan of Arc to cross-dressing *franc-tireur* Antoinette Lix. By contrast, Bergasse du Petit-Thouars admired women in their capacities as women. They had not taken on a masculine stoicism but rather showed their fear in a way that was comfortingly feminine and dependent.

Looking back, later authors also admired the women of Strasbourg collectively for activities considered feminine. In his 1893 book of anecdotes about women during the invasion, Joseph Turquan praised the women of Strasbourg because they encouraged the soldiers to fight well and "went through the streets to seek out provisions necessary to their family."[55] Turquan recognized that simply stepping out into the street posed a risk to life and limb. So long as women did not stay cowering in cellars, they were worthy of honor. Similarly, Beaunis, writing in the 1880s, applauded women who maintained their mental fortitude during the siege. While some succumbed to nervous disorders, most did not. Beaunis deemed their mental stability an act of bravery. "In general," he concluded, "for the women of Strasbourg, courage was pushed to heroism."[56] Turquan and Beaunis did not expect women to do anything but provide for their families; they admired women simply for maintaining their composure. Women's everyday, domestic activities became heroic during the siege because women were not expected to endure combat.

Indeed, all of these authors preferred to see Strasbourg's female citizens as the quintessence of womanhood. The raucous flirt that Reuss had alluded to in the early days of the war disappeared. Turquan claimed that the women of Strasbourg "responded to this calculated barbarity with the most beautiful attitude that women have ever had in the history of besieged cities."[57] Similarly, Bergasse du Petit-Thouars praised the women's bravery, "the most admirable example of resolution [and] patriotism ever recorded in history."[58] These observers believed that prayerful, domestic, trembling, yet resolute women represented the best that womanhood had to offer.

All of these portraits of female heroism in Strasbourg disregarded the range of activities that besieged women have historically undertaken. During the early modern period, many women openly defended their cities. They built barricades, repaired fortifications, and dug ditches. Occasionally, they fought alongside men to protect their homes, their families, and their own bodies. These actions fell outside normal gender-defined roles of the time, but they earned praise in the extraordinary circumstance of war. Numerous women won royal citation and national fame for their actions. Strasbourgeois would likely have been most familiar with Jeanne Hachette, the hatchet-wielding heroine of fifteenth-century Beauvais, but other examples underscore the many possibilities for female activities. Kenau Simons Hasselaar of Haarlem organized and equipped a battalion of three hundred women against the Spanish in 1572–1573. In 1622, the Protestant women of Montpellier took up swords and daggers to fight off and kill Catholic besiegers. More recently, Agustina Zaragoza y Doménech of Saragossa aimed a cannon at the encroaching French during the Napoleonic Wars. From 1940 through 1944, during the siege of Leningrad, women took on prominent roles and extensive responsibilities as doctors, civil defense workers, factory workers, and government officials.[59]

It was possible, too, for women elsewhere in France to earn praise for individual, extraordinary actions during the Franco-Prussian War. *Cantinières*, women who traveled with the army to sell soldiers food and drink, often received unofficial decorations or the Military Medal, the lowest grade of the Legion of Honor, for acts of bravery. One *cantinière*, Marie Jarrethout, later received the Cross of the Legion of Honor (for which she was technically not eligible) for carrying ammunition to soldiers in battle, nursing the wounded under fire, and escaping from Prussian captivity. Jarrethout furthermore fought at three battles, including the siege of Châteaudun, where she dressed as a man, but her combat role was deemphasized in her citation for the Legion of Honor. In addition, throughout the early Third Republic, civics textbooks aimed at girls praised certain individuals for their unique acts of heroism. Marie-Edmée Pau nursed her wounded brother on the battlefield, organized seamstresses to make clothes for soldiers, and even sketched portraits of dying soldiers for their families. She died of illness in this service. Antoinette Lix fought in male disguise as a *franc-tireur*. In Paris, women were known to have donned uniforms and joined the National Guard or the *francs-tireurs*. Finally, Juliette Dodu, a telegraph operator near Orléans, won fame for hiding her equipment from the enemy and for reportedly tapping the telegraph wires of the occupying Germans. According to legend, the Prussians caught Dodu and condemned her to death, but at the last minute, Prince Friedrich Karl spared her life. Whatever the truth behind this melodramatic story, Dodu was awarded the Legion of Honor in 1878. So, women during the Franco-Prussian War earned praise not just for being patriotic and prayerful mothers and sisters, not just for nursing, but also for risking their own lives. They inspired the generation of women who came of age prior to the Great War.

In Strasbourg, the few women to be singled out for praise—Mlle Ritton, Mlle Lange, and Mme Kiéné—performed their noteworthy actions after the city fell: they all helped French prisoners of war. As Margaret Darrow has noted, women tend to be allowed the status of hero only after men have failed.[60] In Strasbourg, the need to assign to women the role of victim proved so strong that it overcame any desire to produce a heroine story for the city.

Civilian men managed to be both the most visible and the least discussed category of besieged people. Rodolphe Reuss, Frédéric Piton, Max Reichard, and many others kept diaries and published memoirs, and their perspectives have shaped much of our knowledge about civilian life during the siege. Yet they rarely discussed themselves or their compatriots as men. In other words, men were seldom discussed as a group worthy of either pity or praise, the way that authors referred generally to the women of Strasbourg. They were not celebrated as a group for their prayers or for carrying on with business while under fire. Nor can we find admiration for young hotheaded urban revolutionaries, as occurred in other cities.[61]

Civilian men could earn some recognition only by directly contributing to the war effort as medical personnel, national guardsmen, or *francs-tireurs*. Strasbourg's firefighters, too, won praise from several commentators for their important and dangerous work. Forty-nine of Strasbourg's two hundred forty firemen were injured during the siege, and seven died. The casualty rate of firefighters was much higher than that of soldiers, though a higher percentage of soldiers died. A contemporary lithograph by Auguste Münch highlights the efforts of firefighters in the faubourg National to control flames that consume homes, churches, and trees. The firefighters wear uniforms, including helmets, as they push a pump and wagons carrying barrels filled with water. The calm, concerted efforts of the adult male firefighters to the left contrast

Uniformed municipal firefighters bring water pumps to a fire caused by nighttime bombardment in the faubourg National, on Strasbourg's west side. Auguste Münch, *Guerre de 1870: Siège et bombardement de Strasbourg* (1870). (Archives de la Ville et de la Communauté urbaine de Strasbourg)

with the chaos of rearing horses and fleeing women and children to the right. The firefighters have not become individual heroes but a collective heroic force.[62]

Only one author explicitly discussed the dilemmas that civilian men faced while under bombardment. In his detailed memoir, republican journalist Auguste Schneegans described the challenges faced by these men, fearing the imminent deaths of their loved ones and powerless to provide any real protection. He envied warriors of past times, "who, under the open sky, could fight a visible, tangible enemy, exposed like them! . . . They were not constrained by this yoke of impotence, that breaks the most robust courage and destroys the most valiant men."[63]

According to Schneegans, civilian men chose one of two courses of action. Some cowered "in the shadows and the unhealthy air of the cellars," prey to the fear of the unknown. "The less one saw," he wrote, "the less one conversed with others . . . the more one broke down into a sort of mute terror." Schneegans had only contempt for these men. They "did not count for anything during this entire period. They retreated from the world, trembling, not thinking about anything but themselves, caring little for their neighbors."[64] Indeed, no memoirs survive of men who spent the majority of the siege underground (whereas the most detailed female voices, Weiss and Dartein, wrote regularly about life in the cellars). For men, seeking shelter did not seem worth writing about.

The other sort of man, continued Schneegans, overcame his fears: "As for the rest of the population—for the *men*—who, valiant and resolute, traversed the bombardment standing tall, they arrived, toward the second two weeks, at a virile resignation [italics in the original]." Staying in the cellar, Schneegans implied, signaled womanly, weak, and limited men—victims—whereas going outside for any purpose signified strength and allowed for personal growth. He admitted that this "virile resignation" included contradictory elements: "One was convinced that Strasbourg was lost; one had the strong apprehension of losing France itself; and, on the other hand, one was sustained to a high degree by the sentiment of duty to fulfill and by the consciousness of the grandeur of this duty. . . . Do what I must, we told ourselves, come what may! And we knew all too well that nothing good could come, neither for us, nor for our city, nor, alas! for our France."[65] Schneegans tried to establish, without much success, that his own kind of manhood, the civil servant, could be honorable. For the most part, civilian men, stripped of their ability to mitigate the city's suffering, could not be discussed.

"Nothing Comparable"

Wounded male soldiers, too, were left out of the civilian conversation. Although soldiers composed the largest category of wounded, most civilian memoirists of Strasbourg did not mention them at all, perhaps because the civilian experience appeared more pressing and novel, perhaps because combatants were expected to suffer and die. However, two surgeons at the Military Hospital, Henri-Etienne Beaunis and François Poncet, included wounded soldiers in their memoirs, and their descriptions throw the discussion about civilians into sharp relief. In the eyes of Beaunis and Poncet, the soldiers were victims, too: of modern warfare that had far outpaced medical practice and, in retrospect, of callous, unthinking political leaders.

Mornings in the Military Hospital were dedicated to emergency surgeries, three or four at a time, with the nonurgent cases reserved for the afternoons.[66] Poncet recalled the "hours of sadness when the most hardened man would be moved before blood, sorrow, fire [and] death."[67] Beaunis later remembered that in all his years as a military surgeon, "I saw nothing comparable to what I saw in Strasbourg."[68] One morning in early September particularly haunted him. A sudden rush of wounded soldiers inundated the hospital and quickly exhausted their supply of mattresses and sheets. Beaunis and the nursing staff made a rapid triage between those beyond hope and those whose wounds might be healed. His lengthy description manages to convey both the horror of the scene and a clinical detachment from it:

> I lifted the cover thrown over the first wounded man: it's an artilleryman; his right leg had been almost detached by a shell burst; it is next to him, clad still in the standard-issue boot, and holding on only by a shred of flesh; I had him taken up to the operating room to finish the amputation. The second was a young *mobile*, almost a child; his skull had been crushed in, his face bloody, his eyes dull; at his temple an open wound at the bottom of which his brain rose with

each respiratory movement; the projectile is in the cerebral substance; he will die; the chaplain, kneeling at his stretcher, hastily administers [last rites]. The third is dead; do not even look at his wound; time is pressing. This one's chest has been shot through with a bullet, he is hardly breathing, let's move on: nothing to be done. What is that one rasping in the corner? I look: his thigh is crushed; the projectile entered from the rear deeply into the pelvis; this is not a wound, it is something shapeless and without name, a mix of pulsating muscles, loops of still-living intestines, shreds of fabric, pieces of straw and dung, the hint of bones.[69]

Beaunis' account is fast paced and graphic. Fate bears down. Beaunis emphasizes that all this carnage unfolded under the eyes of the soldiers who had brought their comrades to the hospital, "pale, immobilized by horror, and no doubt telling themselves that tomorrow it could be their turn."[70] Beaunis focuses on the horror of the wounds, the limitations of his abilities to cope with them, and his anger at those in power who allowed such suffering to occur. "The glory of a Napoleon I or a Wilhelm means little to a doctor who often sees such scenes," he continues. "These great heroes are for him only assassins."[71] By the time Beaunis authored his memoir, general republican contempt for the imperial regime had solidified into a narrative about the dangers of authoritarian rule for the bodily integrity of the nation. Nowhere do we see the irony so common in narratives of the Great War, even though this account seems to be intended for the same kind of general educated audience that might have read Robert Graves' *Good-Bye to All That* forty years later.[72]

Of all the techniques that surgeons employed, amputation caused the most concern. Although some doctors during the Franco-Prussian War called for conservative surgery, avoiding amputation when at all possible, the surgeons in Strasbourg's Military Hospital took a more radical approach.[73] "Amputate, always amputate," recalled Beaunis.[74] Proponents of swift amputation believed it saved money and lives. It provided surgeons with a decisive solution to a horrifying problem, a clear course of action that was often welcome in stressful and overcrowded surgical wards. But it was also traumatic for both doctors and patients. "It was no longer surgery," remembered Beaunis, "it was a true human butchery."[75] Soldiers whose legs or thighs were amputated stood little chance of recovery: of twenty-seven amputees, only five survived.[76]

While Beaunis focused on the horror of operating on such wounds, Poncet, who oversaw the surgery clinic at the Military Health Service School, sought to analyze the mortality rate of amputees. In a report for medical professionals and policymakers written soon after the war, Poncet linked mortality to three considerations: hygiene, complications, and psychological factors. For Poncet, "hygiene" meant preventing overcrowding in the wards and maintaining medical supplies; it did not include sterilization. Although Louis Pasteur had developed the germ theory of disease during the previous decade and Joseph Lister had published his groundbreaking study on antiseptics in surgery in 1867, antiseptic methods had not been adopted as standard procedure in Strasbourg. In any case, Poncet reported that hygiene declined over the course of the siege. At first, wounds healed quickly, and suppurations were healthy. All soldiers under treatment at the Military Hospital had shelter, a bed, a mattress, and covers, as well as food and wine. Unlike soldiers in other arenas of the war, they did not need to be transported over long distances by cart or train. Strasbourg's wounded also escaped the scourges of dysentery and typhus. However, trained doctors and medical supplies soon ran short. Many practicing doctors and surgeons had left Strasbourg at the beginning of August to treat the wounded at battle sites further north, and the Prussians prevented them from returning to Strasbourg. Medical students from the Military Health Service School tried to fill the gap. Strasbourg ran out of chloroform to ease the pain of amputation and quinine to fight against fever; fortunately, Pastor Albert Schillinger obtained permission to cross Prussian lines and secure these medicines in Paris. Then, after the heavy bombardment of August 24 through 27, the ward at the Military Hospital became overcrowded. Infections rose despite the influx of medical supplies and even though convalescents spent six hours in the open air of the hospital's courtyards and breathed freshly ventilated air twenty-four hours a day (a practice that French sanitarians strongly favored though it was still publicly mistrusted). On September 7, pyemia, a blood infection, struck the wards. Many died. Only those who were sent to recover in the homes of individuals escaped.[77]

Poncet also worried about complications to leg wounds, particularly shock and hemorrhages. He attributed the majority of all deaths to shock. Modern artillery caused devastating wounds and triggered a cascade of symptoms: "A man hit by a voluminous burst, having his two legs blown off or crushed, falls struck down, annihilated. . . . His face has a mortal pallor, his features are contracted, immobile, his eyes closed or haggard, fixed, sickly; saliva stains [his] beard. . . . [His] chest is cold, or covered with a viscous sweat (as are the temples). The extremities are . . . insensible and cold. The pulse is light, slow, spindly. . . . It is the image of agony or death."[78] This state could last from two to twenty-four hours, after which the man either died or recovered. Poncet could not do much to affect the outcome beyond administering hot water and alcohol infusions and wrapping the man in blankets and warm bricks. Poncet noted that one could not perform amputations on someone who was in shock; therefore, he argued strongly against battlefield surgery. He warned, "With the predominance of artillery in today's combat, this complication tends to become very frequent, and it will henceforth play the greatest role in military surgery."[79] Continuous changes in warfare made it harder and harder for surgeons to keep up.

Hemorrhages, in which bleeding continues unchecked within the body, also complicated the treatment of leg wounds. Poncet observed that shell wounds in Strasbourg frequently caused a particular kind of hemorrhage, one that he had never seen before and that did not appear in the literature. The bone's spongy tissue itself bled mercilessly, unresponsive to Poncet's ministrations. In serious wounds with such a hemorrhage, only amputation would stop the blood loss. If the patient also suffered from shock, the amputation had to be postponed. Poncet despaired of finding a way out of this new quandary: "We ask, what should a surgeon do?"[80]

Poncet's third concern, psychological damage, presented another potentially fatal complication on top of a serious physical wound. Psychological damage arose from many causes. After the garrison's arsenal caught fire on August 23, *le délire moral* struck many soldiers, even those who had otherwise almost healed from earlier wounds and had never displayed psychological ailments. "It lasted for several hours," wrote Poncet. "It was a hallucination due to overly strong emotions among men who were debilitated by previous blood loss." Once again, Poncet could not offer solutions to this health problem. *Le délire moral* could also arise among men who focused too strongly "on ideas of the afterlife." Poncet resented the presence of religious personnel and believed they caused patients to resign themselves to death too soon.[81] In this narrowly anticlerical way, Poncet attempted to grapple with the psychological strains of warfare. It is worth noting, however, that Poncet did not describe any somatic ailments that lacked an obvious cause, the kind of psychological diseases that so puzzled and frustrated doctors during the Great War. Either such diseases did not manifest themselves in the same ways or in the same numbers as in the later conflict, or Poncet did not possess the words to describe them.

Both Beaunis and Poncet portrayed wounded soldiers as the victims of pitiless warfare rather than as noble, virile warriors. Poncet's report is startling in its humble assessment of the difficulties facing surgeons and their helplessness against the devastating power of modern artillery. "If we want to heal amputees," he argued, "we can no longer have hospitals as we know them today. The health of the operated men is in the dissemination of wounds over the largest space possible. The distribution of wounded men in the homes of individuals is the only way to do it."[82] Remarkably, this trained surgeon trusted the ability of nonprofessionals to handle the difficult task of caring for seriously wounded soldiers. This unusual recommendation fit with the rising desire of individuals to intervene on behalf of the victims of this war. By contrast, Beaunis sought to keep the treatment of soldiers firmly in the hands of medical professionals. Writing in 1887, Beaunis placed warfare within the context of a litany of social problems: "debauchery, drunkenness, superstition, [and] ignorance," causes and consequences of human passion. War was the "social plague that supersedes all others."[83] Beaunis argued that doctors could best diagnose these social maladies and advise legislators with the proper legal remedies. Poncet and Beaunis differed on their conclusions, but on their views of Strasbourg's wounded soldiers, they agreed: these men were the victims of modern war. Whereas the destruction of the New Church appeared to Reuss and Schneegans as a return to uncivilized times, Poncet and Beaunis saw soldiers' wounds as new and troubling. The surgeons' accounts—far more graphic than even the most explicit descriptions of civilians—provide a portrait of suffering that other authors refused to attempt. Indirectly, these memoirs alert us that civilians also experienced shock, hemorrhages, and fever, and render the silence regarding male civilians all the more striking.

Psychological Trauma

Given our modern understanding of the psychological trauma that people often suffer under intense, prolonged stress, we might wonder: Did the bombardment also induce traumatic memories? Were children, women, and soldiers viewed as particularly susceptible to psychological trauma? Did doctors acknowledge that mental illness might be caused by the traumatic experience of a siege, rather than by heredity and biology?[84] The evidence is suggestive, but elusive. Numerous authors writing about the siege of Strasbourg linked the experience of war to temporary psychological trauma. As we have seen, Poncet worried that psychological stress adversely affected the physical recovery of soldiers, and Catherine Weiss occasionally succumbed to nocturnal bouts of anxiety in the midst of shelling. However, Weiss did not describe any ongoing psychological difficulty or traumatic memory. We might read her manuscript as some kind of self-therapy, but she did not recognize it as such. She and other memoirists described loss of mental control as a condition that occurred only during the traumatic event itself, not as a trauma of memory that continued to haunt their lives.

A striking example comes from a man who was trapped alone for four days in the cellar under the rubble of his house. He later recounted, "What passed through my head during the first hour of captivity, I do not know how to describe; I passed from mute rages to a general despondency. Little by little, I came back, because I must say that I had completely lost reason." The man recovered his wits and began to make rational plans for escape: "I gathered my thoughts and I thought I remembered that I had brought down during the day a kerosene lamp." With this modest light as his only companion, the man slowly set about digging himself out. The exhausting days that followed brought periods of "rage" and "despair," but he maintained his sanity. Once he finally succeeded in escaping, his primary concern was no longer his mental state but rather the financial hardship he anticipated following the loss of his home and shop.[85] He did not use traumatic memory as a category to help make sense of the bombardment.

In the early 1870s, however, some medical professionals began to argue that the Franco-Prussian War caused longer-term psychological trauma. The French inspector general for psychiatric services, Ludger Lunier, reported that war-related trauma accounted for 18 percent of the men (both civilians and soldiers) and 13 percent of the women who entered asylums during the year that started on July 1, 1870. These mental disorders stemmed from the experience of invasion, the departure of loved ones into the army, and the political upheavals associated with the war.[86] In addition, Lunier noted that a number of patients suffered from depression, stupor, and suicidal thoughts because of "the fatigues and emotions of the siege of Paris," which included both the Prussian siege and the Paris Commune.[87] Some of these patients recovered within a few months, but others died in treatment or remained hospitalized as late as 1873.

Beaunis also argued that a few women in Strasbourg experienced a series of negative physical and psychological symptoms: "palpitations, fainting, insomnia, nightmares, slight fever, gastralgia, etc." In some women, these symptoms led to "mental alienation," or *nervosisme*. Beaunis attributed this condition to the psychological strains of the siege: "This state of anxiety and perpetual anguish, this alternating rest and noise, hope and discouragement, this ever-present impending fire, produced, especially in certain women, a nervous state that sometimes came close to madness."[88] According to Beaunis, only women fit the diagnosis. After the siege, some doctors termed this condition *maladie des caves*, cellar sickness. In that they believed the experience of war could cause madness, Beaunis's and Lunier's reports ran against the emerging trend in late nineteenth-century psychiatry that blamed mental disorders on heredity and degeneracy. They represented a holdover of early nineteenth-century practitioners who allowed that situational factors (such as war) might account for mental disorders. They also anticipated major changes in the understanding of traumatic disorders. In the following decades, particularly due to trench warfare in World War I, mental trauma gained recognition in medical and legal contexts, and its etiology, classification, and therapy became the subject of increased discussion.[89]

In 1870, most civilians eventually adjusted to the stresses and intense emotions associated with bombardment. Beaunis later described his own experience of adaptation. "One finally came to an astonishing impassivity," he recalled. "One became fatalistic despite oneself, and that was perhaps the only way to live tranquilly in the middle of the din. One becomes used to everything, even to bombardment, and in the last days of the siege it seemed as though one had never known another existence."[90] Many people made a point of going out into the streets daily. Frédéric Piton regularly noted his visits to friends and family throughout the city. Beaunis knew elderly citizens who made their usual walk three times a day, venturing into the most destroyed and dangerous neighborhoods. Like the vast majority of Great War soldiers on the Western Front, most people in Strasbourg managed to cope with intense psychological stress.[91]

■ ■ ■

As the intense nighttime bombardment gave way to the regular siege, Weiss and other civilians told stories about the experience of suffering in which they cast other people as the primary victims. Weiss focused on her children, medical doctors worried about wounded soldiers, and civilian males turned their attention to women like Weiss herself. Accounts of physical and psychological suffering portrayed the war as more terrible than they could have previously imagined. The safe division between civilian and military spheres was revealed to be an illusion. Under these circumstances, it was difficult for any civilian action to achieve the status of heroism, except perhaps for firefighting and the collective fortitude of Strasbourg's women. Civilian men could not be adequately described as either victims or heroes; Schneegans's praise of the male civil servant failed to gain traction. The division of civilians into victims and heroes depended upon, and yet stumbled over, expectations based on gender and combatant status.

CHAPTER FIVE

Carrying On

B Y SEPTEMBER, EVERY FAMILY knew someone who had died.[1] The expense of food, threat of fire, and lack of reliable information triggered a crisis of authority. Just who was in charge of this bombed-out city? To whom could civilians turn for answers? It is easy to see why people in Strasbourg felt a sense of loss, anger, sadness, or bewilderment after having been bombarded unremittingly. However, if we are to take seriously the idea that civilians in Strasbourg were not just victims of the war, but also substantive people with some level of resilience and energy, we must also consider their sense of community, justice, and accountability. In other words, we must try to understand their *well-being.*

Well-being is a category of analysis that provides a way to understand civilians at war without dividing them into victims and heroes. Historians who have borrowed the concept from economist Amartya Sen note that well-being, particularly in a period of crisis, includes not only physical security and the availability of material goods, but also trustworthy institutions, fair processes for redress, and the ability or freedom to act.[2] In other words, it is not enough for us to calculate the number of calories available to each person (for which we do not have adequate records, anyway) or the cost of bread, potatoes, or butter. A discussion of well-being must also include the strategies that people must employ in order to procure food. A pound of potatoes purchased after standing in line for hours is different from a pound of potatoes bought rapidly, without thought, at the corner grocery. Well-being is undermined if the availability of those potatoes is perceived to be unfair or tainted by a black market. Conversely, the long wait for potatoes may bolster well-being if it seems like an appropriate sacrifice helping the cause. To speak of the well-being of someone under bombardment is not to deny their suffering, but rather to respect their human dignity and potential as agents.

Werder now sent his bombs both day and night, and food became scarcer, yet many in the city found themselves able to carry on. Public demands for leadership accountability contributed to the formation of a new municipal commission. Antoine Zopff, the energetic administrator behind the Red Cross, emerged as a dynamic advocate for the civilian population. During the first two weeks of September, the city witnessed an increase in aid to hungry families and newly homeless citizens. Meanwhile, Catherine Weiss and her children managed to escape the city. Despite the continued shelling and lack of answers, some people in Strasbourg found the resources to enhance their well-being.

Out from Under

During the regular siege, Werder aimed his artillery at the fortress walls and the garrison, but the people of Strasbourg continued to suffer from the shells that landed in their homes and streets twenty-four hours a day. "Every time one went out," wrote Henri-Etienne Beaunis, "one risked one's life."[3] Even staying at home, nobody was safe. Frédéric Piton's laundress and her young daughter were killed at the window of their apartment in Finckwiller. One morning, two victims of an explosion were brought into Catherine Weiss's courtyard; they both died the next day.[4]

In September, more public buildings suffered damage, including the Palais de Justice, the Prefecture, and the presbytery of Sainte-Aurélie. The theater caught fire on the morning of September 10 and was completely destroyed.[5] Late summer thunderstorms competed with the cannon in "a savage and grandiose harmony."[6] Dogs howled in the streets, and swallows seeking their nests darted through the air. Rocks

After the intense bombardment of August 24–27, Strasbourg's western neighborhoods, including the faubourg National, were nearly destroyed. Gustave Fischbach, *Le siège de Strasbourg: Strasbourg avant, pendant, et après le siège* (1897). (Charles Deering McCormick Library of Special Collections, Northwestern University Library)

detached from the edifices of buildings, falling on the passersby below. Stores closed, religious services were suspended, bells hung silent. The bombardment chipped away at the rituals that tied this society together, from baptism to burial. With so many fires, basic identification records marking births and marriages were at risk of complete destruction. Starting around August 20, burials took place in the Botanical Gardens, since the three major cemeteries outside the city walls had all become unusable. Throughout the rest of the siege, city workers laid the dead to rest in a vast trench. Funeral ceremonies were strongly curtailed and respect for the dead became a luxury.[7]

Many institutions ceased to function. The Jewish Consistory and the Directory for the Church of the Augsburg Confession stopped meeting. The head of the National Guard deserted.[8] The municipal police also lost credibility. Police indolence was nothing new; everyone knew that the officer charged with monitoring the cathedral area stayed drunk "from the first day of the year to Saint-Sylvestre's Day," December 31.[9] But now, the police lost the trust of the municipal government. On August 22, Central Police *Commissaire* Aymard asked Humann for reimbursement for an auxiliary police corps that he had created two weeks earlier, claiming that he had received the mayor's verbal authorization. Humann denied that he had approved any special police corps, refused payment, and ordered the corps disbanded.[10]

Furthermore, the police increasingly lost jurisdiction to the French military. Uhrich's September 1 decree against pillaging subjected violators to martial law rather than ordinary police authority.[11] Just as indicative of the power shift was the monkey incident. In the early evening of September 5, two police agents approaching Place Gutenberg noted a large crowd. At its center, several military personnel, one of whom inexplicably carried a monkey on his shoulder, demanded to see the mayor. Police Agent Montigny explained that it was forbidden to form crowds by order of General Uhrich. The soldier retorted that Montigny had no business there; this was a military affair. Agent Montigny responded, "The object of the offense was the monkey." The simian changed hands a few times. The soldiers told Montigny, "You're nothing in the streets, we're the ones who give orders now." Agent Montigny filed a complaint, but as a result was himself relieved of duty.[12] Sometimes it is better to accept wounded pride than to try to arrest a monkey.

But not everything was death and disintegration. About three-quarters of functionaries remained at their positions. On the Sunday after the New Church burned, without an altar or pulpit, on a floor still warm from the fire, Max Reichard preached to the faithful. Journalists did the best they could to continue informing the public. During the heaviest bombardment, *Le courrier du Bas-Rhin* briefly stopped publication, but on August 30 managed to issue an abbreviated edition filled with important announcements. A brief edition of *L'impartial du Rhin* appeared even on the afternoon of August 25.[13] One grateful resident placed an open letter in *Le courrier du Bas-Rhin* thanking his fellow citizens for helping to put out the fire in his building. A hospital director also expressed gratitude for the "zeal and devotion" of the firefighters, garrison soldiers, and medical students who "saved our population of sick and elderly from a catastrophe that would have had incalculable proportions."[14]

Despite the dangers, some people started to reemerge from hiding during the regular siege.[15] After the intense bombardment ceased, emotions hardened, and the shells seemed more bearable. "So terrible had been the terrors of the first days," wrote Auguste Schneegans, "that the disasters of the days to follow seemed like mere accidents."[16] The area near Saint-Thomas remained largely unscathed, and the cathedral shielded the Imperial Palace. Madame Kiéné, writing in her cellar, even created a positive interpretation of the relentless shelling: "It seems to me that the Prussians must be furious about victories that we have won elsewhere, for it is not possible that France will not emerge victorious from this terrible war."[17]

Although ordinary commerce and productive activity had ceased, crowds gathered larger than ever in public squares. Women and men found community at the religious services and clubs that continued to meet. Piton kept going to the Freemasons, and members of the Commercial and Literary Casino played whist as shells exploded in the street. Reuss dropped by on September 5 to read *David Copperfield*.[18]

Perhaps the most important interactions came in the daily round of social calls with family and friends. "Never so many visits as during this siege," wrote Reuss, "and to say and hear everywhere the same thing!"[19] The calls may have become repetitive, but Weiss understood their real purpose. Friends and her husband's employees came by every morning "not to ask for our news but to see if we were still alive."[20] Reuss used his visits to help distract or amuse his associates. He tutored an adolescent family friend in Latin, requiring him to translate Ovid for an hour every day.[21]

Reuss's fragmented diary for this period reveals the human foibles that escape mention elsewhere. August 29: "Went by the Gymnasium: the [Pastor Georges-Louis] Leblois clique dominated; laughable anecdotes about the extreme devotion of certain of his parishioners. One of the characters who came to find refuge there brought with him, as his sole baggage, a stuffed canary."[22] August 31: "Panic: smoke coming out of the tower of Saint-Thomas; Paul Boegner and I believe the tower is on fire . . . It was a cloud of thousands of gnats! Strolled *[flâné]* through the streets."[23] The *flâneur* under siege could not maintain his detachment; he became emotionally and physically involved. He distributed wine to the soldiers who helped fight fires and helped stack sacks of dirt against the windows of the municipal archives.[24] With his relative wealth and connections intact, Reuss maintained his mobility and his intelligent observations of the city throughout the course of the siege.

"The Real State of Things"

Uhrich attempted to bolster confidence with an August 26 announcement: "Inhabitants of Strasbourg, for three days the city has been bombarded to the limit. Your heroism, at this time, is patience. You suffer for France. All of France will repay your losses. We take up the challenge, in the name of the government that we represent!"[25] Yet Uhrich could do little to ease civilians' distress; his minimalist approach appeared in a statement from defense council member Colonel Du Casse on August 28: "The population deprived of lodging following the fires is invited to construct for itself shelters . . . by leaning wood against the wall of the quai."[26] Anticipating seditious acts, Uhrich armed the three thousand national guardsmen and charged them with keeping internal order.[27] Uhrich wanted calm, but his focus remained on defense rather than on civilian needs.

It was time for the municipality to act. Back on August 16, Prefect Pron had extended the term of the sitting council, whose elections had been disrupted. But as the month of August wore on, that proud bastion of civic responsibility disintegrated. Many members refused to meet or—like Jules Sengenwald—simply fled the city. Of twenty-seven councilmen, eight were gone. Although Humann and his deputy mayors (collectively called the administrative council) had met regularly throughout August, they did not have the manpower to handle the emergency. The municipality's oversight of its property and primary instruction had been all but abandoned, though it did manage to pay for policing and keep records of births, marriages, and deaths. The administrative council gave a one-hundred-franc bonus in gratitude to loyal municipal employees.[28]

As Werder transitioned to the regular siege, Humann managed to call a meeting of the truncated council on August 29. The members knew that they no longer held the city's confidence and voted to expand the council to included men with more community standing. Humann then consulted Pron, who agreed to this extraordinary measure.[29] The council selected twenty new commissioners who "enjoyed the population's confidence," had "a more or less extensive sphere of legitimate influence," and whose "social position [and] patriotism" recommended them.[30] Three of these twenty new men declined to serve: one did not want to join without having been elected, and two had already fled. Pron then extended offers to an additional eleven men, ten of whom agreed to serve. The municipal commission therefore included twenty-seven new members and nineteen members from the municipal council.

Three of the new names stand out: Auguste Schneegans, Antoine Zopff, and Emile Küss. We have already met Schneegans, the staunch republican from *Le courrier du Bas-Rhin,* and Zopff, a Freemason and leader in the Red Cross. Humann praised Zopff, "a man generally esteemed, who has always showed a great devotion to the interests of the laboring classes. At this very moment he is President of one of the aid committees for the wounded. I have seen him at work on several occasions and I must praise his energy and his intelligence."[31] Küss, a doctor and professor at the Faculty of Medicine, had been a local leader in the revolution of 1848. During the Second Empire, he had earned respect for his unbending republican principles, but until recently, he had remained on the margins of political life. In the weeks to come, Küss

Emile Küss. Photographer unknown. Armand Dayot, *L'invasion: Le siège 1870, la commune 1871* (1901). (Charles Deering McCormick Library of Special Collections, Northwestern University Library)

emerged as one of the most important politicians in Strasbourg: by mid-September, he was named mayor, and within a month, he negotiated the difficult German occupation.

The appointment of Schneegans, Zopff, and Küss indicated the political direction of the new municipal commission. Although the municipal council had included only two republican members—Charles Boersch and Stolz—the majority of new commissioners were moderate republicans; men of the far left were excluded.[32] As Schneegans pointed out, Pron's selection of political opponents may have been shrewd: "The city is forced to capitulate? It's the municipal commission that will have to be exposed to all the dangers that always follow in the wake of such a measure. The city, refusing to surrender, will be ruined, burned, decimated? Once again the municipal commission will take the blame."[33]

Posters plastered on city walls during the early morning hours of August 30 announced the new municipal commission. Many citizens believed that it signaled the overthrow of the imperial regime. They noticed that the imperial eagle no longer graced the top of the official proclamation and that the names of the new commissioners included prominent republicans.[34] They were mistaken; a revolution had not yet happened. But perhaps these rumors fueled the demonstration later that morning.

By ten o'clock, some three hundred citizens began to gather outside the municipal commission's offices on Place Gutenberg. The crowd selected a delegation of four men to convey a declaration to the mayor and the commission inquiring into the "situation of the belligerent army" and the garrison's ability to adequately defend against a head-on attack. It also asked about the food supply. In short, it stated, "The municipal commission is invited to make known to the population, through posters, the real state of things."[35]

In other words, the population asked the municipal commission to step over the military's regulations and hold the military accountable to the people of Strasbourg. The demonstrators hoped that the municipal commission would become a new source of authority that could bring popular pressure to bear on General Uhrich and the defense council. For many, the creation of the municipal commission alone was not enough.[36]

Uhrich, hearing about the demonstration secondhand, believed that the crowd directed their anger at him since he refused to capitulate. Uhrich turned the demonstration into an opportunity to defend his honor and courage. He declined to increase his personal guard and reportedly stated, "Whatever happens, there will be no French bullet or bayonet between my chest and them." He confirmed with pleasure that soon "things returned back to calm, and since then there was not the least popular emotion: sufficient proof that this agitation was all on the surface and had no root in the great majority of the population."[37] For Uhrich, this demonstration centered on the population's desire to capitulate and his fortitude against such calls. He did not mention the demand to know "the real state of things."

On August 31, General Uhrich banned public meetings. He expected the citizens of Strasbourg to follow military order and tried to uphold the regulations limiting his engagement with civilians. Uhrich's decree worked; the August 30 demonstration was the last major public meeting of the siege. Uhrich judged it dangerous to publish any information on the city's resources. On September 2, Humann refused to ask Uhrich to have daily bulletins published, for "satisfying public curiosity does not always satisfy national interest."[38] The public demanded answers but did not get them.[39]

The Municipal Commission in Action

After the long period of municipal inaction, the commission dove into its work, meeting almost every afternoon at two o'clock in the Hôtel de Commerce, the same building on Place Gutenberg that housed Mayor Humann's temporary offices and the Commercial and Literary Casino. In the month of September, the municipal commission addressed a series of crises. No member handled more logistical issues than Antoine Zopff. Malartic called Zopff "one of the most fortunate choices that was made," no small praise considering their political differences.[40]

The city had entered 1870 with a surplus of 200,000 francs, almost 12 percent of its total budget of 1,700,000 francs. Prior to August 29, the municipal council had only met six times that year. In its July 1 meeting (the final meeting before August 29), the municipal council concerned itself with acquiring buildings, keeping up churches, and granting pensions to firemen's widows. Rather presciently, it had provided 600,000 francs to the Ministry of War to maintain and enlarge the Military Health Service School, an expression of the mid-century concern for the health of soldiers. With this exception, the municipal council was not particularly visionary, but it kept the city maintained. Under siege conditions, with new membership and significant resources, the commission was poised to expand its purview and purpose.[41]

The Franco-Prussian War created opportunities for power shifts in cities all over France, but they did not all move in the same direction. Bertrand Taithe has demonstrated that in many French cities during the Franco-Prussian War, "social responsibility, and therefore power" was transferred from the department to the commune or municipality in the form of National Guard units and neighborhood Family Councils.[42]

Working-class citizens in Paris, Lyon, and Marseille tried to forge a new social compact within their urban communities. By contrast, in Mulhouse, the war stifled the emerging labor movement.[43]

Strasbourg's municipal commission fell somewhere in the middle of this spectrum. It embodied a moderate republic in which the municipality, not the central state, took responsibility for the well-being of its citizens. The municipal commission wrested from the prefecture control over the civil hospices, the Bureau de Bienfaisance, and other charitable institutions. Commissioners explicitly saw this move as a return to "the principles of [17]89."[44] Still, the municipal commission did not seek to permanently redefine the relationship between civilians and the government, and it resisted actions that would overstep the sanctity of private property.

Homelessness presented an immediate challenge. By September 9, 297 houses had been destroyed, leaving some 3,300 people without shelter. Families found protection wherever they could: under one of the city's many bridges, with family or friends, in brasseries, or in lean-tos that military engineers constructed along the ramparts and on the towpath alongside the canal (but not for long; these "shelters" were in the line of fire). Baron Pron allowed families in the neighborhood to use the basement of the Prefecture, but that refuge immediately proved insufficient.[45]

In response to this need, the municipal commission opened public buildings to the homeless: the covered market, the customs house, schools, the Imperial Palace, the slaughterhouse, and the tobacco factory. Spaces that ordinarily were reserved for one segment of the population suddenly received people from all walks of life: elderly people stayed in schoolrooms, and workers' families filled the theaters. The commission also put public funds toward the construction of shelters, with the added bonus of providing jobs for unemployed workers. Furthermore, the commission coordinated the delicate operation of using abandoned or partially destroyed private buildings as shelters. Although they rejected the idea of allowing the homeless to live in buildings whose owners had fled the city, the commission called for citizens to share their intact houses with newly homeless people. It furthermore requisitioned the cellars of 170 burned buildings in the faubourg National and the faubourg de Saverne and outfitted them with cots and ventilation in order to provide 1,200 people with about four square yards apiece.[46]

The commissioners walked a thin line between the protection of private property and the security of anyone at anytime. Some promoted a policy of leaving the doors of private buildings unlocked so that people could take refuge during a bombardment and firefighters would not have to break the doors down. Others objected that leaving doors open exposed people to theft. Looters had already become a problem. Some thieves rushed into burning buildings on the pretext of preserving property and instead helped themselves to safe-boxes. (Weiss thought the arrest of looters was misplaced: most were just trying to survive, and with the prison in ruins, what was the point?) Humann still recommended that people leave their doors unlocked during the day. The commission tried to use the two problems of homelessness and theft to solve each other. Church in need of a watchman? Send homeless families to live there and keep an eye on it. Finally, a newly formed indemnities subcommittee received individual declarations of material damages, in anticipation of future financial reparations.[47]

Unemployment also presented a difficult problem. By late August, most productive activity had ceased. Most workers did not have large savings to carry them through difficult times. The most fortunate and prudent had placed their savings in the Savings Bank, which the municipal council had created in 1834. Funds deposited in the Savings Bank went directly into the public treasury, with the French government as its backer. As of July 17, the Savings Bank counted 20,693 depositors— almost one in four inhabitants—and nearly seven million francs in deposits. Most clients were artisans, servants, or white-collar clerks earning 3.5 percent interest on their accounts, which were capped by law at 1,000 francs.[48]

During the siege, individual depositors understandably drew upon their savings. Many were disappointed; Savings Bank personnel struggled to keep up with demand, secure the facility, and keep its paperwork in order. The bank limited the days on which it allowed withdrawals. Funds had to be requested on Tuesday morning and could be withdrawn only on the following Sunday and Monday mornings. Even with these restrictions, the bank was unable to meet its clients' needs. The

Savings Bank did not, of course, keep seven million francs in cash on hand, so the money simply was not there. In any case, the average of 334.58 francs per depositor would hardly have made up for a long-term loss of income, considering that daily wages for French workers in the era hovered around 3.75 francs.[49]

Workers scrambled to find employment. About eight to nine hundred continued to help the military build its earthen fortifications, but they were the lucky ones. In this moment of crisis, the municipal commission debated its responsibility to workers. Nobody in authority called for outright unemployment benefits, and they all remembered the National Workshops of the revolutionary period of 1848 that had, to their minds, given workers far too much power.[50] Still, Zopff and others hoped to find a way to help a worker earn pay. The tobacco factory, located in the Krutenau, had let go more than three hundred workers. Since the factory had been granted a state monopoly and the workers were paid by the state, Zopff and others believed that the government should pressure the factory to find work for them. "In moments of crisis," argued M. Henri, "large industries should strive to find work for their workers, not take away the work that they have. The advantages that they enjoy in times of prosperity allow them to do it, and obligate them to do it."[51] It was not enough that the employees still received three-quarters salary. A worker wants to earn his pay, argued Zopff.

In early September, Zopff worked with the Industrial Tribunal (Conseil des Prud'hommes), an institution that arbitrated between workers and employers, to set up Extraordinary Communal Workshops. Unemployed workers signed up with the city to be placed in private workshops, as firefighters or, as a last resort, as temporary city employees paid two francs a day to clear debris. Registration took place at the Hôtel du Commerce between nine o'clock and noon or between two and four o'clock, the traditional two-hour lunch being respected even during the siege.[52]

The commission also worried about public health. It arranged to clear away horse cadavers, which had to this point just been covered with debris. It restarted the collection of waste, though it was difficult to find a place to put it all. The commission furthermore kept an eye on the provisional burials in the Botanical Gardens to prevent well-water contamination. The administration never did resolve the problem of dumping fecal waste into the stagnant waters of the Ill River. Up until the end of the siege, the dammed up river grew ever more fetid.[53]

Fire also continued to pose a serious problem. Sacks of grain, piles of animal fodder, and abandoned wood-framed houses turned into menacing fuel for conflagration. Neighborhood watches continued to locate fires quickly, but the professionals struggled to put them out. Chief Goerner needed twice as many firefighters. The municipal commission wanted individuals to clear out flammable material, but the gardeners' and cultivators' syndicate resisted losing their precious compost and fodder.[54]

The municipal commission furthermore discussed a wide variety of emergency measures: the protection of the archives, the preservation of the cathedral's stained glass and sculptures, the confiscation of medicines from an abandoned pharmacy, the offer of five hundred francs to any person who could smuggle in a recent Parisian newspaper, the decentralized recording of births and deaths so individuals did not have to make their way to the Hôtel de Ville. Beer shortages, too, presented a serious issue. Many brasseries—the heart of Alsatian sociability and political life—closed around September 10 as they ran out of beer, putting an end to the fellowship that had formed there under duress. The commission assured brewers that the tax on beer would be suspended in order to encourage more production.[55]

Overall, Strasbourg did not suffer a food shortage. Most of the harvest had been completed before the siege, and bakers had ample stores of flour. The siege did not last long enough to use up these resources. In the early August, refugees from the countryside had herded in sheep and cattle, and Uhrich had secured additional provisions. When those animals had all been slaughtered, residents ate horsemeat. Reuss noted that flour, wine, and salt remained available throughout the siege, and that horsemeat really was not so bad "when it is well seasoned."[56] Nobody had to resort to eating dogs, cats, and rats as Parisians did later that winter. Food became expensive and the menu tedious, but bodies did not become so depleted of nutrients as to lead to mass epidemics.[57]

Nevertheless, Strasbourgeois began to note high prices and found it difficult to acquire and preserve the food present in the city. Many neighborhood bakers and grocers closed, so "the need of an egg or a little milk for the children and the sick often necessitated long trips."[58] Locating an open store entailed treks across town but also yielded the prize of gossip. By the beginning of September, the damp cellar rotted Catherine Weiss's meat and flour. Fresh meat could only be bought at a high price (almost three francs per pound of beef on September 9), and eggs and butter were rarely available at all. Even dried legumes became scarce.[59]

These shortages affected some populations more than others. Children died disproportionately due to disease and malnutrition. The lack of milk caused an important health concern for the parents of newborns. The municipal commission declined to take on the responsibility of procuring milk for distribution so as to avoid the risk of failure and dampen escalating demands on their powers. Instead, Zopff called on citizens with cows to donate their extra milk to pharmacies so it could be distributed to those with sick children or elderly relatives. Nevertheless, many newborns continued to die.[60]

We might wonder whether women and men experienced the shortages differently. In Paris, men received food and wages through their service in the National Guard, while women suffered from food shortages more acutely; there is no evidence of such distributions in Strasbourg.[61] Certainly, as in Paris, where the wealthy famously dined on elephant and camel while their poorer neighbors went without, the food shortages in Strasbourg affected rich and poor differently.[62] No effort seems to have been made to ration food, so the wealthy could afford to purchase the dwindling supply more readily than the poor. With most restaurants closed, Reuss went "out for dinner" by bringing his own share to a friend's house.[63] He feasted with Schillinger and Carrière on September 20: "very comfortable, picnic, roast, legumes, pâté, fine wine: we drink for dessert the oldest of Grandmother's wines, her last bottle from 1748; it is so bad that we pour it out the window."[64]

Most citizens did not have such resources. Furthermore, most people did not know the status of the food supply. The municipal commission was privy to this confidential information, so Zopff wanted to make it known to the public to help individuals calculate their own provisions.[65] He was overruled in the administrative council, which decided that "each property owner [was] the better judge of what he should do to safeguard his goods."[66] This lack of information undermined citizens' sense of well-being.

Starting in late August, private citizens began to distribute food in institutions they called *restaurants populaires*. The first opened at the *estaminet* of Théodore Piton (probably a relative of the diarist). Soon, thousands of Strasbourgeois took advantage of the free meals every day, including both the chronically indigent and people who ordinarily did not depend upon charity. A meal typically included half a pound of bread, a glass of wine or coffee, and a plateful of dry legumes. By the first week of October, eight *restaurants populaires* located in a communal school, the covered market, four brasseries or eateries, a religious house, and the theater had distributed a total of 309,102 rations. At first, these operations relied upon private donations, but on September 8, the municipal commission voted 180,000 francs—90 percent of its surplus—toward funding the *restaurants populaires,* with the energetic Antoine Zopff as administrator.[67]

A second tier of privately funded establishments, the *cuisines économiques,* offered slightly better meals at a low cost. By charging for their meals, the *cuisines économiques* "preserved the dignity of the laboring class" as well as the city's funds.[68] At five locations (including the Polar Bear on Place Kléber), they provided two meals per day, a large noon meal of hot food, bread, and wine for twenty-five centimes, and a lighter meal of soup, bread, and coffee at six o'clock for fifteen centimes.[69]

Just what kind of establishments were these *restaurants populaires*? Not space for political debate or illicit activities. Zopff indicated that *restaurants populaires* were intended to keep up spirits and health. He understood that bread was the key to social peace within the walls of Strasbourg, and thus, the restaurants were a "work of public safety *[salut]*."[70] This was not a new attitude. In the early modern period, the city had stored grain on Place du Petit Broglie to protect against famine. In the nineteenth century, it maintained sixty windmills to aid in milling grain into flour in case drought dried up water for private watermills. These municipal precautions had helped the city stave off hunger as recently as 1846–1847. Commissioners also used charity to buffer against unrest. Zopff echoed the rhetoric of mid-century industrial bosses who provided their workers with housing, insurance, and inexpensive food in order to inspire gratitude and acceptance for the existing

This bilingual ticket probably dates from the winter of 1870–71, when the
restaurants populaires started to charge twenty centimes for a meal with wine
(fifteen centimes without wine). (Archives de la Ville et de la Communauté
urbaine de Strasbourg)

social order. The same fear of revolt and care for the hungry motivated
the *restaurants populaires*.[71]

We have detailed information about the donors to these restaurants
primarily through the self-congratulatory reports of those who ran them,
but we know little about the people who actually ate there. We do not
know their class or neighborhood or whether they associated themselves
with one particular language or confession. Perhaps that was the point.
The organizers of these charities wanted to give moral courage to the
people of Strasbourg whatever their background, a stance that tended to
support the French cause and shore up the standing of the French-
speaking civilian elite.

In September, the people of Strasbourg collectively had enough
food, but not everyone had the financial resources to purchase it.
Handing out food as charity threatened to undermine a sense of self-
worth; the handouts had to be framed as *restaurants populaires,* with
connotations of a paid establishment, or even as low-cost *cuisines
économiques.* The *restaurants populaires* also played the crucial role
of giving the civilian males who provided the funds and food an activity that could genuinely help others. They may not have been privy to

information on the city's defenses, and they certainly could not stop the bombardment, but they could at least help alleviate the suffering of their fellow civilians and thus elevate their own sense of well-being.

"Calm Succeeded This Storm"

During the regular siege, some civilians managed to leave the city. As we have seen, Werder and Uhrich continually negotiated the release of a small trickle of civilians. The Weiss and Reuss families both took advantage of these passes, so we have firsthand accounts of the logistical tricks and emotional strains involved in such departures from the perspectives of a woman who left and a man who stayed behind.

On September 2, over lunch, the Reuss family suddenly received word that they had been granted a safe-conduct. "Great emotion!" Rodolphe Reuss recorded in his journal: "Papa does not want to leave, Aunt Elise insists, Hélène [Reuss's sister] yells and cries. Stormy deliberation."[72] It is little wonder that the family felt torn over the decision to depart. Accepting a safe-conduct meant leaving family, friends, and home. It meant becoming a refugee, rather than a resister. Moreover, a pass guaranteed passage through the Prussian lines but did not provide food, transportation, or a secure shelter on the outside. Just a week earlier, on August 27 and 28, several families had been quietly allowed to slip out of Austerlitz Gate. Some were able to find refuge in Neuhof, a village about three miles south of the city, but many women and children had returned when they realized that there was no shelter to be found.[73] In another case, an unflappable servant named Grethel attempted to leave with a young boy strapped to her shoulders but turned back when caught in the crossfire.[74]

After some discussion, Reuss's father decided to depart along with Reuss's mother, grandmother, sister, four female cousins, and two female servants. "I naturally did not dream of leaving, and *maman* did not insist too much," Reuss reported. "She knows that I am only doing my duty in staying."[75] His uncles and a third female servant, Henriette, also stayed behind. The family secured a carriage and horses with a deposit of 5,000 francs, and a newly homeless man offered his services as coachman. By four o'clock that afternoon, they said their good-byes at

Nationale Gate. Later, Reuss, back in his father's study, smoked a cigar by the open window, wondering, "Where, when will we see each other again?"[76]

Around the same time, Weiss's husband came home "radiant." He had been trying for days to secure a passport for Weiss and their children; "he met every morning with the American consul" even though "his position did not allow him" to leave. For eight days, Weiss herself had refused to depart with just a "simple passport signed by [the consul]." This time, however, twenty-one days after the bombardment began, her husband had made more secure arrangements.[77]

Now that departure became an imminent reality, Weiss grew fearful of leaving her husband. "And to think," she later wrote, "that my fortune was envied by all the mothers who like me had little children."[78] At their parting, her husband's restraint helped Weiss to calm her "flood of tears."[79] She now took full responsibility for leading her two small children out of the city. They joined five other refugees packed into a four-person carriage, with nothing but a white flag to protect them. After passing through the gate, she recorded, "Your father, seeing the door close on us, was the happiest of mortals. Alas, it was not the same for me, seeing myself outside, alone, without support, and your father in that hell, not knowing if I [would] see him again one day. . . . All my courage abandoned me . . . I no longer had the strength to think."[80]

The carriage slowly approached the Prussian checkpoint. It took at least an hour to move less than a mile. "I politely present[ed] my safe-conduct to the officer of the Prussian guards for him to sign it for me." The officer refused. Weiss had not taken the route specified on the pass. "I [told] him that that path is impassable; it is under a rain of fire, and that leaving in that case is almost certain death."[81] He agreed but said that he could not disobey orders. He dispatched two soldiers at a gallop to consult his superior officer. For two long hours, Weiss waited as bombs fell all around. Finally, she received word that they could continue, but without their carriage and therefore without any baggage.

Weiss set off on foot carrying Emile, while Marie walked as best she could.[82] To her surprise, Weiss soon experienced a remarkable lifting of spirits. "You will say perhaps that at this point I should have been crushed, broken; it was not like that, calm succeeded this storm, there are incomprehensible turnabouts in these major crises, and I experienced one; thinking of the past, seeing your darling father, light, happy, myself seeing you sheltered from the fire, I let myself imagine the happiness of seeing you saved, I no longer doubted God at that moment, I gave him thanks."[83] Having successfully faced a major obstacle to her escape and reclaimed a small measure of independence, Weiss felt a boost in her well-being.

Several miles further, at the next checkpoint, Weiss encountered more resistance. Since she was unexpectedly traveling by foot, Weiss now needed another day of safe passage to make it out of the combat zone. The Prussians refused. She was told to continue on during the night. She replied, "I will stay here despite you, I will not continue my voyage tomorrow, maybe that will be your vengeance but I am staying here and I will stay this time until the opening of the city."[84] Her brisk, dramatic reply "had its effect," and the Prussian gave way. This is the strongest example of Weiss's self-assertion in her entire account of the siege, her clearest moment of self-dramatization and effectiveness, though it came at the cost of suffering the indignity of the Prussian's condescension. "He asked for my passport and put his mark on it, laughing; me, I was hardly disposed to gaiety and I promptly left."[85] She continued to Graffenstaden, about five miles south of Strasbourg, where she managed to secure, somehow, a pass for her ill sister-in-law.

Over the next several weeks, Weiss traveled by carriage, boat, and train, despite the illnesses of both children and the difficulty of finding transport, even at exorbitant prices. They first stopped in Offenburg (Baden), where they encountered some two hundred other refugees from Strasbourg. After a few days, however, the police commissioner asked her to leave for Switzerland. Weiss headed for the safety of Basel, but upon arrival, immediately changed course to find her parents in Colmar. She had heard rumors that they, too, were bombarded. Fortunately, Colmar had escaped a siege, and Weiss stayed with her family until the end of September.[86]

How should we interpret Weiss's escape from Strasbourg? It may be tempting to analyze it using the categories of hero and victim, to ask whether Weiss was a victimized refugee who fled the city or a heroic actor standing up to the Prussians. Applying the lens of well-being to

Weiss's escape, however, gives us a richer set of issues to explore, including civilian views of authority, fairness, and familial relationships in this time of crisis. Weiss valued the protection of her two children as well as that of her parents, and was willing to sacrifice her own comfort in order to assure their safety. In her encounters with the Prussians, Weiss demanded recognition for her authorized pass and argued for the commonsense observation of safety over the rigorous interpretation of the rules. With flexibility, endurance, and luck, Weiss furthered her ability to act and thus enhanced her well-being.

Rumors

Back in the city, Strasbourg hungered for information. As early as August 21, the rumor that a copy of an external newspaper had been smuggled into Strasbourg caused a near riot as publisher Berger-Levrault hurried to reproduce copies.[87] By the first week of September, Strasbourg was awash in rumors both true and false. Not surprisingly, stories of French victories kept popping up. Some thought they heard the distant sound of military music or perceived the hazy shape of an approaching regiment. Even the French Consul in Basel, Switzerland, sent completely false information to the minister of war on September 7: a French sortie had purportedly "killed eight to ten thousand men and taken cannon," and Prussian soldiers on the approach to Strasbourg "had been machine-gunned to the last man."[88] The recurring belief that General Dumont was about to arrive from Rome with 60,000 troops became "a veritable monomania."[89] Even police commissioner Aymard spread this story, for which the municipal commission formally chastised him. Each "victory" proved distressingly chimerical.[90]

On September 5, *francs-tireurs* making their morning rounds came across newspapers that German soldiers had nailed to trees for them to find: France defeated at Sedan. Napoleon III and 80,000 soldiers captured in battle. A new republic declared in Paris. So this explained the recent loud hurrahs and singing in the Prussian camps, the impromptu performance of Beethoven's "The Battle of Vitoria," featuring muskets and artillery.[91] The rumor of France's defeat spread rapidly in Strasbourg. Further confirmation came with the arrival of a few outside letters and two editions of a Karlsruhe newspaper smuggled into the city on September 7 and 10. Soon, rumors of the republic reached even a political outsider like Miss Jacot, an English nanny.[92]

Officially, however, neither Uhrich nor Pron would confirm these stories. On September 3, Werder informed Uhrich of Napoleon III's defeat and capture. On September 9, Werder sent Uhrich newspaper clippings on the political revolution and demanded that Uhrich share them with the city. Uhrich refused. It ran against regulations to circulate demoralizing information. As far away as Berlin, German readers knew that Uhrich had been informed about Sedan, but the people of Strasbourg did not. The municipal commission could not pry information out of Pron. The truth soon came out, but in a way that nobody had expected.[93]

■ ■ ■

As in many cities during the Franco-Prussian War, the war in Strasbourg undermined imperial leadership. The municipality asserted itself as the guardian of civilians. It would be misleading to describe this shift as democratic-republican or socialist. Such movements existed elsewhere in France during and after the Franco-Prussian War, but not in Strasbourg. If anything, the extraordinary circumstance of war allowed a moderate bourgeois republican government to uphold some of the ideals of nineteenth-century French moderate bourgeois republicanism, notably the desire to volunteer and the protection of women, children, and property.

Still, civilians' quest for accountability from the military authorities remains noteworthy. Their well-being—their ability to act—required access to official information, knowledge of the "real state of things," and influence over the decision of whether and when to bargain with the Prussians. Many civilians assumed that the rise of a republican municipality entailed cooperation with the military authorities. Their attempt to transform the relationship between the municipality and the French military happened as the rules governing violence seemed to be slipping from under their feet (or rather, as the sky was falling). When a new opportunity to protect civilians arose, they embraced it and, in the process, helped to change the landscape of war.

CHAPTER SIX

A Fraternal Hand

O N SEPTEMBER 10, IN the middle of their daily meeting, Mayor Théodore Humann announced to the municipal commission that he had just received a remarkable letter. He started to read it aloud but could only manage few words before he was overcome with emotion. What news could have affected him so strongly? Humann's secretary picked up where the mayor left off: a self-appointed delegation of Swiss men had arranged to lead hundreds of women, children, and elderly out of Strasbourg and into Switzerland. The Swiss emphasized both "the moral effect and the practical result of neutral Switzerland's Christian intervention in favor of the unfortunate."[1] With the blessings of the Swiss federal government, this group had secured the agreement of both the French and the Prussian commanders. For many, the ordeal of the siege would soon be over.

The municipal commissioners, too, were overcome by emotion. Auguste Schneegans later reported, "All these men, who had been hardened against emotion by two weeks of bombardment and by the spectacle of unspeakable miseries, cried like children. It was a moment full of religious silence; outside the thunder of the cannon rolled; in the streets and on the rooftops shells exploded; here, what immense and sad joy had just filled all these hearts!"[2] The unabashed "transports of enthusiasm" in the municipal commission should attune us to the unexpectedness of the Swiss offer.[3] It was a creative reimagining of earlier practices, the first example of wartime international humanitarian aid on behalf of civilians that the world had ever witnessed.

When the Swiss arrived at Nationale Gate on the following day, the emotional intensity continued. For half an hour in the late morning, the bombs stopped. A crowd watched as the gate opened and five Swiss men stepped forward, accompanied by the United States Consul in Strasbourg, C. M. Felix Petard, and escorts from Baden and France. The municipal commissioners, dressed in sober black, their eyes stinging with tears, greeted these newcomers with restrained joy.[4] Humann implored the Swiss to bear witness: "Report to Europe the spectacle . . . within our walls; tell what war is in the nineteenth century! It is no longer against the ramparts, against soldiers that fire is directed; it is against the population . . . Women and children are the principle victims. Our ramparts, as you have seen, are intact, but our residences are burned. Our churches, secular and historic monuments, are shamefully mutilated or destroyed, and our admirable library is forever annihilated. Will the conscience of nineteenth-century Europe allow civilization to revert to this point of vandalism, and allow us to fall back under the sway of barbarian codes?"[5] The Swiss, Humann hoped, would not only save Strasbourg's civilians but also reveal to the world the suffering that the city had endured. The small delegation of Swiss men then stepped forward to greet the municipal leaders. "Solemn moment!" wrote Schneegans. "We no longer found the words to welcome them." His voice choked, "smothered by sobs." With "tears in our eyes, we shook these loyal hands; with tears in their eyes, they returned our grip."[6] Librarian Frédéric Piton, too, reported shedding "tears of joy" upon hearing the news. "The Swiss people are a great people," he recorded in his diary. "They alone did not abandon us . . . they alone extended a fraternal hand."[7] The crowd erupted with cheers of *Vive la Suisse!*

In the days that followed, between 1,250 and 2,000 Strasbourgeois left the city. Thousands more experienced the relief of knowing that their loved ones would no longer be prey to shells and bombs. The story of international intervention is usually told from the perspective of the givers, but the interest here is the perspective of the people receiving aid, the civilians of Strasbourg. Humanitarian aid was an "innovative reinvention" of older traditions, distinct from but related to military custom, the Just War tradition, charity, international humanitarian law, and human rights.[8] Contrary to common definition, humanitarianism was not always independent, neutral, or impartial. Its distinguishing characteristics were the physical displacement of the humanitarians to the site of suffering, the primacy of aiding the people defined as victims, and the belief that concrete action could lead to an alteration of the status quo and even transcendence. The Swiss envisioned a new arena for humanitarianism, interventions on behalf of civilians at war.

The Swiss intervention resonated strongly with Strasbourg's municipal leaders because it fit the ways that these civilian men conceptualized their plight and placed women and children at its center. In their eyes, the Swiss intervention provided a happy turn in their narrative of the siege, a moment of redemption within the story of villains and victims. The Swiss offered a "fraternal hand" to Strasbourg's men, but a paternal hand to the city's women and children.

A few questions lingered: Who would be able to take advantage of the Swiss offer? Would civilian women actually want to leave? Why, exactly, had the Swiss decided to help? And why had Prussian General August von Werder changed his mind and agreed to allow the departure of hundreds of civilians? From the beginning, humanitarianism was fraught and filled with contradictions.

"An Act of Humane Assistance"

On the same day that the Swiss arrived in Strasbourg, a populist, spontaneous demonstration took place in Paris. At the foot of the statue personifying Strasbourg on Place de la Concorde, the public was invited to sign a book in honor of Strasbourg's defenders, to be sent to the municipal authorities. The statue, created by James Pradier in the 1830s, became a pilgrimage site for Parisians on the eve of their own siege ordeal. In the exaggerated estimation of *Le moniteur universel,* "more than a million people" filed past the statue on Sunday, September 11. Victor Hugo himself, just returned from a nineteen-year exile, paid his respects. One man reportedly signed the book in his own blood.[9]

This Parisian demonstration, "part social festival, part patriotic and nationalist ritual, and part happening-style participatory artwork or potlatch" fit more closely with revolutionary-era festivals and oath-taking ceremonies than with emerging modern wartime humanitarianism.[10] As we saw earlier, the strategies that societies had long used to protect non-combatants were not working in Strasbourg. Neither military custom nor international treaty extended far enough to protect noncombatants. Neither the Just War tradition nor moral education had convinced Werder to protect civilians. Furthermore, many internal charities had collapsed, and external ones did not extend their purview to include bombarded civilians. Like other early humanitarians, the Swiss delegation believed that the traditional sources of protection had failed and asserted themselves as the standard-bearers of human betterment.

The idea for the Swiss aid originated with Dr. Théophile Bischoff, the secretary of state of Basel, Switzerland, who had read newspaper reports about the bombardment of Strasbourg. By September 7, Bischoff assembled a group of Swiss professionals and politicians with the standing to influence military and civilian authorities in Switzerland, France, and Prussia.[11] These men were well connected, but they did not organize through traditional power structures; none of them was a religious leader, and they did not formally represent any level of the Swiss government. Instead, they formed an ad hoc organization. After receiving permission from the Swiss Federal Council, Bischoff and his colleagues traveled to Strasbourg to negotiate the terms of civilian departure with Werder and Uhrich. Upon admittance into the city, they observed and reported on siege conditions. If the Swiss plan achieved its fullest expression, warfare would have to change. Besieged civilians would no longer be treated as pawns in military strategy but as protected individuals. With their intervention, the Swiss delegates tried to transform the centuries-old practice of siege warfare.

Bischoff and his colleagues called their work an "act of humane assistance" that their humanity compelled them to perform.[12] Although the Swiss did not use the word *humanitär* (humanitarian), they identified their intervention as an emotional act in which they themselves traveled to the site of suffering. They understood their work as transcendent in that it was not a purely secular intervention, but rather "a work of Christian humanity," connecting spirituality with experiences here on earth.[13]

The Swiss delegation was motivated by the timeless concern for human suffering and expressed their concern in a way that resonated with their particular historical conditions. Humanitarianism shared some characteristics with other expressions of care, but its particular constellation of qualities made humanitarianism a unique phenomenon. What distinguished humanitarianism from similar traditions? Unlike the Just War tradition or military custom, humanitarianism tended to stem not from traditional power structures but from civil society and connected concrete action to transcendent emotional or spiritual fulfillment. Unlike charity, humanitarianism envisioned a fundamental altering to the status quo and a transformation of the traditional power structures. Humanitarianism focused on the recipients of aid, whereas charity tended to emphasize the salvation of the giver. Humanitarianism also entailed physical displacement, going to the site of suffering—whether across town or across the globe; it therefore implied distance and difference between the givers and the receivers of humanitarian aid. Charity either allowed donors to give their money without traveling to the site of suffering, or addressed the problems before one's eyes, as with the aid that Richard Wallace and U.S. ambassador Elihu Washbourne extended to besieged Parisians.[14] Unlike human rights advocates, humanitarians tended to regard some people as victims whom the more fortunate (or more civilized) must save; they divided the world into the strong and the weak, a bifurcation that has often fallen along racial or geographical lines. In the context of a European war, women and children were viewed as the weak in need of protection.[15]

It may also be useful to state clearly what humanitarianism was not. It was not necessarily neutral, independent, or impartial, though these characteristics have long been associated with humanitarianism, and the International Committee of the Red Cross enshrined them as fundamental principles in 1965.[16] The fact that the Swiss promoted certain interests—not least their own reputation—and aided a city that shared its historical roots did not make their actions any less sincere or unworthy of the label "humanitarian." Furthermore, humanitarianism did not contain a stable ideology: it could sow the seeds of radical transformation or bolster conservative expressions of hierarchy. Its goals were not stable, either, as the meaning of victimhood and the perceived sources of suffering changed over the decades.

The modern use of the word "humanitarian" dates from the early nineteenth century, though it was generally used pejoratively to describe an overly sentimental attachment to human welfare.[17] The British abolition movement can be seen as an early humanitarian effort that sought to pressure the government to help the victims of slavery. More surprising to our sensibilities, the French colonial enterprises of the 1830s and 1840s were conceptualized as humanitarian missions spreading civilization, just as, it was believed, the ancient Greeks had done in their own colonies.[18] Emergency humanitarianism in response to war or natural disaster developed in mid-century. The International Committee of the Red Cross, founded in 1863, was founded to heal sick and wounded soldiers on either side of a conflict and inspired the Red Cross committee in Strasbourg. But prior to 1870, no third party had extended humanitarian aid across borders to civilians at war. Why now?

Why Humanitarianism?

Civilians in Strasbourg explained the Swiss intervention with the following story. On June 20, 1576, one of the longest, hottest days of the year, in the midst of Strasbourg's summer festival, the people of Zurich rowed a pot of boiling millet down the Rhine toward Strasbourg. It took the entire day to pass from river to river and from canal to canal, but in the end, the well-cooked grain arrived at its destination, still hot. The Zürchers demonstrated just how fast they could aid Strasbourg in the event of need.[19] A celebratory nineteenth-century engraving by German artist Arthur Langhammer portrays idealized Strassburgers in jerkins, capes, and puffed trunkhose, doffing their tall black hats in welcome as the garlanded boat approaches the city. The pot found its way into the city library collection in the New Church, where it barely survived the bombardment; its broken remains are now displayed in Strasbourg's Historic Museum. The Fountain of the Zurichois (built in 1884) commemorates the feat on the street that has been paved over the original arrival spot, not far from the site of Austerlitz Gate.

In the wake of the Swiss intervention of 1870, Auguste Schneegans and Rodolphe Reuss recounted this sixteenth-century story with relish. In their eyes, the long-standing relationship between Strasbourg and independent Swiss cities explained the current extension of aid. Zurich and Strasbourg had first signed a treaty of mutual assistance in 1474, not long after Gutenberg's death. In 1588, the three Protestant cities of Zurich, Bern, and Strasbourg had formally agreed to counter the Catholic cantons' alliances with the pope and Spain. In the eighteenth century, Strasbourg had aided Bischoff's own city of Basel after an earthquake. It seemed natural in 1870 that the Swiss should come to Strasbourg's aid.[20]

With the benefit of hindsight, however, we can see that the boiling pot of millet represented a very different kind of aid: military help against Strasbourg's enemies during the period of religious wars. The early modern riverine rowers promised nothing to suffering civilians. The historical bond among these cities shaped the emergence of modern humanitarianism, but it does not tell the whole story.

In order to better understand the particular case of the Swiss of 1870, we need to analyze the large-scale changes that fostered the emergence of humanitarianism in general. It developed in the context of profound changes at the start of the modern period. In the eighteenth and nineteenth centuries, urbanization and industrial capitalism weakened traditional communities structured around kinship, village, and religious affiliation. What would take their places? For many Europeans, nationalism, racial thinking, and international associations filled the gap and created new "imagined communities."[21] Humanitarianism, too, provided a new way to imagine the relationship between oneself and the outside world. To explain the emergence of humanitarianism, scholars have examined profound changes in technology, civil society, political philosophy, emotions, and spirituality. The Swiss intervention in Strasbourg reveals that the relationship between men and women—particularly between noncombatant males and women—also profoundly shaped the development of humanitarianism.

Humanitarians like those of the Swiss delegation relied upon modern communication and transportation, including the railroad, the telegraph, and cheap newspapers written by professional journalists. These new technologies allowed people to be aware of suffering at a distance and to react quickly enough to make a difference. Media furthermore helped to expose violations of norms, including violations of the Geneva Convention, allowing public pressure to hold each side accountable for its actions. Still, these technological changes do not in themselves explain compassionate actions on behalf of strangers in other countries. During the Crimean War, the telegraph and newspaper reportage allowed the British public to be outraged over the shabby treatment of their own soldiers and famously inspired and immortalized Florence Nightingale's volunteer nurses. But new communications technologies did not lead to international aid on behalf of foreign civilians like the 40,000 displaced Tatar peasants living in the streets of Evpatoria or the refugees fleeing besieged Sevastopol.[22] Knowledge of suffering was not a sufficient catalyst.

Civil society provides another partial explanation and helps us to uncover the workings of many humanitarian operations. In the nineteenth century, civil society became more sophisticated, allowing private individuals to organize themselves and exert influence on the state. Whereas the Just War tradition remained reserved for the elites involved in politics, humanitarianism was open to grassroots activism, primarily among the bourgeoisie. Civil society allowed individuals to address issues of importance to them, even if they did not hold positions of state power. The Just War tradition set guidelines before combat or punished transgressions afterward, while a robust civil society allowed humanitarians to act as a conflict unfolded. Individuals pooled their financial and social resources to raise money, use the press effectively, and gain access to suffering people. By working together, they tackled the logistics of gathering, transporting, and distributing food or bandages. They developed guidelines for vetting and training volunteers and for dismissing unworthy helpers.

Related to the growth of civil society was the underlying modern philosophy that individuals can and must work together to change the world for the better. This belief stemmed in part from Enlightenment philosophies promoting progress, in part from the increasing rationalization of governance and in part from evangelical calls for social reform.[23] Like Protestant congregations in other countries, nineteenth-century Swiss Protestants began to shift attention to "the social question," especially the effects of industrialization on the poor.[24] (Official Catholic doctrine did not turn to issues of social justice until Leo XIII's 1891 papal encyclical *Rerum novarum,* and there is little evidence of concerted Swiss Catholic efforts to address social issues prior to the 1880s.[25]) Nineteenth-century humanitarians believed that one definition of human progress was the spread of European civilization. European missionaries to Asia and Africa conceived of their projects in part as humanitarian, bringing European civilization and morality to areas of the world deemed deficient in those respects.[26] As the Swiss example indicates, humanitarians also hoped to shore up European civilization when it was under threat from within. In its faith in progress and societal transformation, humanitarianism differed from charity, though the line between the two was often blurry. Whereas the highest forms of charity might have transformed the lives of the individuals receiving it, as in the formulation of twelfth-century Jewish philosopher Moses Maimonides, charities in general did not seek to transform the structures of society. Charity, instead, focused on the spiritual benefit to the giver. Still, we have not yet dug deeply enough into the reasons for the extension of aid to people outside of one's immediate experience and the willingness of some individuals to physically go to the sites of suffering in order to alleviate distress.

Lynn Hunt argues that the expansion of the range of compassion is linked to modern concepts of individualism and autonomy. Individualism has its roots in ideas about bodies. Over a long period of time starting around the 1300s, Norbert Elias tells us, European notions of bodily shame began to rise, so that excretions, outbursts of emotion, the blowing of noses, and so forth all became more private. Adherence to these rules became a marker of class distinction as well as of the separation of the self from others. By the 1750s, audiences listened to musical performances in silence, and individuals more commonly had their portraits made. People increasingly valued the autonomous individual, deemed capable of reasoning and making moral judgments.[27] This emphasis on the body also encouraged respect for an individual's physical integrity. The materiality of the body took on fundamental importance.

Likewise, Protestants as early as Martin Luther preached the liberty and autonomy of the Christian soul. Swiss theologian Alexandre Vinet wrote in his *Essay on the Manifestations of Religious Convictions* (1842), "Religion is the choice which the soul has to make over and over again between the world and God, between the visible and the invisible. Man

must be able to choose. . . . Freedom and individuality stand in so intimate a relation that they can be seen as synonymous."[28] Autonomy was
deemed to be a natural quality, not endowed by a monarch or by man-
made law, but by God or nature.

This greater respect for the separation of individual bodies and for
autonomous choices contributed to profound political, social and economic transformations. If one's own body was separate and worthy of
respect, then that same respect might be accorded to other people, if
only to guard one's own autonomy.[29] In the words of Craig Calhoun,
people began to conceive humanity "as a series of equivalent individuals," creating new connections across borders and around the globe,
encouraging them to imagine themselves as part of a larger community
with increased responsibilities to a broader range of people.[30] The valu-
ation of the autonomous individual unleashed a series of new ideas.
Liberal political philosophy posited citizens with theoretically equivalent standing in the eyes of the state. The modern market and understanding of contracts assumed the individual's responsibility for his
signature and his word. Legally sanctioned torture came to an end at
least in part because people recognized their own bodily integrity and
extended the same recognition to others.[31] Humanitarianism, too,
emerged out of this increased respect for the autonomy of the individual,
regardless of social or geographic origin. This process of increasing the
range of compassion was slow and incomplete. It was easiest when the
individuals in question came from a similar background and history. It
should not be surprising, then, that the first international humanitarian
intervention on behalf of civilians—in itself a conceptual leap—occurred
between the Swiss and the people of Strasbourg.

"Delivered of Their Most Cruel Cares"

We have seen that nineteenth-century Europeans embraced advanced
communications technologies, sophisticated civil society, faith in
European civilization, and growing respect for the autonomy and physical integrity of others. While these changes affected other expressions
of concern (such as charity), they also led to the development of humanitarianism, a distinct social and ethical movement. Humanitarianism is

not the same as human rights. Michael Geyer explains that human rights views people as actors, often as revolutionaries seizing rights for themselves. Humanitarianism regards some people as victims whom the more fortunate, or more civilized, must save.[32] The key terms guiding human rights are "rights," "demands," and "actors"; the key terms in humanitarianism are "needs," "duties," and "victims." In 1870, Europeans had not yet articulated civilians' right to wartime protection as a fundamental human right (indeed, rights talk in the nineteenth century was so circumscribed that it may not be appropriate to speak of human rights at that time).[33] Humanitarianism in Strasbourg valued each individual life but did not treat all individuals equally. It particularly valued the lives of the people believed to be the most powerless: women, children, the sick, and the elderly. These "innocents" were not viewed as equal actors bearing rights but as the victims of aggression. This particular aspect of humanitarianism is related to three additional elements: the valorization of sympathy as a motivator of moral action, a new understanding of spiritual atonement, and a particularly sharp separation between male and female activities.

Modern Europe's emotional landscape, in particular its emphasis on sympathy—suffering others' pain along with them—contributed to the formation of humanitarianism. This feeling was not new, of course, but its value had increased during the Enlightenment. As Lynn Hunt argues, popular eighteenth century works like Jean-Jacques Rousseau's *Julie, or the New Heloise* (1761) helped readers to imagine the aspirations of protagonists and to extend their emotional range to include people outside of their traditional social circles.[34] In the nineteenth century, sympathy was generally accepted as the foundation of moral sensibility for both women and men.[35] The valorization of sympathy explains a difference between human rights and humanitarianism; the sympathizer retains separateness and difference from the object of sympathy. It implies pity rather than the equality we associate with human rights.

Humanitarianism also has a spiritual dimension, one that further distinguishes it from human rights. It is possible to see humanitarianism as a new form of community atonement for suffering and sin. In early modern Europe, the torture and suffering of criminals in public view served to repair the harm that crime had done to the community. By the end of the eighteenth century, spectators came to see such displays as abhorrent rather than redeeming.[36] Individual perpetrators were still punished for their crimes, but the public spectacle of punishment was no longer intended to heal the community.

Yet, as Michael Barnett argues, cataclysmic events—crimes, wars, and natural disasters—continued to harm entire communities, not just those who suffered directly. In the modern world, the "community" might include people from other countries. Such events could cause a crisis of faith, which led to "a process of atonement," including self-reflection, the recognition of committing a sin, repentance, and the reparation of a relationship through sacrifice, prayer, and (often) an outward expression of a spiritual awakening. That outward expression sometimes included the construction of moral institutions to help communities "become the people that [they] said [they] were."[37] Thus, the need for atonement could lead to a charitable or humanitarian act, extending across borders or to the other side of the globe. If Barnett is right, then one reason for the rise of humanitarianism is a change in spirituality. Community atonement of sins shifted from the torturer's wheel to the mobile ambulance. Pity for the suffering innocent began to displace punishment of the suffering guilty as a way for community expiation of harm. Concrete action became linked to transcendence and transformation.

Just who should be considered part of the suffering innocent? To fully understand the emergence of humanitarianism, we must consider one more development, one that has not appeared in histories of humanitarianism before: the relationship between men and women. A gender dynamic that became tightly linked to the very concept of European civilization developed in the most routine of spaces: the domestic arrangements of millions of families. These relationships shaped the specific aims of many humanitarians and help to explain the emotional resonance of the Swiss intervention.

In 1870, women and children had long been considered particularly innocent in wartime, more so than civilian males. In the nineteenth century, the dominant gender paradigm argued that civilized society was divided between a male public sphere for political and economic life and a female domestic private sphere that should not be sullied by politics or the market. The nineteenth century cult of female purity restabilized gender relations after the egalitarian politics of the 1790s had crippled traditional patriarchy. Men now joined, at least in theory, a fraternity of equals from which women were excluded. Middle-class male citizens, such as the Swiss delegates, assumed access to political channels and the mobility to go wherever necessary. Women were believed to be the guardians of the household, society, and civilization. They were increasingly seen as biologically inferior to men and constitutionally unfit for the strains of public life, let alone the difficulties of war. Men were supposed to provide their wives and children with financial and physical protection.[38] Yet male civilians had few real options for doing so during war.

The Swiss intervention was a boon for Strasbourg's civilian men. The Swiss did not try to shelter those who were actually the most likely to be harmed—civilian men—and intervened instead on behalf of "women, children [and] in general . . . those unable to defend themselves," such as the elderly or sick. The municipal leadership echoed these criteria without a second thought.[39] Mayor Humann, Schneegans, Piton, and other civilian males were moved to tears because the Swiss helped them to restore the protection that they had failed to provide on their own and thus repair the damage to European civilization. Suddenly, they could help participate in the protection of the people for whom they felt responsible. They could prepare lists of refugees, pack them up, and oversee their departure. For many, the exodus of so many women and children also solidified the desire to resist capitulation.[40] Not only would women and children be safe, but also men would be "delivered of their most cruel cares" and "continue the resistance with a new vigor and a new courage."[41]

Neutral Switzerland

The Strasbourgeois thought that the Swiss intervened to save their traditional ally. We know that humanitarianism grew out of myriad changes in modern life. For the Swiss, however, the key to their intervention was not their historical friendship, but rather their investment in neutrality. Since the sixteenth century, neutrality had formed an important part of

Switzerland's identity and interface with the European great powers. The Swiss claimed to remain disinterested from the outcome of the conflict between France and the German states. Swiss geopolitical neutrality shaped the specific intervention in Strasbourg and has come to be associated with humanitarian aid in general, but neutrality was not simply a beautiful ideal, nor was it a necessary characteristic of humanitarianism. It was a strategic position: every step of the Swiss rescue operation required negotiation and planning between the municipal commission, the French commander, and the German commander.[42] The Swiss faced formidable opposition. By its very presence, humanitarian aid could not help but critique military conduct. The Swiss recognized that military regulations, strictly interpreted, would not allow large numbers of women and children to depart. As Werder argued, a successful siege relied on the suffering of women and children; only a few exceptions might be worked out through intermediaries. Military custom, steeped in its honor code, held humanitarianism to be sentimental kitsch that distracted from military goals (today we might interpret the nineteenth-century military code of honor as equally sentimental). The Swiss hoped that a neutral stance would help to overcome these obstacles.

A stance of neutrality furthermore helped to confirm Swiss identity and exceptionalism as a people who believed that they had risen above the morass of war. Switzerland, in 1870 as well as today, presented an alternative model of government and national identity. A confederation of Swiss cantons formed in the High Middle Ages and developed its Alpine, communal, nonhierarchical identity over the course of the following centuries. Switzerland's adherence to neutrality in European conflicts dated back to the sixteenth century and allowed the Swiss to thrive while the rest of the continent nearly destroyed itself during the Thirty Years' War. Although France tried to dominate Switzerland during the early 1800s, the Vienna Congress reasserted Swiss neutrality. Over the years, Switzerland's many cantons struggled over language, religion, and form of government, sometimes to the point of revolutionary violence. But by 1848 the country had achieved political stability through federalist compromise and semidirect democracy, which gave its varied groups a stake in the nation. While linguistic purity became a preoccupation for French and Germans in the nineteenth century, Switzerland officially maintained its distinct French-, German-, Italian-, and Romansch-speaking populations.

When war began between France and the German states in 1870, the Swiss Federal Council wanted above all to maintain Switzerland's neutrality. In August, the Federal Council decried "the lying, calumnious rumor that the Swiss population favors one or another of the belligerent parties," adding, "one publishes in Germany that [Switzerland] sympathizes with France, and in France that it is for Prussia." The Federal Council deemed it necessary to direct the cantonal governments to "energetically and immediately intervene against attempts to compromise the neutrality of Switzerland, whether verbal, written or otherwise." They were to pay particular attention to the newspapers and to the attitudes of suspicious foreigners in public houses along the borders. The Federal Council regretted undertaking actions that "are unknown in free Switzerland" but felt that the demands of wartime justified the additional surveillance: "The Federal Assembly [has] unanimously and with the assent of the nation proclaimed the neutrality of Switzerland. It is our duty to observe it in the most loyal manner and, in doing so, to avoid even the appearance of wrong."[43]

Swiss neutrality included a confessional dimension as well. The Federal Constitution of 1848 had helped Protestants and Catholics to share power peacefully for over twenty years.[44] The Swiss delegates to Strasbourg did not openly associate themselves with Protestantism, despite the fact that they hailed from predominantly Protestant cities (Basel, Zurich, and Bern). Whatever they believed in their hearts about Protestantism, Catholicism, or Judaism, the Swiss formulated their intervention such that it did not differentiate among faiths. Confessional neutrality helped the Swiss to avoid accusations that they favored France or Germany and reflected the fact that significant Protestant and Catholic populations lived in both belligerent countries. Confessional neutrality also helped the Swiss avoid mentioning the uncomfortable fact that Prussian Protestants were bombing fellow Protestants.

This neutral, humanitarian stance became the cornerstone of Bischoff's committee. When it sought approval from the Swiss Federal Council, it hit hard the message of Swiss exceptionalism: "The city of

Strasbourg can do nothing for [its people]; the country is under enemy occupation; the Badenese, direct neighbors, have become enemies . . . Only we, the Swiss, are capable of offering them a hand."[45] Calling upon the cantons to gather aid for the refugees, the committee hoped that "neutral Switzerland" would "show again that its duty does not consist in opening wounds but in healing them."[46] Indeed, municipal commissioner Antoine Zopff immediately connected the Swiss offer with the Red Cross: "Switzerland . . . covered with its flag the humanitarian work undertaken in favor of soldiers wounded on the battlefield; today it gives the world a yet nobler example."[47] Both the Swiss Federal Council and the Prussian ambassador in Bern approved the mission.

By September 10, the committee arrived at the military camps outside Strasbourg. Negotiations progressed smoothly. Uhrich, Werder, and Friedrich I, Grand Duke of Baden, all approved. To maintain its neutrality, the Swiss delegation carefully balanced its judgments of France and Prussia. It blamed both the Prussians for their cruel bombardment and the French commander for forcing the population to hold on against its will.[48] But the Swiss were pleased that both sides welcomed them: "Our reception at Nationale Gate showed us that Strasbourg had well understood Switzerland, and we do not attach a less moral significance to the sympathetic benevolence that the leaders of the German army testified toward us, on whom the hard and heavy task of such a siege falls."[49] Even the delegation's report on civilian conditions bore the marks of neutrality. They included a detailed description of the cellars in which civilians lived in order to confirm that "everything bore the traces of a siege, and a rigorous siege."[50] They justified their intervention with careful observation, not inflamed rhetoric or biased hearsay.

Furthermore, the Swiss worried about the welfare of both French and Germans. They dreaded "the terrible calamity that the last military act of this siege, the assault of Strasbourg, will bring upon both the unfortunate city and on the soldiers that are laying siege."[51] They understood that the brutalization of war destroyed soldiers as well as civilians. They did not hope to end the war, but strove to prevent the cruel tragedy of rape and pillage at the siege's end. The real enemy was not one nation or the other, but the dynamics of war itself.

We often think that neutrality is a defining characteristic of humanitarianism. Neutrality did indeed shape many humanitarian interventions, but not simply because being neutral is a nice thing to do. It is a useful self-definition and a strategy upheld in order to gain access to suffering populations, as well as a moral ideal. Neutrality is not always neutral.

"We Could Not Recommend Them"

The morning after the Swiss arrival, the city got down to business. Individuals and families who wanted to leave registered at the Hôtel du Commerce. The municipality forwarded the lists to Werder for the final decision.[52] Up to four thousand individuals requested letters of safe-conduct, although fewer than two thousand left with the Swiss between September 15 and 22 before Werder cut off the flow of refugees.[53] Although the Swiss and the municipal commission agreed in principle that women and children should be the beneficiaries of the Swiss intervention, the composition of the departing convoys did not uniformly conform to this assumption.

Many "victims" declined to take the Swiss up on their offer. Some worried that the Swiss did not address any of their previous concerns about leaving the city safely. The trip would be expensive, dangerous, and physically difficult. The Prussians could not be trusted to respect their safe passage. Malartic advised women to stay put rather than lay themselves open to enemy attack. Separating men from their loved ones, he argued, would have a negative effect on morale. Others did not want to leave their homes and family. After some debate, young diarist Cécile de Dartein and her sisters and mother decided to stay in Strasbourg because they would not abandon their house or Cécile's brother Henri, a *franc-tireur*. It was falsely rumored, too, that the Prussians would press departing adolescent males into military service.[54] When Rodolphe Reuss's Aunt Pauline wavered over whether to stay or go, he finally snapped, "Heads or tails will decide!" and, the verdict given, he packed up the women of the family to go.[55] Here, as in any humanitarian intervention, the desire to liberate was mixed with a measure of paternalism. Only the powerful can define "liberation" for someone else.[56]

Still, hundreds of women, like English tutor Miss Jacot, agreed to leave. Many feared a brutal final assault that would lead to pillage, rape, fire, and murder.[57] Information is available on 787 refugees who departed on September 15, 17, and 19. It is not surprising that a sizable number of the refugees were children: at least 193. It is also not surprising that far more women than men departed, including 300 adults and 111 adolescents old enough to be called "demoiselle" or "mademoiselle." A full 20 percent of the total were women traveling without family members.[58] These included eight females associated with the Asylum of Saint-Antoine, the orphanage whose bombardment had shocked the city in mid-August. In addition, 128 women took responsibility for shepherding out 200 children and adolescents without male support. Two of these women, Madame von Essen and Madame Goettelmann, traveled alone with five children each. Men who facilitated women's departures may have thought that they were looking out for their women, but in practice, women had to take responsibility for themselves and often cared for multiple young children over miles of uncertain territory.

Yet, despite the overwhelming rhetoric that only women, children, and the elderly could depart, 116 refugees (about 15 percent) were adult males, including 9 foreigners, such as a Swiss painter who left with his wife, and 4 residents of other French cities.[59] Sixty-nine heads of household left along with their wives and children. They avoided attracting comments for or against their decision. However, the thirty-seven adult male Strasbourg residents who departed without women and children in tow—4.7 percent of all refugees—won derision. Rodolphe Reuss mocked an acquaintance, the archivist Louis Spach, for his fearfulness and eventual departure. Spach had run into Reuss at Place Gutenberg on September 19 and said, "Oh, my dear sir, we will all be violated [violés]!" Reuss "laughed in his face."[60] Frédéric Piton sneered at the "young and able-bodied men who ha[d] the cowardice to leave the city."[61] He believed they must have served the now-defunct imperial regime. The list of refugees indicates the profession of only about half of the adult men, none of whom were unquestionably civic functionaries, so it is impossible to substantiate Piton's contention. Furthermore, we do not know whether these men fit the categories of elderly, sick, or wounded. Still, it is notable that, though the rhetoric of manly protection resonated

The Departures. A female servant in traditional Alsatian dress (lower right) holds a young child as the lady of the house takes leave of her husband near Austerlitz Gate. This scene reiterates the presumption that only women, children, and the elderly should take advantage of the Swiss humanitarian intervention. Auguste Münch, *Guerre de 1870: Siège et bombardement de Strasbourg* (1870). (Archives de la Ville et de la Communauté urbaine de Strasbourg)

strongly among many politicians and journalists, it did not extend into every male soul.

In addition to the gender of the refugees, it would be interesting to know their religious affiliations. Did Werder or the Swiss favor Protestants? Did Jews have equal access to these passes? The lists do not say. Swiss neutrality apparently led those compiling the lists not to ask for this piece of information. Nor did those who stayed behind comment on the religious background of those departing. Confessional identity, which had earlier caused fears that Strasbourg's Protestants would disloyally support their coreligionists, had been pushed to the background.

We can, however, gain some insight into the wealth of the refugees. We might expect that the refugees would primarily come from the poorest classes, those least able to take care of themselves. In fact, however, the Swiss insisted that only those with some financial resources be allowed to depart, so they would not find themselves destitute and dependent on charity upon arrival in Switzerland: "We will absolutely separate out indigent and unsuitable individuals, for we could not recommend them to our compatriots."[62] The Swiss made it clear that they intended to provide diplomatic leverage and logistical support to save civilians from bombs, not financial resources to those who had experienced prewar poverty.

The municipal commission did not follow the Swiss recommendation to the letter. It reported in its minutes for September 13 that those registering to leave had to place themselves into one of three groups: those who could travel at their own expense, those with limited resources, and those without resources. The 568 safe-conducts granted in the second round of departures favored the first category: 380 (over two-thirds) who could travel at their own expense, 78 with limited resources, and 110 without resources. *Le courrier du Bas-Rhin* observed that in the first two convoys, preference had been given to those who had lost their homes due to fire. The list of refugees also suggests the overrepresentation of the wealthy and connected: the fifty-seven adult males whose occupations are known included fourteen in the liberal professions (doctors, professors, judges, teachers, and a civil engineer), six businessmen, and six independently wealthy *rentiers*.[63] Despite its initial reluctance to support the poorer refugees, the Swiss committee called for financial contributions from all the cantons of Switzerland and created a *Damencomite* (ladies' committee) to focus on clothes, shoes, and medical care. The Swiss Federal Council promised support in case private charitable offerings would not suffice.[64]

Some departing civilians had not emerged from their cellars since the early days of the siege and had to readjust to the rays of the sun. Stunned and blinking, they looked as though they had just woken up from a nightmare, their emotions mixed between relief, sorrow at leaving their loved ones behind, and fear of facing the unknown on the other side of the gate.[65] Convoys of refugees in whatever form of carriage they could cobble together slowly made their way toward Austerlitz Gate early in the morning on September 15, 17, 19, 20, 21, and 22. Werder instructed his artillery units to "avoid with particular care shots that could damage the city" but did not allow a ceasefire.[66]

It took over three hours for each convoy to clear through the Prussian line. Many refugees had to change their vehicles to take ones the Prussians approved. Others were obliged to continue on foot, as had Catherine Weiss and her children.[67] Even after they passed out of the city, the path was not smooth. Deputy mayor Antoine Zopff accompanied and oversaw the third convoy's departure. Carriages crammed full of ninety-seven refugees and their few belongings passed through the Austerlitz Gate and headed south. At a crossroads not far from the city, three German soldiers halted the convoy, claiming they lacked orders to allow passage. Zopff replied, "In that case, I do not present myself as representative of the city of Strasbourg, I become the executor of orders from your general in chief; if you refuse to execute them, be so kind as to give me your refusal in writing." The soldiers referred him to their commander, stationed at the Plaine des Bouchers about a mile due south of the city walls. This officer sent Zopff four miles further southwest to the Prussian headquarters in Illkirch. There, Zopff recognized a young Prussian officer who protested that the deputy mayor asked too much. Zopff presented this young officer with the same dilemma: "Take a look at this order from M. von Werder, your general in chief, which authorizes the depart of a convoy of emigrants. If you refuse to comply . . . please do so in writing, so I can cover my own responsibility to my fellow citizens." The young officer hesitated a few minutes before finally allowing them to proceed.[68]

This episode reveals the uncertainties inherent in the departure, Werder's lack of interest in truly ensuring the safety of the refugees, and Zopff's self-conception as a heroic figure, turning the following of orders into a defiant act of bravery. Zopff had also personally shouldered the financial burden for some of the refugees.[69] For male civic leaders like Zopff, it was mightily important to see themselves as gallantly helping women to depart. Their distinctive role was less evident to those observing from the outside. *Le Paris-journal* of September 13 reported that all "elderly, women and children have left Strasbourg and are in safety *[sic]*. Remaining are General Uhrich and his valiant brothers in arms."[70] To the outside world, civilian men had disappeared once again.

Werder's Reasons

Why did Prussian general August von Werder allow this exodus of women and children, when he had explicitly resisted it earlier in the siege? Werder's own bare-bones records do not tell us, but other evidence provides insight. Let's go back to September 10, when the Swiss delegation first approached the Prussian commander. According to the Swiss report, at first, Werder was no more interested in releasing civilians than he had been before. He worried that an exodus of civilians would prolong the siege and force the Germans into a costly all-out assault on the city.[71]

Nevertheless, Werder soon changed his mind. Was this a humanitarian impulse? Schneegans believed that Werder only relented due to the influence of his chief advisor, Lieutenant Colonel von Leszczynski, "Werder's 'good angel.'"[72] But Werder's unwillingness to pause bombardment as the convoys departed and his failure to give his subordinates clear orders suggest that he did not particularly focus on the well-being of departing civilians. Whether on Leszczynski's advice or not, it seems likely that Werder changed his mind for strategic reasons. Ever since September 3, when he had received the news of Prussia's victory at Sedan and the capture of Napoleon III, Werder had come under increased pressure to take Strasbourg. What if the French sued for peace before Strasbourg fell into German hands?[73] Upon hearing about Sedan, Werder immediately notified Uhrich, hoping to weaken his resolve. Uhrich found the news unbelievable and exaggerated. Werder then allowed Uhrich to send out scouts to confirm the truth. Even with this knowledge, Uhrich again refused Werder's demand of surrender, stating, "Whatever may be my desire to spare the inhabitants of Strasbourg the evils resulting from the bombardment to which they are submitted, I cannot dream of handing over the city with whose defense I have been entrusted."[74] On September 7, eager for victory, Werder pressed central command for permission for a stronger bombardment. Moltke replied on September 9, "A serious bombardment of the city is admissible as an extreme measure, but it must be avoided if at all possible, and, in any case, the [French] commander must be warned first."[75] Moltke told Werder to focus on controlling the surrounding areas and disarming the population.[76]

Werder wanted to convince Uhrich to capitulate, but he needed to find a way other than bombardment to do it. The Swiss delegation held the key. They brought trustworthy confirmation of the disastrous battle of Sedan and the declaration of a new republic. Werder likely calculated that this news would signal the end to any hope of exterior relief. Morale would plummet, and civilians would clamor for surrender. Werder may also have reckoned that allowing women and children to depart would reassure the city of Prussia's good intentions. News of the fall of Napoleon III would furthermore permit the replacement of imperial municipal leaders with native republicans who felt less invested in the war and wanted to spare the city total destruction. This is indeed what happened. In fact, some found the news of Sedan so distressing that they believed the Swiss were actually Prussian spies sent to demoralize the population and take women and children hostage. The Swiss visit also reassured the German reading public that the city was still standing. Rumors that the famous cathedral lay in rubble were false. The *National-Zeitung* (Berlin) reproduced Otto von Büren's account of the Swiss visit to Strasbourg. The Germans even allowed an edited version of Humann's speech to the Swiss to be reproduced, one that cut out any specific references to the German states and King Wilhelm. Meanwhile, despite the bad news from the outside, the city experienced one last gasp of heroic resolve.[77]

▪ ▪ ▪

Humanitarianism is one of the defining features of the modern age. It developed not because people were suffering more than they had in the past, but because responses to suffering had changed. Humanitarianism's emphasis on traveling to the site of suffering to alleviate the distress of victims and thereby improve the human condition differentiated it from other expressions of concern. Humanitarians believed that fulfilling "a duty to help people who have no right to expect it" conferred transcendence.[78] In 1870, that meant restoring civilian men's ability to protect women and children and therefore shoring up civilization. The Swiss intervention in Strasbourg was a small step in terms of helping all of humanity—the Swiss aided a city whose history was closely intertwined with their own, and the action did not inspire similar interventions in Paris a few months later—but a big change in the fact that civilians from nonbelligerent nations claimed responsibility for the suffering of civilians caught in war.

It is easy to see the shortcomings in the Swiss intervention. Any sympathetic response lays itself open to the charge of hypocrisy. We might view humanitarian aid as a mask for self-interest, condescension, self-aggrandizement, and even pleasure at not being one of the victims. The Swiss oversimplified the events in Strasbourg, took the liberty of defining the narrative of victimhood, and supplied themselves as the victims' salvation. They primarily offered aid to those with financial resources rather than to those with the greatest needs.

We might also recognize the fragility of using sympathy as a basis for moral action. Eighteenth-century philosophers, even those like Bishop Joseph Butler who rooted morality in sympathy, worried that sympathy could wear thin from overuse. Immanuel Kant rejected sympathy as a basis for morality because of the limits of human feelings: not everyone will feel sufficiently sympathetic by nature, and so it cannot provide universal grounds for right action.[79] "Suffering" and "victim" are in the eyes of the humanitarian; the emotional basis for humanitarianism means that humanitarian aims will always shift as emotional resonances change.[80] The Swiss could not assume that everyone would act in the same way that they did, and sympathy alone proved to be insufficient protection. Just seventeen years later, in 1887, German philosopher Friedrich Nietzsche argued that a morality rooted in sympathy is worthy only of slaves.

The most devastating critique of the Swiss intervention is that it succeeded only because General Werder manipulated its purpose. The Swiss could never have helped the civilians of Strasbourg without Werder's acceptance, and he agreed to it only because he could use the Swiss to further his own war aims. The Swiss did not, in the end, change the nature of siege warfare. From its very earliest days, then, savvy military and political leaders manipulated humanitarianism for their own ends. In the words of Alain Destexhe, former secretary-general of Doctors Without Borders, many strategists treat humanitarianism as "the continuation of politics by other means. If he were still alive, Clausewitz surely would have added a chapter entitled 'On the Proper Use of Humanitarianism' to his monument *On War*."[81]

The Swiss fell into all of these pitfalls, yet they achieved their primary goal of protecting noncombatants from violence. Under their auspices, between 1,250 and 2,000 individuals safely left the city. The Swiss intervention saved lives and alleviated anxiety. The Swiss also managed to keep their own borders calm, enhance their reputation as neutral arbitrators, and avoid retaliation for their interference from either France or Germany. The Swiss furthermore helped to change the reputation of humanitarianism from overbearing do-goodism to an exceptional but appropriate expression of human sympathy. The Swiss intervened when older mechanisms to protect "innocents" had failed, during a period when human rights exerted little influence. In retrospect, the Swiss intervention was less problematic than were humanitarian interventions in colonial contexts. The Swiss work did not become a "disciplining tool of Western institutions and colonialist agendas" that redefined widespread non-European practices as elements of human suffering.[82] Emergency humanitarianism such as the kind practiced in Strasbourg seems to provoke fewer objections than do long-term efforts to change cultural practices deemed harmful by outsiders.

Humanitarianism now offered a new and appealing kind of safety net that included people from outside one's immediate community. Werder's machinations may have been worth it.

For better or worse, the Swiss set some of the patterns of early humanitarian efforts on behalf of civilians. In the decades to come, humanitarian aid for civilians remained fragmented. It tended to be improvised, temporary, and aimed primarily at people with a shared history. In addition, the Swiss muddied the already murky distinction between civilian and military spheres of influence, even as they argued that civilians and military personnel should have separate fates. They believed that the removal of women, children, and the elderly from the arena of war was a mark of civilization. The position of women, who were believed to both safeguard civilization and to need protection themselves, resonated with the paradox of liberation and domination that characterized humanitarianism.[83]

Finally, the Swiss intervention in Strasbourg embodied fundamental dilemmas that humanitarian organizations continue to face today: Who is worthy of aid? Should humanitarians consult the wishes of the people that they are trying to help? Can true neutrality exist? How long and how far should aid extend? Can humanitarianism avoid cynical manipulation? Ideally, humanitarian aid protects the most needy universally, without prejudice and without taking sides, while responding intelligently to the overarching military and geopolitical situation. In reality, humanitarian aid is full of tensions, as flawed humans try to operate in an imperfect world.

CHAPTER SEVEN

Heroic Measures

ARLY ON THE morning of September 20, French soldiers brought to General Uhrich a man who had appeared at Strasbourg's gates during the night. Was this a spy? Middle-aged, with a black beard and an aquiline nose, his clothing tattered and dripping from a swim and several days' exposure, the man pulled from his sleeve a sealed letter of appointment. He was Edmond Valentin, sent by the new French Republic to serve as prefect of the Bas-Rhin. He had come to Strasbourg, he proclaimed, "to share your perils and privations, and together we will struggle to the last extremity."[1]

In the days that followed, Valentin shook Strasbourg's political system and gave a firm answer to the question on everyone's mind: "Should we surrender or not?"[2] Everyone talked about Strasbourg's dire situation, but nobody knew what to do about it. Although it is impossible to establish the majority opinion in Strasbourg, it seems clear that city leaders fell into three camps. The municipal commission, including its new leader, Emile Küss, called for a pragmatic surrender to protect the city and its inhabitants. Uhrich and his defense council followed military regulations that provided the appropriate moment for capitulation. Valentin supported a third position: hold on beyond military necessity as a symbol of French tenacity, whatever the consequences.

176

These three positions echoed a timeless debate among three major
ethical traditions: consequentialism (Küss), deontology (Uhrich), and
virtue ethics (Valentin). Each tradition poses a different question as its
guide to action. The consequentialist, aiming to fulfill the good as he
knows it from his experience, asks, "What will be the results of my
action?" The deontologist draws upon a set of principles to answer the
question, "What is my duty toward others?" Finally, the virtue ethicist
looks at society and within herself to demand, "What kind of a person
should I be?" The particular expressions of each of these positions differ
across time: the principles of the deontologist, the good of the consequentialist, and the qualities of the virtuous person change. The aim
here is to discern the specific qualities of these debates in 1870 from the
general characteristics of these ethical traditions.

The study of ethics provides us with another tool for analyzing the
siege experience. The debate among these ethical traditions is one
marker of our humanity; individuals have always differed on these questions. We may never know what causes one person to negotiate and
another to fight, while a third leans on preexisting rules of conduct. To
complicate matters, no individual follows just one ethical tradition;
Küss, Uhrich, and Valentin were complicated people torn in several
directions. Furthermore, it could be that these traditions simply provided post hoc justifications for decisions made irrationally. Still, it is
worth trying to disentangle these various traditions in order to better
understand how people defend their actions. In the crucial moments, we
must make decisions and face the reactions of other people. It behooves
us to try to understand how we do it.

The New Republic

After the Swiss brought news from the outside on September 11, Prefect
Baron Pron could no longer deny the rumors of the capture of Napoleon
III, the overthrow of his regime, and the declaration of the Third
Republic under the provisional leadership of the Government of
National Defense. The republicans on the municipal commission imme-
diately took symbolic measures to assert authority: on police kepis and

uniform buttons, imperial eagles gave way to the city's coat of arms.[3] They crossed out the words "EMPIRE FRANÇAIS" on preprinted stationary and inscribed an X over the imperial eagle. The news spread rapidly, but even stalwart republicans like Rodolphe Reuss could hardly celebrate: "Morning relatively calm. In the afternoon proclamation of the Republic. Resignation of the prefect. People put out their flags, only a little. At the moment that they brought out the flags on Place Kléber, a stretcher passed with a mortally wounded woman, half covered with a military greatcoat: her pale and contracted face gave [me] a shiver; such a spectacle kills all enthusiasm. The bombardment continues."[4]

Meanwhile, political leaders worked out the transition of power. Uhrich publicly declared his loyalty to the new regime and urged soldiers and civilians to do the same. The republicans happily demanded the resignation of the despised and unpopular Pron. The municipal commission furthermore fired Central Police *Commissaire* Aymard, who had participated in the bribes endemic to elections under Napoleon III and was accused of arbitrary abuses of authority and petty embezzlement. On September 13, Mayor Théodore Humann offered his resignation. Over the objections of moderates on all sides, the Orléanist declared that he could not serve a republican regime in good conscience, nor could he exert the influence on the population necessary to keeping order and calm.[5]

The commissioners moved quickly to replace the prefect and mayor, although they were perfectly aware that the central government normally appointed prefects; they did not want to wait for the uncertain arrival of the new appointee, whomever he may be. In the selection of Charles Boersch as prefect and Emile Küss as mayor, the commission chose two Protestant doctors with impeccable republican pedigrees. These "men of duty and experience" embodied the pious and self-cultivated German *Burger*.[6] Boersch, a capable administrator, had stood for election as a liberal candidate in 1869 and served as both deputy mayor and departmental councilor. He also edited *Le courrier du Bas-Rhin*, the newspaper for which Schneegans wrote.[7]

The new mayor, Emile Küss, embodied "an ancient bourgeois of the Republic of Strasbourg."[8] Born in 1815 into an old, well-regarded family, Küss studied at the Protestant Gymnasium and trained in anatomy. In 1848, this moderate republican became a local leader in the revolution. He was arrested along with many others when Louis-Napoleon Bonaparte overthrew the Second Republic on December 2, 1851, but was acquitted by a court in Metz. Küss returned to private life as a practicing doctor and member of the Faculty of Medicine. He committed himself to his family, his medical career, and the cause of public education. Küss's uncompromising republicanism earned respect: under the Second Empire he twice refused the Legion of Honor. Always in need of money to support his large family, Küss frequently lectured for medical students and visited the sick at their bedsides. Perhaps it was through one of these house calls that he contracted the pulmonary infection that kept him periodically bedridden.[9]

Küss was a true son of Alsace, a poet who loved to walk through the Vosges Mountains and the Black Forest. He not only knew how to sketch but also offered courses on anatomical drawing. He furthermore loved music, especially Beethoven. Generous, good-natured, and ethical, Küss demanded the same of his associates.[10] His family life was simple and patriarchal. Some might perceive him as "taciturn and a bit misanthropic," but within his carefully chosen circle of friends, he was cordial and light hearted.[11] He chose the epigraph "Burn what you love" for his modest medical book on the vascular system.[12] Dr. Henri-Etienne Beaunis, who had studied medicine under Küss, fondly recalled his teacher's mannerisms in class: "his slightly slow speech, with an academic correctness, despite a few Germanisms that the milieu explains, his voice, muted and slightly muffled, but with a beautiful musical timbre . . . his meditative attitude, his face radiating intelligence, whose brow, gaze and smile made one forget the bourgeois mask."[13]

Küss reentered politics to campaign for Charles Boersch during the elections of 1869. The following spring, he argued for a "no" vote to Napoleon III's plebiscite. Younger republicans like Auguste Schneegans adored Küss because he never compromised with the empire. His personality augmented his political pedigree: calm, effective, possessing good judgment and clear vision, able to bring men together with his humor and quiet irony. A model of moderation, Küss displayed none of the "flashy bragging of certain showy revolutionaries, more dangerous for their friends than for their adversaries and the most cruel enemies of their own cause." For Schneegans, Küss did not fit the model of a typical French political leader: "the sparkle, the exterior form, the ardent words." Rather, Küss was an Abraham Lincoln playing on a smaller stage, exuding "simple and male virtues." He may never have a statue erected in his honor, but the people would venerate his "honesty and devotion to public life."[14]

No Exit

As Küss set to work, it was increasingly clear that the siege was entering its final stage. The Germans inched their cannon closer to Strasbourg's fortress walls, while the bombardment of the city center continued unabated. At times, shells landed without interruption, "not from minute to minute, but from second to second."[15] From afar, Crown Prince Friedrich Wilhelm recorded in his war diary, "The maddest part of the whole business is, that desiring to make that town German and gain it over to ourselves, we must first reduce it to ashes to attain our object. But what else is left for the besiegers to do?"[16] The final two weeks were the bloodiest of the siege. Between the Swiss promise of deliverance on September 11 and the last shell's detonation on September 27, at least 124 civilians died violently. On September 12, an unexploded shell went off, killing three young people, aged eight, eleven, and eighteen, and seriously wounding three others. A young salesman, the president of a gymnastics club, lost both legs and died soon after (a rare report of a civilian male death).[17]

The city received yet another symbolic blow on September 15 when a shell damaged the cathedral's spire. This highest point of human construction nearly came crashing down, saved only by the lightning rod. For the rest of the siege, the spire hovered crookedly over the platform, Frédéric Piton's former haunt. The attack spurred Uhrich to transform the cathedral into an ambulance, theoretically protected under the Geneva Convention.[18] In a much-reprinted letter dated September 19, Bishop Raess understood Uhrich to mean that the cathedral could now be safely used "as an asylum for the population deprived of shelter." The homeless could occupy nearly all of the cathedral's space, including several chapels and the transept that housed the marvelous mechanical clock. One portion of Saint-Laurent's chapel would suffice for the faithful partaking in daily mass. Raess only asked for watchmen to "assure order, morality, and—during the divine offices—silence."[19]

Across the city, the siege had unfolded unevenly. Piton's walks from his house near the ruins of the New Church revealed startlingly different experiences. Ten minutes to the northwest, in the faubourg de Pierre, nearly every building lay in rubble. Ten minutes to the southwest, shops remained open and people walked freely along the Grand'Rue. Some remained in cellars for the duration regardless of their location. Yet even in the last week of the siege, even in the most heavily bombarded neighborhoods, intrepid inhabitants still managed—right up to (or sometimes beyond) the official eight o'clock closing time—to ferret out a beer.[20]

For many, the siege routine became unbearable. In Piton's daily chats with the tinsmith or other neighbors, talk inevitably focused on the siege, "for no other subject of conversation is possible."[21] At night, Piton set down his impressions, perched in his attic under a turbulent, shell-streaked sky. He tired of recording the day's dose of destruction, this or that building's "daily allotment of projectiles."[22] Yet reporting the damage proved irresistible. An ogival window of the cathedral was hit today, noted Piton; the north transept's pediment dropped heavy fragments to the street below.[23] Had mankind gone mad? Or turned into demons? The clergy "should have cursed the flags of armies instead of blessing them."[24]

Max Reichard sought comfort in the rhythms of the Christian calendar, which seemed to parallel the city's travail: "Right after the declaration of war came the sixth Sunday after Trinitatis with its exhortations for mercy. . . . Around the 13th we experienced the Good Samaritans, as they truly have never been more poignantly administered, and today on the 15th we have once again taken comfort from the words of the Sermon on the Mount . . . ! We let ourselves point to the birds under heaven and the lilies of the valley. . . . We will not long for other days, but rather accept the prevailing measure of daily trials, certain that they will not surpass [our] capabilities, if we consign our burdens to Him, who has up to now never forgotten us."[25]

For his part, Rodolphe Reuss, who had become so enraged by the destruction of the New Church, tried to retreat back into detachment.

Over dinner with his friends, the news that the Prefecture burned warranted only "Oh yes, I heard about that." Many toasts later, though, they could not help but take up the question of—what else—the impending capitulation.[26]

The Case for Surrender

At their daily meeting on September 18, Küss and the municipal commission heard General Uhrich's latest news. On the previous day, Werder had told Uhrich to prepare the population for another intense bombardment. In sharing this information with the commission, Uhrich announced his hope to establish a greater level of mutual trust between himself and civic leaders. He professed to a new level of "sincerity" that would henceforth drive their interactions and smooth relations with the population at large.[27] Sincerity, highly prized since the publication of Jean-Jacques Rousseau's *Confessions* and the public oaths of the First Republic, resonated with the commissioners. They named Uhrich an honorary citizen of Strasbourg.

No record of this September 18 meeting has been preserved in the minutes of the municipal commission. The pages are not torn out nor left blank; the record simply passes from September 17 to 19 as though the commission had not met in between. Yet the minutes include a letter from General Uhrich acknowledging that he had attended the meeting on September 18.[28] What were they trying to hide?

The siege records held by the French Historical Service of the Ground Army yield the answer. After Uhrich left the meeting, Küss and forty-five municipal leaders decided that all hope was lost.[29] On a folded double sheet of paper, they wrote a request for Uhrich to negotiate surrender. The petition honored Uhrich and his troops for having "defended, for five weeks, a place that did not seem at first to be in the military conditions necessary for a defense of any length," and commended the citizens of Strasbourg for their courage, patience, and sacrifice.[30] Everyone had done his duty. Signatures of the forty-six present members followed, including current and former mayors Küss and Humann, diligent civil servants Antoine Zopff and Jacques Kablé, and republican journalists Schneegans and Boersch. Only two commissioners declined to sign the petition: Mallarmé, a lawyer, and businessman Lipp.[31]

The municipal commissioners developed a consequentialist response to their situation. They wanted to hold out only so long as it would be strategically useful to France. But if the city's sacrifice could no longer assure the greater good of the nation, the siege should come to an end. Like medieval burghers, city leaders preferred surrender to continued resistance. Having consulted their "soul and conscience," they decided that a protracted siege would needlessly kill more civilians and could end in a vicious assault, including rape, bombardment, and street fighting.[32] Emile Küss represents the consequentialist approach to capitulation: prudent, thoughtful, and willing to explore new ideas while prizing the preservation of the good.

Schneegans, the most articulate defender of the consequentialist position, later expanded upon the commission's decision: "To bury oneself under ruins and bury with oneself 60,000 men, women and children is certainly marvelously heroic, and if this sacrifice were useful to the *patrie* and could save the country, it would absolutely be demanded of each and every one; but if this heroism is purely in vain it becomes reprehensible, and those who impose it on a population assume responsibility for all the uselessly spilled blood. The moment has come for the leaders of the city to tell themselves that there is more courage in capitulating, to save a city, than to face death on the ramparts to augment the glory of their name."[33]

Schneegans not only argued that the siege had reached its logical end, but also attempted to paint the capitulation as noble. Adherence to a predetermined principle of holding out at all costs seemed foolish and deadly. Instead of deriving a course of action from preexisting ethical principles or dutifully adhering to codes of conduct, the municipal commissioners made their decision based on the anticipated consequences of their actions. As in the Just War tradition, they preferred to allow their decisions to be guided by context.

The notion that one should act in such a way as to increase the good in the world is shared by many complex philosophies, notably classical utilitarianism. The definition of the "good" that one should seek to increase, however, is variable, subject to debate, and difficult to measure.

Should one increase the world's happiness or its sustainability? Is security the ultimate good, or is freedom? Can such goods be quantified or compared? This uncertainty over the good and how to calculate it is a fundamental weakness to consequentialist ethics. Consequentialism, it can be argued, is both illogical and amoral. Doesn't the search for a good outcome suggest some kind of *a priori* knowledge of the good? If consequentialists lack preexisting guidelines, what prevents their moral compass from spinning in the wrong direction?

The municipal commissioners did not worry about such arguments; they were politicians, not philosophers. They were not attempting to create a robust theory of ethics but rather grappling with a difficult situation using the ethical tools that made sense to them. In their view, the "good" outcome was obvious: the physical security of family, friends, and property. They accepted that they were civilians, not soldiers, and accordingly expected separation from the worst of war's violence. They sought protection from both unprecedented weaponry and from the ideological imperative to die for a cause. (In this regard they shared a reaction to modern warfare with American thinkers who, in the wake of the carnage of the U.S. Civil War, lost the "belief in beliefs" and developed pragmatism, a philosophy of how people think and make decisions.[34]) The expression of this desire for security, as with the response to the Swiss intervention, emerged in a paternalistic context, so that women and children were the primary groups deemed in need of protection.

Küss and the commissioners' consequentialism was also strongly informed by the republican tradition, in particular the claim that municipal government has a privileged role in decision-making processes. So while Schneegans acknowledged that military regulations "prohibited the citizens of a besieged city from interfering in military questions," he argued that the commission nevertheless could not remain silent.[35] Schneegans claimed authority and legitimacy for the commission by invoking its charge to "defend the interests of the city," as well as to share the burden of responsibility.[36] The commission acknowledged duties to the nation but placed the city first.[37]

Despite their emphasis on republicanism and sincerity, and although they claimed to be the "organ of near universal sentiment," the commissioners decided to keep their call for capitulation a secret from the population.[38] Naturally, the well-connected Rodolphe Reuss found out about it within just a few days, but the general population did not hear about it until the publication of a letter from Uhrich in *Le moniteur* on March 29, 1871, followed by more details in Schneegans's *The War in Alsace* (1871) and Uhrich's *Documents Related to the Siege of Strasbourg* (1872).[39]

Duty to France and to the Military

Uhrich's duties to France and to the military required him to deny the municipal commission's request. His arguments reflected several ethical traditions. In one light, Uhrich's refusal to surrender followed a consequentialist view, with the "good" being the best outcome for French military strategy. Given the disaster at Sedan and the installation of a new regime, it was reasonable to anticipate that France might sue for peace. If France surrendered, it would be better to do so with Strasbourg unconquered. "If Strasbourg falls," Uhrich recognized, "Alsace inevitably becomes Prussian."[40] On the very day that the commissioners asked for capitulation, Bismarck presented French foreign minister Jules Favre with a demand for the annexation of Alsace.[41] If Strasbourg held on, France had room to negotiate. Uhrich was reasonable in this assessment: when the war finally ended, besieged Belfort under the command of Colonel Pierre Denfert-Rochereau was the only Alsatian city still resisting, and it was the only Alsatian city to remain French following the Treaty of Frankfurt. Without knowing just how long the conflict would continue, Uhrich hoped that Strasbourg could outlast the war. Furthermore, Strasbourg's resistance might inspire other besieged cities to hold on. All of these practical consequences contributed to Uhrich's decision.

Second, and just as important, Uhrich adhered to a code of conduct that dictated his actions. French military regulations required Uhrich to continue to fight, upon pain of death, until the Prussians had created a practicable breach in the defenses and attempted "at least one assault."[42] Such regulations had developed out of siege conditions from earlier centuries in which commanders were expected to conclude honorable surrenders when it became clear that they would lose.[43] By 1870, the prudent flexibility of yesteryear had hardened into unbending regulations. Uhrich took his duty seriously. He had resisted Werder's repeated requests for capitulation. After the library fire, Uhrich had deflected the suggestion that the city pay off the Germans to desist from bombing. Uhrich remained under orders to limit his engagement with civilians and had no official responsibility to shield them from bombardment or from assault. The municipal commission had no formal role in shaping these decisions. Uhrich's loyalty to the military code transcended political regimes; he fought for both Napoleon III and for the Government of National Defense.

In this adherence to the military regulations, Uhrich's position was more closely allied to deontology, the ethical tradition in which duty is paramount. Actions are judged against *a priori* principles or codes of conduct rather than against the anticipated outcome. In this case, military regulations set the standards, and it was Uhrich's duty to ensure that his behavior aligned with them. "Honor" for Uhrich meant following the course of action that allied with the purpose undergirding the military regulations, namely, upholding the security and power of France. It furthermore entailed a reciprocal relationship of polite exchange with the enemy commander. He earned respect by according it to Werder. Uhrich's personal experiences or evaluation of the situation came into play only in the service of these rules. He was not to consult his personal code of ethics either, except insofar as it fostered a sense of duty to uphold the military regulations. He certainly was not supposed to follow public opinion. Uhrich later wrote that "the general opinion [within the defense council] was: that the question of military duty and the interest of France should be separated from the question of humanity, and consequently, as I demanded, the defense would be continued."[44]

To be sure, Uhrich's motive might also have been very simple: the self-interested desire to avoid court martial. Yet his presentation of the ethical dilemma between duty and "humanity"—between deontology and the municipal commission's brand of consequentialism—suggests that he experienced a strong internal struggle. "Believe me," he told the commission, "no one feels more deeply than me the misfortunes caused to the city of Strasbourg; but I am not free to follow the fervor of my heart. Military law dominates me, and it is my honor to obey loyally. What I can promise you is . . . to remember what you are suffering, and to content myself with that which will suffice to absolve the soldier."[45] Uhrich thus committed his conflicted loyalties to paper. He furthermore agreed to hear out a delegation of citizens on September 20, and as a result, he distributed some of the army's bread, blankets, and shoes among the civilian population.[46] Antoine Zopff thanked Uhrich for these gifts and defined the gesture as "one more testament to the intimate union . . . between our population and its valiant defender."[47] There is a nobility in Uhrich's acknowledgement of the heavy choice he faced. He was torn over not only the best choice at hand, but also the right way to make the choice. In this difficult moment, he remained loyal to the military regulations.

To the Last Extremity

Uhrich and Küss followed different ethical traditions, but they arrived at nearly the same conclusion. The siege would end, probably very soon, without a fight to the bitter end. Edmond Valentin's arrival revived another possibility: *guerre à outrance,* war to the extreme.

From a young age, Valentin had a knack for turning his life into a statement of intensity. Like Küss, Valentin was born under the Restoration (1822) into a respected Strasbourg family. Like Küss, he risked his life and reputation for republican ideas. Otherwise, their paths diverged. Küss remained a civilian, whereas Valentin served a decade in the army. Küss built a life in Strasbourg, while Valentin spent nearly two decades in exile. Küss followed a well-worn path in his education, household, and career, while Valentin broke out of the family mold. The second son in a Legitimist, Catholic household—his elder sister served as the Superior General of the Congregation of Notre-Dame de Sion—Valentin became a republican freethinker.[48] At age eighteen, rather than pursue business or follow his father into law, Valentin joined the army. Out of some combination of adventurousness, patriotism, and self-sacrifice, Valentin served in place of his elder brother. A routine report issued by his superior officer in 1849 suggests that Valentin already defined his own code of ethics: "passable conduct, doubtful principles, well groomed, has studied well. . . . He is undisciplined, he is poor with his superiors and his peers, very demanding on his inferiors."[49] Not the kind of man to submit quietly to authority, Valentin required others to live up to a high standard.

Valentin's "doubtful principles" may have referred to his radical republicanism, which had found an outlet in the revolution of 1848. In early 1850, Valentin was placed on nonactive duty for his republican opinions and his unwillingness to aid President Louis-Napoleon Bonaparte in bringing counterrevolutionary "order" to the country. Undeterred, Valentin turned to politics. Emile Küss, whom Valentin had met in 1848, nominated him in his successful campaign to represent the Bas-Rhin in the Legislative Assembly. Soon after, Valentin became embroiled in an affair of honor and fought a duel against Bonapartist Count Clary. When President Bonaparte overthrew the Second Republic on December 2, 1851, Valentin was arrested along with many other republicans. Like novelist Victor Hugo, he spent the Second Empire in exile: eight years in Brussels, where he married, and a decade in Britain teaching military history in Woolwich. Valentin maintained ties with Strasbourg through trips to Kehl and risked deportation to visit his sister in Paris.[50]

Upon hearing the news of hostilities between France and Prussia, Valentin returned to Paris and immediately demanded that the minister of war reinstate him into the regiment that he had served in 1850, to no avail.[51] On September 1, he joined prominent Alsatians living in Paris (including *Le temps* editor Alfred Marchand and Victor Schoelcher, the architect of abolition in the colonies) in a petition protesting the "unjustifiable horrors of the bombardment of Strasbourg by the Prussians" as well as the French "refusal to arm Alsatian national guardsmen in localities not yet invaded."[52] But it did not suit Valentin to wait impotently in Paris.

Three days later, Napoleon III's regime crumbled. Valentin and his compatriot Maurice Engelhardt jumped at the opportunity. Using the radical language of the French Revolution, they asked the newly minted minister of the interior, Léon Gambetta, to appoint them as "representatives on mission" to Alsace, much like Louis Antoine de Saint-Just during the Terror. Instead, Gambetta named Engelhardt as mayor of Strasbourg and Valentin as prefect of the Bas-Rhin.

With a fake American passport and his appointment papers literally up his sleeve, Valentin headed east. He and Engelhardt traveled the first leg together. After a day's train ride, they reached Mulhouse, in the Haut-Rhin, and turned their sights seventy miles north toward Strasbourg. Had Valentin really been interested in acting as prefect, he could have headed to Schlestadt (today Sélestat), one of the few towns in the Bas-Rhin not occupied by the Prussians. Instead, Valentin gave over to Engelhardt his responsibilities for the small portion of the Bas-Rhin that remained in French hands, while he himself continued on to Strasbourg. "I am a soldier," he told Engelhardt. "I have a special mission to fulfill for General Uhrich; I leave alone."[53] Valentin found heroic adventure more appealing than paperwork in Schlestadt.

Meanwhile, at his headquarters in Rheims, Moltke got wind of Valentin's appointment, perhaps simply by reading the notice in Le journal officiel, and telegraphed Werder: "The revolutionary committee in Paris has sent to Alsace, as civil and military commissioners, two individuals named Valentin and Engelhardt. Arrest them and treat them with all the rigor of the law."[54] Valentin was attempting to enter a besieged city with the Prussians on his trail.

The adventure that unfolded over the next twelve days far outstrips Léon Gambetta's famous departure from Paris via hot-air balloon. It echoes the traditional heroic journey that mythologist Joseph Campbell tells us is common to cultures worldwide. Schneegans called Valentin's travels "a heroic story and a splendid odyssey . . . a kind of epic episode that a Homer or a Tacitus might dream up, a radiant deed in the middle of the darkness of our defeats and our weaknesses."[55] Nobody, of course, truly believed that Valentin was a mythical hero. Still, his contemporaries accepted, to a point, the heroic narrative he fashioned about himself.

Leaving his companion behind, Valentin entered on foot into a shadowy, mysterious territory: the Alsatian countryside had transformed into an alien, impenetrable land with dangers lurking behind every half-timbered house.[56] Such a landscape provided the perfect backdrop to displays of heroic courage. Through a combination of tricks, physical prowess, and help at just the right moments, our hero survived a series of tests. In his circuitous route, Valentin paid no mind to warnings from villagers about the impossibility of his quest. After all,

Valentin was a master of disguises who spoke perfect English. He posed as an American so convincingly that he fooled not only the Prussians—twice—but also his unsuspecting Alsatian guide as they traveled together for eight long days. As with the solitary hero of myth, Valentin did not experience male comradeship; he maintained a secretive distance even from those who helped him. Briefly held by Prussians in Kehl, Valentin narrowly escaped recognition from locals who knew him from his many visits while in exile. He managed to evade detection for two days in Werder's own headquarters, hidden in the very building where the general took his meals. The final step was Schiltigheim, just north of Strasbourg, where unsuspecting villagers provided this mysterious ruddy-cheeked traveler with food and shelter.[57]

Finally closing in on Strasbourg in the cover of night, Valentin correctly interpreted the red glow of cigars and pipes to indicate the location of the German lines. He slipped through undetected and crawled alone across a potato field, taking the occasional nip of kirsch from his flask. Valentin dodged bullets as he swam across one of the many waterways toward the French lines. Safely on the other side, he eventually attracted the attention of French sentinels, who held him outside the locked city gates overnight.[58] Just as Odysseus employed disguise and physical courage to enter his palace in Ithaca after a long period of exile, so did Valentin return to his native Strasbourg after a voyage of twenty years. Finally, as soldiers took Valentin to Uhrich, Valentin experienced his own Calvary: the people of his own city mistook the sodden and muddy captive for a spy. Yet, as Campbell tells us, "When [the hero] arrives at the nadir of the mythological round, he undergoes a supreme ordeal and gains his reward."[59] Beard and moustache intact, Valentin was ready to lead Strasbourg out of its darkest moment.

It is at this point that the metaphor of Valentin as mythic hero broke down. The moment that Valentin revealed his appointment papers to Uhrich, the parallels between his voyage and, say, the death and resurrection of the Egyptian god Osiris, wore thin. He passed from the realm of mythology, dream, and symbolism squarely into the reality of history, event, and biography. Valentin's quest to slay the Germanic dragon and liberate the fair city of Strasbourg—or to die trying—became unintelligible to those who had experienced the day-by-day reality of the siege.

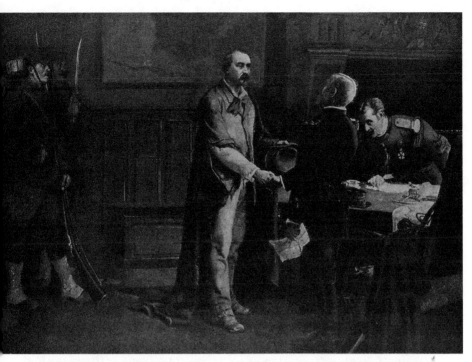

This reproduction of the painting *Valentin's Arrival in Uhrich's Office* by Georges-Louis Poilleux Saint-Ange, which appeared in the Salon of 1880, implies support for the prefect's call to hold out to the last extremity. In reality, both military and civilian leaders in Strasbourg mistrusted this radical position. (Charles Deering McCormick Library of Special Collections, Northwestern University Library)

It is worth noting that Valentin's adventure was not unprecedented. Artillery General de Barral slipped into Strasbourg during the night of August 14 disguised as a worker.[60] Madame Dutailly, a *cantinière* attached to the Third Zouaves, snuck into Strasbourg sometime in September. It was not her first adventure: she had fought at Froeschwiller and killed two Germans while tending to French wounded, then was captured at Sedan but escaped. Dutailly may have made her way into Strasbourg at about the same time as Valentin.[61] Valentin received far more attention than the others because of his public position in the new republican government, his fulfillment of a masculine act at a moment when French men were failing to protect their country, and the consternation that his call to hold out caused among civilians.

All of these factors meant that diarists and memoirists had to comment one way or another about Valentin. His arrival unsettled the authorities in Strasbourg in two ways. First, he threatened to upset the new, locally accepted republican regime. Valentin unseated Boersch as prefect and brought the news that Maurice Engelhardt had been named mayor instead of Küss. It was easy enough for republicans to accept Valentin over Boersch as prefect. Valentin's old friendship with Küss, years of exile for the republican cause, and adventurous entry into the city brought him credibility, even among younger politicians like Schneegans. Furthermore, the commissioners recognized that the central government typically made prefectoral appointments.[62]

The commissioners could not, however, accept Maurice Engelhardt as mayor. Although Engelhardt's republican credentials were sound, he had battled with Küss during the elections of 1869. In a three-way race for their member of the Legislative Corps, Engelhardt had supported the radical republican candidate, while Küss and Schneegans had backed Charles Boersch against the incumbent official candidate, Renouard de Bussierre. Republicans therefore split their vote, allowing the reelection of Bussierre. They clashed again in early 1870 over the controversial plebiscite approving Napoleon III's reforms. In addition, Engelhardt had not suffered the hardships of the siege. He had left Strasbourg for Paris in early August, just after the battle of Froeschwiller.[63] The municipal commission had decided on September 14, perhaps with Engelhardt in mind, that "healthy individuals who left Strasbourg since the opening of the war without good reason are declared unworthy of fulfilling any public function."[64] Furthermore, the commission objected to Gambetta making the appointment at all. The centralized naming of mayors was a mark of authoritarian governments, not of the republic that they had hoped for.[65] The municipal commission voted to reject Engelhardt and keep Küss on September 22 and requested backing from Uhrich, who complied. The next day, Uhrich's confirmation of Küss was printed for the public to see. Valentin, too, recognized the legitimacy of his old comrade. Even if Valentin had been inclined to defend Engelhardt, it was hard to argue that the latter could be an effective mayor from his outpost in Schlestadt.[66]

Second, and more importantly, Valentin exhorted the inhabitants of Strasbourg to hold out *à outrance,* "to the last extremity."[67] Although his appointment papers said nothing about Valentin's relationship to the French army, he presented himself as the man to lead Strasbourg to this heroic end. Instead of focusing on his duty to external rules or calculating the best outcome for all, Valentin practiced virtue ethics. He believed that his actions should follow the demands that society placed on a virtuous man, which he interpreted to mean the courage to die rather than surrender. He cast himself as a latter-day Saint-Just on mission in Alsace, ready to root out the insufficiently committed and model virtuous behavior. He did not want to envision a future in which Strasbourg was a bargaining chip for a defeated France. He felt no obligation to judge his honor against his adherence to a preexisting code of conduct. Valentin saw himself as a military man, but he refused to follow the rules. This position formed the basis for the honor system in which men demanded satisfaction for slights to their reputations. Valentin, who had survived a duel of honor as a younger man, now embodied an ideal expressed well by Captain Bergasse du Petit-Thouars: "To undergo the trials of a siege without weakening, you must withdraw into yourself, becoming absorbed in a single thought, that of resistance: do not discuss, do not see the suffering, the miseries of those around you; live in the past dreaming of the price of the bloody sacrifices our fathers made for the grandeur of the country; live in the future, dreaming of the maledictions that will follow those who, called to the honor of defending the borders, hesitated to cover them with their bodies!"[68]

Valentin's biography de-emphasizes factors that would diminish this heroic story, notably his appointment as prefect, hardly known as a dashing, virile position. We never see the forty-eight-year-old, paunchy Valentin behind a desk drafting formulaic memoranda. One of the few letters he penned during his brief tenure in Strasbourg is, by the standards of the day, notably informal and brisk: "My dear friend," he addressed Küss, "I would be happy if during the course of the day I could speak for a few moments with you."[69] Valentin did not fit into the narrow world of the government bureaucrat, steeped in hierarchy and procedure, parceling out funds to subordinates. In contrast with the ineffectual Pron, Valentin inspired hope for a different future. Schneegans did not agree with Valentin's desire to hold out, but he admitted that their country would never have been defeated "if all of France's servants had been thus."[70]

At the same time, it is notable that Valentin did not perform the tasks that a prefect might need to undertake on behalf of his beleaguered people. Valentin hardly bears comparison with Jean Moulin, prefect of the Eure-et-Loir in 1940, who desperately tried to provide bread, shelter, and gasoline to the citizens of Chartres as the Nazis invaded. Valentin apparently did little of this nature during the week he spent in Strasbourg. Even his faithful biographer could not find much for Valentin to do other than "walk around the worst bombed-out neighborhoods" and "keep the diary of his travels up to date."[71]

Valentin's arrival on September 20 drew people out of their cellars and sparked fresh rumors that the army would soon relieve Strasbourg.[72] It is impossible to know how closely political inclination correlated with willingness to hold out, but there is evidence that Valentin appealed to those who were unhappy with the moderate republican victory. One ardent, anonymous republican, laboring under the belief that Uhrich had been holding back, believed that Valentin's arrival would allow the garrison to fully resist, to "shoot at will."[73] The news also appealed to Bonapartist Raymond-Signouret of *L'impartial du Rhin,* who had been left out of the municipal commission when his rivals Boersch, Schneegans, and Silbermann at *Le courrier du Bas-Rhin* had been included. Raymond-Signouret published editorials calling for the city to hold out and needling republicans for appearing to waver.[74]

Such enthusiasm dismayed the municipal commission. It threatened the cozy understanding the politicians were building with Uhrich. Moreover, the concept of *outrance,* or excess, affronted bourgeois moderation and rationality.[75] Schneegans expressed frustration that, when Valentin arrived, "we suddenly saw reappear that same system of [falsely] comforting telegrams that for a month had worn out our patience."[76] Vague and unjustified statements of hope did no good to the population. Many French fell for even the most *abracadabrante* announcement: "When a nation thus abandons itself, like a child, to its illusions and only wants to feed on chimeras, it is open to whomever wants to take it."[77] Reuss heard about Valentin's arrival almost immediately, but reacted with his typical skepticism. His friend Carrière, he wrote, "calls me a Prussian because this does not excite me."[78]

Valentin's old comrade Emile Küss tried to convince the prefect that the city faced overwhelming difficulties: no hope for an army to relieve the city and the likelihood that continued resistance would bring more hardships. Valentin was undeterred.[79] Similarly, in his first meeting with the municipal commission, Valentin admitted that he could offer no help to the city from the outside but still argued they must hold on to preserve France's "eastern boulevard."[80] The likely dire outcome of an all-out German assault did not concern him. He made no mention of the luxury of home, the value of cultural institutions, or the preciousness of family. He placed no special emphasis on the protection of women and children. The consequentialist argument carried little weight for Valentin, who was puzzled by the "opposition or at least the very marked coldness with which I appear to be welcomed by the municipal commission."[81]

For their part, the commissioners could applaud Valentin's dramatic arrival, but they refused to be drawn into the prefect's heroic vortex.[82] A story from the siege of Leningrad some seventy years later captures this tension. Olga Mikhailovna Freidenberg, who had survived over a year of horrific siege conditions, encountered an outsider in 1943: "[Mariia Veniaminovna] Yudina was pre-war; I was out-and-out a person of the siege. She talked and revealed herself, while I kept silent. I could not find the words. Yudina said that she accepted evil as an inevitability demanded by life. She was rereading *The Idiot,* lived in the world of aesthetics, *understood and accepted heroism* [italics added]. I felt the desecrated soul within me, dying desires, my appreciation of life humiliated and destroyed forever."[83] Yudina, who had not suffered through months of starvation and bombardment, could still find something aesthetically pleasing in facing the evil in the world. Such heroism was no longer possible for Freidenberg.

In Strasbourg, Schneegans and others no longer believed that Valentin or any other man could save the city. The only heroes they recognized were those who had been there all along, experiencing bombardment and striving to ameliorate the suffering of others: the firefighters, the doctors, and the civil servants. For most people in

Strasbourg, virtue meant bravery through the bombardment, carrying on the business of the city, and preparing to protect the population in case of assault. In this view, Valentin's brand of virtue ethics appeared reckless and counterproductive.

The End of the Siege

Captain Bergasse du Petit-Thouars, who had found comfort in the heroic fortitude of Strasbourg's women, now had to maintain the courage of his own men on the northernmost French defenses. Isolated in lunettes out in the flooded defensive plain or stationed back on the heavily bombarded walls, the French defensive artillery labored to slow the Prussian advance. In the night of September 11–12, Prussian engineers constructed the third parallel, which brought their front lines just shy of the defensive flooded area. Within a few days, the Prussians destroyed the outermost French artillery. Communications and provisions to the lunettes became difficult as bridges and gates were rendered unusable. It took 10,000 shells, but eventually the Prussians opened a breach in one of the lunettes.[84] "Like a pearl necklace whose string has been broken," wrote Uhrich, French external strongholds fell. The men retreated to the main walls, leaving the lunettes behind.[85] To ford the floods, a chain of Prussian soldiers built makeshift bridges of sand, stone, and bundles of brushwood. At last, on September 20 and 21, they climbed into two key French lunettes, numbers 53 and 52. The French primary wall of defense was now vulnerable to direct attack from close range.[86]

To the very end, the Prussians used noncombatants as pawns in their strategy, and the French regulations offered Uhrich no guidance on protecting civilians. Werder put a definitive end to emigration to Switzerland on September 22, the same day that he learned of Valentin's arrival. With its typical laconicism, the German logbook noted only that Valentin was trying to thwart Uhrich's intention to capitulate.[87] The following day, Friedrich I, Grand Duke of Baden, who thus far had not intervened, sent Uhrich a long letter calling for surrender. Playing good cop to Werder's bad cop, the Grand Duke assured Uhrich that he had "fulfilled his duty as an officer," defending Strasbourg with "energy and courage." Now, his only responsibility was "before God."[88] Immediate capitulation would prevent a direct assault and help secure better terms for the garrison and the civilians, not to mention for Uhrich himself. Surrender would assuage Uhrich's conscience about the deaths he could prevent. Malartic observed that the Grand Duke twisted the siege to appear as though Uhrich was responsible for maiming and killing civilians, not Werder.[89] Indeed, Friedrich suggested that military law lies beyond the control of humankind, a nonpartisan force in which civilians get caught up as collateral damage.

Uhrich responded to the Grand Duke with surprising candor. "Believe me," he wrote, "it would be very pleasant for me to be able to follow your advice, and to make the sufferings of the resigned and proud population of Strasbourg cease; believe me, it costs a lot to resist all that you tell me. No one is more painfully impressed than I am by the sight of ruins around me, by the spectacle of harmless men, women and poor little children who fall, hit by cannonballs and grapeshot." Uhrich was more explicit here about his feelings towards civilians than in any of the rest of his correspondence. He admitted, "My unfortunate country is in a critical situation." Still, he refused to capitulate. He did not believe that he had yet satisfied all that honor required, and at age sixty-nine, honor became more important than any other ambition. Uhrich personally would have surrendered, but "I do not have the pretention of speaking for myself." Instead, he wrote as "a soldier who obeys the military laws of his country," considering himself devoted to France rather than to any particular French government.[90]

By September 27, the Prussians could fire 146 cannon and 83 mortars against Strasbourg, including 8 cannon positioned on the glacis inside lunettes 52 and 53. The walls shook without cease. Werder's men prepared to cross the moat by lashing together floating bridges of empty barrels taken from the brasseries of surrounding villages.[91] Inside the walls, civilians became desperate. Max Reichard recorded in his diary at noon, "We can no longer think further than the present moment!"[92] He prayed for deliverance and commended the outcome to God. Then, at two o'clock in the afternoon, Uhrich received word from his officers that "the breach in bastion 11 was practicable, that an assault could be given the next morning, that evening, or in two hours: that we were at the mercy of the enemy."[93] In the defense council, each member

Beschießung von Straßburg 1870.—Bombardement de Strasbourg 1870.
Brèche et Passage du Fossé.—Grabenübergang u. Bresche.

After creating a breach in lunette 53, Prussian and Badenese soldiers build a makeshift passage over the flooded areas. (Archives de la Ville et de la Communauté urbaine de Strasbourg)

supported capitulation, with one exception—General de Barral—who suggested that they might hold out until the next day. Later, according to Uhrich, Barral himself admitted that as he uttered these words, he feared that the defense council would take him up on it. They did not.[94]

The German logbook offers the basic facts: "An intermediary delivered the letter from General Uhrich indicating the unconditional surrender of the city, citadel and garrison."[95] For the besieging soldiers, the emotion was less restrained. "Nobody who was not there before Strasbourg on September 27 can have an idea of the profound joy that filled the hearts of the German soldiers," wrote an artilleryman. "Each one was pierced with a feeling of gratitude toward God who blessed our arms. It was as if we woke from a nightmare; soldiers climbed up onto the parapets of their trenches and batteries, joyous hurrahs resounded; we shook hands and embraced."[96] On the French side, the news of capitulation spread through the ranks on the northern defenses, leaving silence in its wake.[97]

In the end, did Uhrich follow military regulations? After consistently prolonging the siege in order to maintain military honor and maximize Strasbourg's strategic potential, Uhrich's humanity (or consequentialism) seems to have won out at the very end. Contrary to regulations, he did not wait for the Germans to assault bastion 11 before surrendering. It was a wise decision. The German logbook confirms that a direct assault was imminent.[98] Nobody knew whether the besiegers would be able to restrain themselves from rape and pillage; after all, as David Bell reminds us, "Armies never pose a greater threat to prisoners and noncombatants than when they have won a major engagement, are shuddering with pent-up tension and fear, and have their enemy at their mercy."[99] From Versailles, the Crown Prince fretted that "unfortunately the storming of the citadel might yet cost much blood."[100] Certainly, the defense council feared the "pillage, fire, massacre and all the horrors that are the usual consequences of [assault]."[101] A continuation of the siege at this point, maintained Colonel Du Casse, would have required "an inhumanity out of season," beyond the demands of "reason and honor."[102] Uhrich told the defense council, "I would have wanted to prolong the defense, but I believe that nobody in my place could have done it without infringing on the laws of humanity."[103]

The White Flag

Frédéric Piton was roosting in his usual observation spot up in his attic at five o'clock on September 27 when he spotted two firemen on the exposed cathedral platform. They hurried across, climbed up the northeast tower, and unfurled a white flag. (Where did they get a white flag? Surely the army did not keep one specially for the purpose of capitulation. Perhaps one of Uhrich's underlings had quietly sewn together a row of sheets.) Piton knew immediately that his city was lost. All their suffering and patience had been in vain.[104]

For many, the surrender came as a relief. "Humanity finally conquered honor," recorded one observer.[105] Red Cross leaders were glad they would no longer have to add a daily tally of wounded to their overburdened hospitals.[106] Rodolphe Reuss noted the "indecent joy" of Max Reichard and other pastors.[107] But the sight of the white flag caught many civilians by surprise. At first sight, Madame Kiéné hoped that the flag signaled "an honorable peace or some kind of victory."[108] Cécile de Dartein, who had never lost hope of relief, had thought that the city would suffer "twice the bombardment" before surrendering to the Prussians.[109] Just one hour before the capitulation, in the four o'clock edition, *L'impartial du Rhin* insisted that Strasbourg "will resist so long as there remains a glimmer of hope."[110]

From their offices in the Hôtel du Commerce, Küss and the municipal commission watched and waited. It was an emotional moment. "We cried tears of rage and sadness," reported Schneegans. "Our fate had been decided! We, who had not wanted this war, we became its first victims!"[111] Küss and Uhrich "cried in each others arms."[112] In Place Gutenberg below, the chants of the angry and unbowed grew louder: "Down with traitors! Death to the mayor! Death to the general!"[113] Max Reichard was nervous. "We see people with shotguns bared," he recorded. "With threatening gestures they are pointing to the cathedral."[114] The authorities grew worried. Again, Reichard: "One deputy mayor . . . looked like a cadaver from inner agony. . . . [He] told me, as he pointed to an angry group, 'for the first time I have my revolver in my pocket! We had a hard, hard, day!'"[115] "The timid ones from before became the partisans of resistance to the end," reported Schneegans. "One could see more than one face, pale from staying in the cellar, illuminated suddenly with the fire of an unaccustomed courage."[116] The crowd demanded Valentin, hoping he would oppose the capitulation. Instead, when Valentin appeared, he counseled acceptance: "I am as republican as you are . . . but resistance is impossible, we must surrender. . . . Believe me, it must be done! You only have one thing to do, that is to avoid bringing greater misfortunes on the city!"[117] Like Uhrich, Valentin accepted defeat in the end.

Reuss hurried to Place Gutenberg to see the flag for himself. He later recorded the confusion of the following hours: "At half past six o'clock the drummer of our [National Guard] company passed Place Saint-Thomas, beating the call with rage: ferocious countenance of this old soldier. I took my rifle: slowly the National Guard assembled near the customs house; what was going on? Some spoke of a mass sortie, others of a riot."[118] Although Mayor Küss called up the National Guard to maintain order, some individual guardsmen hoped to rally a last defense. Around nine o'clock, the guardsmen marched to the cathedral. Some tried to force open the doors and take down the flag, but their lieutenant prevented their passage. Foiled in this plan, someone shot a few rounds at the spire. Did he recognize the irony? Ordered to break ranks and go home, one guardsman cried out, "Let's fight and save ourselves afterwards!"[119] Reuss himself, having learned the details from Küss's son, accepted the capitulation with a heavy heart. He went on watch at eleven o'clock to help prevent any hotheaded resistance. Several members of the municipal commission made the rounds that night.[120]

Soon the city returned to its "ordinary tranquility."[121] Of course, tranquility was anything but ordinary after weeks of shelling. "One is amazed," remarked Albert Schillinger, "to be able to walk in the middle of the street—slowly, in security—to no longer slide fearfully along the houses."[122] The peril of bombardment had ceased, but civilians anticipated a new threat: the German occupation. The distant sounds of Prussian victory songs around bonfires heightened "consciousness of permanent danger."[123] Denuded tree branches reminded Schneegans of a gallows.[124]

▪ ▪ ▪

In the end, the moment of capitulation did not quite fit anyone's protocol. The white flag flew long before Strasbourg had reached the last extremity of resistance, well after it had clearly lost, and just a little too soon to accord with military regulations. After all, Küss, Uhrich, and Valentin were not just representations of ethical traditions, but flesh and blood men faced with agonizing decisions. They all understood the value of virtuous behavior, duty, and practical consequences, though they each tended to favor one over the other when defending their course of action.

The siege can be read as a metaphor for human frailty and limitations. We are, after all, incomplete in our knowledge of the outside world, sensitive to the example of our ancestors, concerned about the judgment of the future, subject to the whims of fortune, vulnerable to powerful external forces, and uncertain about when to fight and when to compromise. In the besieged circumstances of our lives, we make decisions rooted in our experiences, our duties, and our self-perception, often a combination of all three. Küss, Uhrich, and Valentin disagreed over the moment to capitulate, not because they had different information, not because some were deceitful or treasonous, not because one reasoned better than the others. They differed on capitulation because they disagreed over the standards by which they should decide. When faced with differences in opinion, it is not enough for us to throw up our hands and accept that there are disagreements without having to think very hard about it. We should strive to understand why we disagree and become more aware of the combinations of ethical frameworks we use to defend our decisions.

Our awareness of ethical traditions requires us to discern the historically specific manifestations of ethics from the elements that transcend time and place. Consequentialism depends on the experience of what we have previously found to be good. For Küss, the good included the protection of family, culture, and property, and prized the ability to plan ahead, acquire physical objects, and develop personal traits. This good placed special emphasis on women as victims, a perspective that need not be shared by all societies. Uhrich elected to follow his duty as a soldier within a particular military tradition, but others in different times and places might obey a religious tradition or honor code. The virtues of Valentin—courage, confidence, sacrifice for the sake of the nation—could be mixed in different proportions with others, such as sexual fidelity or civic education. The fact that this conflict occurred in an era in which women were largely excluded from political, military, and economic life means that the most robust sources to examine the ethical dilemma posed by capitulation were written by men. Women also explored the range of ethical traditions, as hinted in Weiss's imperative to protect her children or Kiéné's desire to hold out for the sake of France.

In Strasbourg, Uhrich made the final call. Still, Küss's consequentialism influenced the general and affected the timing of the surrender. Yet, in the decades that followed, the dominant story of the siege of Strasbourg became one of lost honor. In France, the lived experiences of the siege gave way to abstract stories of wounded national pride.

CHAPTER EIGHT

Strassburg

A S MORNING BROKE ON September 28, civilians began their new lives as German subjects. The republic that many had awaited for two decades was now taken from their grasp. After the departure of General Uhrich and the French army, Mayor Emile Küss and other municipal leaders were left to mediate between the population and the new occupying forces. Civilians in Strasbourg escaped retribution for falling on the losing side of the siege, but their situation remained precarious. Rather than hastening the war's end, the surrender of Strasbourg steeled the provisional French Government of National Defense to fight on for four more months. New armies of poorly trained Frenchmen arose, and bands of *francs-tireurs* threatened to turn this conventional conflict into a people's war. The German armies found themselves in a longer and bloodier fight than they had anticipated. In this situation, it was all the more important for municipal leaders in Strasbourg to tread carefully. Over the course of the winter, Küss continued to protect the city with his tacit policies of calm and compromise. In the end, however, the loss proved too much for him. Küss died on the very day that his beloved city formally joined the German Empire.

In the fall and winter of 1870, the citizens of Strasbourg adjusted to occupation and attempted to reestablish ordinary life. As Michael Walzer reminds us, "Ordinary life is a value, too. It is what most of the citizens of a defeated country most ardently hope for."[1] Unprecedented international aid helped civilians to rebuild. But the price of normalcy was acquiescence to the German Empire. Pride, sorrow, relief, and mistrust converged as newcomers rushed in and longtime citizens debated whether or not they still belonged. In the months and years that followed, the people who had experienced the siege did not control the story of their city and its annexation. Instead, national humiliation and anger over the loss of Strasbourg dominated the discussion of the city's experience. The postwar investigation into Uhrich's conduct and representations of Valentin in the 1890s both turned the siege from a multifaceted experience into a narrower question of honor.

Dignity and Disorder

Nobody slept well in that first night of silence. At two o'clock on the morning of August 28, in a boxcar in Koenigshoffen, representatives from Uhrich and Werder signed the capitulation agreement. The National Guard and the *francs-tireurs* were to be disarmed and sent home on their own recognizance, while military doctors were free to continue their work. To the officers, including Uhrich, the Prussians offered the option of an honorable release if they promised not to engage in further hostilities. Uhrich and about half of his officers accepted this bargain. But some 17,000 soldiers, including the *cantinières* and the customs agents, were to leave their arms behind and march off to Germany as prisoners of war.[2]

Rodolphe Reuss and his friend Pastor Albert Schillinger came out to witness the departure of the French army. On walls throughout the city, they read Uhrich's proclamation to the inhabitants of Strasbourg. The general thanked the citizenry for its "manly attitude," which "allowed me to delay to the last moment the fall of our city. Civil honor and military honor are safe, thanks to you." He thanked his subordinates, from his defense council to the mobilized customs agents, along with the municipal leaders, doctors, and volunteers. "For your part," he concluded, "remember without bitterness your old general, who would have been so happy to spare you the pain, suffering and dangers that have struck you, but who had to close his heart to this sentiment."[3] Uhrich's time had passed. He had little practical advice for the people he now left behind.

Mayor Küss now stepped in as the primary mediator between bitter civilians and the German army. A few groups of angry citizens still prowled the streets, and Werder was commonly called *General Mörder*— General Murderer.[4] Kiéné wrote in her diary for September 27, "It would be better to massacre us all than to be obliged to live, even if for only twenty-four hours, under the domination of the Prussians!"[5] Küss's first act was to call on the city to remain calm during the entrance of German soldiers. In a poster, he publicly supported Uhrich's decision to capitulate, underscoring the imminence of the assault and the impossibility of further resistance. Uhrich's capitulation had thus far won Strasbourg mild treatment, but the situation remained tenuous: "Recall that the least act of aggression will make our situation worse and will attract terrible reprisals on the entire population. The laws of war state that any house from which a shot is fired will be razed and its inhabitants will be put to the sword. Let everyone remember this. . . . The hour of resistance has passed. Let us be resigned to suffer what could not be avoided. . . . You hold in your hands the fortunes of Strasbourg and yourselves. Do not forget!"[6]

By late morning, Reuss and Schillinger joined the crowd at Nationale Gate. German detachments had already taken possession of the major city gates, and Werder awaited his moment. At half past eleven o'clock, Uhrich arrived at the head of the French army. Werder dismounted from his horse, walked quickly with arms open to embrace Uhrich, and proclaimed his respect for the French general and his garrison. The crowd remained silent. One by one, Werder's staff and the Grand Duke of Baden paid their respects to their defeated colleague. Next, the French officers marched through the gates in a dignified display. Such rituals of surrender were intended to reaffirm respect between victor and vanquished.[7]

Then, the long trail of French soldiers began to depart. They had been drinking. Cursing and breaking rank, the soldiers disrupted the ceremony's quiet restraint. Most had already broken their rifles and dumped them into the Ill River.[8] Civilians joined in. "Many among us," recorded Raymond-Signouret, "helped them to break their rifles and their sabers . . . , to disperse and drown the rest of their munitions in the muck of the gutters; so much the less handed over to the Germans."[9]

Perhaps the soldiers' conduct was understandable, as they faced a long march into Germany without guarantee of food or shelter along the way. In the crowd, Auguste Schneegans found himself standing next to American consul C. M. Felix Petard. "This is the second time," offered Petard, "that I have witnessed the capitulation of an army. The first time, it was Lee's army that surrendered to the troops of the North: those men came to us holding their rifles low to the ground, as for a burial, marching in good order, silent and serious. We saluted them as heroes. Here . . ." Schneegans did not repeat the consul's final words.[10] Even Werder's typically laconic logbook noted the indiscipline of the French soldiers now in Prussian custody.[11]

For their part, Reuss and Schillinger felt ashamed at this spectacle. They did not blame the soldiers for their failure to defend the city, only for their disgraceful conduct in defeat. "How sad it is to see this drama finish with so little dignity!" reported Reuss. "We shed hot tears, Schillinger and I, crying one last time: *Vive la France!* I left, I couldn't hold on anymore; I returned for lunch."[12] By six o'clock, Reuss found himself forced to share a glass of wine with eight Prussians.[13]

"Strasbourg Is Ours"

For many Germans from Versailles to Berlin, the news of Strasbourg's fall seemed to set the world to right. King Wilhelm sent Werder a personal telegram of congratulations along with a promotion and the promise of one hundred Iron Crosses for his troops.[14] Crown Prince Friedrich Wilhelm, whose armies were besieging Paris, received the news of Strasbourg's fall just before his morning ride "in warm autumn weather through the noble avenues of the park of Versailles."[15] He was relieved that the city had fallen without great losses; Moltke reported Prussian casualties of 39 officers and 894 men. He also knew that Strasbourg's capture strengthened the Prussian hand in negotiations with the French and allowed the Germans to funnel supplies to the armies surrounding Paris.[16]

To be sure, the German press representing democrats, socialists, or Catholics, wary of a Germany united under Bismarck, opposed the annexation of Alsace. For many others, however, the capture of

Strasbourg confirmed God's favorable view toward the coming German Empire.[17] "I am overjoyed at the recovery of this German city," the crown prince recorded, "which I pray heaven will now for ever remain German, and where, with God's good help, we shall know how to awaken true German sentiments of mind and soul, and the inhabitants come to realize that in the old, ancestral Fatherland better conditions prevail than in an alien land."[18] Berlin's *Volks-Zeitung* announced, "The crown of German cities is today one pearl richer. Strasbourg is ours."[19] Neatly smoothing out the historical reality of the fragmented Holy Roman Empire, the newspaper announced that this capture put an end to the "old humiliation" of Louis XIV's wars from two hundred years earlier.[20]

On the ground, things looked messier. For German journalists following the army into Strasbourg, the handover unleashed a bewildering series of emotions. What a state! Few houses remained standing. Guns of all kinds were strewn about, with destruction on all sides.[21] "The ghastly devastation served by our cannonballs cannot be described in words," reported Moritz Wiggers to his readers in Berlin; it "recalled Pompeii."[22] Wiggers and other journalists made it clear that Prussian cannon had rendered parts of the city uninhabitable. Still, he argued, the French had no one to blame but *der Dezembermann,* Napoleon III, for causing the war. Uhrich, too, should have allowed the city to fall long before this point.[23] Wiggers described the takeover with unabashed pride: "It was almost overpowering when we crossed over the Cathedral Square and our music 'Die Wacht am Rhein' played. . . . I had to hold back my tears."[24] Later, Wiggers was reminded again of the hardships of the siege. He tried to order a beefsteak but had to content himself with horsemeat instead. He was pleased to report, however, that within a few days, stores reopened and the city dwellers seemed livelier.[25]

Strasbourg Is Worth a Service

The job of the occupier, argues Richard Cobb, is to convince the population that all will continue as before. During the Nazi occupation of France, "business as usual" was a policy designed to help the population reassure themselves of the occupiers' good intentions.[26] In 1870, too, the German military sought to return Strasbourg to normal life as quickly as possible, despite the continuing war. In August, the Governor General of Alsace, Count Friedrich Alexander von Bismarck-Bohlen, had told the region's inhabitants that their laws and religion would be respected.[27] He now encouraged the citizens of Strasbourg to "attend to their daily occupations." This normalcy came with an unforgettable price: "From now on, Strasbourg is and will remain a German city."[28] On October 2, the city first saw the black and white flag of Prussia along with the red, black, and white flag of the North German Confederation flying above the cathedral.[29] Although France did not formally accept this reality until March 1, the remaking of Strasbourg as a German city began as soon as the Prussians marched in.

The first order of business was to replace the representatives of the French central government. When Valentin requested safe conduct, Werder called him to his office only to have "this highly insolent man" arrested and sent off to Germany.[30] Former prefect Pron was allowed to escape to Lake Geneva. Werder himself prepared to move on to operations in southern Alsace and the Vosges Mountains. Bismarck-Bohlen and Civil Commissar Friedrich von Kühlwetter established the imperial administration in Alsace, with first General von Mertens and then Royal Governor von Ollech serving as Strasbourg's governor.[31]

The Germans relied on the municipal government to be the keystone in the unbroken arch of administration. When Küss, Boersch, and Zopff met with Werder at nine o'clock on the morning of the handover, the commission's continuation in power did not even come up for discussion; Werder had no interest in disrupting their authority.[32] Nor did the municipal commission question its role in this transfer of power. In a brief discussion that afternoon, commissioner Klein observed that they should "probably execute the orders given by the military authority pure and simple."[33] It was self-evident to the city's leaders that they would mediate between the military authorities and the civilian population to reestablish order and public safety.

On that first day of occupation, Küss and the municipal commission began to learn more about their new responsibilities. Zopff reported back to the municipal commission with relief that the city would not have to pay a war indemnity or empty its public coffers. Civilians would be treated mildly. More orders came throughout the day. The commission was to communicate to the population that the state of siege continued. All crimes were punishable by martial law; all arms should be surrendered. The city was under a nine o'clock curfew, German officers excepted. Any shots fired would lead to the execution of all males in the offending household. The municipality was also responsible for restoring the city's public lighting, clearing the streets, translating orders from German to French and finding lodging for eight thousand men. All letters or petitions from civilians to the municipal or military authorities had to be written in German.[34]

To seal the relationship between city and occupier, the Germans held a special service at the church of Saint-Thomas. A bastion of the Lutheran church in Strasbourg and situated in a neighborhood relatively unscathed by the bombardment, Saint-Thomas provided the ideal space to celebrate and give thanks for the German victory. The date of the service, September 30, was highly symbolic. Not only was it Queen Augusta's birthday, but it was also the date that Strasbourg had fallen into French hands in 1681. In the front pews, surrounded by Werder, Mertens, Prince Wilhelm of Baden, and hundreds of unarmed Prussian soldiers, sat Mayor Küss and at least fifteen of his fellow Protestant municipal commissioners, including Auguste Schneegans.[35]

The commissioners listened as Emil Frommel, the newly appointed chaplain to Prussian troops, portrayed the conquest of Strasbourg as a victory for the inner German soul. With the strains of "Ein' feste Burg ist unser Gott" echoing around them, the commissioners heard Frommel praise the German sacrifice for king and fatherland. Frommel recalled the "wonderful feeling" he experienced upon seeing the white flag wave from the cathedral, an emotion that flowed not from the work of human hands but rather from "Him, who dwells in the hearts of man like rivulets of water."[36] Frommel asked God to help the people of Strasbourg view the Prussians not as victors, but as liberators and brothers.[37]

The service at Saint-Thomas, like the occupation of Strasbourg in general, bears multiple interpretations. As with the debate over capitulation, the service represented a conflict between virtue ethics and consequentialism. The municipality's presence at the service could be seen as shameful submission to—or even acceptance of—a stronger military authority. Paul Raymond-Signouret certainly saw it that way. Still harboring resentment at having been left out of the municipal commission, he harshly criticized the commissioners for retaining their positions and for attending the service. They had failed to embody civic and national virtue. Raymond-Signouret dismissed the argument that the service preempted violence between the Prussian soldiers and the civilians of Strasbourg. He wished, in fact, to stir up the city's population against the occupying soldiers so that they would eventually revolt and deliver France from Prussian dominance.[38]

According to Schneegans, however, the service represented a two-way negotiation between the Prussian military and the local government. Schneegans claimed that armed civilians had killed three German soldiers on the day after the occupation. As revenge, Werder wanted to humiliate Strasbourg with a triumphal march through the streets followed by a public ceremony in which Mayor Küss would present him with the keys to the city on a silver platter. In addition, the city would pay a heavy war indemnity. When Werder informed Küss of this plan, however, the mayor calmly responded that he would never agree to hand over the keys to the city. Furthermore, he made it clear that a triumphal march would only lead to bloodshed, as many citizens remained armed and angry in the first days after the capitulation. Werder reflected on the mayor's scenario and issued a new order. The city would be spared the victory march and the war indemnity if Küss and the Protestant members of the municipal commission would attend a religious service at the church of Saint-Thomas the next morning.[39]

Was Schneegans telling the truth? His account fits with punishments the Prussians inflicted on other localities during the war. The Prussians marched through Paris after it fell, a moment of supreme humiliation for the long-suffering capital. Le Mans, a city of only 50,000 inhabitants, paid a two-million-franc indemnity upon occupation in January.[40] But in this particular case, Schneegans may have exaggerated in order to justify this symbolic act of unity with the invaders. No other author tried to explain the presence of the city leaders at the service, and it does not appear in the minutes of the municipal commission. The dramatic story of the three murdered soldiers is not corroborated elsewhere. Still, the motivation remains plausible and even defendable: the civilian authorities wanted to keep both occupiers and occupied calm and prevent further violence. They claimed an active role in the future of the city. For Schneegans and his colleagues, Strasbourg was worth a service.

We can also interpret the service at Saint-Thomas along more intimate lines. Chaplain Emil Frommel, a native of nearby Karlsruhe, Baden, had grown up visiting his mother's family in Strasbourg. He delighted to see the portrait of his grandfather on the wall of the church of Sainte-Aurélie and to visit his cousin, who was none other than the vicar of the New Church, Max Reichard.[41] Reichard praised Frommel's "tender and reconciliatory" sermon that calmed both sides and placed both besieged and besieger under the hand of the Lord.[42] For Frommel, the service at Saint-Thomas was a return to his childhood home away from home, a reunion with his extended family and mentors. In Frommel's account, the service was all warmth and community and connectivity.

The Occupation

Civilian interpretations of the transition from siege to occupation, of the supposed return to normalcy, ranged widely from forced submission to prudent compromise to sincere expressions of unity. All of these dynamics played out in myriad proclamations and negotiations in the months to come. Make no mistake, the Germans possessed the city and used the municipal commission to assert control. Yet the occupation period—from September 28 until the formal annexation on March 1, 1871—did not prove as onerous as elsewhere in France nor as heinous as observers like Raymond-Signouret claimed.

Frédéric Piton's first days of the occupation demonstrate the ambiguity of this period. After six weeks of separation, Piton took the first opportunity to visit his brother-in-law in Dorlisheim, seventeen miles to the west. To get there, he gratefully accepted a ride from a Prussian wagon.[43] "Nature is magnificent," he recorded. "What happiness to recover one's liberty, to be able to circulate peacefully in the great and beautiful nature of good God," even if such freedom entailed conversing with the victors.[44] Furthermore, Piton, whose "heart was bleeding too much" to watch the Germans march in, managed to see the silver lining in quartering ten soldiers on the third floor of his house.[45] Despite the fact that every windowpane had been shattered, the soldiers seemed pleased to have mattresses on the floor, a table, and chairs. Piton, too, was glad that their presence secured his house from opportunistic marauders.[46] "They are polite," he recorded in his diary, "they don't ask for much and to judge from their conversation, would prefer to go home rather than hold down Strasbourg. . . . I don't detect any hatred or animosity toward our country."[47] Piton remained skeptical but never reported an unpleasant encounter with his lodgers.

The joint proclamations from Mertens and Küss also reveal the uncertainties of this occupation. On October 3, for example, the mayor invited civilians to report any unexploded projectiles in their homes so that German soldiers could safely discharge them. It seems like a reasonable measure aimed to assure the safety of the population, but the final line, added by Mertens, adds a darker note: "Inhabitants who hide projectiles of any nature . . . will be punished with the severity of military law."[48]

The Germans swiftly and firmly took control of Strasbourg's wealth and institutions. By October 1, inhabitants were required not only to lodge but also to feed eight thousand German occupiers and provide them daily with coffee, wine, and five good cigars apiece.[49] Schneegans called these requisitions "a veritable systematic pillage," though they paled in comparison to those of other cities: Le Mans, for instance, sheltered and fed 40,000 soldiers.[50] The Prussians profited far more from Strasbourg's matériel. They captured 1,277 cannon (about one-sixth of the artillery captured in the course of the war), 140,000 rifles, over 350,000 projectiles, thousands of hatchets and knives, some 50,000 tunics and pants, 270,000 yards of sheets, 26,000 pairs of shoes, and large quantities of flour and animal feed. The Prussians shipped this bonanza directly to their armies besieging Paris.[51] Kiéné complained, "I don't know that they won't invent a machine for transporting houses and especially the cathedral."[52] The Prussians also quickly claimed Strasbourg's liquid money but were dismayed to find much of it missing. The treasurer, Malartic, who spoke no German, was held prisoner at the bank for a month, accused of hiding the cash. (The evening he was freed, Malartic ran through the streets with joy, but finding all the hotels booked, he returned to sleep at the bank again that night!)[53]

In addition, the Germans took over the hospitals. In the early days of October, wounded French soldiers healthy enough to be moved were taken to hospitals or prisons in Germany, often without enough warning for the staff to supply the men with warm clothing. This policy violated the 1868 additional articles of the Geneva Convention, which called for wounded soldiers in enemy hands to be sent back to their country upon recovery if they agreed not to take up arms again. Within a week, all the Red Cross hospitals closed down. Only the Military Hospital, including surgeon François Poncet, continued to care for the wounded who could not be transported. Soon, even that hospital was available only to German soldiers.[54]

Still, the occupation of Strasbourg proceeded rather mildly compared with that of other cities in 1870 and with the occupation of France during the world wars of the twentieth century. The records indicate only two fatalities at the hands of Prussian soldiers. First, at the end of September, a French Zouave who had not left the city with the others drunkenly confronted three German soldiers on rue Sainte-Madeleine in the Krutenau. They ignored his insults but took action when he attacked them. They tied the Zouave's hands behind his back with a handkerchief, pushed him against a carriage entrance, and shot him. Then, on October 10, a Prussian soldier killed an ironworker named Alexis Roild for his seemingly threatening behavior. A third incident shows the limits of the Prussian use of force. On October 12, a shot was fired from a house in the faubourg de Saverne. The Prussians arrested the men of the house and evicted the women. But then the Prussians pulled back. On October 20, Ollech announced, via Küss, that he had not been able to put together sufficient evidence to bring the accused civilians to a military tribunal. They were immediately freed and allowed to return home. Schneegans marveled at the good conduct of the Prussian soldiers and the swiftness with which they were punished for any infraction. Although limits on communications and the imbalance of power might have stifled other reports of conflict, these accounts from the winter of 1870–1871 suggest that the occupation passed relatively lightly in Strasbourg. German authorities and municipal leaders combined to make occupation as normal and peaceful as possible.[55]

Other anecdotes of the occupation, however, took a nationalistic approach and emphasized that Strasbourgeois, particularly women, refused to become German. Alfred Marchand, a journalist who was not in Strasbourg during the siege, claimed that Uhrich had put the question of capitulation to a plebiscite and "the immense majority responded with an energetic *non*."[56] In occupied Strasbourg, according to Kiéné, only the Prussians spoke German. Even native German speakers tried to get by in French, denying—in a German accent—that they could understand any of Wilhelm's soldiers.[57] The women of Strasbourg reportedly dressed in mourning, but "under their black corsage . . . they hid a tricolor cockade."[58] Bergasse du Petit-Thouars believed that the heroic women of Strasbourg, the guardians of the domestic foyer, would never raise German sons. A more elaborate story recounted a confrontation between Prussian officers and a group of Strasbourg women. Piqued at the saber-rattlers, one woman walked right up to them and spat out, "*Vive la France! A bas la Prusse!*" She was arrested and condemned to twenty-five lashes. In response, twenty-five women of Strasbourg offered to share the punishment, having taken part, they said, in the crime. In the end, Bismarck-Bohlen purportedly intervened to pardon the brave woman. This story made good reading, but it did not fit with other occupation episodes. In Strasbourg, confrontations between soldiers and civilians tended to happen at night between men and isolated soldiers, not during the day between women and officers. This is the kind of nationalistic story that some French liked to tell in the aftermath of the war as they encouraged their children to read Alphonse Daudet's short story "The Last Class" and G. Bruno's *The Tour of France by Two Children*.[59]

"You Unfortunate, Wrecked City"

After forty-four days of bombardment, nearly every edifice in the city had been damaged. The Prefecture, the art museum, the theater, the New Church, and the Protestant Gymnasium were gone. The Hôtel de Ville, the citadel, and the train station suffered extensive damage. The city's market gardeners and farmers lost stables and animals. In the cemeteries, headstones were cracked and crosses bent over. Over three hundred private buildings had been destroyed, and another four hundred were uninhabitable. The fires could be smelled from six miles away. In the stripped and barren surrounding countryside, Piton could hardly recognize his familiar pathways.[60] The faubourg de Pierre shocked even those who had survived the siege elsewhere. It lived up to its name, strewn with rocks of masonry, partially flooded, and littered with abandoned artillery, iron, and ashes. Emile Schmitt told his cousin to change the lyrics of the famous folksong to "O Strassburg, du unglückliche und zertrümmerte Stadt" (unfortunate and wrecked city).[61]

Amid these ruins, some eight to ten thousand people were now left homeless, and hundreds still recovered from wounds.[62] Their livelihoods and normal sources of sociability had been disrupted. The man who had spent four days trapped in his cellar found the situation overwhelming: "I had entered without a grey hair, today I am completely white; I had aged in four days more than twenty years. As for my shops, everything is burned. I had worked for ten years to be able to give my family modest comfort; I had envisioned for my wife and for myself a happy, carefree old age; today everything must start over again: I envision on the horizon only misery for our old age."[63] He was lucky; in a few cases, the remains of entire families were uncovered months later. Many could not bear to stay in the city. Hundreds made brief trips to Switzerland to rest and recuperate, including both Reuss and Schneegans, who churned out his initial brief siege memoir in Zurich by October 10.[64] Those who had left earlier, like Catherine Weiss, returned with trepidation. What if the war returned to the city? Young Emile wanted to go back to Colmar, for "he still saw shells everywhere, and the German soldiers scared him." Weiss's account ends rather suddenly after her reunion with her husband.[65]

It did not take long for Strasbourg to become a German tourist attraction, or for natives of Strasbourg to resent the newcomers. "Half of Strasbourg resembles a fair, the other half a ruin," reported one observer to his readers back in Berlin.[66] On the very first day of the occupation, journalist Gustave Fischbach received a visitor, a correspondent for a newspaper in Karlsruhe whom he had once met in a hotel in Offenburg. In that encounter a decade earlier, the two reporters had exchanged pleasantries, but the German had sworn he would never visit Strasbourg except with the German army. On September 28, that correspondent made good on his promise, "triumphant, mocking [and] puffed up, as if he had taken Strasbourg by himself."[67]

Within a few days, Badenese peasants and villagers plagued the city—"a human anthill"—with their gaping mouths and cheap patriotism.[68] "The whole family comes," recorded Dr. Henri-Etienne Beaunis, "the men with their large hats, their red vests and their long shiny frockcoats, the women serious and dignified in their patriotic enthusiasm, the young women in their Sunday best, laughing a large and stupid laugh, their mouths slit open to their ears, their staring eyes, while their fiancés strut around them in their soldier's uniform to pay honor to the ruins; bringing up the rear is an interminable parade of nippers of any age and sex whose limpid blue eyes contemplate all these horrors, poor children who have no idea of the hatred accumulating on their heads."[69] Worst of all, the tourists seemed indifferent to civilians' experience of the siege. Piton deplored "the malicious joy, the cynical arrogance . . . I didn't hear a single expression of pity or sympathy."[70] The Badenese seemed to have forgotten that Alsace had welcomed 1848ers by the hundreds a few decades earlier.[71] Civilians took advantage of these newcomers as best they could. Hungry for custom, street sellers hawked beer, tobacco, cigars, charcuterie, and cheese. Over sixteen thousand tourists each paid one thaler (3 francs 75, a little more than the average worker's daily wage) to enter the destroyed citadel. The Prussians gave the proceeds of 60,100 francs to the city.[72]

Rebuilding the city began almost immediately. On September 30, Zopff announced that the Prussians had requisitioned 750 masons, carpenters, joiners, and locksmiths. They were promised a mediocre daily wage (2 francs 50). In a second requisition of construction workers announced a few days later, Küss offered higher wages (up to four francs) while Mertens promised to expel any construction worker who did not show up.[73] Clearing roads, building shelters, and repairing locks all helped to reestablish order and security. From Versailles, the crown prince immediately ordered the restoration of the cathedral, churches, the library, and other cultural edifices: "We must, in fact—so I consider—give immediate proof that we intend to make good again the damage that, alas! is inevitable in war. In such wise are moral conquests made."[74] On October 29, Bismarck-Bohlen called for donations large and small to fix the damages done, particularly to the cathedral roof, before the winter set in.[75] Using "marvels of science and audacity," workers straightened the spire's crooked cross.[76]

The German government eventually reimbursed the city for almost three-quarters of the costs it had incurred during the siege, including the room and board of German soldiers, repairs to military fortifications, and overtime for firemen and those who buried the dead in the Botanical Gardens. The cost to the city, after reimbursement, was 435,240 francs, about a quarter of its annual budget.[77]

In the decades after annexation, Strasbourg experienced an urban renaissance. Recasting the city as a model urban center, the Germans eventually paid the equivalent of 50,181,000 francs—greased by the French war indemnity—for the physical reconstruction of Strasbourg's streets, buildings, and furnishings. As before, Strasbourg served as a frontier city, a university center, and a commercial hub in which religion played a prominent role. In addition, the German Empire imprinted itself onto its new western capital. A new German university quickly became the envy of reformers across Europe and the United States. By August 1871, the university library held 120,000 books donated by publishing houses and private libraries, including 4,000 from the emperor. By 1881, Strasbourg's library contained half a million books, making it the largest collection in the world—a status it maintained until World War I. The redesigned neo-Romanesque New Church reopened in 1877. By 1900, Strasbourg had tripled the size of its residential neighborhoods, established a monumental administrative center (today, Place de la République), constructed a military wall thirteen yards tall, and built seven new religious structures, including two synagogues and two garrison churches. Much as Paris quickly rebuilt its physical spaces to whitewash the violent repression of the Paris Commune, Strasbourg emerged bigger and more vigorous than before, almost as though the bombardment had never happened.[78]

An Outpouring of Aid

Aid to the people of Strasbourg started with the generals. Uhrich left behind one thousand francs, and Werder gave forty head of cattle to be slaughtered and distributed to the poor (the city sold them and distributed the cash instead).[79] This *noblesse oblige,* continued by the Grand Duchesse of Baden, paled in comparison with international donations that helped thousands of civilians recover their losses. Within a week of the capitulation, the newly founded Strasbourg Aid Committee for the Victims of the Bombardment, an independent organization, began to distribute donated money, clothing, and linens that had been sent from Western Europe and the United States.

The scale of this international relief effort on behalf of civilians was unprecedented: at least 471,600 fr. streamed in from outside of Alsace (which donated 16,500 fr.), including 182,700 fr. from Germany, 58,400 fr. from France, and a total of 230,500 fr. from Switzerland, the United States, the Netherlands, Norway, and Britain. In other words, foreign aid alone—money from outside Germany or France—could reimburse 1,829 workers for wages lost during the six weeks of the siege. In addition, many cities and charities (locations unknown) gave directly to the city of Strasbourg a total of 624,800 fr., of which the Aid Committee received 392,700 fr. The Aid Committee also collected and distributed some 185,500 fr. worth of furniture, food, clothing, artificial limbs, and seed. It wasn't enough, but it was a lot more foreign aid than any other war-torn city had ever received.[80]

No such outpouring of international aid had helped civilians in Crimea or in the South after the American Civil War.[81] Rebel Southerners and Muslim Tatars were unlikely to elicit sympathy from Western Europe. Atlanta and Richmond supported their starving and homeless inhabitants through other means: the Freedmen's Bureau, the American Missionary Association, local voluntary associations, their own meager resources, and a few donations from around the United States. Still, the experience of the Civil War may explain why Americans gave a total of 112,151 fr. The city of St. Louis donated to both Atlanta and Strasbourg. American Clara Barton arrived in Strasbourg to deliver donations that she had personally gathered and to oversee the work of mending linens and clothes for distribution. The changes in communication, sympathy, and civil society that had helped to foster humanitarianism also extended the reach of charitable giving.[82]

The vast majority of these funds were distributed—sometimes as a loan, sometimes a gift—to 5,606 families. Most recipients had lost their homes, and 231 of these families (1 in 25) had lost a family member to the bombardment. The Aid Committee devised its own guidelines for aid to families whose breadwinners had died, acknowledging that, contrary to the rhetoric, male civilians had indeed lost their lives in the siege. A widow could receive 200 to 480 fr., depending on her husband's status and her age (more for an older woman), and a widower could receive 67 to 150 fr., depending on his status and his wife's contributions to the household earnings. Workers could claim funds to buy new tools or make up for a loss of clients.[83] Those seeking aid presented their need in stark terms. The widow Hagelberger, whose husband died of wounds on October 5, had two young children and no income. She and her husband had both worked at the tobacco factory, but this business was now under Prussian control, and she had lost her job. Her case was easily accepted. The Aid Committee rejected the request of a couple who had not lost anything except their livelihood, referring them instead to the Bureau de Bienfaisance, the ordinary source of municipal charity. The label "doubtful morality" fell upon a tailor whose wife refused the work she was offered (not specified), and who sent his two eldest children to beg by the cathedral doors.[84]

Having emerged from the most desperate times, the people of Strasbourg found resources to continue helping soldiers in need. Some members of the Deaconesses left Strasbourg to tend to the wounded on the battlefield throughout Alsace and Lorraine. With this action, they reaffirmed that civilian women need not be seen as victims and demonstrated that female care giving does not have to be interpreted as the embodiment of nationalism. "Without making the least distinction," recorded the Deaconesses, "they cared for French and Germans, wounded and sick, happy to be able to put into practice the teaching that the Lord gives us in the story of the Good Samaritan."[85] They found comfort in the belief that the Lord had created an indivisible heaven, large enough for French and Germans, and hoped to create a world of believers governed by love. By going to the site of suffering and seeing their work as transformative, the Deaconesses crossed the subtle line between charitable work and humanitarian action.[86]

Civilians also mobilized to aid prisoners of war. In the fall and winter, the Strasbourg Red Cross sent ten thousand correspondence cards along with care packages of clothing and food to soldiers interned in Germany. Upon the urging of Madame Kiéné, the Red Cross opened up an ambulance in the train station to serve those passing from France to Germany. Female volunteers in the train station, including Mlle Ritton and Mlle Lange, handed out clothing, linen, tobacco, food, and wine. The Deaconesses dispersed aid to soldiers in Switzerland, France, and Württemberg. In January, Kiéné visited prisoners in Rastatt, Baden, including Bergasse du Petit-Thouars. She helped arrange for the liberation of a customs agent whose son had been killed in the bombardment and whose wife now lived in poverty. In the spring, released prisoners often passed back through Strasbourg on foot at their own cost. The *restaurants populaires,* which had continued privately through the winter, provided over 82,000 free meals to these returning soldiers.[87]

As individuals and families regained their livelihoods, Strasbourg's religious institutions came back to life. The churches and the synagogue assessed damages, distributed aid, and paid for the extra watchmen and fire pumps they had used during the siege. The congregation of the New Church located a temporary place of worship at Saint-Pierre-le-Vieux. For Catholics, the autumn brought yet more bad news: Italian soldiers had occupied Rome on September 20. For ten years, French troops had protected the papacy from the newly unified Italy, but they withdrew in order to fight Prussia. As a result, Pope Pius IX lost his temporal authority. Catholics in Alsace sent to Rome a letter of protest with seventy thousand signatures.[88]

At every turn, Strasbourg's cultural institutions faced the reality of becoming German. The Commercial and Literary Casino renewed and increased its subscriptions to German newspapers. The Gymnasium resumed teaching in October, reorganized along German (especially Prussian) lines, with new teachers and methods. Newspapers, which were banned for four days after the capitulation, resumed publication under strict conditions not to print anything negative about Germany.[89] Raymond-Signouret's *L'impartial du Rhin* did not start up again, and Schneegans, Boersch, and Fischbach soon resigned from *Le courrier du Bas-Rhin,* which under German management became "more Prussian than the king of Prussia."[90] Starting on October 10, the General Government of Alsace published its official newspaper in Strasbourg, the *Strassburger Zeitung.*[91]

As the waters froze, civilians faced continued hardships. One citizen appealed to Küss for help after ten people in his household had endured typhoid fever and three suffered smallpox. Civilians still lacked sanitation and feared contamination in their wells. Psychological scars also remained. A line of carriages transported men and women who could not cope to the Bas-Rhin asylum.[92] Reuss's parents returned to the city suffering from "nervous irritation" and "obsidional fever."[93] Arthur Faes later recalled a series of bizarre events from the winter of occupation. Crowds would suddenly run to examine windows scratched with indelible, shadowy marks that seemed to represent combat scenes such as "a *Turco* thrusting his bayonet into the chest of a Prussian."[94]

A Funeral

While some of Strasbourg's civilians obsessed over visions of combat, the real war continued in arenas across northern France. Werder fought in the east throughout the winter, including a victory against General Charles Bourbaki.[95] Despite their continual losses, the French refused to surrender. German resources and nerves were stretched as French *francs-tireurs* sabotaged train lines. The German press reported that *francs-tireurs* gouged out the eyes and cut off the tongues of wounded Germans; this experience so shook the Germans that it shaped their harsh response to civilian resistance, real and imagined, during the summer of 1914.[96]

Meanwhile, besieged Paris held out for four months, despite the onset of famine and disease during the harsh winter. In January, the Prussians bombarded Paris. This strategy raised the same questions that had been debated at Strasbourg. Bismarck pushed for a bombardment of civilians in part "as an act of national revenge."[97] Moltke viewed the bombardment of Paris as technically difficult and unlikely to achieve capitulation, but he nevertheless eventually agreed to it. Crown Prince Friedrich Wilhelm struggled to overcome his aversion to shelling, having learned that a hospital for children who had lost limbs had to be established in Strasbourg.[98] In the end, the duties of the future emperor compelled him to justify the violence: "I still think to myself that we are doing the Parisians a favor they have long been hoping for, seeing they can now under present circumstances persuade themselves they were vanquished by their opponent's gun-fire and not simply driven by hunger to submit."[99] The nine-day bombardment started on January 5, but it did relatively little damage. Even a dense city like Paris contained many open spaces, and the bombardment, about three to four hundred shells per day, was never as intense as that of Strasbourg (which averaged 4,220 projectiles per day). Still, the Parisian bombardment killed fifty-one civilians and wounded several hundred more.[100] The bombardment of civilians was becoming an expected, although still controversial, strategy of war.

On January 18, even as the siege of Paris continued, German dignitaries, including the Grand Duke of Baden, declared the founding of the German Empire in a ceremony in the Hall of Mirrors at the Palace of Versailles. "The long-cherished hopes of our ancestors, the dreams of German poets, are fulfilled," wrote the crown prince. At last, Germany had emerged from "its sixty years' eclipse" with his father, Kaiser Wilhelm, at its helm.[101] Despite the chill in the air, Friedrich Wilhelm found the ceremony deeply moving. During a prayer that "consisted of a criticism of Louis XIV," the crown prince turned his eyes to the ceiling inscriptions praising the Sun King and "asked myself more than once if it was really true that we were at Versailles to witness there the re-establishment of the German Empire—so like a dream did the whole thing seem to me."[102]

The princes who raised their voices in acclamation at Versailles knew that Strasbourg would soon be part of the Empire. The formal annexation awaited the signing of a peace treaty. Facing rebellion in Paris and defeat almost everywhere else, France finally signed an armistice late in the evening of January 26, 1871. The French Government of National Defense immediately called for the election of a National Assembly to ratify the postwar settlement and eventually write a new constitution.

In the February election, Emile Küss won one hundred thousand votes, more than any other candidate in Alsace.[103] Despite his weary lungs, Küss traveled six hundred miles to take his seat in the southwestern city of Bordeaux (the government had moved there to escape the Prussians). The deputies faced the humiliating task of approving the preliminaries of peace, signed by Bismarck, Jules Favre, and Adolphe Thiers on February 26, which ceded Alsace and part of Lorraine to the

German Empire. On March 1, Küss joined the twenty-seven deputies of Alsace and Lorraine, including Auguste Schneegans, Charles Boersch, Léon Gambetta, and Auguste Scheurer-Kestner, in declaring "null and void a pact that disposes of us without our consent."[104] It was a symbolic protest, as the Assembly had little choice but to accept the treaty: the Prussians occupied one third of the country, including the forts surrounding Paris, and had captured most of the French army and its matériel. The treaty passed 546 to 107. Küss died the same day.[105]

Küss's eldest son brought his father's body back to Strasbourg to lay in state at the Hôtel de Ville on Place Broglie. At two o'clock on the afternoon of March 8, the casket emerged, decorated with Küss's professorial cap and red robe, along with a civic wreath, "the most glorious emblem that a man can dream of for his tomb."[106] The casket did not indicate his lifelong republicanism or his final act of defiance on the national stage. "By this foolish demonstration," reported his former student Beaunis, the Prussian authorities "tried in vain to reduce [Küss] to the role of a purely local personality."[107]

Under the watchful eye of the Prussian authorities, the casket traced a path through the city center. It passed north of the remains of the New Church and then turned south by the cathedral and Place Gutenberg, where the municipal commission had met during Küss's tenure as mayor. Citizens draped their houses in black.[108] All taverns, workshops, and stores were closed as Strasbourg's citizens of "all religions, all classes, [and] all parties pressed around these venerable remains."[109] Finally, the cortege arrived at Saint-Thomas, the one Protestant church in condition to serve such a momentous event. An ensemble played the funeral march "by that Beethoven that he loved so much and that he understood so well." Its "sublime harmonies and poignant melody" echoed "like a cry of despair."[110]

After the service, the funeral cortege made its way north again toward Sainte-Hélène's Cemetery, this time making a detour along rue de la Nuée-Bleue, through the ruins of the faubourg de Pierre. A crowd of men, women, and children gathered in silence to mark Küss's passing with "both a solemn homage and a mute protest."[111] The public outpouring of emotion continued upon reaching the cemetery, which Prussian parallels had cut through just a few months earlier. The

The funeral cortege of Emile Küss passes through a sea of rubble as onlookers cry and kneel in reverence. The women of Strasbourg, who instruct children about the scene, are portrayed as the guardians of memory of the city's struggle and its French past. From a drawing by Frédéric Lix. Armand Dayot, *L'invasion: Le siège 1870, la commune 1871* (1901). (Charles Deering McCormick Library of Special Collections, Northwestern University Library)

Prussian authorities respectfully waited outside the gates while Pastor Leblois of the New Church delivered a prayer and Küss's family, friends, and colleagues said their good-byes.[112]

Küss had played many roles in the drama of Strasbourg. A revolutionary, professor, father, and mayor, Küss had won friends and supporters through his intelligence, good humor, and not least of all, his ability to compromise. Yet as Strasbourg was handed over to the Germans, the story told about Küss lost its nuance. Former Mayor Théodore Humann, who admired Küss despite their political differences, delivered a revealing eulogy. He melodramatically refashioned Küss's life, filling his account of Küss's final weeks with emotional language and building to a stirring climax. Despite his ill health, Küss accepted his selection as mayor "with courage."[113] "The end of his life," continued Humann, "was sadder and more desolate than that of the poor wounded soldier on his hospital bed." Küss struggled with physical pain and the tense responsibility of mediating between invaders and invaded but handled himself with intelligence and calm. Küss agreed to head the delegation of deputies from the Bas-Rhin, "forcing all other sentiment to cede to that of duty." Humann continued: "He left never to return, alas! . . . It was too much for the patriotic heart of our illustrious and dear fellow citizen; it ceased to beat at the moment when they removed its nationality." Nevertheless, cautioned Humann, "Do not pity him; the ancients demanded of their gods a glorious death. Such was that of M. Küss, and I envy his destiny."

Indeed, Küss's final days were sad, even tragic, if we interpret Küss's love for Strasbourg as a tragic flaw that contributed to his death just as much as the pulmonary disease that he had suffered for years. Humann's speech was, after all, a eulogy intended to praise rather than complicate Küss's life. But Humann's portrayal of Küss as an arch-patriot—the kind of man who died rather than accept German rule—glosses over the fact that Küss himself had pursued pragmatic policies, including the offer of surrender and the service at Saint-Thomas, in order to mitigate the suffering of his fellow citizens. Yes, Küss surely was devastated to see Alsace lost to the Germans, but that was not the only facet of his personality nor was it the only reason that he won admiration in his native city. Küss was a French patriot who admired German culture, spoke both languages, and valued his city's unique heritage. He cared more about protecting his city and its people than about French nationalism.

But as Humann's speech indicates, the tide was starting to turn. It was important in March 1871 to speak of Strasbourg as a French city, wrenched from its nation. Humann concluded with a bitter, nationalistic evocation of "our two most patriotic provinces, the most tested, the most French at heart . . . left as prey for the victor."[114] As the first shovels of dirt hit the casket, the crowd cried, *"Vive la France! Vive la République!"*[115]

Caught in the Aftermath

For Uhrich, too, the narrative of the siege changed precipitously. When the general arrived safely in unoccupied Tours, the Government of National Defense greeted him warmly. A street in Paris had already been named for him. A little over a year later, however, Uhrich was publicly disgraced. In the wake of the disastrous war, the army conducted an inquest into the capitulation of two dozen strongholds. On January 8, 1872, the Conseil d'Enquête sur les Capitulations examined the case of Strasbourg and handed down one of its most negative judgments. Although the inquest admitted that Uhrich had never possessed sufficient means for defense, it argued that he could have undertaken more vigorous action.[116] More importantly, it found that Uhrich had not followed the regulations when he decided to capitulate. He had not waited for "one or more assaults." Worse, "the breaches made on bastions 11 and 12 were not practicable and were, besides, defended by a very large, very deep trench full of water."[117] Uhrich had capitulated too soon, a culpable act, "for the question of humanity should have been separated from that of military duty and the interest of the *patrie*."[118]

In addition, the inquest found that Uhrich had made a number of errors in his handling of the siege. The records of the defense council had not been properly kept, and Uhrich's logbook had gone missing.[119] The inquest furthermore judged that Uhrich had failed to make the proper preparations for handing over the city. In the hours between the capitulation and the French evacuation, soldiers should have been busy spiking the cannon, destroying munitions, and pitching water on gun-powder. To preserve the honor of their army, they should have burned their flags rather than allow them to fall into enemy hands. Uhrich had not commanded any of this. Instead, soldiers became drunk and idle. Moreover, Uhrich had failed to demand "the honors of war" for his garrison and had not "stipulate[d] that officers keep their sword, [and] officers and soldiers [keep] their own property." This oversight meant that soldiers led off as prisoners of war could not claim the right to keep food or clothing for their own survival. In addition, Uhrich had not negotiated on behalf of sick and wounded soldiers. Finally, Uhrich had made the damnable decision to forgo a German prison himself for the safety of Tours.[120] He had ignored the French military regulations that stated that a commanding officer "does not separate himself from his officers or from his troops, and he shares their fate afterwards."[121] After Sedan, Napoleon III and Marshal Patrice de MacMahon had become German prisoners. So had 140 French generals. Even Marshal Achille Bazaine, whose capitulation at Metz in October was long deemed treasonous, had served a period of German imprisonment.[122] Not Uhrich. In sum, Uhrich had not followed military regulations closely enough.

Uhrich took to heart the inquest's mission to establish the correct duty and the precise instances in which he had failed to measure up to it. But he disputed many of the facts. In a lengthy published response and in his 1872 memoir, Uhrich noted that the inquest had not interviewed enough witnesses and had not considered key documents. Uhrich had indeed destroyed the flags. The breach in bastion 11 was clearly practicable (Piton corroborated that it was twenty-seven yards wide).[123] Uhrich also disagreed with some of the definitions of honorable action. He argued that it was more honorable to hand over the stronghold in its state at the moment of capitulation than to disable the cannon.[124] Most importantly, Uhrich differed from the inquest on his duties toward civilians: "Should I have exposed Strasbourg to the horrors of an assault, to be sacked perhaps? Should I make myself guilty of such an act of inhumanity? I did not think so, and, on my deathbed, I will congratulate myself again for not having committed this culpable and monstrous folly."[125] Uhrich argued that the inquest should have taken into consideration "this situation without precedent . . . this tempest that surrounded us and that did not always give us time for reflection."[126]

The municipal council of Strasbourg, with a majority of anti-German councilors, also protested against the *conseil d'enquête*'s judgment. Not only did it misrepresent Uhrich, but it also slighted the National Guard and, by implication, the civilian population. The council protested against the inquest's admonition that the guardsmen abandoned their posts as soon as the bombs started to fall. The inquest furthermore had not included a word of sympathy for the damaged city or the slightest recognition of the efforts that civilian men and women had put into hospitals and the *restaurants populaires*.[127] The municipal council might also have noted that the inquest did not acknowledge the three hundred dead civilians, the thousands left homeless, the hopelessness of any relief from the outside, or the burning of the library. Nor did it blame Uhrich for having bombed the open city of Kehl. Military regulations were the only consideration.

The inquest received blame from yet another quarter. Léon Gambetta's republican newspaper interpreted the army's inquest along political lines. It had refused to question Edmond Valentin, argued *La République française,* out of a desire to cover up the misdeeds of the empire.[128] The country had blithely entered a war it was unprepared to fight and then abandoned Strasbourg to its fate. *La République française* did not spare Uhrich, either. What did they expect of commanders? "Audacity, initiative, heroism? No. Simply to execute the military regulations, to obey the laws of their profession, to give the example of firmness and constancy." So far, the newspaper aligned itself with the deontological position and with the inquest's findings. Then, it suddenly swerved into a different interpretation: "We demanded that they hold on to their last morsel of bread, up to the extreme limits of the possible; they didn't do it; they failed in their duty; they are guilty; the *conseil d'enquête* has judged correctly."[129] Despite its claims to the contrary, *La République française* expected heroism. Holding out to the "last morsel of bread, up to the extreme limits of the possible" had nothing to do with following military regulations. The definition of duty had changed abruptly under Uhrich's feet.

This view resonated with civilians who believed that Uhrich had surrendered prematurely. If only the city had manufactured new arms out of the city's metal and wood! The breaches were too small to be attacked. They should have held on through an assault and pillage.[130] If Raymond-Signouret had had his way, the Prussian soldiers would have battled "men, women, children, even the elderly . . . street by street, house by house . . . [in] a relentless slaughter."[131] Then the Germans would have had fewer soldiers to conquer the rest of France, and "what enthusiasm, what irresistible *élan* it would have excited in the ranks . . . !"[132] Just a few more days more of resistance would have inspired troops throughout the country and allowed the new army time to regroup. This fantasy of war, the heroic sacrifice in the name of the *patrie*, like the last stand celebrated in Alphonse de Neuville's painting "The Last Cartridges" (1873), appealed to many in the postwar era. This brand of virtue ethics seeped across political lines. It was not just republicans like Valentin and Gambetta who wanted to hold out to the last extremity, but also Bonapartist Raymond-Signouret.

Uhrich, much praised and much blamed, probably deserved something in between. He failed to undertake inventive or bold measures in Strasbourg's defense, but it was easy enough to find convincing excuses for his shortcomings. Despite the inquest's findings, Uhrich did not face imprisonment. He escaped the fate of Achille Bazaine, who was found guilty of treason for the surrender of Metz, but in Paris, avenue du Général Uhrich was soon renamed after the Bois de Boulogne. Uhrich died in Paris in 1886.

Just as with the capitulation itself, the inquest into Uhrich's decisions brought up conflicts among major ethical traditions. Uhrich and the *conseil d'enquête* agreed that adherence to duty trumped other considerations—the deontological position—though Uhrich believed that his duty should extend to civilians. The municipal council focused on the experience of the siege and the actions of civilians, which resonates with the consequentialist tradition that focuses on context and the outcomes of actions. *La République française* and Raymond-Signouret embraced the virtue ethics that emphasized·courage and sacrifice for the sake of the nation. In the years to come, this latter position came to define the meaning of the siege of Strasbourg.

Unfulfilled Heroism

After his inglorious arrest, Valentin remained a prisoner in Germany until the armistice. In the spring of 1871, he helped to crush the Lyon commune and soon returned to politics. He served as prefect of the Rhône in 1872, deputy of the Seine-et-Oise in 1875, and senator of the Rhône the following year. Due to his heroic conduct, the Royal Military Academy of Woolwich doubled his pension. For reasons that remain unclear, Valentin committed suicide on October 31, 1879, with two bullets to the heart. Some friends believed that once the republican cause had been won, Valentin had nothing left to fight for. He is buried in Montparnasse under a tomb depicting his swim to Strasbourg.[133]

As the Third Republic took shape, Valentin's biography offered an appealing antidote to the stereotypical functionary whose overly cerebral qualities and obsession with getting ahead supposedly stripped him of physicality and fortitude.[134] Valentin's exploits won him a spot in a prominent civics textbook by G. Bruno. Schoolchildren read that Valentin's entrance into Strasbourg embodied the ideal prefect as "the example of patriotism, courage before danger, devotion and fraternity."[135] The textbook details Valentin's adventurous entry, including the American passport, the flying bullets, and the appointment papers up his sleeve.

Valentin's story gained wider exposure in 1898 with the publication of Lucien Delabrousse's biography *A Hero of National Defense: Valentin and the Final Days of the Siege of Strasbourg.* Delabrousse had interviewed Valentin in 1872 but kept silent, he said, due to the sensitivity of his material. The timing of publication suggests that Delabrousse hoped Valentin's adventures could serve a country in desperate need of heroes and consumed with worry over male degeneracy and national decline.[136] In 1898, anyone attuned to national politics had an opinion on the Dreyfus Affair, the conflict over whether a Jewish army officer falsely convicted of espionage should be retried in the name of republican justice or remain imprisoned to protect military honor, hierarchy, and anti-Semitic prejudice. Valentin could bridge the gap. Dreyfusards, who wanted a retrial, could embrace a principled republican like Valentin who choose exile rather than accept Bonapartism. Anti-Dreyfusards might deplore Valentin's republicanism, but they could respect his display of physical courage. In theory, both sides could agree that Valentin represented a formidable combination of brawn and brains, gut-wrenchingly symbolic of a lost cause. It was fitting, too, that in 1898 the French press lionized Captain Jean-Baptiste Marchand's showdown with the British in Fashoda on the Upper Nile.[137] Valentin's story shared Marchand's desperate and nationally humiliating circumstances. Indeed, for many French, the colonial empire was a placeholder for the loss of Strasbourg and Alsace. Delabrousse and his publishers may have hoped that Valentin's story would appeal to a nation enthralled by theatrical productions of martyred heroes Joan of Arc, Napoleon Bonaparte, and Cyrano de Bergerac.[138] Valentin's story also dovetailed with the popular militaristic juvenilia that provided escapism and character formation to the generation of boys coming of age in the late nineteenth century. Delabrousse emphasized Valentin's quick movements and piercing gaze, his "rare energy and admirable valiance," characteristics of a "man of action."[139] With this description of republican vigor, Delabrousse may have been responding to Maurice Barrès's book *The Uprooted* (1897), which contended that the chaotic Third Republic could only produce feminized, listless young men.[140]

Although Valentin's story never became as popular as that of other heroes, it resonated with (but did not quite fulfill) the prevailing ideal of manliness, defined in Edward Berenson's words as "the ability to persist against all odds, to confront physical danger and the perils of the unknown, and to combine strength and fortitude with kindness toward women, 'natives,' and others needing gentle guidance backed by a firm, steady hand."[141] He desperately tried to live out the heroic dream for military men, the individual fighting the odds whose guts and cleverness and skill saved the day. Despite Valentin's failure, such notions of heroism permeated popular understandings about war. It was still an era in which a French author could write, without irony, "If there is glory, it is to die a martyr for the defense of law and justice, for the salvation of the *patrie:* dulce et decorum [est] pro patria mori."[142]

▪ ▪ ▪

The siege in which Prussia wrenched Strasbourg from France contained many meanings beyond the story of national humiliation or national glory. For tens of thousands of individuals, the siege was a life-changing event that destroyed home, work, and bodily integrity. Yet very quickly, for those on the outside, the civilian experience of the siege of Strasbourg was largely forgotten. In part, the dramatic siege of Paris and the bloody springtime Paris Commune overshadowed the events in Strasbourg. Civics textbooks tended to focus on cities that did not fall: Paris, Belfort, Bitche, and Châteaudun.[143] When Strasbourg did win national attention, it came in the context of the loss of Alsace. Anecdotes portrayed the women of Strasbourg primarily as the keepers of French nationality. The funeral of Küss put closure on the siege, but Humann's eulogy emphasized the national story rather than Küss's cautious compromises. Critics of Uhrich focused on the general's lack of adherence to duty and his failure to make extreme sacrifices for the sake of France. Later, the story of Valentin emphasized unrealistic "heroic" sacrifice rather than a subtle reading of the siege. French observers from outside Strasbourg tended to ignore the multifaceted siege experience and focus primarily on its outcome and the resulting national humiliation. In Germany, too, the national story prevailed; in the wake of victory, few discussed suffering (even of German soldiers) or humanitarianism.[144]

This simplification of the siege of Strasbourg was a cause and consequence of European sensitivity to violence. For many, the violence leveled against Europeans in the siege (and elsewhere during the war) was unacceptable. This sensitivity had led the Swiss delegation to believe that it was their duty to intervene. Once the conflict was over, people from the outside did not want to focus on the disturbing experiences of the civilians of Strasbourg. Inscribing the loss of Strasbourg into a narrative that praised individual virtue in the face of national struggle helped people to avoid thinking about the terrible implications of modern warfare: mass, impersonal killing and being killed. The consequentialist ethic that admitted weakness, accepted compromise, and acknowledged the potentially violent consequences of action led to disturbing ideas better left unthought.

For almost fifty years after the loss of Alsace to the German Empire, the female statue personifying Strasbourg in Paris's Place de la Concorde became a favored locale for nationalist rallies.[145] Strasbourg, seated atop a cannon with sword in hand and draped in black on state occasions, suggested to many the pain of defeat and the hope of eventual liberation. As horse and carriage gave way to bicycle and automobile, the statue of Strasbourg came to symbolize narrow *revanchisme,* the obsession with revenge on Germany cultivated within certain nationalist circles. Meanwhile, in Berlin, Germans inaugurated the Victory Column to celebrate the three wars of unification and, in the 1890s, constructed the Kaiser Wilhelm Memorial Church. The siege and the civilians who endured it were largely forgotten.

Conclusion

F RÉDÉRIC PITON DIED on July 12, 1871, from an illness he had contracted during the siege. At his funeral, Pastor Georges-Louis Leblois of the New Church praised Piton's love of country, his historical studies, and his courage in speaking out against the war.[1] This eulogy reminds us of the many interpretations of the siege of Strasbourg. The siege was, of course, partly about love of country: an important episode in a war between two nations, contributing to the founding of the German Empire and the humiliation of France. It was also, however, the story of a city with a rich history whose civilians both confronted and worked with the authorities in order to protect it. Piton and other male civilians felt tension between their dual roles as men and as noncombatants. They eschewed the label of victim and pursued strategies to enhance their well-being but recognized the severe limitations of their situation. The siege also witnessed a debate among three ethical traditions, with honor-bound virtue ethics coming to dominate narratives of the siege. Most importantly, the siege heralded an era of international humanitarian aid for civilians alongside ever-increasing intensity of warfare that disregarded civilian life.

It is not surprising that historians of Alsace after 1870 have largely focused on the tricky issues of identity and national integration. The region lays bare for all to see the impermanence of national borders and the constructedness of national identity. Such issues were thrust in the face of Alsatians in the wake of the annexation to Germany. A clause in the Treaty of Frankfurt allowed native Alsatians to keep their French nationality if they established a domicile in France. Madame Kiéné and former mayor Théodore Humann, like thousands of others (including the family of Alfred Dreyfus), elected to leave Alsace for Paris and thereby retain their French citizenship. Humann returned to his native soil only in death; he was buried in 1873 in Sainte-Hélène's Cemetery.[2]

For those who stayed in Strasbourg, national and regional identity issues remained important. In the decades after 1870, the German government attempted to turn its new subjects into Germans through education, military service, and national holidays, while Alsatians helped to shape their own political and personal destinies. Auguste Schneegans provides a case in point. After his brief service as an Alsatian deputy in the French National Assembly, Schneegans moved to Lyon as editor in chief of *Le journal de Lyon*.[3] He remained vocal in his anger at the Germans: "No! The German people will never see Alsace rush into their arms. [German] armies may occupy our territory; they will never turn us into Germans."[4] Despite this resistance, Schneegans soon returned to Strasbourg to take up politics and journalism again. He founded the first Alsatian autonomist party in 1875 to fight for greater self-government and more equity within the German Empire. Before his death in 1898, Schneegans had made peace enough with Germany to represent it as consul in Messina and consul general in Genoa.[5]

The biography of Rodolphe Reuss suggests, however, that national and regional identities were not the only issues at stake in the period after the siege of Strasbourg. Certainly, Reuss grappled with the dilemma of identity, but he also cared about preserving and disseminating knowledge. He resumed his position at the Protestant Gymnasium when it reopened in October 1870. Two years later, Reuss refused a position at the new Kaiser Wilhelm University, whereas his Germanophile father, Eduard, accepted. Over the next fifty years, Reuss published over 150 titles on a wide variety of topics, including the history of Protestantism, the Eighteenth Brumaire in Alsace, the evolution of the Commercial and Literary Casino, and David Livingstone. Like others of the francophone elite, Reuss possessed the linguistic, social, and cultural resources to maintain ties with France. After twenty-five years as a German subject,

Reuss left Alsace for Paris so that his sons would not have to perform military service for Germany. In 1896, he presented his work at the Sorbonne and became a director at the Ecole Pratique des Hautes Etudes.[6]

The siege, particularly the destruction of the New Church libraries, made Reuss self-conscious as a historical actor and as a conserver of the documents of history. Throughout his career, in addition to his own voluminous work, he edited and published collections of Alsatian documents, disseminating his heritage beyond a few fragile copies that could be easily destroyed. In 1880, he transcribed and completed the notes he took in his siege diary in order to provide a document base for posterity, for "who knows if collections of our newspapers will still exist in one hundred years?"[7] In 1900, he added a new preface in which he mused that his protest against the library destruction, "a page that does honor to the young man who wrote it!" had defined and guided his subsequent work.[8] Twenty years later, having survived another Franco-German war, Reuss wrote one final preface, commending the work to his grandsons.[9] He used his siege notes in his *History of Alsace,* one of his final publications before his death in 1924.

War and Humanity

For those who lived through the siege, the experience was unforgettable and harrowing. They believed they had survived the worst of modern warfare and hoped that their children would not have to experience the same devastation. The Aid Committee's final report concluded, "May an era of justice finally open up for the world, and may future times no longer see the return of these acts, whose bloody trace we would like to see erased from the book of humanity!"[10] Pastor Wilhelm Horning opened the published version of his diary (1894) with a message to his children: "May the younger generation, that is so fortunate not to have experienced war, learn from these pages the horrors of war . . . [and] pray from the heart: 'From war and bloodletting / Protect us dear Lord God!' "[11]

Unfortunately, the siege of Strasbourg and the Franco-Prussian War did not lead to the end of bloodletting but rather heralded the future of

European warfare. Europeans thought that the siege offered a choice between unrestrained warfare and humanitarianism, between barbarism and civilization. But in fact, Europe followed both paths: European nations chose to emulate the German army after 1870, including its ability to destroy cities, and at the same time, Europeans attempted to mitigate war with international law and humanitarian organizations.

In the decades after 1870, most European armies instituted the German model of rapid, integrated mobilization of men and matériel and the near-universal conscription of male citizens. Expanded conscription forced most men to exchange the distress of civilian male vulnerability for the challenges of military service. The terms of service and the kind of training were highly contested, especially among the middle class in France, but the army nevertheless became a fundamental part of life for European males. Army service cultivated the virtue of self-sacrifice for the nation. At the same time, the French army tried to iron out some of the ambiguities of status that it had experienced during the war with Prussia. Between 1875 and 1906, the French army phased out the female *cantinières*, whose position somewhere between soldiers and civilians was no longer tolerated.[12]

In later conflicts, the destruction of cultural sites also signaled the escalation of war. In August 1914, the German occupation of the Belgian city of Louvain devolved into panic and massacre; German soldiers broke into and deliberately set fire to the university library. In the following month, the Germans shelled Rheims cathedral, the site of the coronation of generations of French monarchs.[13] Cultural destruction had evolved from an unfortunate by-product of war during the siege of Strasbourg to a central and deliberate aspect of combat in World War I.

At the same time, armies also increased their capacity to damage cities using artillery and aerial bombardment. The development of recoilless artillery increased the rate of fire from three or four shells per minute during the Franco-Prussian War to fifteen to thirty per minute by the early twentieth century. Armies also became more willing to kill civilians directly or through neglect. The distinction between undefended cities and fortresses eroded such that the concept of the open city became almost obsolete by World War I. The salient issue was no longer whether or not a city was being defended, but whether or not it served a military purpose. In World War II, belligerents on both sides used aerial bombardment more frequently than siege warfare to destroy industry or to punish or pressure civilians, but the few sieges that occurred took on enormous proportions. The German siege of Leningrad killed 700,000 Soviets, while the Allied use of aerial bombing killed 400,000 German civilians. On September 25, 1944, American bombers descended upon Strasbourg, a city with no strategic interest. This bombardment killed 158 inhabitants, wounded 333, and left 3,845 homeless. During the Franco-Prussian War, less than 4 percent of combat deaths were civilians. In World War II, the war in Europe killed some 15 million soldiers and 35 million civilians.[14]

Alongside these developments, Europeans began to debate the ratification of international laws to mitigate civilian suffering in wartime. International law encompassed (at least in theory) a wide variety of issues, including occupation, refugees, food aid, children's rights, labor rights, and minority populations. The brief discussion that follows focuses on the debates over which civilians, if any, could be the target of bombardment and whether civilians should be allowed to leave a stronghold.

In the early 1870s, a few voices, such as Swiss jurist Johann Kaspar Bluntschli, called for limitations to the targeting of civilians. British officer Edward Bruce Hamley argued for a simple rule: "Let the invader treat the population of the hostile State and use its resources as he would an ally's or his own."[15] Still, international law remained silent on the bombardment of civilians within strongholds. The Lieber Code (1863) of the U.S. Army had not discussed the targeted bombardment of civilians in a fortress city and allowed besiegers to prevent the exodus of women and children. Europeans, inspired by the Lieber Code, attempted to create international agreements in the Brussels Declaration (1874, never put into effect) and the Hague Conventions (1899 and 1907). Each of these documents limited bombardment to fortress cities—open cities could not be targeted—but did not distinguish between the fortifications and civilian habitations. Furthermore, they did not discuss the possibility of allowing noncombatants to freely leave besieged cities. In other words, these agreements accepted the bombardment and starvation of civilians as legitimate means of combat. The commanders of besieging forces still occasionally allowed the departure of civilians—the Americans at Santiago in 1898, the Japanese at Port Arthur in 1905—but such gestures came only when victory was already assured.

Even as late as World War II, Europeans had not codified the protection of besieged civilians. During the siege of Leningrad, German Field Marshall Wilhelm Ritter von Leeb issued the order that artillery be used "to prevent [civilians from attempting to flee Leningrad] . . . by opening fire as early as possible, so that the infantry is spared . . . shooting at civilians."[16] Civilians were not allowed to leave the Soviet city, and if they attempted to do so, they would be shelled. After the war, the Allies put Leeb on trial for war crimes at Nuremburg.[17] He defended himself with the argument that he had followed the customary treatment of civilians under siege. Reluctantly, the judges agreed. If the attacking army allowed civilians to leave, it would lose its superior position, and the judges ruled that international law permitted armies to pursue their advantage. The judges lamented, "We might wish the law were otherwise, but we must administer it as we find it."[18] The category of "civilian" was inscribed in international treaty in the 1977 additional protocols to the Geneva Convention.[19]

Although we might find that these documents do not go far enough to protect civilians, German military and legal theorists of the time found them to be too restrictive. In an extended response to Bluntschli, General Julius von Hartmann (1877) argued that the fortress and its city formed an inseparable unit. Making war against the fortress entailed bombarding the city, and it was no better for a city to experience lingering starvation than to submit to a short period of bombardment.[20] Hartmann's ideas were confirmed in the 1902 *German War Book*, a quasi-official document that, according to Isabel Hull, is in all likelihood "an accurate snapshot of what officers believed about the laws of war."[21] The *German War Book* argued that siege warfare "should tend" to the destruction of "material and moral resources"; therefore, "humanitarian consideration . . . toward persons or goods cannot be asked."[22] Given that the city and its fortifications "constitute an ensemble and an inseparable unity," bombardment "extends and *should* extend to the city itself."[23] A commander wishing to protect women, children, the elderly, the sick, and the wounded (no mention of civilian men) should do so before the city was invested. Afterward, there was no reason to allow civilian departures, as "the presence of these people can in certain circumstances hasten the capitulation of the place." Such departures contravened "the principles of war."[24] To be sure, several German commentators noted that the bombardment of Strasbourg in particular had been ineffective—it had turned the population against the Germans, and Uhrich had not given in to civilian pressure—but in theory, the bombardment of civilians remained acceptable practice.[25]

What about the responsibilities of a defending commander, like Uhrich, to the civilians of the stronghold? Although international law did not discuss this perspective, the French military regulations decreed on October 23, 1883, made a small but significant change. Instead of requiring an assault against a practicable breach, the decree allowed a commander to capitulate if he had "exhausted all means of defense" and "done all that duty and honor prescribe."[26] Still, the commander did not have the power to capitulate in order to preserve civilian life or property. This position received a challenge from retired division general Charles Thoumas, who argued in 1886 that the change in technology that allowed for civilian bombardment made the existing military regulations obsolete. He presented several reasons why a commanding officer of a stronghold should take civilians into account when deciding whether to capitulate, including the desire to "spare the civilians the horrors of being taken by assault" and the need to prevent civilians' fears from affecting the troops.[27] Furthermore, "humanity commands . . . that the weak and harmless part of the population not be exposed to assaults and bombardments. It is therefore indispensible to give any governor of a stronghold the means of distancing women, children and the elderly. For it does not suffice . . . to authorize them or even to invite them to leave. Experience has shown . . . that only the rich part of the population will take advantage of it."[28] The commander should therefore be able to provide transportation, food, and money to departing civilians. In this view, humanitarianism was now the duty of the military.

In the decades after 1870, neither international humanitarian law nor military custom extended robust protection to civilians. What about humanitarian aid? The Swiss intervention in Strasbourg did not lead directly to an international humanitarian aid regime aimed at relieving civilians. Prior to 1914, most humanitarian organizations either focused on soldiers or on missionary work; in a few instances, Red Cross aid extended to those suffering from a natural disaster, such as the 1908 earthquake in Sicily. During World War I, however, humanitarian aid to civilians exploded: the Commission for Relief in Belgium, the American organization led by Herbert Hoover, distributed more than five million tons of food over the course of five years, and Britain's Save the Children explicitly aimed to give aid to children regardless of nationality. The Swiss Federal Council helped deportees from occupied Belgium and northern France and facilitated the repatriation of civilian residents of foreign countries interned at the outbreak of war. The International Committee of the Red Cross, in addition to its work on behalf of wounded soldiers and prisoners of war, provided medical aid to wounded civilians. Even though noncombatants were not formally protected by international treaty, when wars actually occurred, some Europeans found the harm to civilians unacceptable and acted accordingly. By this time, humanitarianism also had become tightly interwoven with the modern concepts of international peacemaking and collective security. In the diplomatic meetings following the Great War, humanitarians became deeply involved in the "Paris System," which sought to defend civilization, protect minority populations, yet also, ominously, create ethnically homogenous states.[29]

The Swiss intervention in Strasbourg alerts us that in its early years humanitarian aid for civilians developed in fragmented, improvised form alongside modern warfare. Modern utopias, it seems, arise in tandem with modern nightmares: minority rights and mass deportation, the human right to bodily integrity and the sensationalism of violence, universal equality and dehumanizing crimes.[30] As armies targeted civilians who seemed "like us" and the plight of these civilians could be rapidly communicated to far-flung observers, some segments of the population took it upon themselves to respond. Strasbourg was a harbinger of what Craig Calhoun calls the "emergency imaginary," which posits that the world order usually runs smoothly but sometimes something goes

242 ■ THE SIEGE OF STRASBOURG

horribly wrong, and it is the ethical duty of those in a position to help to do so. Emergencies are now expected, something to prepare for in advance.[31]

■ ■ ■

Only after the bloodbath of World War I did Strasbourg return to France. A generation later, when Nazi Germany invaded France in 1940, Alsace was not just occupied but integrated into the Third Reich. The region was liberated at the end of 1944 and has been French and at peace ever since. Today, Strasbourg is a political center of the European Union and the home of the Council of Europe, the Central Commission for Navigation on the Rhine, and the European Court of Human Rights. The project of the European Union rests upon the deconstruction of the Rhineland frontier, a reconceptualization of the Rhine as a point of exchange rather than as a borderland.[32] Europeans on both sides of the Rhine can walk, bike, or drive freely across bridges from Germany to France and back again. Strasbourg houses the headquarters of ARTE, the European cultural television station. On summer nights, visitors continue to gaze at the rose-colored cathedral. A light show illuminates its lacy stonework, accompanied not by the thunder of shells but by the strains of Beethoven's Ninth Symphony, the hymn of the European Union announcing the brotherhood of man. Directly facing the cathedral, however, is a grim reminder of the conflicts of the past: an unexploded shell dating from 1870 remains lodged in the corner of the Hôtel Cathédrale.

Abbreviations

Notes

Acknowledgments

Index

Abbreviations

ADBR   Archives départementales du Bas-Rhin
AVCUS   Archives de la Ville et de la Communauté urbaine de Strasbourg
SHDV   Service historique de la défense à Vincennes

Notes

Introduction

1. I have chosen to focus on civilians rather than soldiers from either the French or German side. Elite civilian men dominate memoirs and public records; I have located precious few female diaries and memoirs, and no unmediated perspectives from the city's workers or Jewish citizens. Much of the documentation about Strasbourg's Jewish population was destroyed during the Second World War, when the Nazis occupied the city. The Archives of the Consistoire Israélite du Bas-Rhin contains tissue paper copies of the Consistory's official letters. However, the Consistory preserved copies of only two letters written during the siege. The ink has browned and bled through the delicate crinkly paper, rendering the missives completely illegible (CIBR 17, Journal de correspondance, 1870–1872). Non-Jewish authors pass over the experience of Jews as though they did not exist. We might wonder about the relationship between the city Jews and their less-assimilated coreligionists from the countryside who may have sought refuge within the walls. All I know with certainty is that the synagogue served as a small hospital during the entire period of the siege, caring for some twenty-five wounded, and that the Jewish school suffered some damage during the shelling of August 15 (Société Française de Secours aux Blessés et Malades Militaires, *Oeuvre internationale: Rapport du comité auxiliaire de Strasbourg* [Strasbourg: Berger-Levrault, 1871], 14–15; Frédéric Piton, *Siège de Strasbourg: Journal d'un assiégé* [Paris: Schlaeber, 1900], 48).

2. Frédéric Piton, *Strasbourg Illustré; ou, Panorama pittoresque, historique et statistique de Strasbourg et de ses environs* (1855; facsimile, Strasbourg: FNAC, 1987), preface.

3. Goethe's *Dichtung und Wahreit* quoted in Stephan Oettermann, *The Panorama: History of a Mass Medium,* trans. Deborah Lucas Schneider (New York: Zone Books, 1997), 9.

4. Piton, *Strasbourg Illustré,* 360.

5. Ibid., 363.

6. Anthony J. Steinhoff, *The Gods of the City: Protestantism and Religious Culture in Strasbourg, 1870–1914* (Leiden: Brill, 2008), 32–33.

7. Michael Loriaux, *European Union and the Deconstruction of the Rhineland Frontier* (New York: Cambridge University Press, 2008), 7–9; Mark Cioc, *The Rhine: An Eco-Biography, 1815–2000* (Seattle: University of Washington Press, 2002).

8. C. R. Whittaker, *Frontiers of the Roman Empire: A Social and Economic Study* (Baltimore: Johns Hopkins University Press, 1994), 73–74, 130; Loriaux, *Deconstruction*, 52.

9. Friedeburg, *1870: Die Belagerung von Strassburg* (Berlin: Sittenfeld, 1875), 4.

10. Georges Livet and Francis Rapp, *Histoire de Strasbourg* (Toulouse: Privat, 1987), 305; Malartic, *Le siége de Strasbourg pendant la campagne de 1870* (Paris: Librairie du *Moniteur universel*), 166; Stephen L. Harp, *Learning to Be Loyal: Primary Schooling as Nation Building in Alsace-Lorraine, 1850–1940* (Dekalb: Northern Illinois University Press, 1998), 34, 40, 46, 47.

11. Harp, *Learning to Be Loyal*, 15.

12. Max Reichard, *Aus den Tagen der Belagerung Strassburgs* (Bielefeld und Leipzig: Velhagen & Klasing, 1873), 2–3.

13. Piton, *Strasbourg illustré*, 127.

14. "O Strassburg, o Strassburg," accessed December 23, 2012, http://www.volksliederarchiv.de/text1401.html.

15. James J. Sheehan, *Where Have All the Soldiers Gone? The Transformation of Modern Europe* (Boston: Houghton Mifflin Company, 2008), 43–44; Alain Corbin, *The Village of Cannibals: Rage and Murder in France, 1870,* trans. Arthur Goldhammer (Cambridge, MA: Harvard University Press, 1992), 94–96.

16. Corbin, *Village of Cannibals*, 96.

17. Martin J. Wiener, *Men of Blood: Violence, Manliness and Criminal Justice in Victorian England* (New York: Cambridge University Press, 2004), 3.

18. Sheehan, *Soldiers*, 20.

19. Dennis Showalter, *The Wars of German Unification* (London: Hodder Arnold, 2004), 93.

20. Louis Hinckner, *Citoyens-combattants à Paris, 1848–1851* (Villeneuve d'Ascq: Presses Universitaires du Septentrion, 2008).

21. Michael Walzer, *Just and Unjust Wars: A Moral Argument with Historical Illustrations* (New York: Basic Books, 1977), 179.

22. Eliza Earle Ferguson, *Gender and Justice: Violence, Intimacy, and Community in Fin-de-Siècle Paris* (Baltimore: Johns Hopkins University Press, 2010), 213.

23. Osama W. Abi-Mershed, *Apostles of Modernity: Saint-Simonians and the Civilizing Mission in Algeria* (Stanford: Stanford University Press, 2010), 202.

24. Bertrand Taithe, "The Red Cross Flag in the Franco-Prussian War: Civilians, Humanitarians and War in the 'Modern Age,'" in *War, Medicine and Modernity*, eds. Roger Cooter, Mark Harrison and Steve Sturdy (Phoenix Mill: Sutton Publishing Ltd, 1998), 25.

25. Quoted in Geoffrey Wawro, *The Franco-Prussian War: The German Conquest of France in 1870–1871* (Cambridge: Cambridge University Press, 2003), 84.

26. François Roth, *La Guerre de 70* (Paris: Fayard, 1990), 508–510.

27. In World War I, Germany mobilized 197 men per 1000 of the entire population, versus 36 per 1000 in the war of 1870 (Alan Kramer, *Dynamic of Destruction:*

Culture and Mass Killing in the First World War [Oxford: Oxford University Press, 2007], 2).

28. Stéphane Audoin-Rouzeau, *1870: La France dans la guerre* (Paris: Armand Colin, 1989).

29. Christine G. Krüger, "German Suffering in the Franco-German War, 1870/71," *German History* 29, no. 3 (September 2011), 413.

30. Jean-Christoph Rufin, *Le piège humanitaire* (Paris: Jean-Claude Lattès, 1986); Taithe, "Red Cross Flag," 24; Rachel Chrastil, *Organizing for War: France, 1870–1914* (Baton Rouge: Louisiana State University Press, 2010), 127–151.

31. A[uguste] Schneegans, *La guerre en Alsace: Strasbourg* (Neuchâtel: J. Sandoz, 1871), 101.

32. This definition is modified from the one offered in Michael Barnett, *Empire of Humanity: A History of Humanitarianism* (Ithaca: Cornell University Press, 2011), 21: "What distinguishes humanitarianism from previous acts of compassion is that it is organized and part of governance, connects the immanent to the transcendent, and is directed at those in other lands."

33. Michael Barnett and Thomas G. Weiss, "Humanitarianism: A Brief History of the Present," in *Humanitarianism in Question: Politics, Power, Ethics,* eds. Barnett and Weiss (Ithaca: Cornell University Press, 2008), 15–21.

34. Heather Jones, "International or Transnational? Humanitarian action during the First World War," *European Review of History* 16, no. 5 (October 2009), 703–704.

35. The *cantinières,* women who accompanied the army to sell soldiers food and drink and often engaged in fighting, added to the ambiguity. See Thomas Cardoza, *Intrepid Women: Cantinières and Vivandières of the French Army* (Bloomington: Indiana University Press, 2010).

36. Martha Hanna, *The Mobilization of Intellect: French Scholars and Writers during the Great War* (Cambridge: Harvard University Press, 1996), 52.

1. The Grey Areas

1. Frédéric Piton, *Siège de Strasbourg: Journal d'un assiégé* (Paris: Schlaeber, 1900), x.

2. Frédéric Piton, *Strasbourg illustré; ou, Panorama pittoresque, historique et statistique de Strasbourg et de ses environs* (1855; facsimile, Strasbourg: FNAC, 1987), preface; Piton, *Siège de Strasbourg,* vi; AVCUS, 16 Z 26, Frères Réunis, certificates.

3. Piton, *Siège de Strasbourg,* x.

4. Anonymous, "Biographie des verstorbenen Friedrich Piton," *Strassburger Zeitung,* August 22, 1879; Piton, *Strasbourg illustré,* 269–270.

5. Catherine Dunlop, "Borderland Cartographies: Mapping the Lands Between France and Germany, 1860–1940" (Ph.D. diss., Yale University, 2010), 291.

6. Piton, *Siège de Strasbourg,* xi.

7. Ibid.

8. François Igersheim, *Politique et administration dans le Bas-Rhin (1848–1870)* (Strasbourg: Presses Universitaires de Strasbourg, 1993), 68.

9. Georges Livet and Francis Rapp, *Histoire de Strasbourg* (Toulouse: Privat, 1987), 322.

10. G. Foessel, "La vie quotidienne à Strasbourg à la veille de la guerre de 1870," in *L'Alsace en 1870–1871*, ed. F. L'Huillier (Strasbourg: Publications de la Faculté des Lettres de l'Université de Strasbourg, 1971), 15, 22, 24–26; John Craig, *Scholarship and Nation Building: The Universities of Strasbourg and Alsatian Society, 1870–1939* (Chicago: University of Chicago Press, 1984), 103; François Igersheim, *L'Alsace des notables, 1870–1914: La bourgeoisie et le peuple Alsacien* (Strasbourg: Nouvel Alsacien, 1981), 15; Livet and Rapp, *Histoire de Strasbourg*, 320; A. Faes, "Une enfance Strasbougeoise sous le Second Empire (1857–72)" *Annuaire de la Société des Amis du Vieux Strasbourg* (1980), 81–82.

11. Brigitte Fassnacht, "L'armée à Strasbourg (1852–1870)," (Mémoire de Maîtrise, Université des Sciences Humaines de Strasbourg, 1996), 15, 20, 46.

12. Livet and Rapp, *Histoire de Strasbourg*, 326.

13. David Allen Harvey, *Constructing Class and Nationality in Alsace, 1830–1945* (Dekalb: Northern Illinois University Press, 2001), 26; Nadine Schuster, "L'opinion publique et la vie politique à Strasbourg de 1852 à 1870," (Mémoire de Maîtrise, Université des Sciences Humaines de Strasbourg, 1985), 49, 53; Foessel, "Vie quotidienne," 15, 25–26, 28, 38.

14. E. Auguste Hoellbeck, *Almanach du commerce, de l'industrie, des sciences, des arts et des métiers de Strasbourg* (Strasbourg: Silbermann, 1836); AVCUS, 124 Z 3, *Règlement du Casino Commercial et Littéraire* (Strasbourg: Silbermann, 1838); Anthony J. Steinhoff, "Religion as Urban Culture: A View from Strasbourg, 1870–1914," *Journal of Urban History* 30, no. 2 (January 2004), 155; Faes, "Une enfance strasbougeoise," 81–82.

15. Igersheim, *Alsace des Notables*, 21–22; Foessel, "Vie Quotidienne," 14.

16. Rodolphe Reuss, "Chronique strasbourgeoise de la guerre franco-allemande du 16 Juillet au 24 Août 1870," in *Le siège de Strasbourg en 1870: Conférence et chronique strasbourgeoise juillet–août 1870*, ed. Jean Rott (Strasbourg: Libairie Istra, 1971), 37–38.

17. Bernard Le Clère and Vincent Wright, *Les préfets du Second Empire* (Paris: Armand Colin, 1973), Annexe I, n.p.; Roger Price, *The French Second Empire: An Anatomy of Political Power* (New York: Cambridge University Press, 2001), 99; A[uguste] Schneegans, *La guerre en Alsace: Strasbourg* (Neuchâtel: J. Sandoz, 1871), 163–164.

18. G. Erwin Ritter, *Die elsass-lothringische Presse im letzten Drittel des 19. Jahrhunderts* (Strasbourg: Börsendruckerei, 1933), 2–6; Livet and Rapp, *Histoire de Strasbourg*, 316.

19. P. Raymond-Signouret, *Souvenirs du bombardement et de la capitulation de Strasbourg* (Bayonne: P. Cazals, 1872), 207; Igersheim, *Alsace des Notables*, 11, 13, 16; Gustave Fischbach, *Le Siège de Strasbourg: Strasbourg avant, pendant, et après le siège* (Strasbourg: L'Imprimerie Alsacienne, 1897), 307.

20. The Prefect of the Bas-Rhin regarding the appointment of Humann's predecessor in 1852 (Price, *French Second Empire*, 89–90).

21. The proportion of Protestants and Jews nationwide each hovered around 1 in 50. Vicki Caron, *Between France and Germany: The Jews of Alsace-Lorraine, 1871–1918* (Stanford: Stanford University Press, 1988), 17–18; Patrick Cabanel, *Les Protestants et la République: de 1870 à nos jours* (Brussels: Editions Complèxe, 2000), 19; Anthony J. Steinhoff, *The Gods of the City: Protestantism and Religious Culture in Strasbourg, 1870–1914* (Leiden: Brill, 2008), 30, 33–34; Steinhoff, "Religion as Urban Culture," 165, 167; Stephen L. Harp, *Learning to Be Loyal: Primary Schooling as Nation Building in Alsace-Lorraine, 1850–1940* (Dekalb: Northern Illinois University Press, 1998), 12.

22. Piton, *Strasbourg illustré,* 279, 352–353.

23. Ibid., 94, 352–354, 357–359, 362–363.

24. Foessel, "Vie Quotidienne," 36; Steinhoff, "Religion as Urban Culture," 166; AVCUS, 1 MW 203, "Procès-verbaux, Conseil municipal de la ville de Strasbourg," July 1, 1870; Jean-Paul Haas, *Strasbourg, rue du Ciel: L'établissement des Diaconesses de Strasbourg Fête ses 150 ans d'existence européene* (Strasbourg: Editions Oberlin, 1992), 26.

25. Faes, "Une enfance strasbougeoise," 91.

26. Foessel, "Vie quotidienne," 20–21; Raymond-Signouret, *Souvenirs du bombardement,* 32, 328.

27. Piton, *Siège de Strasbourg,* 23.

28. Raymond-Signouret, *Souvenirs du bombardement,* 18–19.

29. A[uguste] Schneegans, *Strasbourg! Quarante jours de bombardement par un refugié strasbourgeois* (Neuchâtel: J. Sandoz, 1871), 14.

30. Armand Dayot, *L'invasion: Le siège 1870; La commune 1871* (Paris: Flammarion, 1901), 47; Baron du Casse, *Journal authentique du siége de Strasbourg* (Paris: Lacroix, Verboeckhoven, 1871), 9; Fischbach, *Siège de Strasbourg,* 491; Raymond-Signouret, *Souvenirs du Bombardement,* 29; Rudolf Wackernager, *Die Unterstützung der Stadt Strassburg durch die Schweiz im Kriegsjahr 1870* (Basel, 1895), 23.

31. Raymond-Signouret, *Souvenirs du bombardement,* 16; Malartic, *Le Siége de Strasbourg pendant la campagne de 1870* (Paris: Librairie du *Moniteur universel*), 66; Schneegans, *Strasbourg!,* 24.

32. H. Beaunis, *Impressions de campagne (1870–1871)* (Paris: Alcan and Berger-Levrault, 1887), 10–11.

33. Ibid., 10.

34. Reuss, "Chronique strasbourgeoise," 31.

35. Ibid.

36. Hollis Clayson, *Paris in Despair: Art and Everyday Life under Siege (1870–71)* (Chicago: The University of Chicago Press, 2002), 78.

37. Reuss, "Chronique strasbourgeoise," 31.

38. Michael Howard, *The Franco-Prussian War: The German Invasion of France, 1870–1871* (New York: The MacMillan Company, 1961), 67–68; Reuss, "Chronique strasbourgeoise," 30, 32; [Heinrich Kayser], *Erinnerungen an Strassburgs trübe Tage 1870 von einem alten Strassburger* (Strasbourg: Neuesten Nachrichten, 1902), 7; Emile Zola, *The Debacle,* trans. John Hands (London: Elek Books, 1968), 9.

252 ■ Notes to Pages 27–31

39. Raymond-Signouret, *Souvenirs du bombardement*, 11; Anonymous, "Strasbourg depuis la déclaration de guerre jusqu'en juin 1871" (unpublished manuscript, 1871), 1; Alan Forrest, "Citizenship and Military Service," in *The French Revolution and the Meaning of Citizenship*, eds. Renée Waldinger et al. (Westport, CT: Greenwood Press, 1993): 153–165; Forrest, "The French Revolution and the First *Levée en masse*," in *The People in Arms: Military Myth and National Mobilization since the French Revolution*, eds. Daniel Moran and Arthur Waldron (Cambridge: Cambridge University Press, 2003): 8–31; David A. Bell, *The First Total War: Napoleon's Europe and the Birth of Warfare as We Know It* (Boston: Houghton Mifflin, 2007), 149.

40. ADBR, 15 M 513, poster, Prefect Pron, 1870; Bertrand Taithe, "Neighborhood Boys and Men: The Changing Spaces of Masculine Identity in France, 1848–71," in *French Masculinities: History, Culture and Politics*, eds. Christopher E. Forth and Bertrand Taithe (New York: Palgrave MacMillan, 2007), 74–75; [Blech], *La défense de Strasbourg jugée par un républicain* (Neuchatel: Attinger, 1871), 13; Howard, *Franco-Prussian War*, 246.

41. Schneegans, *Strasbourg!*, 7–8; Reuss, "Chronique strasbourgeoise," 13, 35; [Blech], *Défense de Strasbourg*, 13; Schneegans, *Guerre en Alsace*, 55.

42. Reuss, "Chronique strasbourgeoise," 33–34.

43. Jean-Jacques-Alexis Uhrich, *Documents relatifs au siége de Strasbourg* (Paris: Dentu, 1872), 26–27, 55.

44. [Blech], *Défense de Strasbourg*, 12–13.

45. *Les murailles d'Alsace-Lorraine: Metz, Sarreguemines, Strasbourg, Haguenau, Saverne, Nancy, etc.* (Paris: L. Le Chevalier, 1874), 164.

46. Howard, *Franco-Prussian War*, 252.

47. Piton, *Siège de Strasbourg*, 58–61.

48. Helmuth von Moltke, *Correspondance militaire du Maréchal de Moltke*, vol. 2, *Guerre de 1870–71* (Paris: H. Charles-Lauvauzelle, n.d., ca.1900), 307, http://gallica .bnf.fr/ark:/12148/bpt6k36507t; Generallandesarchiv Karlsruhe, 456 F 4 no. 162, "Kriegstagebuch des Commandos des Belagerungscorps vor Strassburg," August 24, 1870; Raymond-Signouret, *Souvenirs du bombardement*, 71–72; Uhrich, *Documents*, 76–78.

49. Raymond-Signouret, *Souvenirs du bombardement*, 19; AVCUS, 281 MW 91, letter to Mayor Humann, July 18, 1870; Piton, *Siège de Strasbourg*, xv, 45.

50. Société Française de Secours aux Blessés et Malades Militaires, *Oeuvre internationale: Rapport du comité auxiliaire de Strasbourg* (Strasbourg: Berger-Levrault, 1871), 14–15; Etablissement des Diaconesses de Strasbourg, *Vingt-neuvième rapport* (Strasbourg: Berger-Levrault, 1871), 3–4.

51. ADBR, 2 G 482 F/73, "Procès-verbal du Conseil presbyterial de l'Eglise Reformée"; Max Reichard, *Aus den Tagen der Belagerung Strassburgs* (Bielefeld und Leipzig: Velhagen & Klasing, 1873), 7; Reuss, "Chronique strasbourgeoise," 32.

52. Véronique Harouel, *Histoire de la Croix-Rouge* (Paris: Presses Universitaires de France, 1999), 5–14; Sketch of Kablé in Piton, *Siège de Strasbourg*, 109; Société Française de Secours aux Blessés et Malades Militaires, *Oeuvre internationale*, 7–8.

53. Haas, *Strasbourg, rue du Ciel*, 13, 15, 100; Steinhoff, *Gods of the City*, 53.

54. Diaconesses, *Rapport*, 4.

55. Ibid., 4, 11, 21; Société Française de Secours aux Blessés et Malades Militaires, *Oeuvre internationale*, 14–15.

56. Sketch of Zopff in Piton, *Siège de Strasbourg*, 105; AVCUS, 16 Z 24, Frères Réunis, "Tableau général," 1870; Eric Burst, "La franc-maçonnerie strasbourgeoise au 19ème siècle: Une institution de bienfaisance méconnue (1803–1872)" (DEA d'Histoire de la Science Juridique Européene, 1994), 39–41, 58–60; Société Française de Secours aux Blessés et Malades Militaires, *Oeuvre internationale*, 10–11.

57. ADBR, 2 V 74, letter, Ministre de la Justice et des Cultes, Emile Ollivier to président du Directoire de l'Eglise de la Confession d'Augsburg, July 26, 1870; 2 V 38, "Procès-verbal, Directoire de l'Eglise de la Confession d'Augsburg," August 2 and 11, 1870.

58. Reichard, *Belagerung Strassburgs*, 6.

59. Ibid., 25.

60. Steinhoff, *Gods of the City*, 37–38.

61. René Epp, *Mgr Raess, Evêque de Strasbourg (1842–1887)* (Griesheim-sur-Souffel: Culture alsacienne, 1979), 139–140.

62. Steinhoff, *Gods of the City*, 38.

63. Wilhelm Horning, *Erlebnisse während der Belagerung von Strassburg 1870 aus seinem Tagebuch* (Strasbourg: Hubert, 1894), 5, 16.

64. Rodolphe Reuss, "Le siège de Strasbourg en 1870: conférence faite à l'Institut Populaire de Versailles, le 1er Avril 1902," in *Le siège de Strasbourg en 1870: Conférence et chronique strasbourgeoise juillet–août 1870*, ed. Jean Rott (Strasbourg: Libairie Istra, 1971), 15.

65. Letter from Charles Gerhardt to his son Charles, written in Strasbourg, dated August 9, 1870, quoted in Miss Jacot, *Le journal de Miss Jacot: 1870, siège de Strasbourg*, ed. and trans. Jean-Claude Ménégoz and René Kappler (Aubenas: Le Verger, 1996), 26.

66. Raymond-Signouret, *Souvenirs du bombardement*, 67.

67. AVCUS, 272 MW 84, "Souvenirs—à mes enfants," 1.

68. Cynthia Simmons and Nina Perlina, *Writing the Siege of Leningrad: Women's Diaries, Memoirs, and Documentary Prose* (Pittsburgh: University of Pittsburgh Press, 2002), 16.

69. Leslie Page Moch and Rachel G. Fuchs, "Getting Along: Poor Women's Networks in Nineteenth-Century Paris," *French Historical Studies* 18, no. 1 (Spring 1993), 36.

70. AVCUS, 272 MW 84, "Souvenirs," 1.

71. AVCUS, 272 MW 84, "Souvenirs," 3.

72. Zola, *The Debacle*, 11–13.

73. Reuss, "Chronique strasbourgeoise," 32.

74. AVCUS, 272 MW 84, "Souvenirs," 4.

75. Ibid.

76. Schneegans, *Strasbourg!*, 14–15.

77. Uhrich, *Documents,* 6; Du Casse, *Journal authentique,* 15.

78. Geoffrey Wawro, *The Franco-Prussian War: The German Conquest of France in 1870–1871* (Cambridge: Cambridge University Press, 2003), 41–45.

79. Howard, *Franco-Prussian War,* 63; Wawro, *Franco-Prussian War,* 67–68.

80. Howard, *Franco-Prussian War,* 63; Wawro, *Franco-Prussian War,* 75.

81. Wawro, *Franco-Prussian War,* 86.

82. Of 123 personnel in the naval detachment, only 43 were truly sailors, the rest being men demanded by the admiral. Other detachments of men came under the direct orders of Rear-admiral Excelmans, a total of about 3,000. Bergasse du Petit-Thouars, "Le siége de Strasbourg: Août et septembre 1870," *Le correspondant,* December 25, 1871, 992; Du Casse, *Journal authentique,* 16.

83. Wawro, *Franco-Prussian War,* 93–96.

84. Howard, *Franco-Prussian War,* 82–83; Wawro, *Franco-Prussian War,* 47–48, 75, 84; Geoffrey Wawro, *The Austro-Prussian War: Austria's War with Prussia and Italy in 1866* (New York: Cambridge University Press, 1996), 283.

85. Howard, *Franco-Prussian War,* 82; Wawro, *Franco-Prussian War,* 19–20, 24, 80–81; Dennis Showalter, *The Wars of German Unification* (London: Hodder Arnold, 2004), 50; Ebergard Gömer and Günther Haselier, *Baden-Württemberg: Geschichte seiner Länder und Territorien* (Würzburg: Ploetz KG, 1975), 68.

86. Howard, *Franco-Prussian War,* 102; Wawro, *Franco-Prussian War,* 101–102.

87. Reuss, "Chronique strasbourgeoise," 34.

88. Howard, *Franco-Prussian War,* 108, 116, 118; Wawro, *Franco-Prussian War,* 103, 121–137.

89. Du Casse, *Journal authentique,* 17; Reuss, "Chronique strasbourgeoise," 35.

90. AVCUS, 272 MW 84, "Souvenirs," 6.

91. Reuss, "Chronique strasbourgeoise," 34.

92. Beaunis, *Impressions de campagne,* 14–15; Howard, *Franco-Prussian War,* 116.

93. Reuss, "Chronique strasbourgeoise," 35.

2. Insiders and Outsiders

1. *Le courrier du Bas-Rhin,* August 7, 1870, supplement; Rodolphe Reuss, "Chronique strasbourgeoise de la guerre franco-allemande du 16 juillet au 24 août 1870," in *Le siège de Strasbourg en 1870: Conférence et chronique strasbourgeoise juillet–août 1870,* ed. Jean Rott (Strasbourg: Libairie Istra, 1971), 35; AVCUS, MS 204, letter from Emile Schmitt to his cousin Georg Schmidt, October 24, 1870.

2. Max Reichard, *Aus den Tagen der Belagerung Strassburgs* (Bielefeld und Leipzig: Velhagen & Klasing, 1873), 18.

3. Reuss, "Chronique strasbourgeoise," 35–36; Reichard, *Belagerung Strassburgs,* 19–20.

4. Bergasse du Petit-Thouars, "Le siége de Strasbourg: Août et septembre 1870," *Le correspondant,* December 25, 1871, 995.

5. Reuss, "Chronique strasbourgeoise," 36.

6. Quoted in Jean-Pierre Klein, "La vie quotidienne et la lutte à outrance à Strasbourg pendant le siège de 1870," *Revue historique de l'Armée* 29, no. 1 (1973), 172.

7. Geoffrey Best, *Humanity in Warfare* (New York: Columbia University Press, 1980), 61; Michael Wolfe, *Walled Towns and the Shaping of France: From the Medieval to the Early Modern Era* (New York: Palgrave MacMillan, 2009), 154.

8. Geoffrey Parker, *The Military Revolution: Military Innovation and the Rise of the West, 1500–1800* (Cambridge: Cambridge University Press, 1988), 9, 13, 43, 164, 166.

9. Michael Walzer, *Just and Unjust Wars: A Moral Argument with Historical Illustrations* (New York: Basic Books, 1977), 160; Simon Pepper, "Siege Law, Siege Ritual, and the Symbolism of City Walls in Renaissance Europe," in *City Walls: The Urban Enceinte in Global Perspective,* ed. James D. Tracy (New York: Cambridge University Press, 2000), 578–580; John A. Lynn II, *Women, Armies, and Warfare in Early Modern Europe* (Cambridge: Cambridge University Press, 2008), 159; Best, *Humanity in Warfare,* 93.

10. Lynn, *Women, Armies, and Warfare.*

11. Quoted in Leon Friedman, ed., *The Law of War: A Documentary History,* 2 vols (Westport, CT: Greenwood Press, 1972), 1:13.

12. Geoffrey Wawro, *Warfare and Society in Europe 1792–1914* (London: Routledge, 2000), 59–64; Brigitte Fassnacht, "L'armée à Strasbourg (1852–1870)," (Mémoire de Maîtrise, Université des Sciences Humaines de Strasbourg, 1996), 162.

13. Geoffrey Wawro, *The Franco-Prussian War: The German Conquest of France in 1870–1871* (Cambridge: Cambridge University Press, 2003), 58.

14. Wawro, *Franco-Prussian War,* 57; Wawro, *Warfare and Society,* 9.

15. AVCUS, MS 204, letter from Schmitt to Schmidt. On Henry Shrapnel: Wawro, *Warfare and Society,* 9.

16. Michael Howard, *The Franco-Prussian War: The German Invasion of France, 1870–1871* (New York: The MacMillan Company, 1961), 118; Wawro, *Franco-Prussian War,* 64.

17. Bergasse du Petit-Thouars, "Siége de Strasbourg," 991.

18. Fassnacht, "L'armée à Strasbourg," 41.

19. Bergasse du Petit-Thouars, "Siége de Strasbourg," 991.

20. Miss Jacot, *Le journal de Miss Jacot: 1870, siège de Strasbourg,* ed. and trans. Jean-Claude Ménégoz and René Kappler (Aubenas: Le Verger, 1996), 11.

21. Klein, "Vie quotidienne," 173; Grégory Lamarche, "L'urbanisme à Strasbourg de 1848 a 1870" (D.E.A., Université des Sciences Humaines de Strasbourg, 1996), 97, 100; Fassnacht, "L'armée à Strasbourg," 86.

22. ADBR, 14 M 2, Uhrich to Pron, August 18, 1870.

23. P. Raymond-Signouret, *Souvenirs du bombardement et de la capitulation de Strasbourg* (Bayonne: P. Cazals, 1872), 38.

24. Jacot, *Journal,* 14.

25. Howard, *Franco-Prussian War,* 273.

26. Quoted in Malartic, *Le siége de Strasbourg pendant la campagne de 1870* (Paris: Librairie du *Moniteur universel*), 29.

27. G. Foessel, "La vie quotidienne à Strasbourg à la veille de la guerre de 1870," in *L'Alsace en 1870–1871,* ed. F. L'Huillier (Strasbourg: Publications de la Faculté des Lettres de l'Université de Strasbourg, 1971), 13.

28. Quoted in Colin Jones, *Paris: The Biography of a City* (New York: Penguin, 2005), 301.

29. Foessel, "Vie quotidienne," 13; Georges Livet and Francis Rapp, *Histoire de Strasbourg* (Toulouse: Privat, 1987), 320; Anthony J. Steinhoff, *The Gods of the City: Protestantism and Religious Culture in Strasbourg, 1870–1914* (Leiden: Brill, 2008), 31; Lamarche, "L'urbanisme à Strasbourg," 69–70, 77.

30. Lamarche, "L'urbanisme à Strasbourg," 69–70, 85, 100; Fassnacht, "L'armée à Strasbourg," 127–128.

31. Foessel, "Vie quotidienne," 13; Lamarche, "L'urbanisme à Strasbourg," 85–86; H. Magnus, "Erlebnisse eines Land-Pfarrers in der Nähe Strassburgs" (unpublished manuscript, October 1870), 3, 6, 10–11; Howard, *Franco-Prussian War,* 254.

32. Michael Sorgius, *Schiltigheim während der Belagerung von Strassburg im Jahre 1870* (Schiltigheim: Bartl and Reimann, 1907), 7; Bergasse du Petit-Thouars, "Siége de Strasbourg," 991; Gustav Waltz, *Erlebnisse eines Feldarztes der badischen Division im Kriege 1870–71* (Heidelberg: Carl Winter's Universistätsbuchhandlung, 1872), 27.

33. Baron du Casse, *Journal authentique du siége de Strasbourg* (Paris: Lacroix, Verboeckhoven, 1871), 20; G. Bodenhorst, *Campagne de 1870–1871: Le siège de Strasbourg en 1870* (Paris: Dumaine, 1876), 45.

34. Emile Ehrhardt, *Siège de Strasbourg: Souvenirs d'un habitant de Schiltigheim* (Strasbourg: Imprimerie Alsacienne, 1909), 27.

35. Ehrhardt, *Siège de Strasbourg,* 34–35.

36. Bergasse du Petit-Thouars, "Siége de Strasbourg," 995.

37. H. Beaunis, *Impressions de campagne (1870–1871)* (Paris: Alcan and Berger-Levrault, 1887), 23.

38. Magnus, "Erlebnisse," 21.

39. Ehrhardt, *Siège de Strasbourg,* 27–28.

40. Jules-Edouard Dufrenoy, *Journal du siège de Strasbourg: 13 août–26 septembre 1870,* ed. Emmanuel Amougou (Paris: L'Harmattan, 2004), 36–37.

41. ADBR, 14 M 1, "Proclamation," Crown Prince Friedrich Wilhelm, n.d.; Société Française de Secours aux Blessés et Malades Militaires, *Oeuvre internationale: Rapport du comité auxiliaire de Strasbourg* (Strasbourg: Berger-Levrault, 1871), 11–12; Waltz, *Erlebnisse eines Feldarztes,* 19.

42. Isabel V. Hull, *Absolute Destruction: Military Culture and the Practices of War in Imperial Germany* (Cornell: Cornell University Press, 2005), 125; Anonymous, *Strasbourg: Journal des mois d'août et septembre 1870* (Paris: Sandoz et Fischbacher, 1874), 344–346; Felix Dahn, *Das Kriegsrecht: Kurze, volksthümliche Darstellung für Jedermann zumal für den deutschen Soldaten* (Würzburg: Stuber, 1870), 3.

43. Anonymous, *Strasbourg journal,* 22.

44. A[uguste] Schneegans, *La guerre en Alsace: Strasbourg* (Neuchâtel: J. Sandoz, 1871), 71–72.

45. Reuss, "Chronique strasbourgeoise," 36.

46. Wolfe, *Walled Towns*, 13.

47. Bergasse du Petit-Thouars, "Siége de Strasbourg," 992; Raymond-Signouret, *Souvenirs du bombardement*, 105–106.

48. *Bulletin des lois de l'Empire français*, July–December 1863, 914–915; Jacot, *Journal*, 27; Bergasse du Petit-Thouars, "Siége de Strasbourg," 994–995; Raymond-Signouret, *Souvenirs du bombardement*, 108–109; *Les murailles d'Alsace-Lorraine: Metz, Sarreguemines, Strasbourg, Haguenau, Saverne, Nancy, etc.* (Paris: L. Le Chevalier, 1874), 167.

49. *Bulletin des lois*, 1863/07–12, 914.

50. *Le courrier du Bas-Rhin*, August 7, 1870, supplement; Beaunis, *Impressions de campagne*, 25; Raymond-Signouret, *Souvenirs du bombardement*, 77; ADBR, 15 M 513, Uhrich and Pron, poster, August 14, 1870.

51. Bergasse du Petit-Thouars, "Siége de Strasbourg," 988–989.

52. Reichard, *Belagerung Strassburgs*, 19–20.

53. AVCUS, 272 MW 84, "Souvenirs—à Mes Enfants," 7.

54. Ibid., 30.

55. Ibid.

56. Guy Trendel, *Racontez-moi Strasbourg: Les très riches heures d'une ville libre* (Strasbourg: La Nuée Bleue, 2006), 223.

57. Raymond-Signouret, *Souvenirs du bombardement*, 42–43.

58. Ibid., 49–50.

59. Du Casse, *Journal authentique*, 19, 25; Malartic, *Siége de Strasbourg*, 27; Reuss, "Chronique strasbourgeoise," 31.

60. Malartic, *Siége de Strasbourg*, 111.

61. [Heinrich Kayser], *Erinnerungen an Strassburgs trübe Tage 1870 von einem alten Strassburger* (Strasbourg: Neuesten Nachrichten, 1902), 30–32.

62. *Bulletin des lois*, 1863/07–12, 919.

63. Ibid., 918.

64. *Murailles d'Alsace-Lorraine*, 160–161.

65. ADBR, 14 M 2, Uhrich and Pron, proclamation, August 10, 1870.

66. Raymond-Signouret, *Souvenirs du bombardement*, 62.

67. Bergasse du Petit-Thouars, "Siége de Strasbourg," 988.

68. Ibid., 988–989.

69. [Blech], *La défense de Strasbourg jugée par un républicain* (Neuchatel: Attinger, 1871), 12–13.

70. AVCUS, 272 MW 84, "Souvenirs," 8.

71. Foessel, "Vie quotidienne," 13.

72. Frédéric Piton, *Strasbourg illustré; ou, Panorama pittoresque, historique et statistique de Strasbourg et de ses environs* (1855; facsimile, Strasbourg: FNAC, 1987), 356–357; A. Faes, "Une enfance strasbougeoise sous le Second Empire (1857–72)" *Annuaire de la Société des Amis du Vieux Strasbourg* (1980), 85.

73. *Murailles d'Alsace-Lorraine*, 163.

74. AVCUS, 272 MW 14, letter from the inhabitants of the Faubourg de Pierres to Mayor Humann, August 15, 1870.

75. Anonymous, *Strasbourg journal*, 314.

76. AVCUS, 272 MW 14, letter Faubourg de Pierres to Humann, August 15, 1870.

77. Raymond-Signouret, *Souvenirs du bombardement*, 68–69.

78. Engraving in Rudolf von Pirscher, *Ingenieure und Pioniere im Feldzuge 1870–71: Belagerung von Strassburg* (Berlin: Schall, 1905), n.p.

79. Waltz, *Erlebnisse eines Feldarztes*, 42.

80. A[uguste] Schneegans, *Strasbourg! Quarante jours de bombardement par un refugié strasbourgeois* (Neuchâtel: J. Sandoz, 1871), 10.

81. E. von Conrady, *Das Leben des Grafen August von Werder* (Berlin: Ernst Siegfried Mittler und Sohn, 1889), 1, 5, 8, 110–11; Frederick III (Crown Prince Friedrich Wilhelm), *The War Diary of the Emperor Frederick III, 1870–1871*, ed. and trans. A. R. Allinson (New York: Howard Fertig, 1988), 35; Best, *Humanity in Warfare*, 202.

82. Howard, *Franco-Prussian War*, 107–112.

83. Helmuth von Moltke, *Correspondance militaire du Maréchal de Moltke*, vol. 2, *Guerre de 1870–71* (Paris: H. Charles-Lauvauzelle, n.d., ca.1900), 283, http://gallica .bnf.fr/ark:/12148/bpt6k36507t 283.

84. Stig Förster, "The Prussian Triangle of Leadership in the Face of a People's War: A Reassessment of the Conflict between Bismarck and Moltke, 1870–71," in *On the Road to Total War: The American Civil War and the German Wars of Unification, 1861–1871*, ed. Stig Förster and Jörg Nagler (New York: Cambridge University Press, 1997), 135.

85. Conrady, *Werder*, 110–111.

86. Engraving in Pirscher, *Ingenieure*, n.p.; Conrady, *Werder*, 110.

87. Helmuth von Moltke, *La guerre de 1870*, trans. E. Jaeglé, 8th ed. (Paris: H. Le Soudier, 1891), 163–164, http://gallica.bnf.fr/ark:/12148/bpt6k39959w; Du Casse, *Journal authentique*, 26; Frédéric Piton, *Siège de Strasbourg: Journal d'un assiégé* (Paris: Schlaeber, 1900), 42; Anonymous, *Ephémérides du siège et du bombardement de Strasbourg* (Strasbourg: Simon, 1871), 2–3.

88. Schneegans, *Strasbourg!*, 11.

89. Du Casse, *Journal authentique*, 26.

90. Bergasse du Petit-Thouars, "Siége de Strasbourg," 995.

91. Schneegans, *Strasbourg!*, 12.

92. AVCUS, 272 MW 84, "Souvenirs," 9–10; Schneegans, *Strasbourg!*, 9–10.

93. Gordon Wright, *France in Modern Times* (New York, W.W. Norton, 1983), 141; Livet and Rapp, *Histoire de Strasbourg*, 316; Klein, "Vie quotidienne," 172.

94. Sudhir Hazareesingh, *The Saint-Napoleon: Celebrations of Sovereignty in Nineteenth-Century France* (Cambridge: Harvard University Press, 2004), 3–4, 10; Fassnacht, "L'armée à Strasbourg," 159; Schneegans, *Strasbourg!*, 16.

95. ADBR, 14 M 1, letter (draft) Uhrich and Pron to clergy of Strasbourg, August 12, 1870.

96. Quoted in Gustave Fischbach, *Le siège de Strasbourg: Strasbourg avant, pendant, et après le siège* (Strasbourg: L'Imprimerie Alsacienne, 1897), 86–87 and Raymond-Signouret, *Souvenirs du bombardement*, 82.

97. Fischbach, *Siège de Strasbourg*, 87; Schneegans, *Strasbourg!*, 16.

98. W., *Erlebnisse eines schweizerischen Malers in Strassburg während der Belagerung im Jahre 1870* (Laufen: Köchlin, 1870), 8; Etablissement des Diaconesses de Strasbourg, *Vingt-neuvième rapport* (Strasbourg: Berger-Levrault, 1871), 3; Reichard, *Belagerung Strassburgs,* 24–25; Malartic, *Siége de Strasbourg,* 44–45.

99. Raymond-Signouret, *Souvenirs du bombardement,* 80–81; Reichard, *Belagerung Strassburgs,* 24–25.

100. AVCUS, 272 MW 84, "Souvenirs," 8.

101. Beaunis, *Impressions de campagne,* 13–14.

102. Reuss, "Chronique strasbourgeoise," 37.

103. W., *Erlebnisse eines schweizerischen Malers,* 9; Conrady, *Werder,* 112.

104. Generallandesarchiv Karlsruhe, 456 F 4 no. 162, "Kriegstagebuch des Commandos des Belagerungscorps vor Strassburg," August 15, 1870.

105. W., *Erlebnisse eines schweizerischen Malers,* 8.

106. AVCUS, 272 MW 84, "Souvenirs," 9–10.

107. Piton, *Siège de Strasbourg,* 48.

108. Anonymous, *Ephémérides,* 3.

109. Schneegans, *Strasbourg!,* 16; Beaunis, *Impressions de campagne,* 26.

110. Raymond-Signouret, *Souvenirs du bombardement,* 84.

3. Every Twenty Seconds

1. AVCUS, 272 MW 84, "Souvenirs—à mes enfants," 13.

2. E. von Conrady, *Das Leben des Grafen August von Werder* (Berlin: Ernst Siegfried Mittler und Sohn, 1889), 113–114; "Kriegschronik," *Illustrirte Zeitung* (Leipzig), September 3, 1870, 166; "Strasburg," [sic] *Illustrirte Zeitung* (Leipzig), September 10, 1870, 187; *Königlich Preußischer Staats-Anzeiger* account of the siege of Strasbourg, quoted in "Der Krieg," *Kölnische Zeitung,* October 1, 1870, 2; M. de Malartic, *Le siége de Strasbourg pendant la campagne de 1870* (Paris: Librairie du Moniteur universel, 1872), 80–81.

3. AVCUS, 272 MW 84, "Souvenirs," 11, 17.

4. Ibid., 18.

5. A[uguste] Schneegans, *La guerre en Alsace: Strasbourg* (Neuchâtel: J. Sandoz, 1871), 220.

6. Frédéric Piton, *Strasbourg illustré; ou, Panorama pittoresque, historique et statistique de Strasbourg et de ses environs* (1855; facsimile, Strasbourg: FNAC, 1987), 284, 288–290 ("peccadillo" quotation appears on 288).

7. Georges Livet and Francis Rapp, *Histoire de Strasbourg* (Toulouse: Privat, 1987), 322; François Igersheim, *Politique et administration dans le Bas-Rhin (1848–1870)* (Strasbourg: Presses Universitaires de Strasbourg, 1993), 276.

8. AVCUS, 272 MW 84, "Souvenirs," 29.

9. H. Beaunis, *Impressions de campagne (1870–1871)* (Paris: Alcan and Berger-Levrault, 1887), 5–6.

10. Piton, *Strasbourg illustré,* 270–271.

11. Ludger Lunier, *De l'influence des grandes commotions politiques et sociales sur le développement des maladies mentales: Mouvement de l'aliénation mentale en France pendant les années 1869 à 1873* (Paris: F. Savy, 1874), 28.

12. Schneegans, *Guerre en Alsace,* 12.

13. Ch. Thoumas, *Les capitulations: Etude d'histoire militaire sur la responsabilité du commandement* (Pairs: Librairie Militaire Berger-Levrault, 1886), 221.

14. Schneegans, *Guerre en Alsace,* 21; Anonymous, *Ephémérides du siége et du bombardement de Strasbourg* (Strasbourg: Simon, 1871), 6; Baron du Casse, *Journal authentique du siége de Strasbourg* (Paris: Lacroix, Verboeckhoven, 1871), 31; P. Raymond-Signouret, *Souvenirs du bombardement et de la capitulation de Strasbourg* (Bayonne: P. Cazals, 1872), 112; Max Reichard, *Aus den Tagen der Belagerung Strassburgs* (Bielefeld und Leipzig: Velhagen & Klasing, 1873), 31.

15. Raymond-Signouret, *Souvenirs du bombardement,* 110; Eissen, *Le service médical du bataillon de sapeurs-pompiers pendant le Siége de Strasbourg* (Strasbourg: Berger-Levrault, 1871), 13–14; Meyret, *Carnet d'un prisonnier de guerre* (Paris: Lecène and Oudin, 1888), 216; Schneegans, *Guerre en Alsace,* 113–114; Jules-Edouard Dufrenoy, *Journal du siège de Strasbourg: 13 août–26 septembre 1870,* ed. Emmanuel Amougou (Paris: L'Harmattan, 2004), 32; Jean-Jacques-Alexis Uhrich, *Documents relatifs au siége de Strasbourg* (Paris: Dentu, 1872), 55; *Le courrier du Bas-Rhin,* September 6, 1870; Du Casse, *Journal authentique,* 31–32.

16. Malartic, *Siége de Strasbourg,* 97.

17. Frédéric Piton, *Siège de Strasbourg: Journal d'un assiégé* (Paris: Schlaeber, 1900), 81.

18. Raymond-Signouret, *Souvenirs du bombardement,* 126.

19. Schneegans, *Guerre en Alsace,* 101.

20. AVCUS, 272 MW 84, Anonymous, letter, September 8, 1870, 4.

21. Malartic, *Siége de Strasbourg,* 79.

22. Ibid., 79.

23. Ibid., 97; Raymond-Signouret, *Souvenirs du bombardement,* 158; Oscar Berger-Levrault, *Le courrier du Bas-Rhin,* September 13, 1870.

24. Paul and Henry de Trailles, *Les femmes de France pendant la guerre et les deux siéges de Paris* (Paris: F. Polo, 1872), 40; Anonymous, *Ephémérides,* 6.

25. Quoted in Gustave Fischbach, *Le siège de Strasbourg: Strasbourg avant, pendant, et après le siège* (Strasbourg: L'Imprimerie Alsacienne, 1897), 378.

26. Beaunis, *Impressions de campagne,* 43.

27. AVCUS, 272 MW 84, "Souvenirs," 20, 27.

28. Ibid., 28.

29. Ibid., 14.

30. Ibid., 16.

31. Ibid., 13.

32. Léon Caïn, *Souvenirs du siège de Strasbourg 1870: Le combat du pont d'Illkirch (sortie du 16 août)* (Paris: Société Française d'Imprimerie et de Librairie, 1902); Conrady, *Werder,* 112; AVCUS, 272 MW 84, Anonymous, letter "à mon cher Gustave," August 22, 1870, 1; Gustav Waltz, *Erlebnisse eines Feldarztes der badischen Division im Kriege 1870–71* (Heidelberg: Carl Winter's Universistäts-buchhandlung, 1872), 25; Du Casse, *Journal authentique,* 35–36.

33. Quoted in Fischbach, *Siège de Strasbourg,* 108.

34. Reichard, *Belagerung Strassburgs,* 30; Raymond-Signouret, *Souvenirs du bombardement,* 196; Du Casse, *Journal authentique,* 32.

35. Reichard, *Belagerung Strassburgs,* 34.

36. AVCUS, 272 MW 84, "Souvenirs," 2–3.

37. Quoted in Raymond-Signouret, *Souvenirs du bombardement,* 137.

38. Sahr Conway-Lanz, *Collateral Damage: Americans, Noncombatant Immunity, and Atrocity after World War II* (New York: Routledge, 2006), 3.

39. My thanks to Phil Wynn for alerting me to this text, the *Cáin Adomnán* or "Law of the Innocents."

40. Davis Brown, *The Sword, the Cross, and the Eagle: The American Christian Just War Tradition* (Lanham: Rowman & Littlefield Publishers, 2008); Daryl Charles, "Presumption against War or Presumption against Injustice?: The Just War Tradition Reconsidered," *Journal of Church & State* 47, no. 2 (2005), 339; James Turner Johnson, "The Broken Tradition," *National Interest* 45 (1996): 27–36.

41. Mona Fixdal and Dan Smith, "Humanitarian Intervention and Just War," *Mershon International Studies Review* 42 (1998): 283–312, 288.

42. Jill Lepore, *The Name of War: King Philip's War and the Origins of American Identity* (New York: Vintage Books, 1999), 107–108; Conway-Lanz, *Collateral Damage,* 4.

43. Geoffrey Best, *Humanity in Warfare* (New York: Columbia University Press, 1980), 67.

44. David A. Bell, *The First Total War: Napoleon's Europe and the Birth of Warfare as We Know It* (Boston: Houghton Mifflin Company, 2007), 140.

45. Best, *Humanity in Warfare,* 126.

46. C. Lueder, *La Convention de Genève au point de vue historique, critique et dogmatique* (Paris: Edouard Besold, 1876), 232; for an example at Strasbourg, see "Der Krieg," *Kölnische Zeitung,* September 2, 1870, 1.

47. Uhrich, *Documents,* 28–30.

48. Schneegans, *Guerre en Alsace,* 136.

49. Malartic, *Siége de Strasbourg,* 107–108.

50. Miss Jacot, *Le journal de Miss Jacot: 1870, siège de Strasbourg,* ed. and trans. Jean-Claude Ménégoz and René Kappler (Aubenas: Le Verger, 1996), 49.

51. Michael Walzer, *Just and Unjust Wars* (New York: Basic Books, 1977), 169.

52. Quoted in Sergei Varshavsky and Boris Rest, *The Ordeal of the Hermitage: The Siege of Leningrad, 1941–1944,* trans. Arthur Shkarovsky-Raffé (Leningrad: Aurora Art Publishers, 1985), 272.

53. Isabel V. Hull, *Absolute Destruction: Military Culture and the Practices of War in Imperial Germany* (Cornell: Cornell University Press, 2005), 220, 224.

54. Helmuth von Moltke, *Correspondance militaire du Maréchal de Moltke,* vol. 2, *Guerre de 1870–71* (Paris: H. Charles-Lauvauzelle, n.d., ca.1900), 302, http://gallica.bnf.fr/ark:/12148/bpt6k36507t.

55. Michael Howard, *The Franco-Prussian War: The German Invasion of France, 1870–1871* (New York: The MacMillan Company, 1961), 273.

56. Bell, *First Total War,* 283.

57. Quoted in Conrady, *Werder*, 123.
58. Dennis Showalter, *The Wars of German Unification* (London: Hodder Arnold, 2004), 292; Thomas E. Kaiser, "From the Austrian Committee to the Foreign Plot: Marie-Antoinette, Austrophobia, and the Terror," *French Historical Studies* 26, no. 4 (Fall 2003), 594–595.
59. Hull, *Absolute Destruction*, 224; Rodolphe Reuss, *Les bibliothèques publiques de Strasbourg incendiées dans la nuit du 24 août 1870* (Paris: Fischbacher, 1871), 18–19.
60. Hull, *Absolute Destruction*, 103.
61. Ibid., 98.
62. Stig Förster, "The Prussian Triangle of Leadership in the Face of a People's War: A Reassessment of the Conflict between Bismarck and Moltke, 1870–71," in *On the Road to Total War: The American Civil War and the German Wars of Unification, 1861–1871*, ed. Stig Förster and Jörg Nagler (New York: Cambridge University Press, 1997), 122–123.
63. Showalter, *Wars of German Unification*, 292.
64. Förster, "Prussian Triangle," 128.
65. Quoted in Alexander B. Downes, *Targeting Civilians in War* (Ithaca: Cornell University Press, 2008), 181.
66. Conrady, *Werder*, 109.
67. Quoted in Conrady, *Werder*, 123.
68. Best, *Humanity in Warfare*, 155.
69. Leon Friedman, ed., *The Law of War: A Documentary History* (Westport, CT: Greenwood Press, 1972), 1:161.
70. Ibid., 1:162.
71. Ibid., 1:165.
72. Ibid., 1:152.
73. Bertrand Taithe, *Defeated Flesh: Welfare, Warfare and the Making of Modern France*, (Manchester, England: Manchester University Press, 1999), 162.
74. Helmuth von Moltke, *La guerre de 1870*, trans. E. Jaeglé, 8th ed. (Paris: H. Le Soudier, 1891), 574–575, http://gallica.bnf.fr/ark:/12148/bpt6k39959w.
75. Quoted in Best, *Humanity in Warfare*, 202.
76. Moltke, *Guerre de 1870*, 163.
77. Anonymous, *Éphémérides*, 4–5.
78. Schneegans, *Guerre en Alsace*, 78.
79. Georges Foessel, "Journal du siège de Strasbourg par Cécile de Dartein," *Annuaire de la Société des Amis du Vieux-Strasbourg* 15 (1985), 85; Piton, *Siège de Strasbourg*, 190–193; Schneegans, *Guerre en Alsace*, 135–136.
80. Quoted in Conrady, *Werder*, 155.
81. Ute Frevert, *A Nation in Barracks: Modern Germany, Military Conscription and Civil Society*, trans. Andrew Boreham with Daniel Brückenhaus (Oxford: Berg, 2004), 222.
82. Simon Pepper, "Siege Law, Siege Ritual, and the Symbolism of City Walls in Renaissance Europe," in *City Walls: The Urban Enceinte in Global Perspective*, ed. James D. Tracy (New York: Cambridge University Press, 2000), 574.

83. SHDV, Ln 10, Werder to Uhrich, August 20, 1870.
84. SHDV, Ln 10, Werder to Uhrich, August 19, 1870.
85. SHDV, Ln 10, Uhrich to Werder, August 20, 1870.
86. Ibid.
87. SHDV, Ln 10, Werder to Uhrich, August 20, 1870.
88. Schneegans, *Guerre en Alsace,* 250–251.
89. AVCUS, 272 MW 84, "Souvenirs," 7.
90. Uhrich, *Documents,* 38.
91. SHDV, Ln 10, Werder to Uhrich, August 20, 1870.
92. SHDV, Ln 10, Uhrich to Werder, August 21, 1870.
93. Ibid.
94. Ibid.
95. SHDV, Ln 10, Werder to Uhrich, August 21, 1870.
96. Uhrich, *Documents,* 38.
97. SHDV, Ln 10, Werder to Uhrich, August 22, 1870; Uhrich, *Documents,* 40.
98. Malartic, *Siége de Strasbourg,* 56–57.
99. Rodolphe Reuss, "Le siège de Strasbourg en 1870: Conférence faite à l'Institut Populaire de Versailles, le 1er Avril 1902," in *Le siège de Strasbourg en 1870: Conférence et chronique Strasbourgeoise juillet–août 1870,* ed. Jean Rott (Strasbourg: Libairie Istra, 1971), 18.
100. Reuss, "Conférence," 18.
101. Raymond-Signouret, *Souvenirs du bombardement,* 123.
102. Piton, *Siège de Strasbourg,* 80.
103. Ibid., 83.
104. Rodolphe Reuss, "Chronique strasbourgeoise de la guerre franco-allemande du 16 juillet au 24 août 1870," in *Le siège de Strasbourg en 1870: Conférence et chronique strasbourgeoise juillet–août 1870,* ed. Jean Rott (Strasbourg: Libairie Istra, 1971), 37.
105. Julius von Wickede, "Kriegsfahrten," *Kölnische Zeitung,* September 10, 1870, 2.
106. Hermann Bartholomä, *Erlebnisse eines Badischen Lazareth-Unteroffiziers im Feldzuge 1870/71* (Karlsruhe: J. J. Reiff, 1897), 52–53.
107. Wickede, "Kriegsfahrten," *Kölnische Zeitung,* September 10, 1870, 2.
108. Quoted in Reichard, *Belagerung Strassburgs,* 57.
109. Ibid., 60.
110. Ibid., 61.
111. Ibid., 61.
112. Piton, *Strasbourg illustré,* 282.
113. Piton, *Siège de Strasbourg,* v–vii.
114. Willa Z. Silverman, *The New Bibliopolis: French Book Collectors and the Culture of Print, 1880–1914* (Toronto: University of Toronto Press, 2008), 3.
115. Piton, *Strasbourg illustré,* 291.
116. Generallandesarchiv Karlsruhe, 456 F 4 no. 183, letter from Mühler to Bismarck-Bohlen, August 27, 1870.
117. Ibid., 292.
118. Reuss, "Chronique strasbourgeoise," 38.

119. "Diabolical": Reuss, "Chronique strasbourgeoise," 56; "marvelous" and "stupefying": Reuss, *Bibliothèques publiques,* 18.

120. Reuss, "Conférence," 19–20.

121. A. G. Heinhold in *L'impartial du Rhin,* quoted in Raymond-Signouret, *Souvenirs du bombardement,* 88.

122. Holger H. Herwig, "An Introduction to Military Archives in West Germany," *Military Affairs* 36, no. 4 (December 1972): 121–124.

123. Johann Wilemn Baum, quoted in John Craig, *Scholarship and Nation Building: The Universities of Strasbourg and Alsatian Society, 1870–1939* (Chicago: University of Chicago Press, 1984), 31.

124. Best, *Humanity in Warfare,* 160.

125. Schneegans, *Guerre en Alsace,* 96.

126. Ibid.

127. Ibid., 97.

128. Christine G. Krüger, "German Suffering in the Franco-German War, 1870/71," *German History* 29, no. 3 (September 2011), 404.

129. Reuss, *Bibliothèques publiques,* 21.

130. Norbert Elias, *The Civilizing Process: Sociogenetic and Psychogenetic Investigations,* trans. Edmund Jephcott, ed. Eric Dunning, Johan Goudsblom, and Stephen Mennell (Oxford: Blackwell Publishers, 2000), 6.

131. Reuss, "Chronique strasbourgeoise," 55.

132. Reuss, *Bibliothèques publiques,* 19.

133. A[uguste] Schneegans, *Strasbourg! Quarante jours de bombardement par un refugié Strasbourgeois* (Neuchâtel: J. Sandoz, 1871), 10.

134. Schneegans, *Guerre en Alsace,* 94.

135. Martha Hanna, *The Mobilization of Intellect: French Scholars and Writers during the Great War* (Cambridge: Harvard University Press, 1996), 9–10.

136. Taithe, *Defeated Flesh,* 163–164.

137. Craig, *Scholarship and Nation Building,* 31.

138. Raymond-Signouret, *Souvenirs du bombardement,* 90.

139. Osama W. Abi-Mershed, *Apostles of Modernity: Saint-Simonians and the Civilizing Mission in Algeria* (Stanford: Stanford University Press, 2010), 11.

140. Reuss, "Chronique strasbourgeoise," 56.

141. Ibid.

142. Ibid., 55.

143. Ibid., 56.

144. Ibid., 56.

145. "Der Krieg," *Kölnische Zeitung,* September 2, 1870, 1.

146. "Vom Kriegschauplatz," *Volks-Zeitung* (Berlin), September 12, 1.

147. Reuss, "Chronique strasbourgeoise," 55.

148. Schneegans, *Guerre en Alsace,* 98.

149. Du Casse, *Journal authentique,* 30.

4. Victims in the Eye of the Beholder

1. Quoted in Jean-Jacques-Alexis Uhrich, *Documents relatifs au siége de Strasbourg* (Paris: Dentu, 1872), 44–45.

2. Generallandesarchiv Karlsruhe, 456 F 4 no. 162, "Kriegstagebuch des Commandos des Belagerungscorps vor Strassburg," August 26, 1870; quoted in Reinhold Wagner, *Geschichte der Belagerung von Strassburg im Jahre 1870* (Berlin: F. Schneider, 1878), 85*.

3. Uhrich, *Documents*, 45.

4. Quoted in ibid., 49.

5. Uhrich, *Documents*, 51.

6. A[uguste] Schneegans, *La guerre en Alsace: Strasbourg* (Neuchâtel: J. Sandoz, 1871), 147.

7. Frédéric Piton, *Siège de Strasbourg: Journal d'un assiégé* (Paris: Schlaeber, 1900), 91.

8. Schneegans, *Guerre en Alsace*, 22.

9. P. Raymond-Signouret, *Souvenirs du bombardement et de la capitulation de Strasbourg* (Bayonne: P. Cazals, 1872), 149.

10. Schneegans, *Guerre en Alsace*, 22.

11. Uhrich, *Documents*, 50.

12. Ibid.

13. Fernand L'Huillier, "L'attitude politique de Mgr Raess entre 1859 et 1879," *Etudes alsaciennes* (F.X. Le Roux: Strasbourg, 1947), 251; René Epp, *Mgr Raess, Evêque de Strasbourg (1842–1887)* (Griesheim-sur-Souffel: Culture Alsacienne, 1979), 6.

14. Uhrich, *Documents*, 50.

15. Helmuth von Moltke, *La guerre de 1870*, trans. E. Jaeglé, 8th ed. (Paris: H. Le Soudier, 1891), 163–164, http://gallica.bnf.fr/ark:/12148/bpt6k39959w.

16. Gustave Fischbach, *Le siège de Strasbourg: Strasbourg avant, pendant, et après le siège* (Strasbourg: L'Imprimerie Alsacienne, 1897), 171.

17. "Der Krieg," *Kölnische Zeitung*, September 2, 1870, 1; *National-Zeitung* (Berlin), August 30, 1870; Quoted in Anonymous, *Strasbourg: Journal des mois d'août et septembre 1870* (Paris: Sandoz et Fischbacher, 1874), 75.

18. L'Huillier, "Mgr Raess," 249.

19. Malartic, *Le siége de Strasbourg pendant la campagne de 1870* (Paris: Librairie du Moniteur universel), 75.

20. Quoted in E. von Conrady, *Das Leben des Grafen August von Werder* (Berlin: Ernst Siegfried Mittler und Sohn, 1889), 124.

21. Robert Asmus, "Drei Tage vor Strasburg," *Illustrirte Zeitung* (Leipzig), October 8, 1870, 251.

22. Fischbach, *Siège de Strasbourg*, 171.

23. Malartic, *Siége de Strasbourg*, 76.

24. Rodolphe Reuss, "Chronique strasbourgeoise de la guerre franco-allemande du 16 juillet au 24 août 1870," in *Le siège de Strasbourg en 1870: Conférence et chronique strasbourgeoise juillet–août 1870*, ed. Jean Rott (Strasbourg: Libairie Istra, 1971), 39.

25. Malartic, *Siége de Strasbourg*, 81.

26. Uhrich, *Documents*, 53.

27. AVCUS, 272 MW 18, Jules Sengenwald, letter to Acting Mayor Klein, August 7, 1871.

28. Ibid.

29. Michael Howard, *The Franco-Prussian War: The German Invasion of France, 1870–1871* (New York: The MacMillan Company, 1961), 274–275.

30. "Der Krieg," *Kölnische Zeitung*, October 1, 1870, 2; Emil Frommel, *O Strassburg, du Wunderschöne Stadt! Alte und Neue, Freudvolle und Leidvolle, Fremde und Eigene: Erinnerungen eines Feldpredigers vor Strassburg im Jahr 1870* (Stuttgart: Steinkopf, 1872), 69; "Vom Kriegschauplatz," *Volks-Zeitung* (Berlin), September 7, 1870, 2.

31. Uhrich, *Documents*, 61–62; Baron du Casse, *Journal authentique du siége de Strasbourg* (Paris: Lacroix, Verboeckhoven, 1871), 46–47; Anonymous, *Ephémérides du siége et du bombardement de Strasbourg* (Strasbourg: Simon, 1871), 9.

32. Moltke, *Guerre de 1870*, 164–165; "Vom Kriegschauplatz," *Volks-Zeitung* (Berlin), September 7, 1870, 2; *Neue Preussische Zeitung*, September 8, 1870, 2; Julius von Wickede, "Kriegsfahrten," *Kölnische Zeitung*, September 12, 1870, 1.

33. Société Française de Secours aux Blessés et Malades Militaires, *Oeuvre internationale: Rapport du comité auxiliaire de Strasbourg* (Strasbourg: Berger-Levrault, 1871), 12; H. Beaunis, *Impressions de campagne (1870–1871)* (Paris: Alcan and Berger-Levrault, 1887), 46; Raymond-Signouret, *Souvenirs du bombardement*, 355.

34. Beaunis, *Impressions de campagne*, 46; Société Française de Secours aux Blessés et Malades Militaires, *Oeuvre internationale*, 12–15; Jacques Flach, *Strasbourg après le bombardement: 2 octobre 1870–30 septembre 1872; Rapport sur les travaux du Comité de Secours Strasbourgeois pour les Victimes du Bombardement* (Strasbourg: Fischbach, 1873), 3.

35. François Poncet, *Hôpital militaire, service de la 1re division de blessés, siége de Strasbourg (1870)* (Montpellier: Boehm et fils, 1872); Société Française de Secours aux Blessés et Malades Militaires, *Oeuvre internationale*, 12; Beaunis, *Impressions de campagne*, 46.

36. Wagner, *Geschichte der Belagerung von Strassburg*, 151–52*; Flach, *Strasbourg*, 4; Fischbach, *Siège de Strasbourg*, 521–528; Beaunis, *Impressions de campagne*, 42.

37. Wagner, *Geschichte der Belagerung von Strassburg*, 152*; Raymond-Signouret, *Souvenirs du bombardement*, 333.

38. Raymond-Signouret, *Souvenirs du bombardement*, 111.

39. Malartic, *Siége de Strasbourg*, 46; Raymond-Signouret, *Souvenirs du bombardement*, 138–139.

40. Schneegans, *Guerre en Alsace*, 93.

41. Ibid., 95.

42. Malartic, *Siége de Strasbourg*, 107.

43. "Vom Kriegschauplatz," *Volks-Zeitung* (Berlin), September 14, 1870, 2.

44. I consider all individuals listed with an occupation or marital status to be adults. This includes all individuals age nineteen and older, and about half of those age seventeen and eighteen (Fischbach, *Siège de Strasbourg*, 521–527).

45. Raymond-Signouret, *Souvenirs du bombardement*, 355.

46. Anonymous, "Strasbourg depuis la déclaration de guerre jusqu'en juin 1871" (unpublished manuscript, 1871), 8.

47. Beaunis, *Impressions de campagne*, 42.

48. Men's and women's actions are differentiated in the vast majority of accounts, with one exception. The municipal council of Strasbourg praised "men and women" without difference in a public announcement issued May 29, 1871 (quoted in Fischbach, *Siège de Strasbourg,* 501).

49. Georges Foessel, "Journal du siège de Strasbourg par Cécile de Dartein," *Annuaire de la Société des Amis du Vieux-Strasbourg* 15 (1985), 89.

50. Ibid., 76.

51. Cynthia Simmons and Nina Perlina, *Writing the Siege of Leningrad: Women's Diaries, Memoirs, and Documentary Prose* (Pittsburgh: University of Pittsburgh Press, 2002), 120.

52. Bergasse du Petit-Thouars, "Le siége de Strasbourg: Août et septembre 1870," *Le correspondant,* December 25, 1871, 997.

53. Ibid.

54. Ibid.

55. Joseph Turquan, *Les femmes de France pendant l'invasion* (Paris: Berger-Levrault, 1893), 228.

56. Beaunis, *Impressions de campagne,* 45.

57. Turquan, *Femmes de France,* 227–228.

58. Bergasse du Petit-Thouars, "Siége de Strasbourg," 997.

59. Margaret H. Darrow, "In the Land of Joan of Arc: The Civic Education of Girls and the Prospect of War in France, 1871–1914," *French Historical Studies,* 31, no. 2 (Spring 2008): 279–280; John A. Lynn II, *Women, Armies, and Warfare in Early Modern Europe* (Cambridge: Cambridge University Press, 2008), 63–64, 204, 205–8; David A. Bell, *The First Total War: Napoleon's Europe and the Birth of Warfare as We Know It* (Boston: Houghton Mifflin Company, 2007), 281; Simmons and Perlina, *Writing the Siege of Leningrad,* 5.

60. Thomas Cardoza, *Intrepid Women: Cantinières and Vivandières of the French Army* (Bloomington: Indiana University Press, 2010), 163–164, 172–173; Darrow, "In the Land of Joan of Arc," 284–287, 290–291; Margaret H. Darrow, "Nursing Heroines of the Franco-Prussian War," paper presented at the Western Society for French History Annual Conference, Quebec, Canada, November 2008; Hollis Clayson, *Paris in Despair: Art and Everyday Life under Siege (1870–71)* (Chicago: The University of Chicago Press, 2002), 130.

61. Bertrand Taithe, "Neighborhood Boys and Men: The Changing Spaces of Masculine Identity in France, 1848–71," in *French Masculinities: History, Culture and Politics,* eds. Christopher E. Forth and Bertrand Taithe (New York: Palgrave MacMillan, 2007), 73, 81.

62. Uhrich, *Documents,* 139; Fischbach, *Siège de Strasbourg,* 520–521; Auguste Münch, *Guerre de 1870: Siège et Bombardement de Strasbourg* (1870).

63. Schneegans, *Guerre en Alsace,* 145–146.

64. Ibid., 154.

65. Ibid., 154–155.

66. Beaunis, *Impressions de campagne,* 46.

67. Poncet, *Hôpital militaire,* 3.

68. Beaunis, *Impressions de campagne,* 46.

69. Ibid., 47–48.

70. Ibid., 47.

71. Ibid., 48.

72. Robert Graves, *Good-Bye to All That* (New York: Anchor Books, 1985).

73. Bertrand Taithe, *Defeated Flesh: Welfare, Warfare and the Making of Modern France* (Manchester, England: Manchester University Press, 1999), 180–190.

74. Beaunis, *Impressions de campagne,* 46.

75. Ibid.

76. Poncet, *Hôpital militaire,* 47.

77. Joseph Lister, "On the Antiseptic Principle in the Practice of Surgery," *British Medical Journal* 2, no. 351 (September 21, 1867): 246–248; Uhrich, *Documents,* 41; Société Française de Secours aux Blessés et Malades Militaires, *Oeuvre internationale,* 12–13; David S. Barnes, *The Great Stink of Paris and the Nineteenth-Century Struggle Against Filth and Germs* (Baltimore: Johns Hopkins University Press, 2006), 101–102; Poncet, *Hôpital militaire,* 59–61.

78. Poncet, *Hôpital militaire,* 62.

79. Ibid., 64.

80. Ibid., 68.

81. Ibid., 78.

82. Ibid., 60–61.

83. Beaunis, *Impressions de campagne,* 3.

84. Robert A. Nye, *Crime, Madness, and Politics in Modern France: The Medical Concept of National Decline* (Princeton: Princeton University Press, 1984).

85. Quoted in Raymond-Signouret, *Souvenirs du bombardement,* 129–131.

86. Ludger Lunier, *De l'influence des grandes commotions politiques et sociales sur le développement des maladies mentales: Mouvement de l'aliénation mentale en France pendant les années 1869 à 1873* (Paris: F. Savy, 1874), 3, 32–33.

87. Ibid., 223. Overall, however, admissions in occupied territories dropped by about 25 percent compared with the previous years. Lunier attributed the drop in admissions partly to disruptions in services and government funding. He also believed that the war served as a diversion from the ordinary causes of alienation, including civilian alcohol abuse (20, 23).

88. Beaunis, *Impressions de campagne,* 44–45.

89. Thanks to Jessie Hewitt for her insight on this issue. Mark S. Micale and Paul Lerner, "Trauma, Psychiatry, and History: A Conceptual and Historiographical Introduction," in Micale and Lerner, ed., *Traumatic Pasts: History, Psychiatry, and Trauma in the Modern Age, 1870–1930* (New York: Cambridge University Press, 2001), 11.

90. Beaunis, *Impressions de campagne,* 44.

91. Piton, *Siège de Strasbourg,* 99, 116, 157–158; Alexander Watson, *Enduring the Great War: Combat, Morale and Collapse in the German and British Armies, 1914–1918* (Cambridge: Cambridge University Press, 2008).

5. Carrying On

1. *Blaetter aus dem Tagebuche eines Strassburgers waehrend der Belagerung in den Monaten August und September 1870* (Altona: Prinz, 1870), 9.

2. Jay M. Winter, "Paris, London, Berlin 1914–1919: Capital Cities at War," in *Capital Cities at War: Paris, London, Berlin 1914–1919,* ed. Jay M. Winter and Jean-Louis Robert (Cambridge: Cambridge University Press, 1997), 11–19.

3. H. Beaunis, *Impressions de Campagne (1870–1871)* (Paris: Alcan and Berger-Levrault, 1887), 42.

4. Frédéric Piton, *Siège de Strasbourg: Journal d'un assiégé* (Paris: Schlaeber, 1900), 100; AVCUS, 272 MW 84, "Souvenirs—à mes enfants," 25–26.

5. Anonymous, *Ephémérides du siége et du bombardement de Strasbourg* (Strasbourg: Simon, 1871), 8, 11; Malartic, *Le siége de Strasbourg pendant la campagne de 1870* (Paris: Librairie du *Moniteur universel*), 85–86; Piton, *Siège de Strasbourg,* 105.

6. Piton, *Siège de Strasbourg,* 123.

7. Rodolphe Reuss, *Les bibliothèques publiques de Strasbourg incendiées dans la nuit du 24 août 1870* (Paris: Fischbacher, 1871), 19; Anonymous, *Strasbourg: Journal des mois d'août et septembre 1870* (Paris: Sandoz et Fischbacher, 1874), 314; Rodolphe Reuss, "Le Siège de Strasbourg en 1870: Conférence Faite à l'Institut Populaire de Versailles, le 1er Avril 1902," in *Le Siège de Strasbourg en 1870: Conférence et Chronique Strasbourgeoise Juillet–Août 1870,* ed. Jean Rott (Strasbourg: Libairie Istra, 1971), 18; Gustave Fischbach, *Le siège de Strasbourg: Strasbourg avant, pendant, et après le siège* (Strasbourg: L'Imprimerie Alsacienne, 1897), 362.

8. ADBR, 2 V 38, "Procès-verbal, Directoire de l'Eglise de la Confession d'Augsbourg," August 11, 1870; Archives of the Consistoire Israelite du Bas-Rhin, CIBR 17, "Journal de correspondance, 1870–1872"; Rodolphe Reuss, "Chronique strasbourgeoise de la guerre franco-allemande du 16 juillet au 24 août 1870," in *Le siège de Strasbourg en 1870: Conférence et chronique strasbourgeoise juillet–août 1870,* ed. Jean Rott (Strasbourg: Libairie Istra, 1971), 41.

9. P. Raymond-Signouret, *Souvenirs du bombardement et de la capitulation de Strasbourg* (Bayonne: P. Cazals, 1872), 18.

10. AVCUS, 1 MW 204, "Procès-verbaux, Conseil d'administration de la ville de Strasbourg," August 22, 1870, 15.

11. A[uguste] Schneegans, *La guerre en Alsace: Strasbourg* (Neuchâtel: J. Sandoz, 1871), xxxv–xxxvi.

12. ADBR, 14 M 2, agents Montigny and Fleck to the Inspector of Police, September 5, 1870.

13. Jean-Pierre Klein, "La vie quotidienne et la lutte à outrance à Strasbourg pendant le siège de 1870," *Revue historique de L'Armée* 29, no. 1 (1973), 180; Max Reichard, *Aus den Tagen der Belagerung Strassburgs* (Bielefeld und Leipzig: Velhagen & Klasing, 1873), 37–39; Raymond-Signouret, *Souvenirs du bombardement,* 143.

14. *Le courrier du Bas-Rhin,* August 30, 1870.

15. AVCUS, 272 MW 84, "Souvenirs," 24.

16. A[uguste] Schneegans, *Strasbourg! Quarante jours de bombardement par un refugié strasbourgeois* (Neuchâtel: J. Sandoz, 1871), 27.

17. Kiéné, quoted in Paul and Henry de Trailles, *Les femmes de France pendant la guerre et les deux siéges de Paris* (Paris: F. Polo, 1872), 40.

18. Piton, *Siège de Strasbourg,* 116; Anonymous, "Strasbourg depuis la déclaration de guerre jusqu'en juin 1871" (unpublished manuscript, 1871), 8–9; Reuss, "Chronique strasbourgeoise," 42.

19. Reuss, "Chronique strasbourgeoise," 42–43.

20. AVCUS, 272 MW 84, "Souvenirs," 25.

21. Reuss, "Chronique strasbourgeoise," 42–43.

22. Ibid., 39.

23. Ibid., 40.

24. Ibid., 37–38, 39.

25. *Le courrier du Bas-Rhin,* August 30, 1870.

26. Ibid.

27. Baron du Casse, *Journal authentique du siége de Strasbourg* (Paris: Lacroix, Verboeckhoven, 1871), 39–40.

28. Malartic, *Siége de Strasbourg,* 88; P. Raymond-Signouret, *L'impartial du Rhin,* August 30, 1870; AVCUS, 1 MW 204, "Conseil d'administration," August 15, 1870, 3.

29. AVCUS, 1 MW 203, "Procès-verbaux, Conseil municipal de la ville de Strasbourg," August 29, 1870, 354–355.

30. AVCUS, 1 MW 203, "Conseil municipal," August 30, 1870, 360–361.

31. ADBR, 14 M 2, Mayor Humann to Prefect Pron, August 30, 1870.

32. Schneegans, *Guerre en Alsace,* xxxiii, 161, 164–165.

33. Ibid., 158–159.

34. Ibid., 160.

35. Schneegans, *Guerre en Alsace,* 162; Raymond-Signouret, *Souvenirs du bombardement,* 171; Malartic, *Siége de Strasbourg,* 93–94.

36. Raymond-Signouret, *Souvenirs du bombardement,* 171.

37. Jean-Jacques-Alexis Uhrich, *Documents relatifs au siége de Strasbourg* (Paris: Dentu, 1872), 53–54.

38. AVCUS, 1 MW 203, "Conseil municipal," September 2, 1870, 393.

39. Piton, *Siège de Strasbourg,* 109; Malartic, *Siége de Strasbourg,* 93–94.

40. Malartic, *Siége de Strasbourg,* 93.

41. G. Foessel, "La vie quotidienne à Strasbourg à la veille de la guerre de 1870," in *L'Alsace en 1870–1871,* ed. F. L'Huillier (Strasbourg: Publications de la Faculté des Lettres de l'Université de Strasbourg, 1971), 25, 32; AVCUS, 1 MW 203, "Conseil municipal," July 1, 1870.

42. Bertrand Taithe, *Citizenship and Wars: France in Turmoil 1870–1871* (London and New York: Routledge, 2001), 45–46.

43. Ibid., 18; Sudhir Hazareesingh, "Republicanism, War and Democracy: The *Ligue du Midi* in France's War Against Prussia, 1870–1871," *French History* 17, no. 1 (March 2003): 48–78; David Allen Harvey, *Constructing Class and Nationality in Alsace, 1830–1945* (Dekalb: Northern Illinois University Press, 2001), 66.

44. Fischbach, *Siège de Strasbourg,* 432.

45. Malartic, *Siége de Strasbourg,* 83–84; AVCUS, 1 MW 203, "Conseil municipal," August 30, 1870, 367; 1 MW 204, "Conseil d'administration," September 9, 1870, 46–47; 272 MW 15, "Avis," poster, September 9, 1870.

46. *Le courrier du Bas-Rhin,* August 30, 1870; AVCUS, 1 MW 203, "Conseil munic-ipal," August 31, 379–380; September 25, 1870, 560; 1 MW 204, "Conseil d'administration," September 9, 1870, 47; *Les murailles d'Alsace-Lorraine: Metz,*

Sarreguemines, Strasbourg, Haguenau, Saverne, Nancy, etc. (Paris: L. Le Chevalier, 1874), 181.

47. AVCUS, 1 MW 203, "Conseil municipal," August 30, 1870, 378–379; September 26, 1870, 564–565; AVCUS, 272 MW 84, "Souvenirs," 21–22.

48. AVCUS MS 397, Eric Burst, "L'assistance à Strasbourg au 19ème siècle (1800–1870)" (unpublished MS,), 11; AVCUS, 272 MW 20, President of the Administration of the Caisse d'Epargne et de Prévoyance de Strasbourg to Mayor Küss, October 16, 1870.

49. AVCUS, 272 MW 20, President of the Caisse d'Epargne to Mayor Küss, October 16, 1870; 272 MW 92, poster, Caisse d'Epargne de Strasbourg, September 2, 1870; Michelle Perrot, *Les ouvriers en grève: France 1871–1890* (Paris: Mouton, 1974), 346.

50. Raymond-Signouret, *Souvenirs du bombardement,* 189–190; AVCUS, 1 MW 204, "Conseil d'administration," September 6, 1870, 36.

51. AVCUS, 1 MW 203, "Conseil municipal," September 5, 1870, 413–414.

52. AVCUS, 1 MW 204, "Conseil d'administration," September 9, 1870, 47–48; 272 MW 93, Conseil de Prud'hommes de la Ville de Strasbourg, poster, September 10, 1870.

53. AVCUS, 1 MW 204, "Conseil d'administration," September 5, 1870, 32; September 6, 1870, 34; September 24, 1870, 86; September 25, 1870, 89–90.

54. AVCUS, 1 MW 203, "Conseil municipal," August 30, 1870, 366–367; September 2, 1870, 396; September 5, 1870, 415; September 7, 1870, 430–432.

55. AVCUS, 1 MW 203, "Conseil municipal," August 30, 1870, 370; September 6, 1870, 421–423; September 10, 1870, 451; September 15, 1870, 504–506; September 27, 1870, 583; 1 MW 204, "Conseil d'administration," September 17, 1870, 71.

56. Reuss, "Conférence," 24.

57. Malartic, *Siége de Strasbourg,* 27; Du Casse, *Journal authentique,* 19, 25; Reuss, "Chronique strasbourgeoise," 31; Jules-Edouard Dufrenoy, *Journal du siège de Strasbourg: 13 août–26 septembre 1870,* ed. Emmanuel Amougou (Paris: L'Harmattan, 2004), 41.

58. Anonymous, "Strasbourg depuis la déclaration de Guerre," 8.

59. AVCUS, 272 MW 84, "Souvenirs," 29; Kiéné, quoted in De Trailles, *Femmes de France,* 40; Dufrenoy, *Journal,* 41.

60. Fischbach, *Siège de Strasbourg,* 267; *Murailles d'Alsace-Lorraine,* 188.

61. Hollis Clayson, *Paris in Despair: Art and Everyday Life under Siege (1870–71)* (Chicago: The University of Chicago Press, 2002), 179; Taithe, *Citizenship and Wars,* 56–57.

62. Clayson, *Paris in Despair,* 164, 175.

63. Reuss, "Conférence," 24.

64. Reuss, "Chronique strasbourgeoise," 47.

65. AVCUS, 1 MW 203, "Conseil municipal," August 30, 1870, 369.

66. AVCUS, 1 MW 204, "Conseil d'administration," September 5, 1870, 32.

67. Schneegans, *Guerre en Alsace,* 140–141; Fischbach, *Siège de Strasbourg,* 267; AVCUS, 272 MW 69, Compte rendu des opérations du restaurant populaire et réception des prisonniers de passage à Strasbourg à la Halle Couverte 1870–1871

(Strasbourg: Heitz, 1871), 4; Raymond-Signouret, *Souvenirs du bombardement*, 231–232.

68. Anonymous, *Strasbourg: Journal*, 157–158.

69. *Murailles d'Alsace-Lorraine*, 180.

70. Anonymous, *Strasbourg: Journal*, 157–158.

71. Guy Trendel, *Racontez-moi Strasbourg: Les très riches heures d'une ville libre* (Strasbourg: La Nuée Bleue, 2006), 105–108; Harvey, *Class and Nationality in Alsace*, 25–26, 39, 48, 52; Frédéric Piton, *Strasbourg illustré; ou, Panorama pittoresque, historique et statistique de Strasbourg et de ses environs* (1855; facsimile, Strasbourg: FNAC, 1987), 36.

72. Reuss, "Chronique strasbourgeoise," 40.

73. Malartic, *Siége de Strasbourg*, 88–89; Uhrich, *Documents*, 55–56; Jean-Paul Haas, *Strasbourg, rue du Ciel: L'établissement des Diaconesses de Strasbourg fête ses 150 ans d'existence européene* (Strasbourg: Editions Oberlin, 1992), 36.

74. Louise Weiss, *Mémoires d'une européenne*, vol. 1, *1893–1919* (Paris: Payot, 1968), 63–64. My thanks to Margaret Darrow for this reference.

75. Reuss, "Chronique strasbourgeoise," 41.

76. Ibid., 41.

77. AVCUS, 272 MW 84, "Souvenirs," 30–31.

78. Ibid., 32.

79. Ibid., 33.

80. Ibid., 34.

81. Ibid., 35.

82. Ibid., 36–37.

83. Ibid., 38.

84. Ibid.

85. Ibid., 40.

86. Ibid., 43, 48, 51.

87. Raymond-Signouret, *Souvenirs du bombardement*, 132–133.

88. AN, F 7, 12680, telegram, French Consul in Basel to Minister of War, September 7, 1870.

89. Beaunis, *Impressions de campagne*, 41.

90. AVCUS, 1 MW 203, "Conseil municipal," September 10, 1870, 452–453; Anonymous, "Strasbourg depuis la déclaration de Guerre," 141; Kiéné, quoted in De Trailles, *Femmes de France*, 40.

91. E. von Conrady, *Das Leben des Grafen August von Werder* (Berlin: Ernst Siegfried Mittler und Sohn, 1889), 135.

92. Piton, *Siège de Strasbourg*, 126–128; Bergasse du Petit-Thouars, "Le Siége de Strasbourg: Août et Septembre 1870," *Le Correspondant*, December 25, 1871, 1001; Reuss, "Chronique strasbourgeoise," 42; Schneegans, *Guerre en Alsace*, 170; Miss Jacot, *Le journal de Miss Jacot: 1870, siège de Strasbourg*, ed. and trans. Jean-Claude Ménégoz and René Kappler (Aubenas: Le Verger, 1996), 31.

93. Uhrich, *Documents*, 64–65, 71, 75; "Vom Kriegschauplatz," *Volks-Zeitung* (Berlin), September 9, 1870, 2; AVCUS, 1 MW 203, "Conseil municipal," September 6, 423–424; September 7, 429.

6. A Fraternal Hand

1. Swiss Report of September 17, 1870, reproduced in Gustave Fischbach, *Le siège de Strasbourg: Strasbourg avant, pendant, et après le siège* (Strasbourg: L'Imprimerie Alsacienne, 1897), 312.
2. A[uguste] Schneegans, *La guerre en Alsace: Strasbourg* (Neuchâtel: J. Sandoz, 1871), 172.
3. AVCUS, 1 MW 203, "Procès-verbaux, Conseil municipal de la ville de Strasbourg," September 10, 1870, 454–455.
4. Fischbach, *Siège de Strasbourg*, 286; Schneegans, *Guerre en Alsace*, 175, 177, 198–199; Jules-Edouard Dufrenoy, *Journal du siège de Strasbourg: 13 août–26 septembre 1870*, ed. Emmanuel Amougou (Paris: L'Harmattan, 2004), 39.
5. Quoted in Schneegans, *Guerre en Alsace*, 178.
6. Schneegans, *Guerre en Alsace*, 177.
7. Frédéric Piton, *Siège de Strasbourg: Journal d'un assiégé* (Paris: Schlaeber, 1900), 142–143.
8. Adam J. Davis and Bertrand Taithe, "From the Purse and the Heart: Exploring Charity, Humanitarianism, and Human Rights in France," *French Historical Studies* 34, no. 3 (Summer 2011), 414.
9. Quoted in P. Raymond-Signouret, *Souvenirs du bombardement et de la capitulation de Strasbourg* (Bayonne: P. Cazals, 1872), 214.
10. Hollis Clayson, *Paris in Despair: Art and Everyday Life under Siege (1870–71)* (Chicago: The University of Chicago Press, 2002), 332.
11. In addition to Bischoff, the Swiss delegation included a federal councilor (Schenk), the president of the commune of Zurich (Dr. Römer), the president of the commune of Bern (Colonel Otto von Büren), a federal officer (Hans de Wattenwyl), a professor from Bern (Munzinger), a banker originally from Strasbourg (Staehling), and another man named Brunner (Schneegans, *Guerre en Alsace*, 173, 191–193; Lucien Delabrousse, *Un héros de la défense nationale: Valentin et les derniers jours du siège de Strasbourg* [Paris: Berger-Levrault, 1898], 69).
12. Swiss Federal Archives, Official Digital Publication, *Diplomatische Dokumente der Schweiz* 2, no. 280, "Proposition du Chef du Département politique, J. Dubs, au Conseil fédéral," September 1, 1870, 423.
13. Dr. Römer quoted in Rudolf Wackernagel, *Die Unterstützung der Stadt Strassburg durch die Schweiz im Kriegsjahr 1870* (Basel: 1895), 19.
14. Alistair Horne, *The Fall of Paris: The Siege and the Commune, 1870–71* (New York: Penguin, 2007), 167–168.
15. This discussion owes much to Michael Barnett, *Empire of Humanity: A History of Humanitarianism* (Ithaca: Cornell University Press, 2011), to the comments of Michael Geyer in the roundtable "Human Rights and Humanitarianism, 1870s to 1970s," at the American Historical Association Annual Meeting, Boston, January 2011, and to many conversations with colleagues.
16. Barnett, *Empire of Humanity*, 10, 137.
17. "humanitarianism, n." OED Online (Oxford University Press, June 2011), http://www.oed.com/view/Entry/272189?redirectedFrom=humanitarianism;

humanitaire dates to at least 1835 in French (http://www.cnrtl.fr/definition /humanitaire); the German *humanitär* is derived from French: http://wortschatz .uni-leipzig.de/cgi-bin/wort_www.exe?site=2&Wort_id=7084034.

18. Naomi J. Andrews, "'The Universal Alliance of All Peoples': Romantic Socialists, the Human Family, and the Defense of Empire during the July Monarchy, 1830– 1848," *French Historical Studies* 34, no. 3 (Summer 2011): 473–502; Osama W. Abi-Mershed, *Apostles of Modernity: Saint-Simonians and the Civilizing Mission in Algeria* (Stanford: Stanford University Press, 2010).

19. Schneegans, *Guerre en Alsace,* 172–173, 188; Rodolphe Reuss, "Chronique stras- bourgeoise de la guerre franco-allemande du 16 juillet au 24 août 1870," in *Le siège de Strasbourg en 1870: Conférence et chronique strasbourgeoise juillet–août 1870,* ed. Jean Rott (Strasbourg: Libairie Istra, 1971), 22; Fischbach, *Siège de Strasbourg,* 278; Guy Trendel, *Racontez-moi Strasbourg: Les très riches heures d'une ville libre* (Strasbourg: La Nuée Bleue, 2006), 128–130.

20. Trendel, *Racontez-moi Strasbourg,* 129; Paul Besson, *Etude sur Jean Fischart* (Paris: Hachette, 1889), 301; Schneegans, *Guerre en Alsace,* 172–173; Fischbach, *Siège de Strasbourg,* 455–456.

21. Samuel Moyn, *The Last Utopia: Human Rights in History* (Cambridge: The Belknap Press of Harvard University Press, 2010), 38–39 (international associa- tions); Benedict Anderson, *Imagined Communities: Reflections on the Origins and Spread of Nationalism* (London and New York: Verso, rev. ed., 1991).

22. Orlando Figes, *The Crimean War, A History* (New York: Metropolitan Books, 2010), 339, 378.

23. Craig Calhoun, "The Imperative to Reduce Suffering: Charity, Progress, and Emergencies in the Field of Humanitarian Action," in *Humanitarianism in Question: Politics, Power, Ethics,* eds. Michael Barnett and Thomas G. Weiss (Ithaca: Cornell University Press, 2008), 77; Barnett, *Empire of Humanity,* 54; Michael Barnett, "Humanitarianism as a Scholarly Vocation," in Barnett and Weiss, eds., *Humanitarianism in Question,* 246–247.

24. Jonathan Steinberg, *Why Switzerland?,* 2nd ed. (New York: Cambridge University Press, 1996), 219.

25. Gregor Beuret, *Die Katholisch-Soziale Bewegung in der Schweitz 1848–1919* (Winterthur: P. G. Keller, 1959), 70–84.

26. Calhoun, "Imperative to Reduce Suffering," 77–78.

27. Lynn Hunt, *Inventing Human Rights: A History* (New York: W. W. Norton, 2007), 29–30, 82–92; Norbert Elias, *The Civilizing Process: Sociogenetic and Psychogenetic Investigations,* trans. Edmund Jephcott, eds. Eric Dunning, Johan Goudsblom, and Stephen Mennell (Oxford: Blackwell Publishers, 2000); Barnett, *Empire of Humanity,* 51.

28. Quoted in Steinberg, *Why Switzerland,* 218.

29. Michelle Brady, "Locke's *Thoughts* on Reputation," *The Review of Politics* 75, no. 3 (Summer 2013): 335–356.

30. Quotation is Calhoun, "Imperative to Reduce Suffering," 78; see also Barnett, *Empire of Humanity,* 52; Barnett, "Humanitarianism as a Scholarly Vocation," 246–247.

31. Calhoun, "Imperative to Reduce Suffering," 78; Hunt, *Inventing Human Rights,* 111–112.

32. Comments of Michael Geyer in the roundtable "Human Rights and Humanitarianism, 1870s to 1970s," at the American Historical Association Annual Meeting, Boston, January 2011.

33. Moyn, *Last Utopia.*

34. Hunt, *Inventing Human Rights,* 33–34.

35. Susan Lanzoni, "Sympathy in *Mind* (1876–1900)," *Journal of the History of Ideas* 70, no. 2 (April 2009), 285.

36. Hunt, *Inventing Human Rights,* 94, 97; still, such spectacles continued, occasionally, right up to 1870: see Alain Corbin, *Village of Cannibals: Rage and Murder in France, 1870,* trans. Arthur Goldhammer (Cambridge: Harvard University Press, 1992).

37. Barnett, *Empire of Humanity,* 28.

38. Stephanie Coontz, *Marriage, A History: How Love Conquered Marriage* (New York: Penguin, 2005), 159–160, 168; Calhoun, "Imperative to Reduce Suffering," 78.

39. Swiss letter of September 7, 1870, quoted in Schneegans, *Guerre en Alsace,* 173; Théodore Humann, quoted in Schneegans, *Guerre en Alsace,* 177; Antoine Zopff, quoted in Fischbach, *Siège de Strasbourg,* 274.

40. H. Beaunis, *Impressions de campagne, 1870–1871* (Paris: Alcan and Berger-Levrault, 1887), 50–51.

41. Fischbach, *Siège de Strasbourg,* 276.

42. *L'impartial du Rhin,* September 13, 1870.

43. Swiss Federal Archives, Official Digital Publication, *Diplomatische Dokumente der Schweiz* 2, no. 278, "Le Conseil fédéral aux cantons," August 20, 1870, 420–421.

44. Steinberg, *Why Switzerland,* 48–49.

45. Quoted in Fischbach, *Siège de Strasbourg,* 279.

46. Quoted in Wackernagel, *Unterstützung,* 38.

47. Zopff, speaking at the municipal commission of September 11, 1870, quoted in Fischbach, *Siège de Strasbourg,* 274.

48. Fischbach, *Siège de Strasbourg,* 279, 285–286; Generallandesarchiv Karlsruhe, 456 F 4 no. 162, "Kriegstagebuch des Commandos des Belagerungscorps vor Strassburg," September 9 and 10, 1870; Swiss report, quoted in Fischbach, *Siège de Strasbourg,* 288–289; Schneegans, *Guerre en Alsace,* 191–193, 200–201.

49. Swiss report, quoted in Fischbach, *Siège de Strasbourg,* 312.

50. Ibid., 309.

51. Ibid., 312.

52. Fischbach, *Siège de Strasbourg,* 283.

53. Four thousand requests: Georges Foessel, "Journal du siège de Strasbourg par Cécile de Dartein," *Annuaire de la Société des Amis du Vieux-Strasbourg* 15 (1985), 58 n. 25. Numbers that left: Convoys of 254 on Sept. 15, 412 on Sept. 17, 97 on Sept. 19, 155 on Sept. 20, 9 on Sept. 21, and 334 on Sept. 22, for a total of 1,261 (Wackernagel, *Unterstützung,* 89–93); *Le courrier du Bas-Rhin,* September 18, 1870; 272 MW 18, "Liste de refugiés." A few authors put the number higher: Schneegans puts the total number of refugees at about two thousand (*Guerre en*

Alsace, 210), and A.-G. Heinhold reported in *L'impartial du Rhin* on September 22, 1870 that 768 left on September 21 (instead of 9). These higher figures are corroborated in the *Journal de Genève* (cited in Anonymous, *Strasbourg: Journal des mois d'août et septembre 1870* [Paris: Sandoz et Fischbacher, 1874], 301).

54. Piton, *Siège de Strasbourg,* 165; Malartic, *Le siége de Strasbourg pendant la campagne de 1870* (Paris: Librairie du *Moniteur universel*), 88–89; Wilhelm Horning, *Erlebnisse während der Belagerung von Strassburg 1870 aus seinem Tagebuch* (Strasbourg: Hubert, 1894), 68; Foessel, "Dartein," 54–56, 76.

55. Reuss, "Chronique strasbourgeoise," 45.

56. Barnett, *Empire of Humanity,* 11–12, 55.

57. Miss Jacot, *Le journal de Miss Jacot: 1870, siège de Strasbourg,* ed. and trans. Jean-Claude Ménégoz and René Kappler (Aubenas: Le Verger, 1996), 32; Anonymous, "Strasbourg depuis la déclaration de guerre jusqu'en juin 1871" (unpublished manuscript, 1871), 15.

58. AVCUS, 272 MW 18, "Liste de refugiés": 159 women without family members.

59. AVCUS, 272 MW 18, "Liste de refugiés." The numbers of adult females, adolescent females, adult males, and children do not add up to 787 because several records list only the number of people in a group; W., *Erlebnisse eines schweizerischen Malers in Strassburg während der Belagerung im Jahre 1870* (Laufen: Köchlin, 1870), 15.

60. Reuss, "Chronique strasbourgeoise," 47.

61. Piton, *Siège de Strasbourg,* 176.

62. Swiss letter to the mayor, quoted in Schneegans, *Guerre en Alsace,* 206.

63. AVCUS, 1 MW 203, "Conseil municipal," September 13, 1870, 480–481; Anonymous, *Strasbourg: Journal,* 158; 272 MW 18, "Liste de refugiés"; *Le courrier du Bas-Rhin,* September 18, 1870.

64. Swiss report, quoted in Fischbach, *Siège de Strasbourg,* 291; Dufrenoy, *Journal,* 39; Wackernagel, *Unterstützung,* 38, 42.

65. Fischbach, *Siège de Strasbourg,* 309; D. Goldschmidt, *Souvenirs de 1870: Autour de Strasbourg assiégé* (Strasbourg: Imprimerie Alsacienne, 1909), 18; Piton, *Siège de Strasbourg,* 176.

66. Uhrich, *Documents relatifs au Siége de Strasbourg* (Paris: Dentu, 1872), 88.

67. A.-G. Heinhold, *L'impartial du Rhin,* September 22, 1870.

68. AVCUS, 1 MW 203, "Conseil municipal," September 19, 1870, 527–528.

69. Raymond-Signouret, *Souvenirs du bombardement,* 208.

70. Quoted in ibid., 319.

71. Generallandesarchiv Karlsruhe, 456 F 4 no. 162, "Kriegstagebuch," September 9 and 10, 1870; Wackernagel, *Unterstützung,* 19.

72. Schneegans, *Guerre en Alsace,* 194–195; the Swiss account of their meeting with Werder is reproduced in Fischbach, *Siège de Strasbourg,* 285.

73. E. von Conrady, *Das Leben des Grafen August von Werder* (Berlin: Ernst Siegfried Mittler und Sohn, 1889), 135.

74. Uhrich, *Documents,* 68–69.

75. Helmuth von Moltke, *La guerre de 1870,* trans. E. Jaeglé, 8th ed. (Paris: H. Le Soudier, 1891), 360, http://gallica.bnf.fr/ark:/12148/bpt6k39959w.

76. Generallandesarchiv Karlsruhe, 456 F 4 no. 162, "Kriegstagebuch," September 9, 1870.

77. Michael Howard, *The Franco-Prussian War: The German Invasion of France, 1870–1871* (New York: The MacMillan Company, 1961), 275; Schneegans, *Guerre en Alsace,* 181; Beaunis, *Impressions de campagne,* 53; Fischbach, *Siège de Strasbourg,* 276, 422–23; "Vom Kriegschauplatz," *Volks-Zeitung* (Berlin), September 25, 1870, 2; *National-Zeitung* (Berlin), September 27, 1870; Raymond-Signouret, *Souvenirs du bombardement,* 192–193.

78. Mona Fixdal and Dan Smith, "Humanitarian Intervention and Just War," *Mershon International Studies Review* 42 (1998), 290.

79. Samuel Moyn, "Empathy in History, Empathizing with Humanity," *History and Theory* 45 (October 2006), 400, 410.

80. Hunt, *Inventing Human Rights,* 26.

81. Alain Destexhe, *L'humanitaire impossible, ou Deux siècles d'ambiguïté* (Paris: Armand Colin, 1993), 14.

82. Keith David Watenpaugh, "The League of Nations' Rescue of Armenian Genocide Survivors and the Making of Modern Humanitarianism, 1920–1927," *American Historical Review* 115, no. 5 (December 2010), 1321–1322.

83. Barnett, *Empire of Humanity,* 82–83; Bertrand Taithe, *Defeated Flesh: Welfare, Warfare and the Making of Modern France* (Manchester, England: Manchester University Press, 1999), 156.

7. Heroic Measures

1. Lucien Delabrousse, *Un héros de la défense nationale: Valentin et les derniers jours du siège de Strasbourg* (Paris: Berger-Levrault, 1898), 113–114; P. Raymond-Signouret, *Souvenirs du bombardement et de la capitulation de Strasbourg* (Bayonne: P. Cazals, 1872), 240–241.

2. A. Schillinger, *Souvenirs pour ses amis par Rodolphe Reuss,* ed. Rodolphe Reuss (Strasbourg: J. H. Ed. Heitz, 1883), 194.

3. A[uguste] Schneegans, *La guerre en Alsace: Strasbourg* (Neuchâtel: J. Sandoz, 1871), 182–183; AVCUS, 1 MW 203, "Procès-verbaux, Conseil municipal de la ville de Strasbourg," September 12, 1870, 467, 469.

4. Rodolphe Reuss, "Chronique strasbourgeoise de la guerre franco-allemande du 16 juillet au 24 août 1870," in *Le siège de Strasbourg en 1870: Conférence et chronique strasbourgeoise juillet–août 1870,* ed. Jean Rott (Strasbourg: Libairie Istra, 1971), 44.

5. *Les murailles d'Alsace-Lorraine: Metz, Sarreguemines, Strasbourg, Haguenau, Saverne, Nancy, etc.* (Paris: L. Le Chevalier, 1874), 184; AVCUS, 272 MW 14, letter, Küss to Uhrich, September 15, 1870; AVCUS, 1 MW 203, "Conseil municipal," September 10, 1870, 452–453; September 13, 1870, 475–476; AVCUS, 1 MW 204, "Procès-verbaux, Conseil d'administration de la ville de Strasbourg," September 14, 1870, 59–60; September 15, 1870, 64–65; September 23, 1870, 78–79; AVCUS, 271 MW 86, "Arrête," Mayor Küss, September 25, 1870; Edouard Ebel, "La police en Alsace de 1800 a 1870," (Doctoral Thesis, Université des Sciences Humaines de Strasbourg, 1995), 515–516.

6. Frédéric Piton, *Siège de Strasbourg: Journal d'un assiégé* (Paris: Schlaeber, 1900), 161.

7. Schneegans, *Guerre en Alsace,* 158–159; Gustave Fischbach, *Le siège de Strasbourg: Strasbourg avant, pendant, et après le siège* (Strasbourg: L'Imprimerie Alsacienne, 1897), 336.

8. Schneegans, *Guerre en Alsace,* 165–166.

9. Jean-Pierre Klein, "La vie quotidienne et la lutte à outrance à Strasbourg pendant le siège de 1870," *Revue historique de L'Armée* 29, no. 1 (1973), 176; H. Beaunis, *Impressions de campagne (1870–1871)* (Paris: Alcan and Berger-Levrault, 1887), 234–237 (Beaunis's obituary on Küss originally appeared in *Le journal de Lyon* on July 22, 1871).

10. Beaunis, *Impressions de campagne,* 239, 241.

11. Ibid., 241.

12. Ibid., 232.

13. Ibid., 233.

14. Schneegans, *Guerre en Alsace,* 166.

15. AVCUS, 272 MW 84, anonymous letter, September 15, 1870, 5.

16. Frederick III (Crown Prince Friedrich Wilhelm), *The War Diary of the Emperor Frederick III, 1870–1871,* ed. and trans. A. R. Allinson (New York: Howard Fertig, 1988), 129.

17. Fischbach, *Siège de Strasbourg,* 521–528; Raymond-Signouret, *Souvenirs du bombardement,* 198–199, 333–343; *Blaetter aus dem Tagebuche eines Strassburgers waehrend der Belangerung in den Monaten August und September 1870* (Altona: Prinz, 1870), 67–68.

18. Jean-Jacques-Alexis Uhrich, *Documents relatifs au siége de Strasbourg* (Paris: Dentu, 1872), 115.

19. Quoted in ibid., 117.

20. Piton, *Siège de Strasbourg,* 157–158, 165.

21. Ibid., 162.

22. Ibid., 149.

23. Ibid., 190–194.

24. Ibid., 179.

25. Max Reichard, *Aus den Tagen der Belagerung Strassburgs* (Bielefeld und Leipzig: Velhagen & Klasing, 1873), 163.

26. Reuss, "Chronique strasbourgeoise," 47.

27. Uhrich, *Documents,* 102, 104–105.

28. AVCUS, 1 MW 203, "Conseil municipal," 537–538.

29. Schneegans, *Guerre en Alsace,* 285.

30. SHDV, Ln 10, "Extrait du registre des procès-verbaux du Conseil municipal de la ville de Strasbourg," September 18, 1870.

31. Delabrousse, *Héros,* 147–148; Bergasse du Petit-Thouars, "Le siége de Strasbourg: Août et septembre 1870," *Le correspondant,* December 25, 1871, 1005. Lipp is not to be confused with the bar owner.

32. Quotation is SHDV, Ln 10, "Extrait du registre des procès-verbaux du Conseil municipal de la ville de Strasbourg," September 18, 1870; Schneegans, *Guerre en Alsace,* 92, 97–98.

33. Schneegans, *Guerre en Alsace,* 277.

34. Louis Menand, *The Metaphysical Club: A Story of Ideas in America* (New York: Farrar, Straus and Giroux, 2002), 4.

35. Schneegans, *Guerre en Alsace,* 285–286.

36. Ibid., 289.

37. Not all consequentialists were republicans. Malartic, the empire's man, also feared an all-out assault and urged the city to capitulate (Malartic, *Le siége de Strasbourg pendant la campagne de 1870* [Paris: Librairie du *Moniteur universel*], 146).

38. SHDV, Ln 10, "Extrait du registre des procès-verbaux du Conseil municipal de la ville de Strasbourg," September 18, 1870.

39. Reuss, "Chronique strasbourgeoise," 47; Fischbach, *Siège de Strasbourg,* 357; Maurice Engelhardt, "Lettre de M. Maurice Engelhard *[sic]* à M. A. Schnéegans" (Lyon: J. Jossier, 1871), n.p.

40. Uhrich, *Documents,* 107.

41. Stig Förster, "The Prussian Triangle of Leadership in the Face of a People's War: A Reassessment of the Conflict between Bismarck and Moltke, 1870–71," in *On the Road to Total War: The American Civil War and the German Wars of Unification, 1861–1871,* ed. Stig Förster and Jörg Nagler (New York: Cambridge University Press, 1997), 128.

42. *Bulletin des lois de l'Empire français,* July–December 1863, 919.

43. Geoffrey Best, *Humanity in Warfare* (New York: Columbia University Press, 1980), 61.

44. Uhrich, *Documents,* 107–108; see also Baron du Casse, *Journal authentique du siége de Strasbourg* (Paris: Lacroix, Verboeckhoven, 1871), 55–56.

45. Uhrich, *Documents,* 122.

46. Uhrich, *Documents,* 119, 126; AVCUS, 1 MW 204, "Conseil d'administration," September 23, 1870, 81.

47. Quoted in Uhrich, *Documents,* 126.

48. Vincent Wright, *Les préfets de Gambetta: Texte complété, mis à jour et présenté par Eric Anceau et Sudhir Hazareesingh* (Paris: Presses de l'Université Paris-Sorbonne, 2007), 409–411.

49. Quoted in Wright, *Préfets,* 410.

50. Fischbach, *Siège de Strasbourg,* 366; Delabrousse, *Héros,* 23–24.

51. Wright, *Préfets,* 409–411; Delabrousse, *Héros,* 44.

52. Quoted in Delabrousse, *Héros,* 204.

53. Quoted in Delabrousse, *Héros,* 49–50; Delabrousse based his account on an interview with Valentin held in 1872.

54. Delabrousse, *Héros,* 47–48; Helmuth von Moltke, *La guerre de 1870,* trans. E. Jaeglé, 8th ed. (Paris: H. Le Soudier, 1891), 360, http://gallica.bnf.fr/ark:/12148/bpt6k39959w.

55. Schneegans, *Guerre en Alsace,* 234.

56. Bertrand Taithe, *Citizenship and Wars: France in Turmoil 1870–1871* (London and New York: Routledge, 2001), 104.

57. Delabrousse, *Héros,* 57–59, 69; Valentin's own account, written in October 1871, is quoted in Raymond-Signouret, *Souvenirs du bombardement,* 236–239; Emile

Ehrhardt, *Siège de Strasbourg: Souvenirs d'un habitant de Schiltigheim* (Strasbourg: Imprimerie Alsacienne, 1909), 62, 66–67.

58. Delabrousse, *Héros,* 103–108; Raymond-Signouret, *Souvenirs du bombardement,* 238.

59. Joseph Campbell, *The Hero with a Thousand Faces* (1949; Princeton: Princeton University Press, 1973), 246.

60. Du Casse, *Journal authentique,* 71; A[uguste] Schneegans, *Strasbourg! Quarante jours de bombardement par un refugié strasbourgeois* (Neuchâtel: J. Sandoz, 1871), 14–15.

61. Thomas Cardoza, *Intrepid Women: Cantinières and Vivandières of the French Army* (Bloomington: Indiana University Press, 2010), 158–159; Luce Larcade, "Les cantinières, 'Ces dames du Champ d'Honneur,'" *Revue de la Société des Amis du Musée de l'Armée* 96 (1987): 60.

62. Schneegans, *Guerre en Alsace,* 231.

63. François Igersheim, *L'Alsace des notables, 1870–1914: La bourgeoisie et le peuple alsacien* (Strasbourg: Nouvel Alsacien, 1981), 20; Delabrousse, *Héros,* 26; Schneegans, *Strasbourg!,* 41.

64. Schneegans, *Guerre en Alsace,* 227.

65. Ibid., 230, 232–233.

66. AVCUS, 1 MW 203, "Conseil municipal," September 22, 548; Uhrich, *Documents,* 123–125; Schneegans, *Guerre en Alsace,* 238–239.

67. Delabrousse, *Héros,* 113–114.

68. Bergasse du Petit-Thouars, "Siége de Strasbourg," 1002.

69. AVCUS, 272 MW 25, letter, Valentin to Küss, September 22, 1870.

70. Schneegans, *Strasbourg!,* 50.

71. Delabrousse, *Héros,* 124.

72. Reichard, *Belagerung Strassburgs,* 143.

73. [Blech], *La défense de Strasbourg jugée par un républicain* (Neuchatel: Attinger, 1871), 19.

74. D. Rosenstiehl, *L'impartial du Rhin,* September 22, 1870; Raymond-Signouret, *Souvenirs du bombardement,* 229–230. His mother, Madame Raymond-Signouret, died on September 23, apparently due to illness (Raymond-Signouret, *Souvenirs du bombardement,* 5).

75. Bertrand Taithe, *Defeated Flesh: Welfare, Warfare and the Making of Modern France,* (Manchester, England: Manchester University Press, 1999), 35.

76. Schneegans, *Strasbourg!,* 52.

77. Ibid., 54.

78. Reuss, "Chronique strasbourgeoise," 46.

79. Delabrousse, *Héros,* 114–115.

80. Ibid., 116–117.

81. AVCUS, 272 MW 25, letter, Valentin to Küss, September 22, 1870.

82. Schneegans, *Guerre en Alsace,* 237.

83. Quoted in Cynthia Simmons and Nina Perlina, *Writing the Siege of Leningrad: Women's Diaries, Memoirs, and Documentary Prose* (Pittsburgh: University of Pittsburgh Press, 2002), 74.

84. Bergasse du Petit-Thouars, "Siége de Strasbourg," 1005–1006; Moltke, *Guerre de 1870*, 165–166; Friedeburg, *1870: Die Belagerung von Strassburg* (Berlin: Sittenfeld, 1875), 31.

85. Uhrich, *Documents*, 131.

86. "Aus den Parallelen vor Strassburg," *Kölnische Zeitung*, September 25, 1870, 1; "Der Krieg," *Kölnische Zeitung*, October 1, 1870, 2.

87. Fischbach, *Siège de Strasbourg*, 353; Generallandesarchiv Karlsruhe, 456 F 4 no. 162, "Kriegstagebuch des Commandos des Belagerungscorps vor Strassburg," September 22, 1870.

88. Quoted in Uhrich, *Documents*, 127–128 and Fischbach, *Siège de Strasbourg*, 403.

89. Malartic, *Siége de Strasbourg*, 141.

90. Uhrich, *Documents*, 129–130; an abbreviated version appears in Fischbach, *Siège de Strasbourg*, 404.

91. Bergasse du Petit-Thouars, "Siége de Strasbourg," 1006; "Der Krieg," *Kölnische Zeitung*, October 1, 1870, 2; Du Casse, *Journal authentique*, 60.

92. Reichard, *Belagerung Strassburgs*, 172.

93. Uhrich, *Documents*, 132.

94. Ibid., 133.

95. Generallandesarchiv Karlsruhe, 456 F 4 no. 162, "Kriegstagebuch," September 27, 1870.

96. SHDV, Ln 10, Meier, "Le siége de Strasbourg," trans. L. Durieux (unpublished MS, October 27, 1873), 55.

97. Bergasse du Petit-Thouars, "Siége de Strasbourg," 1007.

98. Generallandesarchiv Karlsruhe, 456 F 4 no. 162, "Kriegstagebuch," September 27, 1870.

99. David A. Bell, *The First Total War: Napoleon's Europe and the Birth of Warfare as We Know It* (Boston: Houghton Mifflin Company, 2007), 174.

100. Frederick III, *War Diary*, 132.

101. Du Casse, *Journal authentique*, 59.

102. Ibid., 61.

103. Quoted in ibid., 67.

104. Piton, *Siège de Strasbourg*, 205–206.

105. *Blaetter*, 71.

106. Société Française de Secours aux Blessés et Malades Militaires, *Oeuvre internationale: Rapport du comité auxiliaire de Strasbourg* (Strasbourg: Berger-Levrault, 1871), 13.

107. Reuss, "Chronique strasbourgeoise," 49.

108. Quoted in Paul and Henry de Trailles, *Les femmes de France pendant la guerre et les deux siéges de Paris* (Paris: F. Polo, 1872), 42.

109. Georges Foessel, "Journal du siège de Strasbourg par Cécile de Dartein," *Annuaire de la Société des Amis du Vieux-Strasbourg* 15 (1985), 90.

110. Quoted in Anonymous, *Strasbourg: Journal des mois d'août et septembre 1870* (Paris: Sandoz et Fischbacher, 1874), 196.

111. Schneegans, *Guerre en Alsace*, 302.

112. Ibid., 294–295.

113. Ibid., 296.
114. Reichard, *Belagerung Strassburgs,* 177.
115. Ibid.
116. Schneegans, *Guerre en Alsace,* 296.
117. Valentin quoted in Schneegans, *Guerre en Alsace,* 297.
118. Reuss, "Chronique strasbourgeoise," 49.
119. Quoted in ibid.
120. Schneegans, *Strasbourg!,* 57.
121. AVCUS, 272 MW 84, anonymous letter, September 27, 1870, 7.
122. Schillinger, *Souvenirs,* 203.
123. Fischbach, *Siège de Strasbourg,* 441.
124. Schneegans, *Guerre en Alsace,* 298; Schneegans, *Strasbourg!,* 58.

8. Strassburg

1. Michael Walzer, *Just and Unjust Wars: A Moral Argument with Historical Illustrations* (New York: Basic Books, 1977), 178–179.
2. Rodolphe Reuss, "Chronique strasbourgeoise de la guerre franco-allemande du 16 juillet au 24 août 1870," in *Le siège de Strasbourg en 1870: Conférence et chronique strasbourgeoise juillet–août 1870,* ed. Jean Rott (Strasbourg: Libairie Istra, 1971), 49; Max Reichard, *Aus den Tagen der Belagerung Strassburgs* (Bielefeld und Leipzig: Velhagen & Klasing, 1873), 180; Georges Livet and Francis Rapp, *Histoire de Strasbourg* (Toulouse: Privat, 1987), 332; Baron du Casse, *Journal authentique du siége de Strasbourg* (Paris: Lacroix, Verboeckhoven, 1871), 62; Gustave Fischbach, *Le siège de Strasbourg: Strasbourg avant, pendant, et après le siège* (Strasbourg: L'Imprimerie Alsacienne, 1897), 458; "Kriegschronik," *Illustrirte Zeitung* (Leipzig), October 1, 1870, 230; Anonymous, *Strasbourg: Journal des mois d'août et septembre 1870* (Paris: Sandoz et Fischbacher, 1874), 349; Luce Larcade, "Les cantinières: Ces dames du champs d'honneur," *Revue des Amis du Musée de l'Armée* 96 (1987), 60.
3. Jean-Jacques-Alexis Uhrich, *Documents relatifs au siége de Strasbourg* (Paris: Dentu, 1872), 138–140.
4. Frédéric Piton, *Siège de Strasbourg: Journal d'un assiégé* (Paris: Schlaeber, 1900), 207–208; P. Raymond-Signouret, *Souvenirs du bombardement et de la capitulation de Strasbourg* (Bayonne: P. Cazals, 1872), 263.
5. Quoted in Paul and Henry de Trailles, *Les femmes de France pendant la guerre et les deux siéges de Paris* (Paris: F. Polo, 1872), 42.
6. Quoted in Jules Claretie, *Revolution de 1870–71* (Paris: Aux Bureaux du Journal L'éclipse, 1872), 288.
7. Uhrich, *Documents,* 140; Du Casse, *Journal authentique,* 62; Dennis Showalter, *The Wars of German Unification* (London: Hodder Arnold, 2004), 291.
8. Du Casse, *Journal authentique,* 62; Malartic, *Le siége de Strasbourg pendant la campagne de 1870* (Paris: Librairie du *Moniteur universel*), 149.
9. Raymond-Signouret, *Souvenirs du bombardement,* 262.
10. A[uguste] Schneegans, *Strasbourg! Quarante jours de bombardement par un refugié strasbourgeois* (Neuchâtel: J. Sandoz, 1871), 62–63.

11. Generallandesarchiv Karlsruhe, 456 F 4 no. 162, "Kriegstagebuch des Commandos des Belagerungscorps vor Strassburg," September 28, 1870.

12. Quote is Reuss, "Chronique strasbourgeoise," 50; A. Schillinger, *Souvenirs pour ses amis par Rodolphe Reuss*, ed. Rodolphe Reuss (Strasbourg: J. H. Ed. Heitz, 1883), 205.

13. Reuss, "Chronique strasbourgeoise," 49–50.

14. E. von Conrady, *Das Leben des Grafen August von Werder* (Berlin: Ernst Siegfried Mittler und Sohn, 1889), 151.

15. Frederick III (Crown Prince Friedrich Wilhelm), *The War Diary of the Emperor Frederick III, 1870–1871*, ed. and trans. A. R. Allinson (New York: Howard Fertig, 1988), 138.

16. Helmuth von Moltke, *La guerre de 1870*, trans. E. Jaeglé, 8th ed. (Paris: H. Le Soudier, 1891), 169, http://gallica.bnf.fr/ark:/12148/bpt6k39959w; Frederick III, *War Diary*, 138; François Roth, *La guerre de 70* (Paris: Fayard, 1990), 228.

17. Christine G. Krüger, "German Suffering in the Franco-German War, 1870/71," *German History* 29, no. 3 (September 2011), 408.

18. Frederick III, *War Diary*, 139.

19. "Strassburg," *Volks-Zeitung* (Berlin), September 29, 1870, 1.

20. Ibid.

21. Rudolf Wilckens, *Kriegsfahrten eines Freiwilligen Badischen Dragoners anno 1870/71*, 2nd ed. (Karlsruhe: J. J. Reiff, 1894), 34–35; Dr. Max Hirsch, "Briefe vom Kriegsschauplatz," *Volks-Zeitung* (Berlin), October 12, 1870, 2; "Aus den Parallelen vor Strassburg," *Kölnische Zeitung*, October 2, 1870, 2.

22. Moritz Wiggers, "Aus Strassburg," *Volks-Zeitung* (Berlin), October 3, 1870, 1.

23. Moritz Wiggers, "Aus Strassburg," *Volks-Zeitung* (Berlin), October 5, 1870, 1–2; "Vom Kriegsschauplatz," *Volks-Zeitung* (Berlin), August 31, 1870, 3; "General Uhrich," *Illustrirte Zeitung* (Leipzig), September 24, 1870, 219.

24. Moritz Wiggers, "Aus Strassburg," *Volks-Zeitung* (Berlin), October 6, 1870, 1–2.

25. Moritz Wiggers, "Aus Strassburg," *Volks-Zeitung* (Berlin), October 3, 1.

26. Richard Cobb, *French and Germans, Germans and French: A Personal Interpretation of France under Two Occupations, 1914–1918/1940–1944* (Hanover, NH: University Press of New England, 1983), 150.

27. Generallandesarchiv Karlsruhe, 456 F 4 no. 185, "Nouvelles officielles pour le Gouvernement Général de l'Alsace," August 30, 1870.

28. Announcement of October 8, quoted in Anonymous, *Strasbourg: Journal*, 351.

29. Piton, *Siège de Strasbourg*, 229.

30. Conrady, *Werder*, 154.

31. Schneegans, *Strasbourg!*, 24; Stephen L. Harp, *Learning to Be Loyal: Primary Schooling as Nation Building in Alsace-Lorraine, 1850–1940* (Dekalb: Northern Illinois University Press, 1998), 49–50.

32. AVCUS, 1 MW 203, "Procès-verbaux, Conseil municipal de la ville de Strasbourg," September 28, 1870, 569–570.

33. Ibid., 570.

34. Ibid., 585–586; Piton, *Siège de Strasbourg*, 229–230; Anonymous, *Strasbourg: Journal*, 351.

35. Raymond-Signouret, *Souvenirs du bombardement,* 277–278.
36. Emil Frommel, *O Strassburg, du Wunderschöne Stadt! Alte und Neue, Freudvolle und Leidvolle, Fremde und Eigene: Erinnerungen eines Feldpredigers vor Strassburg im Jahr 1870* (Stuttgart: Steinkopf, 1872), 124–125.
37. Ibid., 116; "Der Krieg," *Kölnische Zeitung,* October 5, 1870, 2.
38. Raymond-Signouret, *Souvenirs du bombardement,* 276–277.
39. A[uguste] Schneegans, *La guerre en Alsace: Strasbourg* (Neuchâtel: J. Sandoz, 1871), 313–315.
40. Rachel Chrastil, *Organizing for War: France 1870–1914* (Baton Rouge: Louisiana State University Press, 2010), 24.
41. Anthony J. Steinhoff, *The Gods of the City: Protestantism and Religious Culture in Strasbourg, 1870–1914* (Leiden: Brill, 2008), 58–59; Frommel, *O Strassburg,* 45–46.
42. Reichard, *Belagerung Strassburgs,* 194–195.
43. Piton, *Siège de Strasbourg,* 218.
44. Ibid., 220.
45. Ibid., 213.
46. Ibid., 217–218.
47. Ibid., 222–223.
48. Quoted in Anonymous, *Strasbourg: Journal,* 350.
49. Fischbach, *Siège de Strasbourg,* 459–460.
50. Quotation is Schneegans, *Guerre en Alsace,* 74; Chrastil, *Organizing for War,* 24.
51. Fischbach, *Siège de Strasbourg,* 452–454; "Kriegschronik," *Illustrirte Zeitung* (Leipzig), October 8, 1870, 246.
52. Quoted in De Trailles, *Femmes de France,* 42–43.
53. Malartic, *Siége de Strasbourg,* 182.
54. H. Beaunis, *Impressions de campagne (1870–1871)* (Paris: Alcan and Berger-Levrault, 1887), 68; "Additional Articles relating to the Condition of the Wounded in War," October 20, 1868, http://www.icrc.org/ihl.nsf/FULL/125?OpenDocument; F. Poncet, *Hôpital Militaire, Service de la 1re Division de Blessés, Siége de Strasbourg (1870)* (Montpellier: Boehm et fils, 1872); Société Française de Secours aux Blessés et Malades Militaires, *Oeuvre internationale: Rapport du comité auxiliaire de Strasbourg* (Strasbourg: Berger-Levrault, 1871), 20.
55. Fischbach, *Siège de Strasbourg,* 450, citing a story reported by Raymond-Signouret during the period of occupation; Anonymous, *Strasbourg: Journal,* 352; AVCUS, 272 MW 23, letter from Küss quoting Ollech, October 20, 1870; Schneegans, *Guerre en Alsace,* 73.
56. Alfred Marchand, *Siége de Strasbourg: 1870, La Bibliothèque—La Cathédrale* (Paris: Cherbuliez, 1871), 104.
57. De Trailles, *Femmes de France,* 47.
58. Ibid., 52–53.
59. Bergasse du Petit-Thouars, "Le siége de Strasbourg: Août et septembre 1870," *Le correspondant,* December 25, 1871, 1008; the story of the twenty-five lashes came from Jules Claretie and was reprinted in Joseph Turquan, *Les Femmes de France pendant l'Invasion* (Paris: Berger-Levrault, 1893), 230; Elizabeth Vlossak,

Marianne or Germania?: Nationalizing Women in Alsace, 1870–1946 (New York: Oxford University Press, 2010), 10.

60. M. Ruhlmann, *Le courrier du Bas-Rhin*, September 26, 1870 (supplement); Reuss, "Chronique strasbourgeoise," 25; A. Faes, "Une enfance strasbougeoise sous le Second Empire (1857–72)" *Annuaire de la Société des Amis du Vieux Strasbourg* (1980), 93; Piton, *Siège de Strasbourg*, 211–212.

61. AVCUS, MS 204, letter, Emile Schmitt to Georg Schmidt, October 24, 1870.

62. Schneegans, *Guerre en Alsace*, 142.

63. Quoted in Raymond-Signouret, *Souvenirs du bombardement*, 129–131.

64. Schneegans, *Guerre en Alsace*, 143–144; Reuss, "Chronique strasbourgeoise," 50; *Strasbourg!* (1871) and the more extensive *Guerre en Alsace* (1871) were both published in Neuchâtel.

65. AVCUS, 272 MW 84, "Souvenirs—à mes enfants," 63.

66. Dr. Max Hirsch, "Briefe vom Kriegsschauplatz," *Volks-Zeitung* (Berlin), October 12, 1870, 2.

67. Quoted in D. Goldschmidt, *Souvenirs de 1870: Autour de Strasbourg assiégé* (Strasbourg: Imprimerie Alsacienne, 1909), 23.

68. Piton, *Siège de Strasbourg*, 225.

69. Beaunis, *Impressions de campagne*, 64–65.

70. Piton, *Siège de Strasbourg*, 225–226.

71. Ibid.

72. Fischbach, *Siège de Strasbourg*, 462.

73. Fischbach, *Siège de Strasbourg*, 457–458; Anonymous, *Strasbourg: Journal*, 353–354.

74. Frederick III, *War Diary*, 139.

75. Anonymous, *Strasbourg: Journal*, 355–356.

76. Fischbach, *Siège de Strasbourg*, 329.

77. Annual budget: G. Foessel, "La vie quotidienne à Strasbourg à la veille de la guerre de 1870," in *L'Alsace en 1870–1871*, ed. F. L'Huillier (Strasbourg: Publications de la Faculté des Lettres de l'Université de Strasbourg, 1971), 25; Fischbach, *Siège de Strasbourg*, 461–462.

78. Anthony J. Steinhoff, "Religion as Urban Culture: A View from Strasbourg, 1870–1914," *Journal of Urban History* 30, no. 2 (January 2004), 153, 165; Fischbach, *Siège de Strasbourg*, 467; Brigitte Fassnacht, "L'armée à Strasbourg (1852–1870)," (Mémoire de Maîtrise, Université des Sciences Humaines de Strasbourg, 1996), 174; John Craig, *Scholarship and Nation Building: The Universities of Strasbourg and Alsatian Society, 1870–1939* (Chicago: University of Chicago Press, 1984), 60, 100; Jules Sengenwald, *Exposé des faits relatifs à la reconstruction du Temple-Neuf* (Strasbourg: Fischbach, 1876), 6–8; Catherine Dunlop, "Borderland Cartographies: Mapping the Lands Between France and Germany, 1860–1940" (Ph.D. diss., Yale University, 2010), 304–314.

79. AVCUS, 1 MW 203, "Procès-verbaux, Conseil municipal de la ville de Strasbourg," September 29, 1870, 573; Fischbach, *Siège de Strasbourg*, 462.

80. Fischbach, *Siège de Strasbourg*, 466; Jacques Flach, *Strasbourg après le bombardement: 2 octobre 1870-30 septembre 1872; Rapport sur les travaux du Comité de*

Secours Strasbourgeois pour les Victimes du Bombardement (Strasbourg: Fischbach, 1873), 66; wages calculated at 3 francs 50 per day, six days per week.

81. No such aid is discussed in Amanda Foreman, *A World on Fire: Britain's Crucial Role in the American Civil War* (New York: Random House, 2010) or Orlando Figes, *The Crimean War, A History* (New York: Metropolitan Books, 2010).

82. Elna C. Green, *This Business of Relief: Confronting Poverty in a Southern City, 1740–1940* (Athens: University of Georgia Press, 2003), 85–102; James Michael Russell, *Atlanta 1847–1890: City Building in the Old South and the New* (Baton Rouge: Louisiana State University Press, 1988), 174–175; Fischbach, *Siège de Strasbourg,* 466; Flach, *Strasbourg,* 63–64, 66.

83. Flach, *Strasbourg,* 4; AVCUS, 272 MW 68, Comité Strasbourgeois de Secours aux Victimes du Bombardement, *Bases de secours adoptées en assemblée générale du 3 janvier 1871* (Strasbourg: J. H. Ed. Heitz [1871]), n.p.

84. AVCUS, 272 MW 48, requests to the Aid Committee. Distributions continued from October 2, 1870, to September 30, 1872.

85. Etablissement des Diaconesses de Strasbourg, *Vingt-neuvième rapport* (Strasbourg: Berger-Levrault, 1871), 5.

86. Ibid., 12.

87. Société Française de Secours aux Blessés et Malades Militaires, *Oeuvre internationale,* 23–24, 48, 53–57; De Trailles, *Femmes de France,* 43; Turquan, *Femmes de France,* 231; Diaconesses, *Rapport,* 6–11; De Trailles, *Femmes de France,* 46; AVCUS, 272 MW 69, *Compte rendu des opérations du restaurant populaire et réception des prisonniers de passage à Strasbourg à la Halle couverte 1870–1871* (Strasbourg: Heitz, 1871), 4–6.

88. ADBR, 2 G 482 K/14, "Registre des délibérations de la Consistoire de Ste.-Aurélie," November 6, 1870; 172 AL 228, "Extrait du registre des délibérations du Conseil presbyteral de St.-Guillaume," March 14, 1871; 2 V 38, "Procès-verbal, Directoire de l'Eglise de la Confession d'Augsburg," December 6, 1870; AVCUS, 86 Z 83, "Délibérations du Consistoire du Temple-Neuf," October 7–December 5, 1870; Archives of the Consistoire Israelite du Bas-Rhin, CIBR 17, Journal de correspondance 1870–1872, December 15, January 11, 1871; René Epp, *Mgr Raess, Evêque de Strasbourg (1842–1887)* (Griesheim-sur-Souffel: Culture Alsacienne, 1979), 124.

89. AVCUS, 124 Z 3, "Procès-verbaux, Casino commercial et littéraire," October 3, 1870; Rodolphe Reuss, *À la mémoire de M. Charles-Frédéric Schneegans, Directeur du Gymnase Protestant de Strasbourg, 1822–1890* (Strasbourg: Heitz, 1890), 12–13; Steinhoff, "Religion as Urban Culture," 172; Anonymous, *Strasbourg: Journal,* 353; Raymond-Signouret, *Souvenirs du bombardement,* 274.

90. Malartic, *Siège de Strasbourg,* 169.

91. The newspaper used this name starting January 1, 1871 (G. Erwin Ritter, *Die elsass-lothringische Presse im letzten Drittel des 19. Jahrhunderts* [Strasbourg: Börsendruckerei, 1933], 34–35).

92. AVCUS, 272 MW 17, letter, Klotz to Küss, January 15, 1871; Schneegans, *Guerre en Alsace,* 156.

93. Reuss, "Chronique strasbourgeoise," 50.

94. Faes, "Enfance strasbourgeoise," 95.

95. Frederick III, *War Diary*, 262, 284.

96. Krüger, "German Suffering," 412; John Horne and Alan Kramer, *German Atrocities, 1914: A History of Denial* (New Haven, CT: Yale University Press, 2001), 141–142.

97. Michael Howard, *The Franco-Prussian War: The German Invasion of France, 1870–1871* (New York: The MacMillan Company, 1961), 353.

98. Ibid., 356; Frederick III, *War Diary*, 253.

99. Frederick III, *War Diary*, 257.

100. Howard, *Franco-Prussian War*, 361; Roth, *Guerre de 70*, 356.

101. Frederick III, *War Diary*, 269.

102. Ibid., 272.

103. Beaunis, *Impressions de campagne*, 230.

104. AVCUS 272 MW 96, Poster, "La protestation des députés de l'Alsace et de la Lorraine lue à l'Assemblée nationale le 1er mars 1871."

105. Beaunis, *Impressions de campagne*, 230.

106. Gustave Fischbach, *Le courrier du Bas-Rhin*, March 9, 1871.

107. Beaunis, *Impressions de campagne*, 238.

108. Ibid., 239.

109. Gustave Fischbach, *Le courrier du Bas-Rhin*, March 9, 1871.

110. Beaunis, *Impressions de campagne*, 238.

111. Ibid., 239.

112. Gustave Fischbach, *Le courrier du Bas-Rhin*, March 9, 1871.

113. The following is from Théodore Humann, "Discours sur la tombe de M. Emile Küss, maire de Strasbourg," (no publication data [1871]; held in the Bibliothèque nationale et universitaire de Strasbourg), 2–3.

114. Ibid., 3.

115. Beaunis, *Impressions de Campagne*, 239.

116. Du Casse, *Journal authentique*, 63; today the former avenue du Général Uhrich is avenue Foch http://www.v2asp.paris.fr/commun/v2asp/v2/nomenclature_voies/Voieactu/3711.nom.htm; Roth, *Guerre de 70*, 563–564; the inquest's report is reproduced in Fischbach, *Siège de Strasbourg*, 488–491 and Uhrich, *Documents*, 155–159.

117. SHDV, Lo 72, Le Conseil d'enquête, Ministère de la guerre, *Extrait du procès-verbal de la séance du 8 janvier 1872.*

118. Quoted in Fischbach, *Siège de Strasbourg*, 458.

119. Fischbach, *Siège de Strasbourg*, 489–490.

120. Uhrich, *Documents*, 158–159.

121. *Bulletin des lois de l'Empire français*, July–December 1863, 919.

122. Geoffrey Wawro, *The Franco-Prussian War: The German Conquest of France in 1870–1871* (Cambridge: Cambridge University Press, 2003), 252.

123. Piton, *Siège de Strasbourg*, 212.

124. Fischbach, *Siège de Strasbourg*, 498–499.

125. Quoted in ibid., 497.

126. Quoted in ibid., 499.

127. Fischbach, *Siège de Strasbourg*, 456, 500, 501.

128. *La République française* of May 25 and 27, 1872, quoted in Lucien Delabrousse, *Un héros de la défense nationale: Valentin et les derniers jours du siège de Strasbourg* (Paris: Berger-Levrault, 1898), 165–167.

129. Quoted in Delabrousse, *Héros*, 168.

130. Georges Foessel, "Journal du siège de Strasbourg par Cécile de Dartein," *Annuaire de la Société des Amis du Vieux-Strasbourg*, 15 (1985), 90; [Blech], *La défense de Strasbourg jugée par un républicain* (Neuchâtel: Attinger, 1871), 14; Raymond-Signouret, *Souvenirs du bombardement*, 294.

131. Raymond-Signouret, *Souvenirs du bombardement*, 295.

132. Ibid., 296.

133. Delabrousse, *Héros*, 2, 38–39, 41, 135–136.

134. Christopher E. Forth, "*La Civilisation* and its Discontents: Modernity, Manhood and the Body in the Early Third Republic," in *French Masculinities: History, Culture and Politics,* eds. Christopher E. Forth and Bertrand Taithe (New York: Palgrave MacMillan, 2007), 93.

135. G. Bruno, *Les enfants de Marcel: Instruction morale et civique en Action: Livre de lecture courante cours moyen, conforme aux programmes du 27 juillet 1882,* 8th ed. (Paris: Eugene Belin, 1887), 136–137. My thanks to Peggy Darrow for this find.

136. Christopher E. Forth, *The Dreyfus Affair and the Crisis of French Manhood* (Baltimore: The Johns Hopkins University Press, 2004), 7–9; Venita Datta, *Heroes and Legends of Fin-de-Siècle France: Gender, Politics, and National Identity* (New York: Cambridge University Press, 2011), 11–13, 78.

137. Edward Berenson, *Heroes of Empire: Five Charismatic Men and the Conquest of Africa* (Berkeley: University of California Press, 2011), 168.

138. Datta, *Heroes and Legends*.

139. Delabrousse, *Héros*, 2, 1.

140. Datta, *Heroes and Legends,* 125–127.

141. Berenson, *Heroes of Empire,* 10.

142. E. Barré, *Religion et patrie: Le héros de Strasbourg: Le Commandant de génie Ducrot* (Rouen: Deshays, 1871), 22.

143. Margaret Darrow, "The Franco-Prussian War in French Elementary Schools, 1882–1910," paper presented at the Society for French Historical Studies Annual Meeting, Tempe, April 2010.

144. Krüger, "German Suffering," 421.

145. Danielle Tartakowsky, "La construction sociale de l'espace politique: Les usages politiques de la Place de la Concorde des années 1880 à nos jours," *French Historical Studies* 27, no. 1 (Winter 2004), 151–152; Hollis Clayson, *Paris in Despair: Art and Everyday Life under Siege (1870–71)* (Chicago: The University of Chicago Press, 2002), 334.

Conclusion

1. Frédéric Piton, *Siège de Strasbourg: Journal d'un assiégé* (Paris: Schlaeber, 1900), vi.

2. Paul and Henry de Trailles, *Les femmes de France pendant la guerre et les deux siéges de Paris* (Paris: F. Polo, 1872), 52; Gustave Fischbach, *Le siège de Strasbourg: Strasbourg avant, pendant, et après le siège* (Strasbourg: L'Imprimerie Alsacienne, 1897), 314.

3. Recent treatments include Christopher J. Fischer, *Alsace to the Alsatians? Visions and Divisions of Alsatian Regionalism, 1870–1939* (New York: Berghahn Books, 2010); Elizabeth Vlossak, *Marianne or Germania?: Nationalizing Women in Alsace, 1870–1946* (New York: Oxford University Press, 2010), 6–7, 23–24; Maurice Engelhardt, "Lettre de M. Maurice Engelhard à M. A. Schnéegans" (Lyon: J. Jossier, 1871), n.p.

4. Quoted in Anonymous, *Strasbourg: Journal des mois d'août et septembre 1870* (Paris: Sandoz et Fischbacher, 1874), 355.

5. Áine McGillicuddy, *René Schickele and Alsace: Cultural Identity between the Borders* (Bern: Peter Lang, 2011), 56; *Stammbaum der Familie Schneegans* (1894), located in the Bibliothèque nationale et universitaire in Strasbourg.

6. Vlossak, *Marianne*, 6–7; Fischer, *Alsace to the Alsatians?*, 14–15; Bernard Vogler, "Les protestants alsaciens entre leurs coreligionnaires allemands et français, 1815–1914," *Bulletin de la Société de l'Histoire du Protestantisme Français* 137 (1991), 572–573.

7. Rodolphe Reuss, "Chronique strasbourgeoise de la guerre franco-allemande du 16 juillet au 24 août 1870," in *Le siège de Strasbourg en 1870: Conférence et chronique strasbourgeoise juillet–août 1870*, ed. Jean Rott (Strasbourg: Libairie Istra, 1971), preface, September 1880, 29.

8. Ibid., preface, August 8, 1900, 29.

9. Ibid., preface, January 5, 1920, 30.

10. Jacques Flach, *Strasbourg après le bombardement: 2 octobre 1870–30 septembre 1872; Rapport sur les travaux du Comité de Secours Strasbourgeois pour les Victimes du Bombardement* (Strasbourg: Fischbach, 1873), 88.

11. Wilhelm Horning, *Erlebnisse während der Belagerung von Strassburg 1870 aus seinem Tagebuch* (Strasbourg: Hubert, 1894), forward.

12. Thomas Cardoza, *Intrepid Women: Cantinières and Vivandières of the French Army* (Bloomington: Indiana University Press, 2010), 11, 184–185.

13. Alan Kramer, *Dynamic of Destruction: Culture and Mass Killing in the First World War* (Oxford: Oxford University Press, 2007), 7–8, 18–19.

14. Geoffrey Wawro, *Warfare and Society in Europe 1792–1914* (London: Routledge, 2000), 153; Christian Geinitz, "The First Air War Against Noncombatants: Strategic Bombing of German Cities in World War I," in *Great War, Total War: Combat and Mobilization on the Western Front, 1914–1918*, eds. Roger Chickering and Stig Förster (Cambridge: Cambridge University Press, 2000), 214; Susan R. Grayzel, *At Home and Under Fire: Air Raids and Culture in Britain from the Great War to the Blitz* (New York: Cambridge University Press, 2012); Nadezhda Cherepenina, "Assessing the Scale of Famine and Death in the Besieged City," in *Life and Death in Besieged Leningrad, 1941–44*, eds. John Barber and Andrei Dzeniskevich (Houndmills: Palgrave Macmillan, 2005), 63–64; Randall Hansen, "War, Suffering and Modern German History," *German History* 29, no. 3

(September 2011), 373; Guy Trendel, *Racontez-moi Strasbourg: Les très riches heures d'une ville libre* (Strasbourg: La Nuée Bleue, 2006), 33, 313; Robert A. Doughty, et al., *Warfare in the Western World*, vol. 2, *Military Operations since 1871* (Lexington, MA: D.C. Heath and Company, 1996), 637.

15. E. B. Hamley, "The Conduct of War," *The Times* (London), January 24, 1871, 8, *The Times Digital Archive 1785–1985*. Avishai Margalit and Michael Walzer advocate the same principle in "Israel: Civilians and Combatants," *The New York Review of Books* 56, no. 8 (May 14, 2009), http://www.nybooks.com/articles /22664.

16. Quoted in Michael Walzer, *Just and Unjust Wars: A Moral Argument with Historical Illustrations* (New York: Basic Books, 1977), 166.

17. Cherepenina, "Assessing the Scale of Famine and Death," 43, 63–64.

18. Quoted in Walzer, *Just and Unjust Wars,* 167.

19. Geoffrey Best, *Humanity in Warfare* (New York: Columbia University Press, 1980), 157; Leon Friedman, ed., *The Law of War: A Documentary History* (Westport, CT: Greenwood Press, 1972), 1:152, 197, 229–231, 318–319; Walzer, *Just and Unjust Wars,* 167.

20. J. von Hartmann, "Militärische Nothwendigkeit und Humanität: Ein kritischer Versuch," *Deutsche Rundschau* 13 (1877), 467, 469.

21. Isabel V. Hull, *Absolute Destruction: Military Culture and the Practices of War in Imperial Germany* (Cornell: Cornell University Press, 2005), 120–121.

22. *Les lois de la guerre continentale* [Kriegsbrauch im Landkriege], trans. Paul Carpentier (Paris: Librairie Générale de Droit et de Jurisprudence, 1904), 2–3.

23. Ibid., 45.

24. Ibid., 47–48.

25. Felix Dahn, "Der deutsch-französische Krieg und das Völkerrecht," *Bausteine* 5, no. 1 (Berlin: Janke, 1884), 132–133; Rudolf von Pirscher, *Ingenieure und Pioniere im Feldzuge 1870–71: Belagerung von Strassburg* (Berlin: Schall, 1905), 42.

26. *Bulletin des lois de la République française,* October 23, 1883, article 208, 1141.

27. Ch. Thoumas, *Les capitulations: Etude d'histoire militaire sur la responsabilité du commandement* (Pairs: Librairie Militaire Berger-Levrault, 1886), 31.

28. Thoumas, *Capitulations,* 92–93.

29. Rachel Chrastil, *Organizing for War: France, 1870–1914* (Baton Rouge: Louisiana State University Press, 2010), 142; Michael Barnett, *Empire of Humanity: A History of Humanitarianism* (Ithaca: Cornell University Press, 2011), 82–87; Pierre Dubois, "L'action humanitaire de la Suisse durant la Première Guerre Mondiale," *Revue d'Allemagne* 28, no. 3 (July 1996): 377–389; Heather Jones, "International or Transnational? Humanitarian action during the First World War," *European Review of History* 16, no. 5 (October 2009), 708; Eric D. Weitz, "From the Vienna to the Paris System: International Politics and the Entangled Histories of Human Rights, Forced Deportations, and Civilizing Missions," *The American Historical Review* 113, no. 5 (December 2008): 1313–1343.

30. Lynn Hunt, *Inventing Human Rights: A History* (New York: W. W. Norton, 2007), 212; Eric D. Weitz, "From the Vienna to the Paris System," 1314.

31. Craig Calhoun, "The Imperative to Reduce Suffering: Charity, Progress, and Emergencies in the Field of Humanitarian Action," in *Humanitarianism in Question: Politics, Power, Ethics,* eds. Michael Barnett and Thomas G. Weiss (Ithaca: Cornell University Press, 2008), 85.

32. Michael Loriaux, *European Union and the Deconstruction of the Rhineland Frontier* (New York: Cambridge University Press, 2008), 10–11.

Acknowledgments

A Fulbright-Alsace Regional Council Award, along with Xavier University's faculty development leave and summer fellowship, supported research for this book. Martha Hanna, Peggy Darrow, Carol Harrison, the late and much missed Frank Turner, and the inestimable John Merriman encouraged its development. I am indebted to the staffs of the Bibliothèque nationale et universitaire (especially in Salle 5), the Archives de la Ville et de la Communauté urbaine de Strasbourg, the Archives départementales du Bas-Rhin, the Bibliothèque nationale de France, the Service historique de la défense, the Generallandesarchiv Karlsruhe, the Charles Deering McCormick Library of Special Collections at Northwestern University (especially R. Russell Maylone and Scott Krafft), the Consistoire Israélite du Bas-Rhin, and the McDonald Library at Xavier University. In Strasbourg, Nicolas Bourguinat welcomed me at the Université de Strasbourg, and I enjoyed the company of Alison Carrol and Kate Lemay. Rick Gangloff, whose great-grandfather served with the *pontonniers* at Strasbourg and who shares a love of the city and its besieged fighters, swapped sources with me. Back in Cincinnati, I wrote this salute to vibrant urban life in lively and welcoming neighborhood spaces, notably the Red Tree Gallery and Essencha Tea House. I am grateful as well that Kathleen McDermott, along with Andrew Kinney and Harvard University Press, took on this project.

I presented early versions of several chapters at the annual meetings of the American Historical Association, the Society for French Historical Studies, the Western Society for French History, and the German Studies Association, and benefitted from the comments of Naomi Andrews, Sophie De Schaepdrijver, Robert Zaretksy, Peggy Darrow, Anthony Steinhoff, Martha Hanna, Stephen Harp, Michael Geyer, and Sheryl Kroen. Audiences at the University of North Florida and the Pennsylvania State University particularly engaged with the dilemmas facing Strasbourg's besieged people; Alison Bruey, Dale Clifford, and Jennifer Boittin supported these visits. The Annual Lecture of the Pi of Ohio Chapter of Phi Beta Kappa also provided a welcome opportunity to hone my ideas.

Ellen Atkinson, Michelle Brady, Alison Bruey, Stephen Harp, Christine Haynes, Jessie Hewitt, Andrew Orr, and Erin Prus provided careful comment on certain chapters, as did members of the Cincinnati French History Group: Ethan Katz, Judith Zinsser, Janine Hartman, Andrew Thompson, and Bela Kashyap. Two anonymous readers for Harvard University Press helped me clarify and shape my arguments. I learned from insightful conversations with Howard Brown, Sahr Conway-Lanz, J. P. Daughton, Catherine Dunlop, Michael Goldweber, Paul Hanson, David Mengel, Deborah Neill, Steve Porter, Paul O'Hara, Andrew Orr, Devin Pendas, Kathleen Smythe, Pam Stewart, and Phil Wynne. Undergraduates at Xavier University in European History II and A History of Saving the World also commented, notably Christine Connolly, Angela DiGangi, Annie Golemboski, David Miller, Betsy Moore, Molly Ritchie, and Ivanna Stefanyshyn. Steve Yandell and Vanessa Sorensen helped me to think spatially about Strasbourg. Isabelle Lewis produced the maps, which were made possible through a grant from Dean Janice Walker of the Xavier University College of Arts and Sciences.

Jacob Melish listened and asked questions over the course of many months, and at a crucial moment, gave a wise piece of advice. Esmeralda Năstase and Steph Brzuzy have provided a steady stream of encouragement. Amy Whipple's capacity for schemes and she-nanigans in the doing and teaching of history has carried me through many a day in the office. Beeto Lyle has long shared and inspired unbounded curiosity and mental disci-pline. John Fairfield has discussed this project in countless sessions in our kitchen and at the bar down the street. Our improbable romance has enriched every part of my life. Finally, I want to thank my family, Mom and Dad and Mike and Liz, for music, veggies, stories, and adventures. This book is dedicated to my parents, Roger Chrastil and Mary Chrastil.

Index